To Mother with Love
on Mothers' Day 1961
From - Eileen - Ben
Victoria & Wm. John

THE NEW
ENGLISH BIBLE

THE BIBLE
A NEW ENGLISH TRANSLATION

Planned and Directed by Representatives of

THE BAPTIST UNION OF GREAT BRITAIN AND IRELAND

THE CHURCH OF ENGLAND

THE CHURCH OF SCOTLAND

THE CONGREGATIONAL UNION OF ENGLAND AND WALES

THE COUNCIL OF CHURCHES FOR WALES

THE LONDON YEARLY MEETING OF
THE SOCIETY OF FRIENDS

THE METHODIST CHURCH OF GREAT BRITAIN

THE PRESBYTERIAN CHURCH OF ENGLAND

THE UNITED COUNCIL OF CHRISTIAN CHURCHES AND
RELIGIOUS COMMUNIONS IN IRELAND

THE BRITISH AND FOREIGN BIBLE SOCIETY

THE NATIONAL BIBLE SOCIETY OF SCOTLAND

THE NEW ENGLISH BIBLE

NEW TESTAMENT

OXFORD UNIVERSITY PRESS
CAMBRIDGE UNIVERSITY PRESS
1961

Eighth Printing, April 1961

Printed in the United States of America

PREFACE

In May 1946 the General Assembly of the Church of Scotland received an overture from the Presbytery of Stirling and Dunblane recommending that a translation of the Bible be made in the language of the present day. As a result of this, delegates of the Church of England, the Church of Scotland, and the Methodist, Baptist, and Congregationalist Churches met in conference in October. They recommended that the work should be undertaken, and that a completely new translation should be made, rather than a revision, once previously contemplated, of any earlier version. In January 1947 a second conference, held like the first in the Central Hall, Westminster, included representatives of the University Presses of Oxford and Cambridge. At the request of this conference, the Churches named above appointed representatives to form the Joint Committee on the New Translation of the Bible. This Committee met for the first time in July of the same year. By January 1948, when its third meeting was held, invitations to be represented had been sent to the Presbyterian Church of England, the Society of Friends, the Churches in Wales, the Churches in Ireland, the British and Foreign Bible Society, and the National Bible Society of Scotland: these invitations were accepted.

The Bishop of Truro (Dr J. W. Hunkin) acted as Chairman from the beginning. He gave most valuable service until his death in 1950, when the Bishop of Durham (Dr A. T. P. Williams, later Bishop of Winchester) was elected to succeed him. The Reverend Dr G. S. Hendry and the Reverend Professor J. K. S. Reid, both of the Church of Scotland, have successively held the office of Secretary, to the Committee's great advantage.

The actual work of translation was entrusted by the Committee to four panels dealing respectively with the Old Testament, the Apocrypha, the New Testament, and the literary revision of the whole. Denominational considerations played no part in the appointment to membership of these panels.

Since January 1948 the Joint Committee has met regularly twice a year in the Jerusalem Chamber, Westminster Abbey, with four exceptions during 1954–1955 when the Langham Room in the precincts of the Abbey was kindly made available. At these meetings the Committee has received reports on the progress of the work from the Conveners of the four panels, and its members have had in their hands typescripts of the books so far translated and revised. They have made such comments and given such advice or decisions as they judged to be necessary, and from time to time they have met members of the panels in conference. The Committee has warmly appreciated the courteous hospitality of the Dean of Westminster and of the Trustees of the Central Hall.

Work upon the Old Testament and the Apocrypha is actively going forward. Much has been done: much remains to do. At a later time, when the whole translation has been completed, further and more particular acknowledgements will doubtless be made. But this brief preface to the translation of the New Testament must not end without an expression of the Joint Committee's thanks to all those who have given their time and knowledge to a task both long and difficult. We owe a great debt to the support and the experienced counsel of the University Presses of Oxford and Cambridge, and we acknowledge our obligation, an obligation impossible to exaggerate, to the Reverend Dr C. H. Dodd who, as Director of our enterprise, has devoted to it in full measure his scholarship, his patience, and his wisdom.

ALWYN WINTON:
Chairman of the Joint Committee

INTRODUCTION

This translation of the New Testament (to be followed in due course by the Old Testament and by the Apocrypha) was undertaken with the object of providing English readers, whether familiar with the Bible or not, with a faithful rendering of the best available Greek text into the current speech of our own time, and a rendering which should harvest the gains of recent biblical scholarship.

It is just three hundred and fifty years since King James's men put out what we have come to know as the Authorized Version. Two hundred and seventy years later the New Testament was revised. The Revised Version, which appeared in 1881, marked a new departure especially in that it abandoned the so-called Received Text, which had reigned ever since printed editions of the New Testament began, but which the advance of textual criticism had antiquated. The Revisers no longer followed (like their predecessors) the text of the majority of manuscripts, which, being for the most part of late date, had been exposed not only to the accidental corruptions of long-continued copying, but also in part to deliberate correction and 'improvement'. Instead, they followed a very small group of manuscripts, the earliest, and in their judgement the best, of those which had survived. During the eighty years which have passed since their time, textual criticism has not stood still. Manuscripts have been discovered of substantially earlier date than any which the Revisers knew. Other important sources of evidence have been either freshly discovered or made more fully available. Meanwhile the methods of textual criticism have themselves been refined and estimates of the value of manuscripts have sometimes been reconsidered. The problem of restoring a form of text as near as possible to the vanished autographs now appears less simple than it did to our predecessors. There is not at the present time any critical text which would command the same degree of general acceptance as the Revisers' text did in its day. Nor has the time come, in the judgement of competent scholars, to construct such a text, since new material constantly comes to light, and the debate continues. The present translators therefore could do no other than consider variant readings on their merits, and, having weighed the evidence for themselves, select for translation in each passage the reading which to the best of their judgement seemed most likely to represent what the author wrote. Where other readings seemed to deserve serious consideration they have been recorded in footnotes. In assessing the evidence, the translators have taken into account (*a*) ancient manuscripts of the New Testament in Greek, (*b*) manuscripts of early translations into other languages, and (*c*) quotations from the New Testament by early Christian writers. These three sources of evidence are collectively referred to as 'witnesses'. A large number of variants, however, are such as could make no appreciable difference to the meaning so far as it could be represented in translation, and these have been passed over in silence. The translators are well aware that their judgement is at best provisional, but they believe the text they have followed to be an improvement on that underlying the earlier translations.

So much for the text. The next step was the effort to understand the original as accurately as possible, as a preliminary to turning it into English. The Revisers of 1881 believed that a better knowledge of the Greek language made it possible to correct a number of mistranslations in the older version, though in doing so they were somewhat limited by the instruction 'to introduce as few alterations as possible...consistently with faithfulness'. During the past eighty years the study of the Greek language has no more stood still than has textual criticism. In particular, our knowledge of the kind of Greek used by most of the New Testament writers has been greatly enriched since 1881 by the discovery of many thousands of papyrus documents in popular or non-literary Greek of about the same period as the New Testament. It would be wrong to suggest that they lead to any far-reaching change in our understanding of the Greek of the New Testament period, but they have often made possible a better appreciation of the finer shades of idiom, which sometimes clarifies the meaning of passages in the New Testament. Its language is indeed in many respects more flexible and easy-going than the Revisers were ready to allow, and invites the translator to use a larger freedom.

Our task, however, differed in an important respect from that of the Revisers of 1881. They were instructed not only to introduce as few alterations as possible, but also 'to limit, as far as possible, the expression of such alterations to the language of the Authorized and earlier English Versions'. Today that language is even more definitely archaic, and less generally understood, than it was eighty years ago, for the rate of change in English usage has accelerated. The present translators were subject to no such limitation. The Joint Committee which promoted and controlled the enterprise decided at the outset that what was now needed was not another revision of the Authorized Version but a genuinely new translation, in which an attempt should be made consistently to use the idiom of contemporary English to convey the meaning of the Greek. The older translators, on the whole, considered that fidelity to the original demanded that they should reproduce, as far as possible, characteristic features of the language in which it was written, such as the syntactical order of words, the structure and division of sentences, and even such irregularities of grammar as were indeed natural enough to authors writing in the easy idiom of popular Hellenistic Greek, but less natural when turned into English. The present translators were enjoined to replace Greek constructions and idioms by those of contemporary English.

This meant a different theory and practice of translation, and one which laid a heavier burden on the translators. Fidelity in translation was not to mean keeping the general framework of the original intact while replacing Greek words by English words more or less equivalent. A word, indeed, in one language is seldom the exact equivalent of a word in a different language. Each word is the centre of a whole cluster of meanings and associations, and in different languages these clusters overlap but do not often coincide. The place of a word in the clause or sentence, or even in a larger unit of thought, will determine what aspect of its total meaning is in the foreground. The translator can hardly hope to convey in another language every shade of meaning that attaches to the word in the original, but if he is free to exploit a wide range of English words covering a similar area of meaning and association he may hope to carry over the meaning of the sentence as a whole. Thus we have not felt obliged (as did the Revisers of 1881) to make an effort to render the same Greek word everywhere by the same English word. We have in this respect returned to the wholesome practice of King James's men, who (as they expressly state in their preface) recognized no such obligation. We have conceived our task to be that of understanding the original as precisely as we could (using all available aids), and then saying again in our own native idiom what we believed the author to be saying in his. We have found that in practice this frequently compelled us to make decisions where the older method of translation allowed a comfortable ambiguity. In such places we have been aware that we take a risk, but we have thought it our duty to take the risk rather than remain on the fence. But in no passage of doubtful meaning does the rendering adopted represent merely the preference of any single person.

The Joint Committee appointed a panel of scholars, drawn from various British universities, whom they believed to be representative of competent biblical scholarship in this country at the present time. The procedure was for one member of the panel to be invited to submit a draft translation of a particular book or group of books. This draft was circulated in typescript to members of the panel for their consideration. They then met together and discussed the draft round a table, verse by verse, sentence by sentence. Each member brought his view about the meaning of the original to the judgement of his fellows, and discussion was continued until they reached a common mind. There are passages where no one, in the present state of our knowledge, could say with absolute certainty which of two (or even more) meanings is intended. In such cases, after careful discussion, alternative meanings have been recorded in footnotes, but only where the difference was deemed of sufficient importance. There is probably no member of the panel who has not found himself compelled to give up, perhaps with lingering regret, a cherished view about the meaning of this or that difficult or doubtful passage. But each learned much from the others, and from the discipline of working towards a common mind. In the end we accept collective responsibility for the interpretation set forth in the text of our translation.

It should be said that our intention has been to offer a translation in the strict sense, and not a paraphrase, and we have not wished to encroach on the field of the commentator. But if the best commentary is a good translation, it is also true that every intelligent translation is in a sense a paraphrase. But if paraphrase means taking the liberty of introducing into a passage something which is not there, to elucidate the meaning which is there, it can be said that we have taken this liberty only with extreme caution, and in a very few passages, where without it we could see no way to attain our aim of making the meaning as clear as it could be made. Taken as a whole, our version claims to be a translation, free, it may be, rather than literal, but a faithful translation nevertheless, so far as we could compass it.

In doing our work, we have constantly striven to follow our instructions and render the Greek, as we understood it, into the English of the present day, that is, into the natural vocabulary, constructions, and rhythms of contemporary speech. We have sought to avoid archaism, jargon, and all that is either stilted or slipshod. Since sound scholarship does not always carry with it a delicate sense of style, the Committee appointed a panel of literary advisers, to whom all the work of the translating panel has been submitted. They scrutinized it, once again, verse by verse and sentence by sentence, and took pains to secure the tone and level of language appropriate to the different kinds of writing to be found in the New Testament, whether narrative, familiar discourse, argument, rhetoric, or poetry. But always the overriding aims were accuracy and

INTRODUCTION

clarity. The final form of the version was reached by agreement between the two panels.

The translators are as conscious as anyone can be of the limitations and imperfections of their work. No one who has not tried it can know how impossible an art translation is. Only those who have meditated long upon the Greek original are aware of the richness and subtlety of meaning that may lie even within the most apparently simple sentence, or know the despair that attends all efforts to bring it out through the medium of a different language. Yet we may hope that we have been able to convey to our readers something at least of what the New Testament has said to us during these years of work, and trust that under the providence of Almighty God this translation may open the truth of the scriptures to many who have been hindered in their approach to it by barriers of language.

CONTENTS

MARGINAL NUMBERS

The conventional verse divisions in the New Testament date only from 1551 and have no basis in the manuscripts. Any system of division into numbered verses is foreign to the spirit of this translation, which is intended to convey the meaning in continuous natural English rather than to correspond sentence by sentence with the Greek.

For purposes of reference, and of comparison with other translations, verse numbers are placed in the margin opposite the line in which the first word belonging to the verse in question appears. Sometimes, however, successive verses are combined in a continuous English sentence, so that the precise point where a new verse begins cannot be fixed; occasionally in the interests of clarity the order of successive verses is reversed (e.g. at John 4. 7, 8).

THE GOSPEL

THE
GOSPEL ACCORDING TO
MATTHEW

The Coming of Christ

ATABLE of the descent of Jesus Christ, son of David, son 1
of Abraham.
    Abraham was the father of Isaac, Isaac of Jacob, Jacob of 2
Judah and his brothers, Judah of Perez and Zarah (their mother was 3
Tamar), Perez of Hezron, Hezron of Ram, Ram of Amminadab, 4
Amminadab of Nahshon, Nahshon of Salma, Salma of Boaz (his 5
mother was Rahab), Boaz of Obed (his mother was Ruth), Obed of
Jesse; and Jesse was the father of King David. 6
    David was the father of Solomon (his mother had been the wife of
Uriah), Solomon of Rehoboam, Rehoboam of Abijah, Abijah of Asa, 7
Asa of Jehoshaphat, Jehoshaphat of Joram, Joram of Azariah, Azariah 8, 9
of Jotham, Jotham of Ahaz, Ahaz of Hezekiah, Hezekiah of Manasseh, 10
Manasseh of Amon, Amon of Josiah; and Josiah was the father of 11
Jeconiah and his brothers at the time of the deportation to Babylon.
    After the deportation Jeconiah was the father of Shealtiel, Shealtiel 12
of Zerubbabel, Zerubbabel of Abiud, Abiud of Eliakim, Eliakim of 13
Azor, Azor of Zadok, Zadok of Achim, Achim of Eliud, Eliud of 14, 15
Eleazar, Eleazar of Matthan, Matthan of Jacob, Jacob of Joseph, the 16
husband of Mary, who gave birth to*a* Jesus called Messiah.
    There were thus fourteen generations in all from Abraham to 17
David, fourteen from David until the deportation to Babylon, and
fourteen from the deportation until the Messiah.

THIS IS the story of the birth of the Messiah. Mary his mother was 18
betrothed to Joseph; before their marriage she found that she was
with child by the Holy Spirit. Being a man of principle, and at the 19
same time wanting to save her from exposure, Joseph desired to have

[a] *Some witnesses read* Joseph, to whom was betrothed Mary, a virgin, who gave birth
to...; *one early witness has* Joseph, and Joseph, to whom Mary, a virgin, was betrothed,
was the father of...

3

20 the marriage contract set aside quietly. He had resolved on this, when an angel of the Lord appeared to him in a dream. 'Joseph son of David,' said the angel, 'do not be afraid to take Mary home with you as your wife. It is by the Holy Spirit that she has conceived this

21 child. She will bear a son; and you shall give him the name Jesus

22 (Saviour), for he will save his people from their sins.' All this happened in order to fulfil what the Lord declared through the

23 prophet: 'The virgin will conceive and bear a son, and he shall be

24 called Emmanuel', a name which means 'God is with us'. Rising from sleep Joseph did as the angel had directed him; he took Mary

25 home to be his wife, but had no intercourse with her until her son was born. And he named the child Jesus.

2 JESUS WAS BORN at Bethlehem in Judaea during the reign of Herod.

2 After his birth astrologers from the east arrived in Jerusalem, asking, 'Where is the child who is born to be king of the Jews?[a] We observed

3 the rising of his star, and we have come to pay him homage.' King Herod was greatly perturbed when he heard this; and so was the

4 whole of Jerusalem. He called a meeting of the chief priests and lawyers of the Jewish people, and put before them the question:

5 'Where is it that the Messiah is to be born?' 'At Bethlehem in Judaea', they replied; and they referred him to the prophecy which

6 reads: 'Bethlehem in the land of Judah, you are far from least in the eyes of[b] the rulers of Judah; for out of you shall come a leader to be the shepherd of my people Israel.'

7 Herod next called the astrologers to meet him in private, and

8 ascertained from them the time when the star had appeared. He then sent them on to Bethlehem, and said, 'Go and make a careful inquiry for the child. When you have found him, report to me, so that I may go myself and pay him homage.'

9 They set out at the king's bidding; and the star which they had seen at its rising went ahead of them until it stopped above the place

10 where the child lay. At the sight of the star they were overjoyed.

11 Entering the house, they saw the child with Mary his mother, and bowed to the ground in homage to him; then they opened their

12 treasures and offered him gifts: gold, frankincense, and myrrh. And being warned in a dream not to go back to Herod, they returned home another way.

[a] Or Where is the king of the Jews who has just been born? [b] Or least among.

4

After they had gone, an angel of the Lord appeared to Joseph in 13
a dream, and said to him, 'Rise up, take the child and his mother
and escape with them to Egypt, and stay there until I tell you; for
Herod is going to search for the child to do away with him.' So 14
Joseph rose from sleep, and taking mother and child by night he
went away with them to Egypt, and there he stayed till Herod's 15
death. This was to fulfil what the Lord had declared through the
prophet: 'I called my son out of Egypt.'

When Herod saw how the astrologers had tricked him he fell into a 16
passion, and gave orders for the massacre of all children in Bethlehem
and its neighbourhood, of the age of two years or less, corresponding
with the time he had ascertained from the astrologers. So the words 17
spoken through Jeremiah the prophet were fulfilled: 'A voice was heard 18
in Rama, wailing and loud laments; it was Rachel weeping for her
children, and refusing all consolation, because they were no more.'

The time came that Herod died; and an angel of the Lord 19
appeared in a dream to Joseph in Egypt and said to him, 'Rise up, 20
take the child and his mother, and go with them to the land of Israel,
for the men who threatened the child's life are dead.' So he rose, 21
took mother and child with him, and came to the land of Israel.
Hearing, however, that Archelaus had succeeded his father Herod 22
as king of Judaea, he was afraid to go there. And being warned by
a dream, he withdrew to the region of Galilee; there he settled in 23
a town called Nazareth. This was to fulfil the words spoken through
the prophets: 'He shall be called a Nazarene.'

ABOUT THAT TIME John the Baptist appeared as a preacher in the 3
Judaean wilderness; his theme was: 'Repent; for the kingdom of 2
Heaven is upon you!' It is of him that the prophet Isaiah spoke 3
when he said, 'A voice crying aloud in the wilderness, "Prepare a way
for the Lord; clear a straight path for him."'

John's clothing was a rough coat of camel's hair, with a leather 4
belt round his waist, and his food was locusts and wild honey. They 5
flocked to him from Jerusalem, from all Judaea, and the whole
Jordan valley, and were baptized by him in the River Jordan, 6
confessing their sins.

When he saw many of the Pharisees and Sadducees coming for 7
baptism he said to them: 'You vipers' brood! Who warned you to
escape from the coming retribution? Then prove your repentance 8

5

9 by the fruit it bears; and do not presume to say to yourselves, "We have Abraham for our father." I tell you that God can make children
10 for Abraham out of these stones here. Already the axe is laid to the roots of the trees; and every tree that fails to produce good fruit is
11 cut down and thrown on the fire. I baptize you with water, for repentance; but the one who comes after me is mightier than I, and I am not fit to take off his shoes; he will baptize you with the
12 Holy Spirit and with fire. His shovel is ready in his hand and he will winnow his threshing-floor; the wheat he will gather into his granary, but he will burn the chaff on a fire that can never go out.'
13   Then Jesus arrived at the Jordan from Galilee, and came to John
14 to be baptized by him. John tried to dissuade him. 'Do you come
15 to me?' he said; 'I need rather to be baptized by you.' Jesus replied, 'Let it be so for the present; we do well to conform in this way with
16 all that God requires.' John then allowed him to come. After baptism Jesus came up out of the water at once, and at that moment heaven opened; he saw the Spirit of God descending like a dove to alight
17 upon him; and a voice from heaven was heard saying, 'This is my Son, my Beloved,[a] on whom my favour rests.'

4 JESUS WAS THEN led away by the Spirit into the wilderness, to be tempted by the devil.
2   For forty days and nights he fasted, and at the end of them he was
3 famished. The tempter approached him and said, 'If you are the
4 Son of God, tell these stones to become bread.' Jesus answered, 'Scripture says, "Man cannot live on bread alone; he lives on every word that God utters."'
5   The devil then took him to the Holy City and set him on the
6 parapet of the temple. 'If you are the Son of God,' he said, 'throw yourself down; for Scripture says, "He will put his angels in charge of you, and they will support you in their arms, for fear you should
7 strike your foot against a stone."' Jesus answered him, 'Scripture says again, "You are not to put the Lord your God to the test."'
8   Once again, the devil took him to a very high mountain, and
9 showed him all the kingdoms of the world in their glory. 'All these', he said, 'I will give you, if you will only fall down and do me
10 homage.' But Jesus said, 'Begone, Satan; Scripture says, "You shall do homage to the Lord your God and worship him alone."'

[a] *Or* This is my only Son.

Then the devil left him, and angels appeared and waited on him. 11
When he heard that John had been arrested, Jesus withdrew to 12
Galilee; and leaving Nazareth he went and settled at Capernaum on 13
the Sea of Galilee, in the district of Zebulun and Naphtali. This 14
was in fulfilment of the passage in the prophet Isaiah which tells of
'the land of Zebulun, the land of Naphtali, the road by the sea, the 15
land beyond Jordan, heathen Galilee', and says:

'The people that lived in darkness saw a great light;   16
Light dawned on the dwellers in the land of death's dark shadow.'

From that day Jesus began to proclaim the message: 'Repent; for*a* 17
the kingdom of Heaven is upon you.'

JESUS WAS WALKING by the Sea of Galilee when he saw two 18
brothers, Simon called Peter and his brother Andrew, casting a net
into the lake; for they were fishermen. Jesus said to them, 'Come 19
with me, and I will make you fishers of men.' They left their nets at 20
once and followed him.

He went on, and saw another pair of brothers, James son of 21
Zebedee and his brother John; they were in the boat with their
father Zebedee, overhauling their nets. He called them, and at once 22
they left the boat and their father, and followed him.

He went round the whole of Galilee, teaching in the synagogues, 23
preaching the gospel of the Kingdom, and curing whatever illness or
infirmity there was among the people. His fame reached the whole 24
of Syria; and sufferers from every kind of illness, racked with pain,
possessed by devils, epileptic, or paralysed, were all brought to
him, and he cured them. Great crowds also followed him, from 25
Galilee and the Ten Towns,*b* from Jerusalem and Judaea, and from
Transjordan.

The Sermon on the Mount

WHEN HE SAW the crowds he went up the hill. There he took 5
his seat, and when his disciples had gathered round him he 2
began to address them. And this is the teaching he gave:

[a] *Some witnesses omit* Repent; for. [b] *Greek* Decapolis.

7

3   'How blest are those who know that they are poor;
          the kingdom of Heaven is theirs.
4   How blest are the sorrowful;
          they shall find consolation.
5   How blest are those of a gentle spirit;
          they shall have the earth for their possession.
6   How blest are those who hunger and thirst to see right prevail;*a*
          they shall be satisfied.
7   How blest are those who show mercy;
          mercy shall be shown to them.
8   How blest are those whose hearts are pure;
          they shall see God.
9   How blest are the peacemakers;
          God shall call them his sons.
10   How blest are those who have suffered persecution for the cause
          of right;
          the kingdom of Heaven is theirs.

11   'How blest you are, when you suffer insults and persecution and
12   every kind of calumny for my sake. Accept it with gladness and
     exultation, for you have a rich reward in heaven; in the same way
     they persecuted the prophets before you.
13   'You are salt to the world. And if salt becomes tasteless, how is its
     saltness to be restored? It is now good for nothing but to be thrown
     away and trodden underfoot.
14   'You are light for all the world. A town that stands on a hill
15   cannot be hidden. When a lamp is lit, it is not put under the meal-
     tub, but on the lamp-stand, where it gives light to everyone in the
16   house. And you, like the lamp, must shed light among your fellows,
     so that, when they see the good you do, they may give praise to your
     Father in heaven.

17   'DO NOT SUPPOSE that I have come to abolish the Law and the
18   prophets; I did not come to abolish, but to complete. I tell you
     this: so long as heaven and earth endure, not a letter, not a stroke,
     will disappear from the Law until all that must happen has happened.*b*
19   If any man therefore sets aside even the least of the Law's demands,
     and teaches others to do the same, he will have the lowest place in

[a] *Or* to do what is right. [b] *Or* before all that it stands for is achieved.

8

the kingdom of Heaven, whereas anyone who keeps the Law and
teaches others so will stand high in the kingdom of Heaven. I tell 20
you, unless you show yourselves far better men than the Pharisees and
the doctors of the law, you can never enter the kingdom of Heaven.

'You have learned that our forefathers were told, "Do not commit 21
murder; anyone who commits murder must be brought to judgement." But what I tell you is this: Anyone who nurses anger against 22
his brother*a* must be brought to judgement. If he abuses his brother
he must answer for it to the court; if he sneers at him he will have
to answer for it in the fires of hell.

'If, when you are bringing your gift to the altar, you suddenly 23
remember that your brother has a grievance against you, leave your 24
gift where it is before the altar. First go and make your peace with
your brother, and only then come back and offer your gift.

'If someone sues you, come to terms with him promptly while 25
you are both on your way to court; otherwise he may hand you over
to the judge, and the judge to the constable, and you will be put in
jail. I tell you, once you are there you will not be let out till you have 26
paid the last farthing.

'You have learned that they were told, "Do not commit adultery." 27
But what I tell you is this: If a man looks on a woman with a lustful 28
eye, he has already committed adultery with her in his heart.

'If your right eye leads you astray, tear it out and fling it away; 29
it is better for you to lose one part of your body than for the whole
of it to be thrown into hell. And if your right hand is your undoing, 30
cut it off and fling it away; it is better for you to lose one part of your
body than for the whole of it to go to hell.

'They were told, "A man who divorces his wife must give her a 31
note of dismissal." But what I tell you is this: If a man divorces his 32
wife for any cause other than unchastity he involves her in adultery;
and anyone who marries a woman so divorced commits adultery.

'Again, you have learned that they were told, "Do not break your 33
oath", and, "Oaths sworn to the Lord must be kept." But what I tell 34
you is this: You are not to swear at all—not by heaven, for it is God's
throne, nor by earth, for it is his footstool, nor by Jerusalem, for it 35
is the city of the great King, nor by your own head, because you 36
cannot turn one hair of it white or black. Plain "Yes" or "No" is all 37
you need to say; anything beyond that comes from the devil.

[a] *Some witnesses insert* without good cause.

9

38 'You have learned that they were told, "An eye for an eye, and
39 a tooth for a tooth." But what I tell you is this: Do not set yourself
against the man who wrongs you. If someone slaps you on the right
40 cheek, turn and offer him your left. If a man wants to sue you for
41 your shirt, let him have your coat as well. If a man in authority
42 makes you go one mile, go with him two. Give when you are
asked to give; and do not turn your back on a man who wants to
borrow.

43   'You have learned that they were told, "Love your neighbour, hate
44 your enemy." But what I tell you is this: Love your enemies*ᵃ* and
45 pray for your persecutors;*ᵇ* only so can you be children of your
heavenly Father, who makes his sun rise on good and bad alike, and
46 sends the rain on the honest and the dishonest. If you love only
those who love you, what reward can you expect? Surely the tax-
47 gatherers do as much as that. And if you greet only your brothers,
what is there extraordinary about that? Even the heathen do as
48 much. You must therefore be all goodness, just as your heavenly
Father is all good.

6 'BE CAREFUL not to make a show of your religion before men; if
you do, no reward awaits you in your Father's house in heaven.

2   'Thus, when you do some act of charity, do not announce it with
a flourish of trumpets, as the hypocrites do in synagogue and in the
streets to win admiration from men. I tell you this: they have their
3 reward already. No; when you do some act of charity, do not let
4 your left hand know what your right is doing; your good deed must
be secret, and your Father who sees what is done in secret will
reward you.*ᶜ*

5   'Again, when you pray, do not be like the hypocrites; they love
to say their prayers standing up in synagogue and at the street-
corners, for everyone to see them. I tell you this: they have their
6 reward already. But when you pray, go into a room by yourself,
shut the door, and pray to your Father who is there in the secret
place; and your Father who sees what is secret will reward you.*ᵈ*

7   'In your prayers do not go babbling on like the heathen, who
imagine that the more they say the more likely they are to be heard.

[*a*] *Some witnesses insert* bless those who curse you, do good to those who hate you.
[*b*] *Some witnesses insert* and those who treat you spitefully. [*c*] *Some witnesses add*
openly. [*d*] *Some witnesses add* openly.

Do not imitate them. Your Father knows what your needs are before 8
you ask him.

'This is how you should pray: 9

> "Our Father in heaven,
> Thy name be hallowed;
> Thy kingdom come,   10
> Thy will be done,
> On earth as in heaven.
> Give us today our daily bread.*   11
> Forgive us the wrong we have done,   12
> As we have forgiven those who have wronged us.
> And do not bring us to the test,   13
> But save us from the evil one."*

For if you forgive others the wrongs they have done, your heavenly 14
Father will also forgive you; but if you do not forgive others, then the 15
wrongs you have done will not be forgiven by your Father.

'So too when you fast, do not look gloomy like the hypocrites: 16
they make their faces unsightly so that other people may see that
they are fasting. I tell you this: they have their reward already.
But when you fast, anoint your head and wash your face, so that 17, 18
men may not see that you are fasting, but only your Father who is
in the secret place; and your Father who sees what is secret will give
you your reward.

'DO NOT STORE up for yourselves treasure on earth, where it 19
grows rusty and moth-eaten, and thieves break in to steal it. Store 20
up treasure in heaven, where there is no moth and no rust to spoil
it, no thieves to break in and steal. For where your wealth is, there 21
will your heart be also.

'The lamp of the body is the eye. If your eyes are sound, you will 22
have light for your whole body; if the eyes are bad, your whole body 23
will be in darkness. If then the only light you have is darkness, the
darkness is doubly dark.

'No servant can be slave to two masters; for either he will hate 24
the first and love the second, or he will be devoted to the first and
think nothing of the second. You cannot serve God and Money.

[a] *Or* our bread for the morrow. [b] *Some witnesses add* For thine is the kingdom and
the power and the glory, for ever. Amen.

25 'Therefore I bid you put away anxious thoughts about food and drink to keep you alive, and clothes to cover your body. Surely life
26 is more than food, the body more than clothes. Look at the birds of the air; they do not sow and reap and store in barns, yet your
27 heavenly Father feeds them. You are worth more than the birds! Is there a man of you who by anxious thought can add a foot to his
28 height[a]? And why be anxious about clothes? Consider how the lilies
29 grow in the fields; they do not work, they do not spin;[b] and yet, I tell you, even Solomon in all his splendour was not attired like
30 one of these. But if that is how God clothes the grass in the fields, which is there today, and tomorrow is thrown on the stove, will he
31 not all the more clothe you? How little faith you have! No, do not ask anxiously, "What are we to eat? What are we to drink? What
32 shall we wear?" All these are things for the heathen to run after, not for you, because your heavenly Father knows that you need them all.
33 Set your mind on God's kingdom and his justice before everything
34 else, and all the rest will come to you as well. So do not be anxious about tomorrow; tomorrow will look after itself. Each day has troubles enough of its own.

7 1,2 'PASS NO JUDGEMENT, and you will not be judged. For as you judge others, so you will yourselves be judged, and whatever measure
3 you deal out to others will be dealt back to you. Why do you look at the speck of sawdust in your brother's eye, with never a thought for
4 the great plank in your own? Or how can you say to your brother, "Let me take the speck out of your eye", when all the time there is
5 that plank in your own? You hypocrite! First take the plank out of your own eye, and then you will see clearly to take the speck out of your brother's.
6 'Do not give dogs what is holy; do not feed your pearls to pigs: they will only trample on them, and turn and tear you to pieces.
7 'Ask, and you will receive; seek, and you will find; knock, and the
8 door will be opened. For everyone who asks receives, he who seeks finds, and to him who knocks, the door will be opened.
9 'Is there a man among you who will offer his son a stone when he
10,11 asks for bread, or a snake when he asks for fish? If you, then, bad as you are, know how to give your children what is good for them,

[a] Or a day to his life. [b] One witness reads Consider the lilies: they neither card nor spin, nor labour.

how much more will your heavenly Father give good things to those who ask him!

'Always treat others as you would like them to treat you: that is 12 the Law and the prophets.

'Enter by the narrow gate. The gate is wide that leads to perdition, 13 there is plenty of room on the road,*a* and many go that way; but the 14 gate that leads to life is small and the road is narrow,*b* and those who find it are few.

'Beware of false prophets, men who come to you dressed up as 15 sheep while underneath they are savage wolves. You will recognize 16 them by the fruits they bear. Can grapes be picked from briars, or figs from thistles? In the same way, a good tree always yields good 17 fruit, and a poor tree bad fruit. A good tree cannot bear bad fruit, 18 or a poor tree good fruit. And when a tree does not yield good fruit 19 it is cut down and burnt. That is why I say you will recognize them 20 by their fruits.

'Not everyone who calls me "Lord, Lord" will enter the kingdom 21 of Heaven, but only those who do the will of my heavenly Father. When that day comes, many will say to me, "Lord, Lord, did we 22 not prophesy in your name, cast out devils in your name, and in your name perform many miracles?" Then I will tell them to their face, 23 "I never knew you: out of my sight, you and your wicked ways!"

'What then of the man who hears these words of mine and acts 24 upon them? He is like a man who had the sense to build his house on rock. The rain came down, the floods rose, the wind blew, and beat 25 upon that house; but it did not fall, because its foundations were on rock. But what of the man who hears these words of mine and does not 26 act upon them? He is like a man who was foolish enough to build his house on sand. The rain came down, the floods rose, the wind blew, 27 and beat upon that house; down it fell with a great crash.'

When Jesus had finished this discourse the people were astounded 28 at his teaching; unlike their own teachers he taught with a note of 29 authority.

[a] *Some witnesses read* The road that leads to perdition is wide with plenty of room.
[b] *Some witnesses read* but the road that leads to life is small and narrow.

Teaching and Healing

8 AFTER HE HAD come down from the hill he was followed by
2 a great crowd. And now a leper approached him, bowed low,
3 and said, 'Sir, if only you will, you can cleanse me.' Jesus stretched
out his hand, touched him, and said, 'Indeed I will; be clean again.'
4 And his leprosy was cured immediately. Then Jesus said to him,
'Be sure you tell nobody; but go and show yourself to the priest,
and make the offering laid down by Moses for your cleansing; that
will certify the cure.'
5   When he had entered Capernaum a centurion came up to ask his
6 help. 'Sir,' he said, 'a boy of mine lies at home paralysed and racked
7, 8 with pain.' Jesus said, 'I will come and cure him.'*a* But the centurion replied, 'Sir, who am I to have you under my roof? You need
9 only say the word and the boy will be cured. I know, for I am myself
under orders, with soldiers under me. I say to one, "Go", and he
goes; to another, "Come here", and he comes; and to my servant,
10 "Do this", and he does it.' Jesus heard him with astonishment, and
said to the people who were following him, 'I tell you this: nowhere,
even in Israel, have I found such faith.
11   'Many, I tell you, will come from east and west to feast with
12 Abraham, Isaac, and Jacob in the kingdom of Heaven. But those
who were born to the kingdom will be driven out into the dark, the
place of wailing and grinding of teeth.'
13   Then Jesus said to the centurion, 'Go home now; because of your
faith, so let it be.' At that moment the boy recovered.
14   Jesus then went to Peter's house and found Peter's mother-in-law
15 in bed with fever. So he took her by the hand; the fever left her,
and she got up and waited on him.
16   When evening fell, they brought to him many who were possessed
by devils; and he drove the spirits out with a word and healed all
17 who were ill, to make good the prophecy of Isaiah: 'He took away
our illnesses and lifted our diseases from us.'*b*

18 AT THE SIGHT of the crowds surrounding him Jesus gave word to
19 cross to the other shore. A doctor of the law came up, and said,

[a] Or Am I to come and cure him?   [b] Or and bore the burden of our diseases.

'Master, I will follow you wherever you go.' Jesus replied, 'Foxes 20 have their holes, the birds their roosts; but the Son of Man has nowhere to lay his head.' Another man, one of his disciples, said to 21 him, 'Lord, let me go and bury my father first.' Jesus replied, 22 'Follow me, and leave the dead to bury their dead.'

Jesus then got into the boat, and his disciples followed. All at 23, 24 once a great storm arose on the lake, till the waves were breaking right over the boat; but he went on sleeping. So they came and woke 25 him up, crying: 'Save us, Lord; we are sinking!' 'Why are you such 26 cowards?' he said; 'how little faith you have!' Then he stood up and rebuked the wind and the sea, and there was a dead calm. The 27 men were astonished at what had happened, and exclaimed, 'What sort of man is this, that even the wind and the sea obey him?'

When he reached the other side, in the country of the Gadarenes, 28 he was met by two men who came out from the tombs; they were possessed by devils, and so violent that no one dared pass that way. 'You son of God,' they shouted, 'what do you want with us? Have 29 you come here to torment us before our time?' In the distance a 30 large herd of pigs was feeding; and the devils begged him: 'If you 31 drive us out, send us into that herd of pigs.' 'Begone', he said. 32 Then they came out and went into the pigs; the whole herd rushed over the edge into the lake, and perished in the water.

The men in charge of them took to their heels, and made for the 33 town, where they told the whole story, and what had happened to the madmen. Thereupon the whole town came out to meet Jesus; 34 and when they saw him they begged him to leave the district and go. So he got into the boat and crossed over, and came to his own 9 town.

And now some men brought him a paralytic lying on a bed. 2 Seeing their faith Jesus said to the man, 'Take heart, my son; your sins are forgiven.' At this some of the lawyers said to themselves, 3 'This is blasphemous talk.' Jesus read their thoughts, and said, 4 'Why do you harbour these evil thoughts? Is it easier to say, "Your 5 sins are forgiven", or to say, "Stand up and walk"? But to convince 6 you that the Son of Man has the right on earth to forgive sins'—he now addressed the paralytic—'stand up, take your bed, and go home.' Thereupon the man got up, and went off home. The people were 7, 8 filled with awe at the sight, and praised God for granting such authority to men.

9 AS HE PASSED on from there Jesus saw a man named Matthew at his seat in the custom-house; and he said to him, 'Follow me.' And Matthew rose and followed him.

10 When Jesus was at table in the house, many bad characters—
11 tax-gatherers and others—were seated with him and his disciples. The Pharisees noticed this, and said to his disciples, 'Why is it that your
12 master eats with tax-gatherers and sinners?' Jesus heard them and
13 said, 'It is not the healthy that need a doctor, but the sick. Go and learn what that text means, "I require mercy, not sacrifice." I did not come to invite virtuous people, but sinners.'

14 Then John's disciples came to him with the question: 'Why do we
15 and the Pharisees fast, but your disciples do not?' Jesus replied, 'Can you expect the bridegroom's friends to go mourning while the bridegroom is with them? The time will come when the bridegroom will be taken away from them; that will be the time for them to fast.

16 'No one sews a patch of unshrunk cloth on to an old coat; for then
17 the patch tears away from the coat, and leaves a bigger hole. No more do you put new wine into old wine-skins; if you do, the skins burst, and then the wine runs out and the skins are spoilt. No, you put new wine into fresh skins; then both are preserved.'

18 EVEN AS HE SPOKE, there came a president of the synagogue, who bowed low before him and said, 'My daughter has just died; but
19 come and lay your hand on her, and she will live.' Jesus rose and went with him, and so did his disciples.

20 Then a woman who had suffered from haemorrhages for twelve
21 years came up from behind, and touched the edge of his cloak; for she said to herself, 'If I can only touch his cloak, I shall be cured.'
22 But Jesus turned and saw her, and said, 'My daughter, your faith has cured you.' And from that moment she recovered.

23 When Jesus arrived at the president's house and saw the flute-
24 players and the general commotion, he said, 'Be off! The girl is
25 not dead: she is asleep'; but they only laughed at him. But, when everyone had been turned out, he went into the room and took the
26 girl by the hand, and she got up. This story became the talk of all the country round.

27 As he passed on Jesus was followed by two blind men, who cried
28 out, 'Son of David, have pity on us!' And when he had gone indoors they came to him. Jesus asked, 'Do you believe that I have

the power to do what you want?' 'Yes, sir', they said. Then he 29
touched their eyes, and said, 'As you have believed, so let it be';
and their sight was restored. Jesus said to them sternly, 'See that 30
no one hears about this.' But as soon as they had gone out they 31
talked about him all over the country-side.

They were on their way out when a man was brought to him, who 32
was dumb and possessed by a devil; the devil was cast out and the 33
patient recovered his speech. Filled with amazement the onlookers
said, 'Nothing like this has ever been seen in Israel. He casts out 34
devils*a* by the prince of devils.'

So JESUS went round all the towns and villages teaching in their 35
synagogues, announcing the good news of the Kingdom, and curing
every kind of ailment and disease. The sight of the people moved him 36
to pity: they were like sheep without a shepherd, harassed and
helpless; and he said to his disciples, 'The crop is heavy, but 37
labourers are scarce; you must therefore beg the owner to send 38
labourers to harvest his crop.'

Then he called his twelve disciples to him and gave them authority 10
to cast out unclean spirits and to cure every kind of ailment and
disease.

These are the names of the twelve apostles: first Simon, also 2
called Peter, and his brother Andrew; James son of Zebedee, and his
brother John; Philip and Bartholomew, Thomas and Matthew the 3
tax-gatherer, James son of Alphaeus, Lebbaeus,*b* Simon, a member 4
of the Zealot party, and Judas Iscariot, the man who betrayed him.

These twelve Jesus sent out with the following instructions: 'Do 5
not take the road to gentile lands, and do not enter any Samaritan
town; but go rather to the lost sheep of the house of Israel. And as 6, 7
you go proclaim the message: "The kingdom of Heaven is upon you."
Heal the sick, raise the dead, cleanse lepers, cast out devils. You 8
received without cost; give without charge.

'Provide no gold, silver, or copper to fill your purse, no pack for the 9, 10
road, no second coat, no shoes, no stick; the worker earns his keep.

'When you come to any town or village, look for some worthy 11
person in it, and make your home there until you leave. Wish the 12
house peace as you enter it, so that, if it is worthy, your peace may 13

[a] *Some witnesses read* But the Pharisees said, 'He casts out devils...' [b] *Some witnesses read* Thaddaeus.

17

descend on it; if it is not worthy, your peace can come back to you.
14 If anyone will not receive you or listen to what you say, then as you
15 leave that house or that town shake the dust of it off your feet. I tell
you this: on the day of judgement it will be more bearable for the
land of Sodom and Gomorrah than for that town.

16   'Look, I send you out like sheep among wolves; be wary as
serpents, innocent as doves.

17   'And be on your guard, for men will hand you over to their courts,
18 they will flog you in the synagogues, and you will be brought before
governors and kings, for my sake, to testify before them and the
19 heathen. But when you are arrested, do not worry about what you
are to say; when the time comes, the words you need will be given
20 you; for it is not you who will be speaking: it will be the Spirit of
your Father speaking in you.

21   'Brother will betray brother to death, and the father his child;
children will turn against their parents and send them to their death.
22 All will hate you for your allegiance to me; but the man who holds
23 out to the end will be saved. When you are persecuted in one town,
take refuge in another; I tell you this: before you have gone through
all the towns of Israel the Son of Man will have come.

24   'A pupil does not rank above his teacher, or a servant above his
25 master. The pupil should be content to share his teacher's lot, the
servant to share his master's. If the master has been called Beelzebub,
how much more his household!

26   'So do not be afraid of them. There is nothing covered up that
will not be uncovered, nothing hidden that will not be made known.
27 What I say to you in the dark you must repeat in broad daylight;
28 what you hear whispered you must shout from the house-tops. Do
not fear those who kill the body, but cannot kill the soul. Fear him
rather who is able to destroy both soul and body in hell.

29   'Are not sparrows two a penny? Yet without your Father's leave
30 not one of them can fall to the ground. As for you, even the hairs
31 of your head have all been counted. So have no fear; you are worth
more than any number of sparrows.

32   'Whoever then will acknowledge me before men, I will acknow-
33 ledge him before my Father in heaven; and whoever disowns me
before men, I will disown him before my Father in heaven.

34   'You must not think that I have come to bring peace to the earth;
35 I have not come to bring peace, but a sword. I have come to set

a man against his father, a daughter against her mother, a young wife against her mother-in-law; and a man will find his enemies 36 under his own roof.

'No man is worthy of me who cares more for father or mother 37 than for me; no man is worthy of me who cares more for son or daughter; no man is worthy of me who does not take up his cross 38 and walk in my footsteps. By gaining his life a man will lose it; by 39 losing his life for my sake, he will gain it.

'To receive you is to receive me, and to receive me is to receive 40 the One who sent me. Whoever receives a prophet as a prophet will 41 be given a prophet's reward, and whoever receives a good man because he is a good man will be given a good man's reward. And if 42 anyone gives so much as a cup of cold water to one of these little ones, because he is a disciple of mine, I tell you this: that man will assuredly not go unrewarded.'

When Jesus had finished giving his twelve disciples their instruc- 11 tions, he left that place and went to teach and preach in the neighbouring towns.

JOHN, WHO WAS in prison, heard what Christ was doing, and sent 2 his own disciples to him with this message: 'Are you the one who 3 is to come, or are we to expect some other?' Jesus answered, 'Go and 4 tell John what you hear and see: the blind recover their sight, the 5 lame walk, the lepers are clean, the deaf hear, the dead are raised to life, the poor are hearing the good news—and happy is the man 6 who does not find me a stumbling-block.'

When the messengers were on their way back, Jesus began to 7 speak to the people about John: 'What was the spectacle that drew you to the wilderness? A reed-bed swept by the wind? No? Then 8 what did you go out to see? A man dressed in silks and satins? Surely you must look in palaces for that. But why did you go out? 9 To see a prophet? Yes indeed, and far more than a prophet. He is 10 the man of whom Scripture says,

"Here is my herald, whom I send on ahead of you,
And he will prepare your way before you."

I tell you this: never has there appeared on earth a mother's son 11 greater than John the Baptist, and yet the least in the kingdom of Heaven is greater than he.

12 'Ever since the coming of John the Baptist the kingdom of Heaven
13 has been subjected to violence and violent men^a are seizing it. For
    all the prophets and the Law foretold things to come until John
14 appeared, and John is the destined Elijah, if you will but accept it.
15 If you have ears that can hear, then hear.
16   'How can I describe this generation? They are like the children
    sitting in the market-place and shouting at each other,

17   "We piped for you and you would not dance."
            "We wept and wailed, and you would not mourn."

18 For John came, neither eating nor drinking, and they say, "He is
19 possessed." The Son of Man came eating and drinking, and they say,
    "Look at him! a glutton and a drinker, a friend of tax-gatherers and
    sinners!" And yet God's wisdom is proved right by its results.'

20 THEN HE SPOKE of the towns in which most of his miracles had
21 been performed, and denounced them for their impenitence. 'Alas for
    you, Chorazin!' he said; 'alas for you, Bethsaida! If the miracles
    that were performed in you had been performed in Tyre and Sidon,
22 they would long ago have repented in sackcloth and ashes. But it
    will be more bearable, I tell you, for Tyre and Sidon on the day of
23 judgement than for you. And as for you, Capernaum, will you be
    exalted to the skies? No, brought down to the depths! For if the
    miracles had been performed in Sodom which were performed in
24 you, Sodom would be standing to this day. But it will be more
    bearable, I tell you, for the land of Sodom on the day of judgement
    than for you.'
25   At that time Jesus spoke these words: 'I thank thee, Father, Lord
    of heaven and earth, for hiding these things from the learned and
26 wise, and revealing them to the simple. Yes, Father, such^b was thy
27 choice. Everything is entrusted to me by my Father; and no one
    knows the Son but the Father, and no one knows the Father but the
    Son and those to whom the Son may choose to reveal him.
28   'Come to me, all whose work is hard, whose load is heavy; and
29 I will give you relief. Bend your necks to my yoke, and learn from
    me, for I am gentle and humble-hearted; and your souls will find
30 relief. For my yoke is good to bear, my load is light.'

[a] *Or* has been forcing its way forward, and men of force... [b] *Or* Yes, I thank thee,
Father, that such...

Controversy

ONCE ABOUT that time Jesus took a walk on the Sabbath through 12
the cornfields; and his disciples, feeling hungry, began to pluck
some ears of corn and eat them. The Pharisees noticed this, and said 2
to him, 'Look, your disciples are doing something which is forbidden
on the Sabbath.' He answered, 'Have you not read what David did 3
when he and his men were hungry? He went into the House of God 4
and ate the consecrated loaves, though neither he nor his men had a
right to eat them, but only the priests. Or have you not read in the 5
Law that on the Sabbath the priests in the temple break the Sabbath
and it is not held against them? I tell you, there is something greater 6
than the temple here. If you had known what that text means, 7
"I require mercy, not sacrifice", you would not have condemned the
innocent. For the Son of Man is sovereign over the Sabbath.' 8
He went on to another place, and entered their synagogue. 9
A man was there with a withered arm, and they asked Jesus, 'Is it 10
permitted to heal on the Sabbath?' (Their aim was to frame a charge
against him.) But he said to them, 'Suppose you had one sheep, 11
which fell into a ditch on the Sabbath; is there one of you who would
not catch hold of it and lift it out? And surely a man is worth far 12
more than a sheep! It is therefore permitted to do good on the
Sabbath.' Turning to the man he said, 'Stretch out your arm.' He 13
stretched it out, and it was made sound again like the other. But 14
the Pharisees, on leaving the synagogue, laid a plot to do away with
him.
Jesus was aware of it and withdrew. Many followed, and he cured 15
all who were ill; and he gave strict injunctions that they were not to 16
make him known. This was in fulfilment of Isaiah's prophecy: 17

'Here is my servant, whom I have chosen, 18
My beloved, on whom my favour rests;
I will put my Spirit upon him,
And he will proclaim judgement among the nations.
He will not strive, he will not shout, 19
Nor will his voice be heard in the streets.
He will not snap off the broken reed, 20

Nor snuff out the smouldering wick,
Until he leads justice on to victory.
21   In him the nations shall place their hope.'

22 THEN THEY BROUGHT HIM a man who was possessed; he was
blind and dumb; and Jesus cured him, restoring both speech and
23 sight. The bystanders were all amazed, and the word went round:
24 'Can this be the Son of David?' But when the Pharisees heard it they
said, 'It is only by Beelzebub prince of devils that this man drives
the devils out.'

25   He knew what was in their minds; so he said to them, 'Every
kingdom divided against itself goes to ruin; and no town, no house-
26 hold, that is divided against itself can stand. And if it is Satan who
casts out Satan, Satan is divided against himself; how then can his
27 kingdom stand? And if it is by Beelzebub that I cast out devils, by
whom do your own people drive them out? If this is your argument,
28 they themselves will refute you. But if it is by the Spirit of God that
I drive out the devils, then be sure the kingdom of God has already
come upon you.

29   'Or again, how can anyone break into a strong man's house and
make off with his goods unless he has first tied the strong man up
before ransacking the house?

30   'He who is not with me is against me, and he who does not gather
with me scatters.

31   'And so I tell you this: no sin, no slander, is beyond forgiveness
for men, except slander spoken against the Spirit, and that will not
32 be forgiven. Any man who speaks a word against the Son of Man
will be forgiven; but if anyone speaks against the Holy Spirit, for
him there is no forgiveness, either in this age or in the age to come.

33   'Either make the tree good and its fruit good, or make the tree
34 bad and its fruit bad; you can tell a tree by its fruit. You vipers'
brood! How can your words be good when you yourselves are evil?
For the words that the mouth utters come from the overflowing of
35 the heart. A good man produces good from the store of good
within himself; and an evil man from evil within produces evil.

36   'I tell you this: there is not a thoughtless word that comes from
men's lips but they will have to account for it on the day of judgement.
37 For out of your own mouth you will be acquitted; out of your own
mouth you will be condemned.'

At this some of the doctors of the law and the Pharisees said, 38
'Master, we should like you to show us a sign.' He answered: 'It is 39
a wicked, godless generation that asks for a sign; and the only sign
that will be given it is the sign of the prophet Jonah. Jonah was in 40
the sea-monster's belly for three days and three nights, and in the
same way the Son of Man will be three days and three nights in the
bowels of the earth. At the Judgement, when this generation is on 41
trial, the men of Nineveh will appear against it[a] and ensure its
condemnation, for they repented at the preaching of Jonah; and
what is here is greater than Jonah. The Queen of the South 42
will appear at the Judgement when this generation is on trial,[b] and
ensure its condemnation, for she came from the ends of the earth
to hear the wisdom of Solomon; and what is here is greater than
Solomon.

'When an unclean spirit comes out of a man it wanders over the 43
deserts seeking a resting-place; and finding none, it says, "I will go 44
back to the home I left." So it returns and finds the house unoccupied, swept clean, and tidy. Off it goes and collects seven other 45
spirits more wicked than itself, and they all come in and settle down;
and in the end the man's plight is worse than before. That is how
it will be with this wicked generation.'

He was still speaking to the crowd when his mother and brothers 46
appeared; they stood outside, wanting to speak to him. Someone 47
said, 'Your mother and your brothers are here outside; they want
to speak to you.' Jesus turned to the man who brought the message, 48
and said, 'Who is my mother? Who are my brothers?'; and pointing 49
to the disciples, he said, 'Here are my mother and my brothers. Who- 50
ever does the will of my heavenly Father is my brother, my sister,
my mother.'

THAT SAME DAY Jesus went out and sat beside the lake, where so 13 1,2
many people gathered round him that he had to get into a boat. He
sat there, and all the people stood on the shore. He spoke to them in 3
parables, at some length.

He said: 'A sower went out to sow. And as he sowed, some seed 4
fell along the footpath; and the birds came and ate it up. Some seed 5
fell on rocky ground, where it had little soil; it sprouted quickly

[a] Or will rise again together with it. [b] Or At the Judgement the Queen of the South
will be raised to life together with this generation.

6 because it had no depth of earth, but when the sun rose the young
7 corn was scorched, and as it had no root it withered away. Some
seed fell among thistles; and the thistles shot up, and choked the
8 corn. And some of the seed fell into good soil, where it bore fruit,
9 yielding a hundredfold or, it might be, sixtyfold or thirtyfold. If you
have ears, then hear.'
10   The disciples went up to him and asked, 'Why do you speak to
11 them in parables?' He replied, 'It has been granted to you to know
the secrets of the kingdom of Heaven; but to those others it has not
12 been granted. For the man who has will be given more, till he has
enough and to spare; and the man who has not will forfeit even what
13 he has. That is why I speak to them in parables; for they look without
14 seeing, and listen without hearing or understanding. There is a prophecy of Isaiah which is being fulfilled for them: "You will hear and
15 hear, but never understand; you will look and look, but never see. For
this people has grown gross at heart; their ears are dull, and their
eyes are closed. Otherwise, their eyes might see, their ears hear,
and their heart understand, and then they might turn again, and I
would heal them."
16   'But happy are your eyes because they see, and your ears because
17 they hear! Many prophets and saints, I tell you, desired to see
what you now see, yet never saw it; to hear what you hear, yet never
heard it.
18, 19   'You, then, may hear the parable of the sower. When a man hears
the word that tells of the Kingdom but fails to understand it, the evil
one comes and carries off what has been sown in his heart. There
20 you have the seed sown along the footpath. The seed sown on rocky
ground stands for the man who, on hearing the word, accepts it
21 at once with joy; but as it strikes no root in him he has no staying-
power, and when there is trouble or persecution on account of the
22 word he falls away at once. The seed sown among thistles represents
the man who hears the word, but worldly cares and the false glamour
23 of wealth choke it, and it proves barren. But the seed that fell into
good soil is the man who hears the word and understands it, who
accordingly bears fruit, and yields a hundredfold or, it may be,
sixtyfold or thirtyfold.'
24   Here is another parable that he put before them: 'The kingdom
25 of Heaven is like this. A man sowed his field with good seed; but
while everyone was asleep his enemy came, sowed darnel among the

24

wheat, and made off. When the corn sprouted and began to fill out, 26 the darnel could be seen among it. The farmer's men went to their 27 master and said, "Sir, was it not good seed that you sowed in your field? Then where has the darnel come from?" "This is an enemy's 28 doing", he replied. "Well then," they said, "shall we go and gather the darnel?" "No," he answered; "in gathering it you might pull up the 29 wheat at the same time. Let them both grow together till harvest; 30 and at harvest-time I will tell the reapers, 'Gather the darnel first, and tie it in bundles for burning; then collect the wheat into my barn.'"'

And this is another parable that he put before them: 'The kingdom 31 of Heaven is like mustard-seed, which a man took and sowed in his field. As a seed, mustard is smaller than any other; but 32 when it has grown it is bigger than any garden-plant; it becomes a tree, big enough for the birds to come and roost among its branches.'

He told them also this parable: 'The kingdom of Heaven is like 33 yeast, which a woman took and mixed with half a hundredweight of flour till it was all leavened.'

In all this teaching to the crowds Jesus spoke in parables; in fact 34 he never spoke to them without a parable; thus making good the 35 prophecy of Isaiah:[a]

'I will open my mouth in parables;
I will utter things kept secret since the world was made.'

He then dismissed the people, and went into the house, where his 36 disciples came to him and said, 'Explain to us the parable of the darnel in the field.' And this was his answer: 'The sower of the good 37 seed is the Son of Man. The field is the world; the good seed stands 38 for the children of the Kingdom, the darnel for the children of the evil one. The enemy who sowed the darnel is the devil. The harvest 39 is the end of time. The reapers are angels. As the darnel, then, is 40 gathered up and burnt, so at the end of time the Son of Man will 41 send out his angels, who will gather out of his kingdom everything that causes offence, and all whose deeds are evil, and these will be 42 thrown into the blazing furnace, the place of wailing and grinding of teeth. And then the righteous will shine as brightly as the sun in 43 the kingdom of their Father. If you have ears, then hear.

[a] *Some witnesses omit* of Isaiah.

44 'The kingdom of Heaven is like treasure lying buried in a field. The man who found it, buried it again; and for sheer joy went and sold everything he had, and bought that field.

45 'Here is another picture of the kingdom of Heaven. A merchant
46 looking out for fine pearls found one of very special value; so he went and sold everything he had, and bought it.

47 'Again the kingdom of Heaven is like a net let down into the sea,
48 where fish of every kind were caught in it. When it was full, it was dragged ashore. Then the men sat down and collected the good fish
49 into pails and threw the worthless away. That is how it will be at the end of time. The angels will go forth, and they will separate the
50 wicked from the good, and throw them into the blazing furnace, the place of wailing and grinding of teeth.

51 'Have you understood all this?' he asked; and they answered,
52 'Yes.' He said to them, 'When, therefore, a teacher of the law has become a learner in the kingdom of Heaven, he is like a householder who can produce from his store both the new and the old.'

53, 54 WHEN HE HAD finished these parables Jesus left that place, and came to his home town, where he taught the people in their synagogue. In amazement they asked, 'Where does he get this wisdom
55 from, and these miraculous powers? Is he not the carpenter's son? Is not his mother called Mary, his brothers James, Joseph, Simon,
56 and Judas? And are not all his sisters here with us? Where then has
57 he got all this from?' So they fell foul of him, and this led him to say, 'A prophet will always be held in honour, except in his home town,
58 and in his own family.' And he did not work many miracles there: such was their want of faith.

14 It was at that time that reports about Jesus reached the ears of
2 Prince Herod. 'This is John the Baptist,' he said to his attendants; 'John has been raised to life, and that is why these miraculous powers are at work in him.'

3 FOR HEROD had arrested John, put him in chains, and thrown him
4 into prison, on account of Herodias, his brother Philip's wife; for
5 John had told him: 'You have no right to her.' Herod would have liked to put him to death, but he was afraid of the people, in whose
6 eyes John was a prophet. But at his birthday celebrations the daughter of Herodias danced before the guests, and Herod was so

delighted that he took an oath to give her anything she cared to ask. 7
Prompted by her mother, she said, 'Give me here on a dish the head 8
of John the Baptist.' The king was deeply distressed when he heard 9
it; but out of regard for his oath and for his guests, he ordered the
request to be granted, and had John beheaded in prison. The head 10, 11
was brought in on a dish and given to the girl; and she carried it
to her mother. Then John's disciples came and took away the body, 12
and buried it; and they went and told Jesus.

WHEN HE HEARD what had happened Jesus withdrew privately by 13
boat to a lonely place; but people heard of it, and came after him in
crowds by land from the towns. When he came ashore, he saw 14
a great crowd; his heart went out to them, and he cured those of
them who were sick. When it grew late the disciples came up to 15
him and said, 'This is a lonely place, and the day has gone; send
the people off to the villages to buy themselves food.' He answered, 16
'There is no need for them to go; give them something to eat
yourselves.' 'All we have here', they said, 'is five loaves and two 17
fishes.' 'Let me have them', he replied. So he told the people to 18, 19
sit down on the grass; then, taking the five loaves and the two fishes,
he looked up to heaven, said the blessing, broke the loaves, and gave
them to the disciples; and the disciples gave them to the people.
They all ate to their hearts' content; and the scraps left over, which 20
they picked up, were enough to fill twelve great baskets. Some 21
five thousand men shared in this meal, to say nothing of women and
children.

Then he made the disciples embark and go on ahead to the other 22
side, while he sent the people away; after doing that, he went up the 23
hill-side to pray alone. It grew late, and he was there by himself.
The boat was already some furlongs from the shore,[a] battling with 24
a head-wind and a rough sea. Between three and six in the morning 25
he came to them, walking over the lake. When the disciples saw him 26
walking on the lake they were so shaken that they cried out in terror:
'It is a ghost!' But at once he spoke to them: 'Take heart! It is I; 27
do not be afraid.'

Peter called to him: 'Lord, if it is you, tell me to come to you over 28
the water.' 'Come', said Jesus. Peter stepped down from the boat, 29
and walked over the water towards Jesus. But when he saw the 30

[a] *Some witnesses read* already well out on the water.

strength of the gale he was seized with fear; and beginning to sink,
31 he cried, 'Save me, Lord.' Jesus at once reached out and caught
hold of him, and said, 'Why did you hesitate? How little faith you
32 have!' They then climbed into the boat; and the wind dropped.
33 And the men in the boat fell at his feet, exclaiming, 'Truly you are
the Son of God.'
34 So they finished the crossing and came to land at Gennesaret.
35 There Jesus was recognized by the people of the place, who sent
out word to all the country round. And all who were ill were brought
36 to him, and he was begged to allow them simply to touch the edge
of his cloak. And everyone who touched it was completely cured.

15 THEN JESUS was approached by a group of Pharisees and lawyers
2 from Jerusalem, with the question: 'Why do your disciples break
the old-established tradition? They do not wash their hands before
3 meals.' He answered them: 'And what of you? Why do you break
4 God's commandment in the interest of your tradition? For God
said, "Honour your father and mother", and, "The man who curses
5 his father or mother must suffer death." But you say, "If a man says
to his father or mother, 'Anything of mine which might have been
6 used for your benefit is set apart for God', then he must not honour
his father or his mother." You have made God's law null and void
7 out of respect for your tradition. What hypocrisy! Isaiah was right
8 when he prophesied about you: "This people pays me lip-service,
9 but their heart is far from me; their worship of me is in vain, for
they teach as doctrines the commandments of men."'
10 He called the crowd and said to them, 'Listen to me, and under-
11 stand this: a man is not defiled by what goes into his mouth, but
by what comes out of it.'
12 Then the disciples came to him and said, 'Do you know that the
13 Pharisees have taken great offence at what you have been saying?' His
answer was: 'Any plant that is not of my heavenly Father's planting
14 will be rooted up. Leave them alone; they are blind guides,*a* and if
one blind man guides another they will both fall into the ditch.'
15, 16 Then Peter said, 'Tell us what that parable means.' Jesus
17 answered, 'Are you still as dull as the rest? Do you not see that
whatever goes in by the mouth passes into the stomach and so is
18 discharged into the drain? But what comes out of the mouth has its

[a] *Some witnesses insert* of blind men.

28

origins in the heart; and that is what defiles a man. Wicked thoughts, 19
murder, adultery, fornication, theft, perjury, slander—these all proceed from the heart; and these are the things that defile a man; 20
but to eat without first washing his hands, that cannot defile him.'

Jesus and His Disciples

JESUS THEN LEFT that place and withdrew to the region of Tyre 21
and Sidon. And a Canaanite woman from those parts came crying 22
out, 'Sir! have pity on me, Son of David; my daughter is tormented
by a devil.' But he said not a word in reply. His disciples came and 23
urged him: 'Send her away; see how she comes shouting after us.'
Jesus replied, 'I was sent to the lost sheep of the house of Israel, and 24
to them alone.' But the woman came and fell at his feet and cried, 25
'Help me, sir.' To this Jesus replied, 'It is not right to take the 26
children's bread and throw it to the dogs.' 'True, sir,' she answered; 27
'and yet the dogs eat the scraps that fall from their masters' table.'
Hearing this Jesus replied, 'Woman, what faith you have! Be it 28
as you wish!' And from that moment her daughter was restored to
health.

After leaving that region Jesus took the road by the Sea of Galilee 29
and went up to the hills. When he was seated there, crowds flocked 30
to him, bringing with them the lame, blind, dumb, and crippled, and
many other sufferers; they flung them down at his feet, and he
healed them. Great was the amazement of the people when they saw 31
the dumb speaking, the crippled strong, the lame walking, and sight
restored to the blind; and they gave praise to the God of Israel.

Jesus called his disciples and said to them, 'I feel sorry for all these 32
people; they have been with me now for three days and have nothing
to eat. I do not want to send them away unfed; they might turn faint
on the way.' The disciples replied, 'Where in this lonely place can 33
we find bread enough to feed such a crowd?' 'How many loaves have 34
you?' Jesus asked. 'Seven,' they replied; 'and there are a few small
fishes.' So he ordered the people to sit down on the ground; 35
then he took the seven loaves and the fishes, and after giving thanks 36
to God he broke them and gave to the disciples, and the disciples
gave to the people. They all ate to their hearts' content; and the 37

scraps left over, which they picked up, were enough to fill seven
38 baskets. Four thousand men shared in this meal, to say nothing of
39 women and children. He then dismissed the crowds, got into a boat,
and went to the neighbourhood of Magadan.

16   The Pharisees and Sadducees came, and to test him they asked
2,4 him to show them a sign from heaven. His answer was:[a] 'It is
a wicked generation that asks for a sign; and the only sign that will
be given it is the sign of Jonah.' So he went off and left them.

5   In crossing to the other side the disciples had forgotten to take
6 bread with them. So, when Jesus said to them, 'Beware, be on your
7 guard against the leaven of the Pharisees and Sadducees', they began
to say among themselves, 'It is because we have brought no bread!'
8 Knowing what was in their minds, Jesus said to them: 'Why do
9 you talk about bringing no bread? Where is your faith? Do you not
understand even yet? Do you not remember the five loaves for the
10 five thousand, and how many basketfuls you picked up? Or the seven
loaves for the four thousand, and how many basketfuls you picked
11 up? How can you fail to see that I was not speaking about bread?
Be on your guard, I said, against the leaven of the Pharisees and
12 Sadducees.' Then they understood: they were to be on their guard,
not against the baker's leaven of the Pharisees and Sadducees, but
against their teaching.

13 WHEN HE CAME to the territory of Caesarea Philippi, Jesus asked
14 his disciples, 'Who do men say that the Son of Man is[b]?' They
answered, 'Some say John the Baptist, others Elijah, others Jere-
15 miah, or one of the prophets.' 'And you,' he asked, 'who do you
16 say I am?' Simon Peter answered: 'You are the Messiah, the Son
17 of the living God.' Then Jesus said: 'Simon son of Jonah, you are
favoured indeed! You did not learn that from mortal man; it
18 was revealed to you by my heavenly Father. And I say this to you:
You are Peter, the Rock; and on this rock I will build my church,
19 and the forces of death shall never overpower it.[c] I will give you
the keys of the kingdom of Heaven; what you forbid on earth shall
be forbidden in heaven, and what you allow on earth shall be

[a] *Some witnesses here insert* 'In the evening you say, "It will be fine weather, for the
sky is red"; (3) and in the morning you say, "It will be stormy today; the sky is red and
lowering." You know how to interpret the appearance of the sky; can you not interpret
the signs of the times?' [b] *Some witnesses read* that I, the Son of Man, am. [c] *Or* the
gates of death shall never close upon it.

allowed in heaven.' He then gave his disciples strict orders not to 20
tell anyone that he was the Messiah.

From that time Jesus began to make it clear to his disciples that 21
he had to go to Jerusalem, and there to suffer much from the elders,
chief priests, and lawyers; to be put to death and to be raised again
on the third day. At this Peter took him by the arm and began to 22
rebuke him: 'Heaven forbid!' he said. 'No, Lord, this shall never
happen to you.' Then Jesus turned and said to Peter, 'Away with 23
you, Satan; you are a stumbling-block to me. You think as men
think, not as God thinks.'

Jesus then said to his disciples, 'If anyone wishes to be a follower 24
of mine, he must leave self behind; he must take up his cross and
come with me. Whoever cares for his own safety is lost; but if a man 25
will let himself be lost for my sake, he will find his true self.
What will a man gain by winning the whole world, at the cost of his 26
true self? Or what can he give that will buy that self back? For the 27
Son of Man is to come in the glory of his Father with his angels,
and then he will give each man the due reward for what he has done.
I tell you this: there are some standing here who will not taste death 28
before they have seen the Son of Man coming in his kingdom.'

SIX DAYS LATER Jesus took Peter and James and John the brother 17
of James, and led them up a high mountain where they were alone;
and in their presence he was transfigured; his face shone like the sun, 2
and his clothes became white as the light. And they saw Moses 3
and Elijah appear, conversing with him. Then Peter spoke: 'Lord,' 4
he said, 'how good it is that we are here! If you wish it, I will make
three shelters here, one for you, one for Moses, and one for Elijah.'
While he was still speaking, a bright cloud suddenly overshadowed 5
them, and a voice called from the cloud: 'This is my Son, my
Beloved,[a] on whom my favour rests; listen to him.' At the sound 6
of the voice the disciples fell on their faces in terror. Jesus then 7
came up to them, touched them, and said, 'Stand up; do not be
afraid.' And when they raised their eyes they saw no one, but only 8
Jesus.

On their way down the mountain Jesus enjoined them not to tell 9
anyone of the vision until the Son of Man had been raised from the
dead. The disciples put a question to him: 'Why then do our 10

[a] *Or* This is my only Son.

11 teachers say that Elijah must come first?' He replied, 'Yes, Elijah
12 will come and set everything right. But I tell you that Elijah has
already come, and they failed to recognize him, and worked their
will upon him; and in the same way the Son of Man is to suffer at
13 their hands.' Then the disciples understood that he meant John the
Baptist.

14 When they returned to the crowd, a man came up to Jesus, fell
15 on his knees before him, and said, 'Have pity, sir, on my son: he is
an epileptic and has bad fits, and he keeps falling about, often into
16 the fire, often into water. I brought him to your disciples, but they
17 could not cure him.' Jesus answered, 'What an unbelieving and
perverse generation! How long shall I be with you? How much
18 longer must I endure you? Bring him here to me.' Jesus then spoke
sternly to the boy; the devil left him, and from that moment he was
cured.

19 Afterwards the disciples came to Jesus and asked him privately,
20 'Why could not we cast it out?' He answered, 'Your faith is too weak.
I tell you this: if you have faith no bigger even than a mustard-seed,
you will say to this mountain, "Move from here to there!", and it will
move; nothing will prove impossible for you.'[a]

22 THEY WERE going about together in Galilee when Jesus said to
23 them, 'The Son of Man is to be given up into the power of men, and
they will kill him; then on the third day he will be raised again.'
And they were filled with grief.

24 On their arrival at Capernaum the collectors of the temple-tax
came up to Peter and asked, 'Does your master not pay temple-
25 tax?' 'He does', said Peter. When he went indoors Jesus forestalled
him by asking, 'What do you think about this, Simon? From whom
do earthly monarchs collect tax or toll? From their own citizens, or
26 from aliens?' 'From aliens', said Peter. 'Why then,' said Jesus, 'the
27 citizens are exempt! But as we do not want to cause difficulty for
these people, go and cast a line in the lake; take the first fish that
comes to the hook, open its mouth, and you will find a silver coin;
take that and pay it in; it will meet the tax for us both.'

18 At that time the disciples came to Jesus and asked, 'Who is the
2 greatest in the kingdom of Heaven?' He called a child, set him in

[a] *Some witnesses add* (21) But there is no means of casting out this sort but prayer
and fasting.

32

front of them, and said, 'I tell you this: unless you turn round and ₃
become like children, you will never enter the kingdom of Heaven.
Let a man humble himself till he is like this child, and he will be the ₄
greatest in the kingdom of Heaven. Whoever receives one such child ₅
in my name receives me. But if a man is a cause of stumbling to one ₆
of these little ones who have faith in me, it would be better for him to
have a millstone hung round his neck and be drowned in the depths
of the sea. Alas for the world that such causes of stumbling arise! ₇
Come they must, but woe betide the man through whom they come!

'If your hand or your foot is your undoing, cut it off and fling it ₈
away; it is better for you to enter into life maimed or lame, than to
keep two hands or two feet and be thrown into the eternal fire.
If it is your eye that is your undoing, tear it out and fling it away; ₉
it is better to enter into life with one eye than to keep both eyes and
be thrown into the fires of hell.

'Never despise one of these little ones; I tell you, they have their ₁₀
guardian angels in heaven, who look continually on the face of my
heavenly Father.ᵃ

'What do you think? Suppose a man has a hundred sheep. If one ₁₂
of them strays, does he not leave the other ninety-nine on the hill-
side and go in search of the one that strayed? And if he should find ₁₃
it, I tell you this: he is more delighted over that sheep than over
the ninety-nine that never strayed. In the same way, it is not your ₁₄
heavenly Father's will that one of these little ones should be lost.

'If your brother commits a sin,ᵇ go and take the matter up with ₁₅
him, strictly between yourselves, and if he listens to you, you have
won your brother over. If he will not listen, take one or two others ₁₆
with you, so that all facts may be duly established on the evidence
of two or three witnesses. If he refuses to listen to them, report the ₁₇
matter to the congregation; and if he will not listen even to the
congregation, you must then treat him as you would a pagan or a
tax-gatherer.

'I tell you this: whatever you forbid on earth shall be forbidden ₁₈
in heaven, and whatever you allow on earth shall be allowed in
heaven.

'Again I tell you this: if two of you agree on earth about any ₁₉
request you have to make, that request will be granted by my

[a] *Some witnesses add* (11) For the Son of Man came to save the lost. [b] *Some
witnesses insert* against you.

20 heavenly Father. For where two or three have met together in my name, I am there among them.'

21 Then Peter came up and asked him, 'Lord, how often am I to forgive my brother if he goes on wronging me? As many as seven
22 times?' Jesus replied, 'I do not say seven times; I say seventy times seven.

23 'The kingdom of Heaven, therefore, should be thought of in this way: There was once a king who decided to settle accounts with
24 the men who served him. At the outset there appeared before him
25 a man whose debt ran into millions.*a* Since he had no means of paying, his master ordered him to be sold to meet the debt, with
26 his wife, his children, and everything he had. The man fell prostrate at his master's feet. "Be patient with me," he said, "and I will pay
27 in full"; and the master was so moved with pity that he let the
28 man go and remitted the debt. But no sooner had the man gone out than he met a fellow-servant who owed him a few pounds;*b* and catching hold of him he gripped him by the throat and said,
29 "Pay me what you owe." The man fell at his fellow-servant's feet,
30 and begged him, "Be patient with me, and I will pay you"; but he
31 refused, and had him jailed until he should pay the debt. The other servants were deeply distressed when they saw what had happened,
32 and they went to their master and told him the whole story. He accordingly sent for the man. "You scoundrel!" he said to him;
33 "I remitted the whole of your debt when you appealed to me; were you not bound to show your fellow-servant the same pity as I showed
34 to you?" And so angry was the master that he condemned the man
35 to torture until he should pay the debt in full. And that is how my heavenly Father will deal with you, unless you each forgive your brother from your hearts.'

19 WHEN JESUS had finished this discourse he left Galilee and came
2 into the region of Judaea across Jordan. Great crowds followed him, and he healed them there.

3 Some Pharisees came and tested him by asking, 'Is it lawful for
4 a man to divorce his wife on any and every ground?'*c* He asked in return, 'Have you never read that the Creator made them from the
5 beginning male and female?'; and he added, 'For this reason a man

[a] *Literally* who owed 10,000 talents.   [b] *Literally* owed him 100 denarii.   [c] *Or* Is there any ground on which it is lawful for a man to divorce his wife?

34

shall leave his father and mother, and be made one with his wife; and the two shall become one flesh. It follows that they are no 6 longer two individuals: they are one flesh. What God has joined together, man must not separate.' 'Why then', they objected, 'did 7 Moses lay it down that a man might divorce his wife by note of dismissal?' He answered, 'It was because you were so unteach- 8 able that Moses gave you permission to divorce your wives; but it was not like that when all began. I tell you, if a man divorces his 9 wife for any cause other than unchastity, and marries another, he commits adultery.'*a*

The disciples said to him, 'If that is the position with husband 10 and wife, it is better to refrain from marriage.' To this he 11 replied, 'That is something which not everyone can accept, but only those for whom God has appointed it. For while some are 12 incapable of marriage because they were born so, or were made so by men, there are others who have themselves renounced marriage for the sake of the kingdom of Heaven. Let those accept it who can.'

They brought children for him to lay his hands on them with 13 prayer. The disciples scolded them for it, but Jesus said to them, 14 'Let the children come to me; do not try to stop them; for the kingdom of Heaven belongs to such as these.' And he laid his hands 15 on the children, and went his way.

And now a man came up and asked him, 'Master, what good 16 must I do to gain eternal life?' 'Good?' said Jesus. 'Why do you 17 ask me about that? One alone is good. But if you wish to enter into life, keep the commandments.' 'Which commandments?' he asked. 18 Jesus answered, 'Do not murder; do not commit adultery; do not steal; do not give false evidence; honour your father and mother; 19 and love your neighbour as yourself.' The young man answered, 20 'I have kept all these. Where do I still fall short?' Jesus said to him, 21 'If you wish to go the whole way, go, sell your possessions, and give to the poor, and then you will have riches in heaven; and come, follow me.' When the young man heard this, he went away with a 22 heavy heart; for he was a man of great wealth.

Jesus said to his disciples, 'I tell you this: a rich man will find it 23 hard to enter the kingdom of Heaven. I repeat, it is easier for 24

[a] *Some witnesses add* And the man who marries a woman so divorced commits adultery.

35

a camel to pass through the eye of a needle than for a rich man to
25 enter the kingdom of God.' The disciples were amazed to hear this.
26 'Then who can be saved?' they asked. Jesus looked them in the
face, and said, 'For men this is impossible; but everything is possible
for God.'
27   At this Peter said, 'Here are we who left everything to become
28 your followers. What will there be for us?' Jesus replied, 'I tell you
this: in the world that is to be, when the Son of Man is seated on
his throne in heavenly splendour, you my followers will have thrones
of your own, where you will sit as judges of the twelve tribes of
29 Israel. And anyone who has left brothers or sisters, father, mother,
or children, land or houses for the sake of my name will be repaid
30 many times over, and gain eternal life. But many who are first will
be last, and the last first.
20   'The kingdom of Heaven is like this. There was once a landowner
who went out early one morning to hire labourers for his vineyard;
2 and after agreeing to pay them the usual day's wage*a* he sent them off
3 to work. Going out three hours later he saw some more men standing
4 idle in the market-place. "Go and join the others in the vineyard,"
5 he said, "and I will pay you a fair wage"; so off they went. At noon
he went out again, and at three in the afternoon, and made the same
6 arrangement as before. An hour before sunset he went out and found
another group standing there; so he said to them, "Why are you
7 standing about like this all day with nothing to do?" "Because no
one has hired us", they replied; so he told them, "Go and join the
8 others in the vineyard." When evening fell, the owner of the vineyard
said to his steward, "Call the labourers and give them their pay,
beginning with those who came last and ending with the first."
9 Those who had started work an hour before sunset came forward,
10 and were paid the full day's wage.*b* When it was the turn of the men
who had come first, they expected something extra, but were paid
11 the same amount as the others. As they took it, they grumbled at
12 their employer: "These late-comers have done only one hour's work,
yet you have put them on a level with us, who have sweated the whole
13 day long in the blazing sun!" The owner turned to one of them and
said, "My friend, I am not being unfair to you. You agreed on the
14 usual wage for the day,*c* did you not? Take your pay and go home.

[a] *Literally* one denarius for the day. [b] *Literally* one denarius each. [c] *Literally*
You agreed on a denarius.

I choose to pay the last man the same as you. Surely I am free 15
to do what I like with my own money. Why be jealous because I am
kind?" Thus will the last be first, and the first last.'   16

Challenge to Jerusalem

J ESUS WAS journeying towards Jerusalem, and on the way he took 17
the Twelve aside, and said to them, 'We are going to Jeru- 18
salem, and the Son of Man will be given up to the chief priests and
the doctors of the law; they will condemn him to death and hand 19
him over to the foreign power, to be mocked and flogged and
crucified, and on the third day he will be raised to life again.'
The mother of Zebedee's sons then came before him, with her 20
sons. She bowed low and begged a favour. 'What is it you wish?' 21
asked Jesus. 'I want you', she said, 'to give orders that in your
kingdom my two sons here may sit next to you, one at your right,
and the other at your left.' Jesus turned to the brothers and said, 22
'You do not understand what you are asking. Can you drink the cup
that I am to drink?' 'We can', they replied. Then he said to them, 23
'You shall indeed share my cup; but to sit at my right or left is not
for me to grant; it is for those to whom it has already been assigned
by my Father.'
When the other ten heard this, they were indignant with the two 24
brothers. So Jesus called them to him and said, 'You know that 25
in the world, rulers lord it over their subjects, and their great men
make them feel the weight of authority; but it shall not be so with 26
you. Among you, whoever wants to be great must be your servant,
and whoever would be first must be the willing slave of all— 27
like the Son of Man; he did not come to be served, but to serve, and 28
to surrender his life as a ransom for many.'
As they were leaving Jericho he was followed by a great crowd 29
of people. At the roadside sat two blind men. When they heard it 30
said that Jesus was passing they shouted, 'Have pity on us, Son of
David.' The people rounded on them and told them to be quiet. 31
But they shouted all the more, 'Sir, have pity on us, have pity on us,
Son of David.' Jesus stopped and called the men. 'What do you want 32
me to do for you?' he asked. 'Sir,' they answered, 'we want our 33

34 sight.' Jesus was deeply moved, and touched their eyes. At once their sight came back, and they went on after him.

21 THEY WERE now nearing Jerusalem; and when they reached
2 Bethany at the Mount of Olives, Jesus sent two disciples with these instructions: 'Go to the village opposite, where you will at once find a donkey tethered with her foal beside her; untie them, and
3 bring them to me. If anyone speaks to you, say, "Our Master needs
4 them"; and he will let you take them at once.'[a] This was in fulfilment
5 of the prophecy which says, 'Tell the daughter of Zion, "Here is your king, who comes to you in gentleness, riding on an ass, riding on the foal of a beast of burden."'
6, 7   The disciples went and did as Jesus had directed, and brought the donkey and her foal; they laid their cloaks on them and Jesus
8 mounted. Crowds of people carpeted the road with their cloaks,
9 and some cut branches from the trees to spread in his path. Then the crowd that went ahead and the others that came behind raised the shout: 'Hosanna to the Son of David! Hosanna in the heavens!'
10   When he entered Jerusalem the whole city went wild with excite-
11 ment. 'Who is this?' people asked, and the crowd replied, 'This is the prophet Jesus, from Nazareth in Galilee.'
12   Jesus then went into the temple and drove out all who were buying and selling in the temple precincts; he upset the tables of the money-
13 changers and the seats of the dealers in pigeons; and said to them, 'Scripture says, "My house shall be called a house of prayer"; but you are making it a robbers' cave.'
14   In the temple blind men and cripples came to him, and he healed
15 them. The chief priests and doctors of the law saw the wonderful things he did, and heard the boys in the temple shouting, 'Hosanna
16 to the Son of David!', and they asked him indignantly, 'Do you hear what they are saying?' Jesus answered, 'I do; have you never read that text, "Thou hast made children and babes at the breast
17 sound aloud thy praise"?' Then he left them and went out of the city to Bethany, where he spent the night.
18, 19   Next morning on his way to the city he felt hungry; and seeing a fig-tree at the roadside he went up to it, but found nothing on it but leaves. He said to the tree, 'You shall never bear fruit any more!';

[a] *Or* "Our Master needs them and will send them back straight away."

and the tree withered away at once. The disciples were amazed at 20
the sight. 'How is it', they asked, 'that the tree has withered so
suddenly?' Jesus answered them, 'I tell you this: if only you have 21
faith and have no doubts, you will do what has been done to the
fig-tree; and more than that, you need only say to this mountain,
"Be lifted from your place and hurled into the sea", and what you
say will be done. And whatever you pray for in faith you will 22
receive.'

He entered the temple, and the chief priests and elders of the 23
nation came to him with the question: 'By what authority are you
acting like this? Who gave you this authority?' Jesus replied, 'I have 24
a question to ask too; answer it, and I will tell you by what authority
I act. The baptism of John: was it from God, or from men?' This 25
set them arguing among themselves: 'If we say, "from God", he
will say, "Then why did you not believe him?" But if we say, "from 26
men", we are afraid of the people, for they all take John for a prophet.' So they answered, 'We do not know.' And Jesus said: 'Then 27
neither will I tell you by what authority I act.

'But what do you think about this? A man had two sons. He 28
went to the first, and said, "My boy, go and work today in the vineyard." "I will, sir", the boy replied; but he never went. The father 29, 30
came to the second and said the same. "I will not", he replied, but
afterwards he changed his mind and went. Which of these two did 31
as his father wished?' 'The second', they said. Then Jesus answered,
'I tell you this: tax-gatherers and prostitutes are entering the kingdom of God ahead of you. For when John came to show you the 32
right way to live, you did not believe him, but the tax-gatherers and
prostitutes did; and even when you had seen that, you did not change
your minds and believe him.

'Listen to another parable. There was a landowner who planted 33
a vineyard: he put a wall round it, hewed out a winepress, and built
a watch-tower; then he let it out to vine-growers and went abroad.
When the vintage season approached, he sent his servants to the 34
tenants to collect the produce due to him. But they took his servants 35
and thrashed one, murdered another, and stoned a third. Again, 36
he sent other servants, this time a larger number; and they did the
same to them. At last he sent to them his son. "They will respect 37
my son", he said. But when they saw the son the tenants said to 38
one another, "This is the heir; come on, let us kill him, and get his

39 inheritance." And they took him, flung him out of the vineyard,
40 and murdered him. When the owner of the vineyard comes, how
41 do you think he will deal with those tenants?' 'He will bring those
bad men to a bad end', they answered, 'and hand the vineyard over
to other tenants, who will let him have his share of the crop when
42 the season comes.' Then Jesus said to them, 'Have you never read
in the scriptures: "The stone which the builders rejected has
become the main corner-stone. This is the Lord's doing, and it
43 is wonderful in our eyes"? Therefore, I tell you, the kingdom of God
will be taken away from you, and given to a nation that yields the
proper fruit.'*a*
45   When the chief priests and Pharisees heard his parables, they saw
46 that he was referring to them; they wanted to arrest him, but they
were afraid of the people, who looked on Jesus as a prophet.

22 1, 2 THEN JESUS spoke to them again in parables: 'The kingdom of
Heaven is like this. There was a king who prepared a feast for his
3 son's wedding; but when he sent his servants to summon the guests
4 he had invited, they would not come. He sent others again, telling
them to say to the guests, "See now! I have prepared this feast for
you. I have had my bullocks and fatted beasts slaughtered; every-
5 thing is ready; come to the wedding at once." But they took no
6 notice; one went off to his farm, another to his business, and the
others seized the servants, attacked them brutally, and killed them.
7 The king was furious; he sent troops to kill those murderers and set
8 their town on fire. Then he said to his servants, "The wedding-feast
is ready; but the guests I invited did not deserve the honour.
9 Go out to the main thoroughfares, and invite everyone you can find
10 to the wedding." The servants went out into the streets, and collected
all they could find, good and bad alike. So the hall was packed with
guests.
11   'When the king came in to see the company at table, he observed
12 one man who was not dressed for a wedding. "My friend," said the
king, "how do you come to be here without your wedding clothes?"
13 He had nothing to say. The king then said to his attendants, "Bind
him hand and foot; turn him out into the dark, the place of wailing
14 and grinding of teeth." For though many are invited, few are chosen.'

[*a*] *Some witnesses add* (44) Any man who falls on this stone will be dashed to pieces;
and if it falls on a man he will be crushed by it.

THEN THE PHARISEES went and agreed on a plan to trap him in 15
his own words. Some of their followers were sent to him in company 16
with men of Herod's party. They said, 'Master, you are an honest
man, we know; you teach in all honesty the way of life that God
requires, truckling to no man, whoever he may be. Give us your 17
ruling on this: are we or are we not permitted to pay taxes to the
Roman Emperor?' Jesus was aware of their malicious intention and 18
said to them, 'You hypocrites! Why are you trying to catch me out?
Show me the money in which the tax is paid.' They handed him 19
a silver piece. Jesus asked, 'Whose head is this, and whose inscrip- 20
tion?' 'Caesar's', they replied. He said to them, 'Then pay Caesar 21
what is due to Caesar, and pay God what is due to God.' This 22
answer took them by surprise, and they went away and left him
alone.

The same day Sadducees came to him, maintaining that there is 23
no resurrection. Their question was this: 'Master, Moses said, "If 24
a man should die childless, his brother shall marry the widow and
carry on his brother's family." Now we knew of seven brothers. 25
The first married and died, and as he was without issue his wife
was left to his brother. The same thing happened with the second, 26
and the third, and so on with all seven. Last of all the woman died. 27
At the resurrection, then, whose wife will she be, for they had all 28
married her?' Jesus answered: 'You are mistaken, because you know 29
neither the scriptures nor the power of God. At the resurrection 30
men and women do not marry, but are like angels in heaven.

'But about the resurrection of the dead, have you never read what 31
God himself said to you: "I am the God of Abraham, the God of 32
Isaac, and the God of Jacob"? He is not God of the dead but of the
living.' The people heard what he said, and were astounded at his 33
teaching.

Hearing that he had silenced the Sadducees, the Pharisees met 34
together; and one of their number[a] tested him with this question: 35
'Master, which is the greatest commandment in the Law?' He 36, 37
answered, '"Love the Lord your God with all your heart, with all
your soul, with all your mind." That is the greatest commandment. 38
It comes first. The second is like it: "Love your neighbour as your- 39
self." Everything in the Law and the prophets hangs on these two 40
commandments.'

[a] *Some witnesses insert* a lawyer.

41,42 Turning to the assembled Pharisees Jesus asked them, 'What is
your opinion about the Messiah? Whose son is he?' 'The son of
43 David', they replied. 'How then is it', he asked, 'that David by
44 inspiration calls him "Lord"? For he says, "The Lord said to my
Lord, 'Sit at my right hand until I put your enemies under your
45 feet.'" If David calls him "Lord", how can he be David's son?'
46 Not a man could say a word in reply; and from that day forward
no one dared ask him another question.

23 1,2 JESUS THEN addressed the people and his disciples in these words:
'The doctors of the law and the Pharisees sit in the chair of Moses;
3 therefore do what they tell you; pay attention to their words. But
do not follow their practice; for they say one thing and do another.
4 They make up heavy packs and pile them on men's shoulders, but
5 will not raise a finger to lift the load themselves. Whatever they do is
done for show. They go about with broad phylacteries*a* and wear
6 deep fringes on their robes; they like to have places of honour at
7 feasts and the chief seats in synagogues, to be greeted respectfully
in the street, and to be addressed as "rabbi".
8 'But you must not be called "rabbi"; for you have one Rabbi, and
9 you are all brothers. Do not call any man on earth "father"; for you
10 have one Father, and he is in heaven. Nor must you be called
11 "teacher"; you have one Teacher, the Messiah. The greatest among
12 you must be your servant. For whoever exalts himself will be
humbled; and whoever humbles himself will be exalted.
13 'Alas, alas for you, lawyers and Pharisees, hypocrites that you are!
You shut the door of the kingdom of Heaven in men's faces; you
do not enter yourselves, and when others are entering, you stop
them.*b*
15 'Alas for you, lawyers and Pharisees, hypocrites! You travel over
sea and land to win one convert; and when you have won him you
make him twice as fit for hell as you are yourselves.
16 'Alas for you, blind guides! You say, "If a man swears by the
sanctuary, that is nothing; but if he swears by the gold in the sanc-
17 tuary, he is bound by his oath." Blind fools! Which is the more
18 important, the gold, or the sanctuary which sanctifies the gold? Or

[a] See *Deuteronomy 6. 8–9 & Exodus 13. 9.* [b] *Some witnesses add* (14) Alas for you,
lawyers and Pharisees, hypocrites! You eat up the property of widows, while you
say long prayers for appearance' sake. You will receive the severest sentence.

you say, "If a man swears by the altar, that is nothing; but if he swears by the offering that lies on the altar, he is bound by his oath." What blindness! Which is the more important, the offering, or the 19 altar which sanctifies it? To swear by the altar, then, is to swear 20 both by the altar and by whatever lies on it; to swear by the sanc- 21 tuary is to swear both by the sanctuary and by him who dwells there; and to swear by heaven is to swear both by the throne of God 22 and by him who sits upon it.

'Alas for you, lawyers and Pharisees, hypocrites! You pay tithes 23 of mint and dill and cummin; but you have overlooked the weightier demands of the Law, justice, mercy, and good faith. It is these you should have practised, without neglecting the others. Blind 24 guides! You strain off a midge, yet gulp down a camel!

'Alas for you, lawyers and Pharisees, hypocrites! You clean the 25 outside of cup and dish, which you have filled inside by robbery and self-indulgence! Blind Pharisee! Clean the inside of the cup first; 26 then the outside will be clean also.

'Alas for you, lawyers and Pharisees, hypocrites! You are like 27 tombs covered with whitewash; they look well from outside, but inside they are full of dead men's bones and all kinds of filth. So it 28 is with you: outside you look like honest men, but inside you are brim-full of hypocrisy and crime.

'Alas for you, lawyers and Pharisees, hypocrites! You build up 29 the tombs of the prophets and embellish the monuments of the saints, and you say, "If we had been alive in our fathers' time, we 30 should never have taken part with them in the murder of the prophets." So you acknowledge that you are the sons of the men 31 who killed the prophets. Go on then, finish off what your fathers 32 began!*[a]*

'You snakes, you vipers' brood, how can you escape being con- 33 demned to hell? I send you therefore prophets, sages, and teachers; 34 some of them you will kill and crucify, others you will flog in your synagogues and hound from city to city. And so, on you will fall 35 the guilt of all the innocent blood spilt on the ground, from innocent Abel to Zechariah son of Berachiah, whom you murdered between the sanctuary and the altar. Believe me, this generation will bear 36 the guilt of it all.

'O Jerusalem, Jerusalem, the city that murders the prophets and 37

[a] *Or* You too must come up to your fathers' standards.

43

stones the messengers sent to her! How often have I longed to gather your children, as a hen gathers her brood under her wings; but you
38 would not let me. Look, look! there is your temple, forsaken by
39 God.*a b* And I tell you, you shall never see me until the time when you say, "Blessings on him who comes in the name of the Lord."'

Prophecies and Warnings

24 JESUS WAS leaving the temple when his disciples came and pointed
2 to the temple buildings. He answered, 'You see all these buildings? I tell you this: not one stone will be left upon another; all will be thrown down.'
3   When he was sitting on the Mount of Olives the disciples came to speak to him privately. 'Tell us,' they said, 'when will this happen? And what will be the signal for your coming and the end of the age?'
4, 5   Jesus replied: 'Take care that no one misleads you. For many will come claiming my name and saying, "I am the Messiah"; and
6 many will be misled by them. The time is coming when you will hear the noise of battle near at hand and the news of battles far away; see that you are not alarmed. Such things are bound to happen; but
7 the end is still to come. For nation will make war upon nation, kingdom upon kingdom; there will be famines and earthquakes in many
8 places. With all these things the birth-pangs of the new age begin.
9   'You will then be handed over for punishment and execution; and men of all nations will hate you for your allegiance to me.
10 Many will lose their faith; they will betray one another and hate one
11 another. Many false prophets will arise, and will mislead many;
12 and as lawlessness spreads, men's love for one another will grow cold.
13, 14 But the man who holds out to the end will be saved. And this gospel of the Kingdom will be proclaimed throughout the earth as a testimony to all nations; and then the end will come.
15   'So when you see "the abomination of desolation", of which the prophet Daniel spoke, standing in the holy place (let the reader
16 understand), then those who are in Judaea must take to the hills.
17 If a man is on the roof, he must not come down to fetch his goods

[a] *Or* Look, your home is desolate. [b] *Some witnesses add* and laid waste.

from the house; if in the field, he must not turn back for his coat. 18
Alas for women with child in those days, and for those who have 19
children at the breast! Pray that it may not be winter when you 20
have to make your escape, or Sabbath. It will be a time of great 21
distress, such as has never been from the beginning of the world
until now, and will never be again. If that time of troubles were not 22
cut short, no living thing could survive; but for the sake of God's
chosen it will be cut short.

'Then, if anyone says to you, "Look, here is the Messiah", or, 23
"There he is", do not believe it. Impostors will come claiming to be 24
messiahs or prophets, and they will produce great signs and wonders
to mislead even God's chosen, if such a thing were possible. See, 25
I have forewarned you. If they tell you, "He is there in the wilder- 26
ness", do not go out; or if they say, "He is there in the inner room",
do not believe it. Like lightning from the east, flashing as far as the 27
west, will be the coming of the Son of Man.

'Wherever the corpse is, there the vultures will gather.   28

'As soon as the distress of those days has passed, the sun will be 29
darkened, the moon will not give her light, the stars will fall from
the sky, the celestial powers will be shaken. Then will appear in 30
heaven the sign that heralds the Son of Man. All the peoples of
the world will make lamentation, and they will see the Son of Man
coming on the clouds of heaven with great power and glory. With 31
a trumpet blast he will send out his angels, and they will gather his
chosen from the four winds, from the farthest bounds of heaven
on every side.

'Learn a lesson from the fig-tree. When its tender shoots appear 32
and are breaking into leaf, you know that summer is near. In the 33
same way, when you see all these things, you may know that the end
is near,[a] at the very door. I tell you this: the present generation will 34
live to see it all. Heaven and earth will pass away; my words will 35
never pass away.

'But about that day and hour no one knows, not even the angels 36
in heaven, not even the Son; only the Father.

'As things were in Noah's days, so will they be when the Son of 37
Man comes. In the days before the flood they ate and drank and 38
married, until the day that Noah went into the ark, and they knew 39
nothing until the flood came and swept them all away. That is how

[a] *Or* that he is near.

40 it will be when the Son of Man comes. Then there will be two men
41 in the field; one will be taken, the other left; two women grinding
at the mill; one will be taken, the other left.
42 'Keep awake, then; for you do not know on what day your Lord
43 is to come. Remember, if the householder had known at what time
of night the burglar was coming, he would have kept awake and not
44 have let his house be broken into. Hold yourselves ready, therefore,
because the Son of Man will come at the time you least expect him.
45 'Who is the trusty servant, the sensible man charged by his master
to manage his household staff and issue their rations at the proper
46 time? Happy that servant who is found at his task when his master
47 comes! I tell you this: he will be put in charge of all his master's
48 property. But if he is a bad servant and says to himself, "The master
49 is a long time coming", and begins to bully the other servants and
50 to eat and drink with his drunken friends, then the master will
arrive on a day that servant does not expect, at a time he does not
51 know, and will cut him in pieces. Thus he will find his place among
the hypocrites, where there is wailing and grinding of teeth.
25 'When that day comes, the kingdom of Heaven will be like this.
There were ten girls, who took their lamps and went out to meet
2, 3 the bridegroom. Five of them were foolish, and five prudent; when
4 the foolish ones took their lamps, they took no oil with them, but
5 the others took flasks of oil with their lamps. As the bridegroom was
6 late in coming they all dozed off to sleep. But at midnight a cry was
7 heard: "Here is the bridegroom! Come out to meet him." With that
8 the girls all got up and trimmed their lamps. The foolish said to the
prudent, "Our lamps are going out; give us some of your oil."
9 "No," they said; "there will never be enough for us both. You had
10 better go to the shop and buy some for yourselves." While they were
away the bridegroom arrived; those who were ready went in with
11 him to the wedding; and the door was shut. And then the other
five came back. "Sir, sir," they cried, "open the door for us."
12, 13 But he answered, "I declare, I do not know you." Keep awake then;
for you never know the day or the hour.
14 'It is like a man going abroad, who called his servants and put his
15 capital in their hands; to one he gave five bags of gold, to another
two, to another one, each according to his capacity. Then he left the
16 country. The man who had the five bags went at once and employed
17 them in business, and made a profit of five bags, and the man who

46

had the two bags made two. But the man who had been given one 18
bag of gold went off and dug a hole in the ground, and hid his
master's money. A long time afterwards their master returned, and 19
proceeded to settle accounts with them. The man who had been 20
given the five bags of gold came and produced the five he had made:
"Master," he said, "you left five bags with me; look, I have made
five more." "Well done, my good and trusty servant!" said the master. 21
"You have proved trustworthy in a small way; I will now put you
in charge of something big. Come and share your master's delight."
The man with the two bags then came and said, "Master, you left 22
two bags with me; look, I have made two more." "Well done, my 23
good and trusty servant!" said the master. "You have proved trustworthy in a small way; I will now put you in charge of something
big. Come and share your master's delight." Then the man who had 24
been given one bag came and said, "Master, I knew you to be a hard
man: you reap where you have not sown, you gather where you have
not scattered; so I was afraid, and I went and hid your gold in the 25
ground. Here it is—you have what belongs to you." "You lazy 26
rascal!" said the master. "You knew that I reap where I have not
sown, and gather where I have not scattered? Then you ought to 27
have put my money on deposit, and on my return I should have got
it back with interest. Take the bag of gold from him, and give it 28
to the one with the ten bags. For the man who has will always be 29
given more, till he has enough and to spare; and the man who has
not will forfeit even what he has. Fling the useless servant out into 30
the dark, the place of wailing and grinding of teeth!"

'When the Son of Man comes in his glory and all the angels with 31
him, he will sit in state on his throne, with all the nations gathered 32
before him. He will separate men into two groups, as a shepherd
separates the sheep from the goats, and he will place the sheep on his 33
right hand and the goats on his left. Then the king will say to those 34
on his right hand, "You have my Father's blessing; come, enter and
possess the kingdom that has been ready for you since the world
was made. For when I was hungry, you gave me food; when thirsty, 35
you gave me drink; when I was a stranger you took me into your
home, when naked you clothed me; when I was ill you came to my 36
help, when in prison you visited me." Then the righteous will reply, 37
"Lord, when was it that we saw you hungry and fed you, or thirsty
and gave you drink, a stranger and took you home, or naked and 38

39 clothed you? When did we see you ill or in prison, and come to
40 visit you?" And the king will answer, "I tell you this: anything you
did for one of my brothers here, however humble, you did for me."
41 Then he will say to those on his left hand, "The curse is upon you;
go from my sight to the eternal fire that is ready for the devil and
42 his angels. For when I was hungry you gave me nothing to eat, when
43 thirsty nothing to drink; when I was a stranger you gave me no
home, when naked you did not clothe me; when I was ill and in
44 prison you did not come to my help." And they too will reply, "Lord,
when was it that we saw you hungry or thirsty or a stranger or naked
45 or ill or in prison, and did nothing for you?" And he will answer,
"I tell you this: anything you did not do for one of these, however
46 humble, you did not do for me." And they will go away to eternal
punishment, but the righteous will enter eternal life.'

The Final Conflict

26 WHEN JESUS had finished this discourse he said to his disciples,
2 'You know that in two days' time it will be Passover, and the
Son of Man is to be handed over for crucifixion.'
3   Then the chief priests and the elders of the nation met in the
4 palace of the High Priest, Caiaphas; and there they conferred together on a scheme to have Jesus arrested by some trick and put to
5 death. 'It must not be during the festival,' they said, 'or there may
be rioting among the people.'

6,7 JESUS WAS at Bethany in the house of Simon the leper, when a
woman came to him with a small bottle of fragrant oil, very costly;
8 and as he sat at table she began to pour it over his head. The disciples
9 were indignant when they saw it. 'Why this waste?' they said; 'it
could have been sold for a good sum and the money given to the
10 poor.' Jesus was aware of this, and said to them, 'Why must you
make trouble for the woman? It is a fine thing she has done for me.
11 You have the poor among you always; but you will not always have
12 me. When she poured this oil on my body it was her way of pre-
13 paring me for burial. I tell you this: wherever in all the world this
gospel is proclaimed, what she has done will be told as her memorial.'

THEN ONE of the Twelve, the man called Judas Iscariot, went to 14
the chief priests and said, 'What will you give me to betray him to 15
you?' They weighed him out*a* thirty silver pieces. From that moment 16
he began to look for a good opportunity to betray him.

On the first day of Unleavened Bread the disciples came to ask 17
Jesus, 'Where would you like us to prepare for your Passover
supper?' He answered, 'Go to a certain man in the city, and tell 18
him, "The Master says, 'My appointed time is near; I am to keep
Passover with my disciples at your house.'"' The disciples did as 19
Jesus directed them and prepared for Passover.

In the evening he sat down with the twelve disciples; and during 20, 21
supper he said, 'I tell you this: one of you will betray me.' In great 22
distress they exclaimed one after the other, 'Can you mean me,
Lord?' He answered, 'One who has dipped his hand into this bowl 23
with me will betray me. The Son of Man is going the way appointed 24
for him in the scriptures; but alas for that man by whom the Son of
Man is betrayed! It would be better for that man if he had never
been born.' Then Judas spoke, the one who was to betray him. 25
'Rabbi,' he said, 'can you mean me?' Jesus replied, 'The words are
yours.'*b*

During supper Jesus took bread, and having said the blessing 26
he broke it and gave it to the disciples with the words: 'Take this
and eat; this is my body.' Then he took a cup, and having offered 27
thanks to God he gave it to them with the words: 'Drink from it,
all of you. For this is my blood, the blood of the covenant, shed 28
for many for the forgiveness of sins. I tell you, never again shall 29
I drink from the fruit of the vine until that day when I drink it new
with you in the kingdom of my Father.'

After singing the Passover Hymn, they went out to the Mount 30
of Olives. Then Jesus said to them, 'Tonight you will all fall from 31
your faith on my account; for it stands written: "I will strike the
shepherd down and the sheep of his flock will be scattered." But 32
after I am raised again, I will go on before you into Galilee.' Peter 33
replied, 'Everyone else may fall away on your account, but I never
will.' Jesus said to him, 'I tell you, tonight before the cock crows 34
you will disown me three times.' Peter said, 'Even if I must die 35
with you, I will never disown you.' And all the disciples said the
same.

[a] *Or* agreed to pay him...   [b] *Or* It is as you say.

36 JESUS THEN came with his disciples to a place called Gethsemane.
37 He said to them, 'Sit here while I go over there to pray.' He
took with him Peter and the two sons of Zebedee. Anguish and
38 dismay came over him, and he said to them, 'My heart is ready to
39 break with grief. Stop here, and stay awake with me.' He went
on a little, fell on his face in prayer, and said, 'My Father, if it
is possible, let this cup pass me by. Yet not as I will, but as thou
wilt.'
40   He came to the disciples and found them asleep; and he said to
Peter, 'What! Could none of you stay awake with me one hour?
41 Stay awake, and pray that you may be spared the test. The spirit
is willing, but the flesh is weak.'
42   He went away a second time, and prayed: 'My Father, if it is not
possible for this cup to pass me by without my drinking it, thy will
43 be done.' He came again and found them asleep, for their eyes
44 were heavy. So he left them and went away again; and he prayed
the third time, using the same words as before.
45   Then he came to the disciples and said to them, 'Still sleeping?
Still taking your ease? The hour has come! The Son of Man
46 is betrayed to sinful men. Up, let us go forward; the traitor is
upon us.'
47   While he was still speaking, Judas, one of the Twelve, appeared;
with him was a great crowd armed with swords and cudgels, sent by
48 the chief priests and the elders of the nation. The traitor gave them
49 this sign: 'The one I kiss is your man; seize him'; and stepping
50 forward at once, he said, 'Hail, Rabbi!', and kissed him. Jesus
replied, 'Friend, do what you are here to do.'[a] They then came
forward, seized Jesus, and held him fast.
51   At that moment one of those with Jesus reached for his sword
and drew it, and he struck at the High Priest's servant and cut off
52 his ear. But Jesus said to him, 'Put up your sword. All who take
53 the sword die by the sword. Do you suppose that I cannot appeal
to my Father, who would at once send to my aid more than twelve
54 legions of angels? But how then could the scriptures be fulfilled,
which say that this must be?'
55   At the same time Jesus spoke to the crowd. 'Do you take me for
a bandit,' he said, 'that you have come out with swords and cudgels
to arrest me? Day after day I sat teaching in the temple, and you did

[a] *Or* Friend, what are you here for?

not lay hands on me. But this has all happened to fulfil what the 56
prophets wrote.'
Then the disciples all deserted him and ran away.

JESUS WAS led off under arrest to the house of Caiaphas the High 57
Priest, where the lawyers and elders were assembled. Peter fol- 58
lowed him at a distance till he came to the High Priest's courtyard,
and going in he sat down there among the attendants, meaning to
see the end of it all.

The chief priests and the whole Council tried to find some allega- 59
tion against Jesus on which a death-sentence could be based; but 60
they failed to find one, though many came forward with false evidence.
Finally two men alleged that he had said, 'I can pull down the temple 61
of God, and rebuild it in three days.' At this the High Priest rose 62
and said to him, 'Have you no answer to the charge that these
witnesses bring against you?' But Jesus kept silence. The High 63
Priest then said, 'By the living God I charge you to tell us: Are you
the Messiah, the Son of God?' Jesus replied, 'The words are yours.*a* 64
But I tell you this: from now on, you will see the Son of Man seated
at the right hand of God*h* and coming on the clouds of heaven.'
At these words the High Priest tore his robes and exclaimed, 65
'Blasphemy! Need we call further witnesses? You have heard the
blasphemy. What is your opinion?' 'He is guilty,' they answered; 66
'he should die.'

Then they spat in his face and beat him with their fists; and others 67
said, as they struck him, 'Now, Messiah, if you are a prophet, tell 68
us who hit you.'

Meanwhile Peter was sitting outside in the courtyard when a 69
serving-maid accosted him and said, 'You were there too with Jesus
the Galilean.' Peter denied it in face of them all. 'I do not know 70
what you mean', he said. He then went out to the gateway, where 71
another girl, seeing him, said to the people there, 'This fellow was
with Jesus of Nazareth.' Once again he denied it, saying with an 72
oath, 'I do not know the man.' Shortly afterwards the bystanders 73
came up and said to Peter, 'Surely you are another of them; your
accent gives you away!' At this he broke into curses and declared 74
with an oath: 'I do not know the man.' At that moment the cock
crew. And Peter remembered how Jesus had said, 'Before the cock 75

[*a*] *Or* It is as you say. [*b*] *Literally* of the Power.

51

crows you will disown me three times.' He went outside, and wept bitterly.

27 WHEN MORNING came, the chief priests and the elders of the
2 nation met in conference to plan the death of Jesus. They then put him in chains and led him off, to hand him over to Pilate, the Roman Governor.
3 When Judas the traitor saw that Jesus had been condemned, he was seized with remorse, and returned the thirty silver pieces to the
4 chief priests and elders. 'I have sinned,' he said; 'I have brought an innocent man to his death.' But they said, 'What is that to us?
5 See to that yourself.' So he threw the money down in the temple and left them, and went and hanged himself.
6 Taking up the money, the chief priests argued: 'This cannot be
7 put into the temple fund; it is blood-money.' So after conferring they used it to buy the Potter's Field, as a burial-place for foreigners.
8 This explains the name 'Blood Acre', by which that field has been
9 known ever since; and in this way fulfilment was given to the prophetic utterance of Jeremiah: 'They took*a* the thirty silver pieces, the price set on a man's head (for that was his price among the
10 Israelites), and gave the money for the potter's field, as the Lord directed me.'
11 Jesus was now brought before the Governor; and as he stood there the Governor asked him, 'Are you the king of the Jews?'
12 'The words are yours',*b* said Jesus; and to the charges laid against
13 him by the chief priests and elders he made no reply. Then Pilate said to him, 'Do you not hear all this evidence that is brought against
14 you?'; but he still refused to answer one word, to the Governor's great astonishment.
15 At the festival season it was the Governor's custom to release
16 one prisoner chosen by the people. There was then in custody a
17 man of some notoriety, called Jesus*c* Bar-Abbas. When they were assembled Pilate said to them, 'Which would you like me to release
18 to you—Jesus*c* Bar-Abbas, or Jesus called Messiah?' For he knew that it was out of spite that they had brought Jesus before him.
19 While Pilate was sitting in court a message came to him from his wife: 'Have nothing to do with that innocent man; I was much troubled on his account in my dreams last night.'

[a] *Or* I took. [b] *Or* It is as you say. [c] *Some witnesses omit* Jesus.

Meanwhile the chief priests and elders had persuaded the crowd 20 to ask for the release of Bar-Abbas and to have Jesus put to death. So when the Governor asked, 'Which of the two do you wish me to 21 release to you?', they said, 'Bar-Abbas.' 'Then what am I to do 22 with Jesus called Messiah?' asked Pilate; and with one voice they answered, 'Crucify him!' 'Why, what harm has he done?' Pilate 23 asked; but they shouted all the louder, 'Crucify him!'

Pilate could see that nothing was being gained, and a riot was 24 starting; so he took water and washed his hands in full view of the people, saying, 'My hands are clean of this man's blood; see to that yourselves.' And with one voice the people cried, 'His 25 blood be on us, and on our children.' He then released Bar-Abbas 26 to them; but he had Jesus flogged, and handed him over to be crucified.

PILATE'S SOLDIERS then took Jesus into the Governor's head- 27 quarters, where they collected the whole company round him. First 28 they stripped him and dressed him in a scarlet mantle; and plaiting 29 a crown of thorns they placed it on his head, with a cane in his right hand. Falling on their knees before him they jeered at him: 'Hail, King of the Jews!' They spat on him, and used the cane to beat him 30 about the head. Finally, when the mockery was over, they took off 31 the mantle and dressed him in his own clothes.

Then they led him away to be crucified. On their way out they 32 met a man from Cyrene, Simon by name, and pressed him into service to carry his cross.

So they came to a place called Golgotha (which means 'Place of 33 a skull') and there they offered him a draught of wine mixed with 34 gall; but when he had tasted it he would not drink.

After fastening him to the cross they divided his clothes among 35 them by casting lots, and then sat down there to keep watch. 36 Over his head was placed the inscription giving the charge: 'This is 37 Jesus the king of the Jews.'

Two bandits were crucified with him, one on his right and the 38 other on his left.

The passers-by hurled abuse at him: they wagged their heads and 39, 40 cried, 'You would pull the temple down, would you, and build it in three days? Come down from the cross and save yourself, if you are indeed the Son of God.' So too the chief priests with the lawyers 41

42 and elders mocked at him: 'He saved others,' they said, 'but he cannot save himself. King of Israel, indeed! Let him come down 43 now from the cross, and then we will believe him. Did he trust in God? Let God rescue him, if he wants him—for he said he was 44 God's Son.' Even the bandits who were crucified with him taunted him in the same way.

45 Darkness fell over the whole land from midday until three in the 46 afternoon; and about three Jesus cried aloud, '*Eli, Eli, lema sabach-thani?*', which means, 'My God, my God, why hast thou forsaken 47 me?' Some of the bystanders, on hearing this, said, 'He is calling 48 Elijah.' One of them ran at once and fetched a sponge, which he soaked in sour wine, and held it to his lips on the end of a cane. 49 But the others said, 'Let us see if Elijah will come to save him.'

50, 51 Jesus again gave a loud cry, and breathed his last. At that moment the curtain of the temple was torn in two from top to bottom. 52 There was an earthquake, the rocks split and the graves opened, 53 and many of God's people arose from sleep; and coming out of their graves after his resurrection they entered the Holy City, 54 where many saw them. And when the centurion and his men who were keeping watch over Jesus saw the earthquake and all that was happening, they were filled with awe, and they said, 'Truly this man was a son of God.'

55 A NUMBER of women were also present, watching from a distance; 56 they had followed Jesus from Galilee and waited on him. Among them were Mary of Magdala, Mary the mother of James and Joseph, and the mother of the sons of Zebedee.

57 When evening fell, there came a man of Arimathaea, Joseph by name, who was a man of means, and had himself become a disciple 58 of Jesus. He approached Pilate, and asked for the body of Jesus; 59 and Pilate gave orders that he should have it. Joseph took the body, 60 wrapped it in a clean linen sheet, and laid it in his own unused tomb, which he had cut out of the rock; he then rolled a large stone against 61 the entrance, and went away. Mary of Magdala was there, and the other Mary, sitting opposite the grave.

62 Next day, the morning after that Friday, the chief priests and the 63 Pharisees came in a body to Pilate. 'Your Excellency,' they said, 'we recall how that impostor said while he was still alive, "I am 64 to rise after three days." So will you give orders for the grave to be

made secure until the third day? Otherwise his disciples may come, steal the body, and then tell the people that he has been raised from the dead; and the final deception will be worse than the first.' 'You may have your guard,' said Pilate; 'go and make it secure as 65 best you can.' So they went and made the grave secure; they sealed 66 the stone, and left the guard in charge.

THE SABBATH had passed, and it was about daybreak on Sunday, 28 when Mary of Magdala and the other Mary came to look at the grave. Suddenly there was a violent earthquake; an angel of the 2 Lord descended from heaven; he came to the stone and rolled it away, and sat himself down on it. His face shone like lightning; 3 his garments were white as snow. At the sight of him the guards 4 shook with fear and lay like the dead.

The angel then addressed the women: 'You', he said, 'have 5 nothing to fear. I know you are looking for Jesus who was crucified. He is not here; he has been raised again, as he said he would be. 6 Come and see the place where he was laid, and then go quickly and 7 tell his disciples: "He has been raised from the dead and is going on before you into Galilee; there you will see him." That is what I had to tell you.'

They hurried away from the tomb in awe and great joy, and ran 8 to tell the disciples. Suddenly Jesus was there in their path. He gave 9 them his greeting, and they came up and clasped his feet, falling prostrate before him. Then Jesus said to them, 'Do not be afraid. 10 Go and take word to my brothers that they are to leave for Galilee. They will see me there.'

The women had started on their way when some of the guard went 11 into the city and reported to the chief priests everything that had happened. After meeting with the elders and conferring together, 12 the chief priests offered the soldiers a substantial bribe and told 13 them to say, 'His disciples came by night and stole the body while we were asleep.' They added, 'If this should reach the Governor's 14 ears, we will put matters right with him and see that you do not suffer.' So they took the money and did as they were told. This 15 story became widely known, and is current in Jewish circles to this day.

The eleven disciples made their way to Galilee, to the mountain 16 where Jesus had told them to meet him. When they saw him, they 17

18 fell prostrate before him, though some were doubtful. Jesus then
came up and spoke to them. He said: 'Full authority in heaven
19 and on earth has been committed to me. Go forth therefore and
make all nations my disciples; baptize men everywhere in the name
20 of the Father and the Son and the Holy Spirit, and teach them to
observe all that I have commanded you. And be assured, I am with
you always, to the end of time.'

THE
GOSPEL ACCORDING TO
MARK

The Coming of Christ

HERE BEGINS THE GOSPEL of Jesus Christ the 1
Son of God.*
In the prophet Isaiah it stands written: 'Here is my 2
herald whom I send on ahead of you, and he will prepare your way.
A voice crying aloud in the wilderness, "Prepare a way for the Lord; 3
clear a straight path for him."' And so it was that John the Baptist 4
appeared in the wilderness proclaiming a baptism in token of repentance, for the forgiveness of sins; and they flocked to him from the 5
whole Judaean country-side and the city of Jerusalem, and were
baptized by him in the River Jordan, confessing their sins.

John was dressed in a rough coat of camel's hair, with a leather 6
belt round his waist, and he fed on locusts and wild honey. His 7
proclamation ran: 'After me comes one who is mightier than I.
I am not fit to unfasten his shoes. I have baptized you with water; 8
he will baptize you with the Holy Spirit.'

It happened at this time that Jesus came from Nazareth in Galilee 9
and was baptized in the Jordan by John. At the moment when 10
he came up out of the water, he saw the heavens torn open and
the Spirit, like a dove, descending upon him. And a voice spoke 11
from heaven: 'Thou art my Son, my Beloved;* on thee my favour
rests.'

Thereupon the Spirit sent him away into the wilderness, and there 12, 13
he remained for forty days tempted by Satan. He was among the
wild beasts; and the angels waited on him.

[a] *Some witnesses omit* the Son of God.
[b] *Or* Thou art my only Son.

57

In Galilee: Success and Opposition

14 AFTER JOHN had been arrested, Jesus came into Galilee pro-
15 claiming the Gospel of God: 'The time has come; the kingdom
of God is upon you; repent, and believe the Gospel.'
16 Jesus was walking by the shore of the Sea of Galilee when he saw
Simon and his brother Andrew on the lake at work with a casting-
17 net; for they were fishermen. Jesus said to them, 'Come with me,
18 and I will make you fishers of men.' And at once they left their nets
and followed him.
19 When he had gone a little further he saw James son of Zebedee
and his brother John, who were in the boat overhauling their nets.
20 He called them; and, leaving their father Zebedee in the boat with
the hired men, they went off to follow him.
21 They came to Capernaum, and on the Sabbath he went to syna-
22 gogue and began to teach. The people were astounded at his teaching,
for, unlike the doctors of the law, he taught with a note of authority.
23 Now there was a man in the synagogue possessed by an unclean
24 spirit. He shrieked: 'What do you want with us, Jesus of Nazareth?
Have you[a] come to destroy us? I know who you are—the Holy One
25 of God.' Jesus rebuked him: 'Be silent', he said, 'and come out of
26 him.' And the unclean spirit threw the man into convulsions and
27 with a loud cry left him. They were all dumbfounded and began
to ask one another, 'What is this? A new kind of teaching! He
speaks with authority. When he gives orders, even the unclean
28 spirits submit.' The news spread rapidly, and he was soon spoken
of all over the district of Galilee.
29 On leaving the synagogue they went straight to the house
of Simon and Andrew; and James and John went with them.
30 Simon's mother-in-law was ill in bed with fever. They told him
31 about her at once. He came forward, took her by the hand, and
helped her to her feet. The fever left her and she waited upon
them.
32 That evening after sunset they brought to him all who were ill
33 or possessed by devils; and the whole town was there, gathered at
34 the door. He healed many who suffered from various diseases, and

[a] Or You have.

drove out many devils. He would not let the devils speak, because they knew who he was.

Very early next morning he got up and went out. He went away 35 to a lonely spot and remained there in prayer. But Simon and his 36 companions searched him out, found him, and said, 'They are all 37 looking for you.' He answered, 'Let us move on to the country 38 towns in the neighbourhood; I have to proclaim my message there also; that is what I came out to do.' So all through Galilee he went, 39 preaching in the synagogues and casting out the devils.

Once he was approached by a leper, who knelt before him begging 40 his help. 'If only you will,' said the man, 'you can cleanse me.' In warm indignation Jesus stretched out his hand,*a* touched him, 41 and said, 'Indeed I will; be clean again.' The leprosy left him imme- 42 diately, and he was clean. Then he dismissed him with this stern 43 warning: 'Be sure you say nothing to anybody. Go and show your- 44 self to the priest, and make the offering laid down by Moses for your cleansing; that will certify the cure.' But the man went out and 45 made the whole story public; he spread it far and wide, until Jesus could no longer show himself in any town, but stayed outside in the open country. Even so, people kept coming to him from all quarters.

When after some days he returned to Capernaum, the news went 2 round that he was at home; and such a crowd collected that the 2 space in front of the door was not big enough to hold them. And while he was proclaiming the message to them, a man was brought 3 who was paralysed. Four men were carrying him, but because of 4 the crowd they could not get him near. So they opened up the roof over the place where Jesus was, and when they had broken through they lowered the stretcher on which the paralysed man was lying. When Jesus saw their faith, he said to the paralysed man, 'My son, 5 your sins are forgiven.'

Now there were some lawyers sitting there and they thought to 6 themselves, 'Why does the fellow talk like that? This is blasphemy! 7 Who but God alone can forgive sins?' Jesus knew in his own mind 8 that this was what they were thinking, and said to them: 'Why do you harbour thoughts like these? Is it easier to say to this paralysed 9 man, "Your sins are forgiven", or to say, "Stand up, take your

[a] *Some witnesses read* Jesus was sorry for him and stretched out his hand; *one witness has simply* He stretched out his hand.

59

10 bed, and walk"? But to convince you that the Son of Man has the right on earth to forgive sins'—he turned to the paralysed

11, 12 man—'I say to you, stand up, take your bed, and go home.' And he got up, took his stretcher at once, and went out in full view of them all, so that they were astounded and praised God. 'Never before', they said, 'have we seen the like.'

13 Once more he went away to the lake-side. All the crowd came

14 to him, and he taught them there. As he went along, he saw Levi son of Alphaeus at his seat in the custom-house, and said to him, 'Follow me'; and Levi rose and followed him.

15 When Jesus was at table in his house, many bad characters—tax-gatherers and others—were seated with him and his disciples;

16 for there were many who followed him. Some doctors of the law who were Pharisees noticed him eating in this bad company, and said

17 to his disciples, 'He eats with tax-gatherers and sinners!' Jesus overheard and said to them, 'It is not the healthy that need a doctor, but the sick; I did not come to invite virtuous people, but sinners.'

18 Once, when John's disciples and the Pharisees were keeping a fast, some people came to him and said, 'Why is it that John's disciples and the disciples of the Pharisees are fasting, but yours are not?'

19 Jesus said to them, 'Can you expect the bridegroom's friends to fast while the bridegroom is with them? As long as they have the bride-

20 groom with them, there can be no fasting. But the time will come when the bridegroom will be taken away from them, and on that day they will fast.

21 'No one sews a patch of unshrunk cloth on to an old coat; if he does, the patch tears away from it, the new from the old, and leaves

22 a bigger hole. No one puts new wine into old wine-skins; if he does, the wine will burst the skins, and then wine and skins are both lost. Fresh skins for new wine!'

23 One Sabbath he was going through the cornfields; and his dis-

24 ciples, as they went, began to pluck ears of corn. The Pharisees said to him, 'Look, why are they doing what is forbidden on the

25 Sabbath?' He answered, 'Have you never read what David did when

26 he and his men were hungry and had nothing to eat? He went into the House of God, in the time of Abiathar the High Priest, and ate the consecrated loaves, though no one but a priest is allowed to eat them, and even gave them to his men.'

27 He also said to them, 'The Sabbath was made for the sake of

man and not man for the Sabbath: therefore the Son of Man is 28
sovereign even over the Sabbath.'

On another occasion when he went to synagogue, there was a man 3
in the congregation who had a withered arm; and they were watching 2
to see whether Jesus would cure him on the Sabbath, so that they
could bring a charge against him. He said to the man with the 3
withered arm, 'Come and stand out here.' Then he turned to them: 4
'Is it permitted to do good or to do evil on the Sabbath, to save
life or to kill?' They had nothing to say; and, looking round at them 5
with anger and sorrow at their obstinate stupidity, he said to the
man, 'Stretch out your arm.' He stretched it out and his arm was
restored. But the Pharisees, on leaving the synagogue, began plot- 6
ting against him with the partisans of Herod to see how they could
make away with him.

JESUS WENT away to the lake-side with his disciples. Great 7
numbers from Galilee, Judaea and Jerusalem, Idumaea and Trans- 8
jordan, and the neighbourhood of Tyre and Sidon, heard what he
was doing and came to see him. So he told his disciples to have a 9
boat ready for him, to save him from being crushed by the crowd.
For he cured so many that sick people of all kinds came crowding 10
in upon him to touch him. The unclean spirits too, when they 11
saw him, would fall at his feet and cry aloud, 'You are the Son of
God'; but he insisted that they should not make him known. 12

He then went up into the hill-country and called the men he 13
wanted; and they went and joined him. He appointed twelve as his 14
companions, whom he would send out to proclaim the Gospel, with 15
a commission to drive out devils. So he appointed the Twelve: to 16
Simon he gave the name Peter; then came the sons of Zebedee, 17
James and his brother John, to whom he gave the name Boanerges,
Sons of Thunder; then Andrew and Philip and Bartholomew and 18
Matthew and Thomas and James the son of Alphaeus and Thaddaeus
and Simon, a member of the Zealot party, and Judas Iscariot, the 19
man who betrayed him.

He entered a house; and once more such a crowd collected round 20
them that they had no chance to eat. When his family heard of this, 21
they set out to take charge of him; for people were saying that
he was out of his mind.[a]

[a] *Or* of him. 'He is out of his mind', they said.

22 The doctors of the law, too, who had come down from Jerusalem, said, 'He is possessed by Beelzebub', and, 'He drives out devils 23 by the prince of devils.' So he called them to come forward, and 24 spoke to them in parables: 'How can Satan drive out Satan? If a 25 kingdom is divided against itself, that kingdom cannot stand; if a household is divided against itself, that house will never stand; 26 and if Satan is in rebellion against himself, he is divided and cannot stand; and that is the end of him.

27 'On the other hand, no one can break into a strong man's house and make off with his goods unless he has first tied the strong man up; then he can ransack the house.

28 'I tell you this: no sin, no slander, is beyond forgiveness for men; 29 but whoever slanders the Holy Spirit can never be forgiven; he 30 is guilty of eternal sin.' He said this because they had declared that he was possessed by an unclean spirit.

31 Then his mother and his brothers arrived, and remaining outside 32 sent in a message asking him to come out to them. A crowd was sitting round and word was brought to him: 'Your mother and 33 your brothers are outside asking for you.' He replied, 'Who is 34 my mother? Who are my brothers?' And looking round at those who were sitting in the circle about him he said, 'Here are my mother 35 and my brothers. Whoever does the will of God is my brother, my sister, my mother.'

4 ON ANOTHER occasion he began to teach by the lake-side. The crowd that gathered round him was so large that he had to get into a boat on the lake, and there he sat, with the whole crowd on the 2 beach right down to the water's edge. And he taught them many things by parables.

As he taught he said:

3, 4 'Listen! A sower went out to sow. And it happened that as he sowed, some seed fell along the footpath; and the birds came 5 and ate it up. Some seed fell on rocky ground, where it had little soil, and it sprouted quickly because it had no depth of earth; 6 but when the sun rose the young corn was scorched, and as it had 7 no proper root it withered away. Some seed fell among thistles; but the thistles shot up and choked the corn, and it yielded no 8 crop. And some of the seed fell into good soil, where it came up and grew, and bore fruit; and the yield was thirtyfold, sixtyfold,

even a hundredfold.' He added, 'If you have ears to hear, then 9
hear.'

When he was alone, the Twelve and others who were round him 10
questioned him about the parables. He replied, 'To you the secret 11
of the kingdom of God has been given; but to those who are outside
everything comes by way of parables, so that (as Scripture says) 12
they may look and look, but see nothing; they may hear and hear,
but understand nothing; otherwise they might turn to God and be
forgiven.'

So he said, 'You do not understand this parable? How then 13
are you to understand any parable? The sower sows the word. 14
Those along the footpath are people in whom the word is sown, but 15
no sooner have they heard it than Satan comes and carries off the
word which has been sown in them. It is the same with those who 16
receive the seed on rocky ground; as soon as they hear the word,
they accept it with joy, but it strikes no root in them; they have 17
no staying-power; then, when there is trouble or persecution on
account of the word, they fall away at once. Others again receive 18
the seed among thistles; they hear the word, but worldly cares 19
and the false glamour of wealth and all kinds of evil desire come
in and choke the word, and it proves barren. And there are those 20
who receive the seed in good soil; they hear the word and welcome
it; and they bear fruit thirtyfold, sixtyfold, or a hundredfold.'

He said to them, 'Do you bring in the lamp to put it under the 21
meal-tub, or under the bed? Surely it is brought to be set on the
lamp-stand? For nothing is hidden unless it is to be disclosed, 22
and nothing put under cover unless it is to come into the open. If 23
you have ears to hear, then hear.'

He also said, 'Take note of what you hear; the measure you 24
give is the measure you will receive, with something more besides.
For the man who has will be given more, and the man who has not 25
will forfeit even what he has.'

He said, 'The kingdom of God is like this: A man scatters seed 26
on the land; he goes to bed at night and gets up in the morning, 27
and the seed sprouts and grows—how, he does not know. The 28
ground produces a crop by itself, first the blade, then the ear,
then full-grown corn in the ear; but as soon as the crop is ripe, 29
he sets to work with the sickle, because harvest-time has come.'

He said also, 'How shall we picture the kingdom of God, or by 30

31 what parable shall we describe it? It is like the mustard-seed, which
32 is smaller than any seed in the ground at its sowing. But once
sown, it springs up and grows taller than any other plant, and forms
branches so large that the birds can settle in its shade.'
33   With many such parables he would give them his message, so
34 far as they were able to receive it. He never spoke to them except
in parables; but privately to his disciples he explained everything.

Miracles of Christ

35 THAT DAY, in the evening, he said to them, 'Let us cross over
36 to the other side of the lake.' So they left the crowd and took
him with them in the boat where he had been sitting; and there
37 were other boats accompanying him. A heavy squall came on and
38 the waves broke over the boat until it was all but swamped. Now
he was in the stern asleep on a cushion; they roused him and said,
39 'Master, we are sinking! Do you not care?' He stood up, rebuked
the wind, and said to the sea, 'Hush! Be still!' The wind dropped
40 and there was a dead calm. He said to them, 'Why are you such
41 cowards? Have you no faith even now?' They were awestruck and
said to one another, 'Who can this be whom even the wind and the
sea obey?'
5   So they came to the other side of the lake, into the country of the
2 Gerasenes. As he stepped ashore, a man possessed by an unclean
3 spirit came up to him from among the tombs where he had his
dwelling. He could no longer be controlled; even chains were useless;
4 he had often been fettered and chained up, but he had snapped his
chains and broken the fetters. No one was strong enough to master
5 him. And so, unceasingly, night and day, he would cry aloud among
6 the tombs and on the hill-sides and cut himself with stones. When
he saw Jesus in the distance, he ran and flung himself down before
7 him, shouting loudly, 'What do you want with me, Jesus, son of the
8 Most High God? In God's name do not torment me.' (For Jesus
was already saying to him, 'Out, unclean spirit, come out of this
9 man!') Jesus asked him, 'What is your name?' 'My name is Legion,'
10 he said, 'there are so many of us.' And he begged hard that Jesus
would not send them out of the country.

Now there happened to be a large herd of pigs feeding on the 11
hill-side, and the spirits begged him, 'Send us among the pigs and 12
let us go into them.' He gave them leave; and the unclean spirits 13
came out and went into the pigs; and the herd, of about two thousand, rushed over the edge into the lake and were drowned.

The men in charge of them took to their heels and carried the news 14
to the town and country-side; and the people came out to see what
had happened. They came to Jesus and saw the madman who had 15
been possessed by the legion of devils, sitting there clothed and
in his right mind; and they were afraid. The spectators told them 16
how the madman had been cured and what had happened to the
pigs. Then they begged Jesus to leave the district. 17

As he was stepping into the boat, the man who had been possessed 18
begged to go with him. Jesus would not allow it, but said to him, 19
'Go home to your own folk and tell them what the Lord in his
mercy has done for you.' The man went off and spread the news in 20
the Ten Towns*a* of all that Jesus had done for him; and they were
all amazed.

As soon as Jesus had returned by boat to the other shore, a great 21
crowd once more gathered round him. While he was by the lake-
side, the president of one of the synagogues came up, Jairus by 22
name, and, when he saw him, threw himself down at his feet and 23
pleaded with him. 'My little daughter', he said, 'is at death's door.
I beg you to come and lay your hands on her to cure her and
save her life.' So Jesus went with him, accompanied by a great 24
crowd which pressed upon him.

Among them was a woman who had suffered from haemorrhages 25
for twelve years; and in spite of long treatment by doctors, on which 26
she had spent all she had, there had been no improvement; on the
contrary, she had grown worse. She had heard what people were 27
saying about Jesus, so she came up from behind in the crowd and
touched his cloak; for she said to herself, 'If I touch even his 28
clothes, I shall be cured.' And there and then the source of her 29
haemorrhages dried up and she knew in herself that she was cured
of her trouble. At the same time Jesus, aware that power had gone 30
out of him, turned round in the crowd and asked, 'Who touched my
clothes?' His disciples said to him, 'You see the crowd pressing 31
upon you and yet you ask, "Who touched me?"' Meanwhile he was 32

[a] *Greek* Decapolis.

65

33 looking round to see who had done it. And the woman, trembling
with fear when she grasped what had happened to her, came and
34 fell at his feet and told him the whole truth. He said to her, 'My
daughter, your faith has cured you. Go in peace, free for ever
from this trouble.'

35   While he was still speaking, a message came from the president's
36 house, 'Your daughter is dead; why trouble the Rabbi further?' But
Jesus, overhearing the message as it was delivered, said to the
president of the synagogue, 'Do not be afraid; only have faith.'
37 After this he allowed no one to accompany him except Peter and
38 James and James's brother John. They came to the president's house,
39 where he found a great commotion, with loud crying and wailing. So
he went in and said to them, 'Why this crying and commotion? The
40 child is not dead: she is asleep.' But they only laughed at him. After
turning all the others out, he took the child's father and mother and
41 his own companions and went in where the child was lying. Then,
taking hold of her hand, he said to her, '*Talitha cum*', which means,
42 'Get up, my child.' Immediately the girl got up and walked about—
she was twelve years old. At that they were beside themselves with
43 amazement. He gave them strict orders to let no one hear about it,
and told them to give her something to eat.

6   He left that place and went to his home town accompanied by his
2 disciples. When the Sabbath came he began to teach in the synagogue; and the large congregation who heard him were amazed and
said, 'Where does he get it from?', and, 'What wisdom is this that
3 has been given him?', and, 'How does he work such miracles? Is not
this the carpenter, the son of Mary,[a] the brother of James and
Joseph and Judas and Simon? And are not his sisters here with us?'
4 So they fell foul of him. Jesus said to them, 'A prophet will always
be held in honour except in his home town, and among his kinsmen
5 and family.' He could work no miracle there, except that he put
6 his hands on a few sick people and healed them; and he was taken
aback by their want of faith.

7 ON ONE of his teaching journeys round the villages he summoned
the Twelve and sent them out in pairs on a mission. He gave them
8 authority over unclean spirits, and instructed them to take nothing
for the journey beyond a stick: no bread, no pack, no money in

[a] *Some witnesses read* Is not this the son of the carpenter and Mary...

their belts. They might wear sandals, but not a second coat. 'When 9, 10
you are admitted to a house', he added, 'stay there until you leave
those parts. At any place where they will not receive you or listen to 11
you, shake the dust off your feet as you leave, as a warning to them.'
So they set out and called publicly for repentance. They drove out 12, 13
many devils, and many sick people they anointed with oil and cured.

Now King Herod heard of it, for the fame of Jesus had spread; 14
and people were saying,ᵃ 'John the Baptist has been raised to life,
and that is why these miraculous powers are at work in him.' Others 15
said, 'It is Elijah.' Others again, 'He is a prophet like one of the
old prophets.' But Herod, when he heard of it, said, 'This is John, 16
whom I beheaded, raised from the dead.'

For this same Herod had sent and arrested John and put him in 17
prison at the instance of his brother Philip's wife, Herodias, whom
he had married. John had told Herod, 'You have no right to your 18
brother's wife.' Thus Herodias nursed a grudge against him and 19
would willingly have killed him, but she could not; for Herod went 20
in awe of John, knowing him to be a good and holy man; so he kept
him in custody. He liked to listen to him, although the listening
left him greatly perplexed.

Herodias found her opportunity when Herod on his birthday gave 21
a banquet to his chief officials and commanders and the leading
men of Galilee. Her daughter came inᵇ and danced, and so delighted 22
Herod and his guests that the king said to the girl, 'Ask what you
like and I will give it you.' And he swore an oath to her: 'Whatever 23
you ask I will give you, up to half my kingdom.' She went out 24
and said to her mother, 'What shall I ask for?' She replied, 'The
head of John the Baptist.' The girl hastened back at once to the 25
king with her request: 'I want you to give me here and now, on
a dish, the head of John the Baptist.' The king was greatly dis- 26
tressed, but out of regard for his oath and for his guests he could
not bring himself to refuse her. So the king sent a soldier of the 27
guard with orders to bring John's head. The soldier went off and
beheaded him in the prison, brought the head on a dish, and gave 28
it to the girl; and she gave it to her mother.

When John's disciples heard the news, they came and took his 29
body away and laid it in a tomb.

[*a*] *Some witnesses read* and he said... [*b*] *Or* A festive occasion came when Herod on
his birthday gave...of Galilee. The daughter of Herodias came in...

30   The apostles now rejoined Jesus and reported to him all that
31 they had done and taught. He said to them, 'Come with me, by
yourselves, to some lonely place where you can rest quietly.' (For
they had no leisure even to eat, so many were coming and going.)
32 Accordingly, they set off privately by boat for a lonely place.
33 But many saw them leave and recognized them, and came round by
land, hurrying from all the towns towards the place, and arrived
34 there first. When he came ashore, he saw a great crowd; and his
heart went out to them, because they were like sheep without a
35 shepherd; and he had much to teach them. As the day wore on, his
disciples approached him and said, 'This is a lonely place and it
36 is getting very late; send the people off to the farms and villages
37 round about, to buy themselves something to eat.' 'Give them something to eat yourselves', he answered. They replied, 'Are we to
38 go and spend twenty pounds*a* on bread to give them a meal?' 'How
many loaves have you?' he asked; 'go and see.' They found out and
39 told him, 'Five, and two fishes also.' He ordered them to make the
40 people sit down in groups on the green grass, and they sat down in
41 rows, a hundred rows of fifty each. Then, taking the five loaves
and the two fishes, he looked up to heaven, said the blessing, broke
the loaves, and gave them to the disciples to distribute. He also
42 divided the two fishes among them. They all ate to their hearts'
43 content; and twelve great basketfuls of scraps were picked up, with
44 what was left of the fish. Those who ate the loaves numbered five
thousand men.

45   As soon as it was over he made his disciples embark and cross
to Bethsaida ahead of him, while he himself sent the people away.
46, 47 After taking leave of them, he went up the hill-side to pray. It
grew late and the boat was already well out on the water, while
48 he was alone on the land. Somewhere between three and six in the
morning, seeing them labouring at the oars against a head-wind, he
came towards them, walking on the lake. He was going to pass them
49 by; but when they saw him walking on the lake, they thought it was
50 a ghost and cried out; for they all saw him and were terrified. But
at once he spoke to them: 'Take heart! It is I; do not be afraid.'
51 Then he climbed into the boat beside them, and the wind dropped.
52 At this they were completely dumbfounded, for they had not understood the incident of the loaves; their minds were closed.

[a] Literally 200 denarii.

So they finished the crossing and came to land at Gennesaret, 53
where they made fast. When they came ashore, he was immediately 54
recognized; and the people scoured that whole country-side and 55
brought the sick on stretchers to any place where he was reported
to be. Wherever he went, to farmsteads, villages, or towns, they 56
laid out the sick in the market-places and begged him to let them
simply touch the edge of his cloak; and all who touched him were
cured.

Growing Tension

A GROUP of Pharisees, with some doctors of the law who had 7
come from Jerusalem, met him and noticed that some of his 2
disciples were eating their food with 'defiled' hands—in other words,
without washing them. (For the Pharisees and the Jews in general 3
never eat without washing the hands,*a* in obedience to an old-established tradition; and on coming from the market-place they never eat 4
without first washing. And there are many other points on which
they have a traditional rule to maintain, for example, washing of
cups and jugs and copper bowls.) Accordingly, these Pharisees and 5
the lawyers asked him, 'Why do your disciples not conform to the
ancient tradition, but eat their food with defiled hands?' He answered, 6
'Isaiah was right when he prophesied about you hypocrites in these
words: "This people pays me lip-service, but their heart is far
from me: their worship of me is in vain, for they teach as doctrines 7
the commandments of men." You neglect the commandment of God, 8
in order to maintain the tradition of men.'

He also said to them, 'How well you set aside the commandment 9
of God in order to maintain*b* your tradition! Moses said, "Honour 10
your father and your mother", and, "The man who curses his father
or mother must suffer death." But you hold that if a man says to 11
his father or mother, "Anything of mine which might have been
used for your benefit is Corban"' (meaning, set apart for God), 'he is 12
no longer permitted to do anything for his father or mother. Thus by 13
your own tradition, handed down among you, you make God's word
null and void. And many other things that you do are just like that.'

[*a*] *Some witnesses insert* with the fist; *others insert* frequently, *or* thoroughly. [*b*] *Some witnesses read* establish.

14 On another occasion he called the people and said to them,
15 'Listen to me, all of you, and understand this: nothing that goes
into a man from outside can defile him; no, it is the things that
come out of him that defile a man.'*a*
17 When he had left the people and gone indoors, his disciples
18 questioned him about the parable. He said to them, 'Are you as
dull as the rest? Do you not see that nothing that goes from outside
19 into a man can defile him, because it does not enter into his heart
but into his stomach, and so passes out into the drain?' Thus he
20 declared all foods clean. He went on, 'It is what comes out of a
21 man that defiles him. For from inside, out of a man's heart, come
22 evil thoughts, acts of fornication, of theft, murder, adultery, ruthless greed, and malice; fraud, indecency, envy, slander, arrogance,
23 and folly; these evil things all come from inside, and they defile
the man.'

24 Then he left that place and went away into the territory of Tyre.
He found a house to stay in, and he would have liked to remain
25 unrecognized, but this was impossible. Almost at once a woman
whose young daughter was possessed by an unclean spirit heard
26 of him, came in, and fell at his feet. (She was a Gentile, a Phoenician
of Syria by nationality.) She begged him to drive the spirit out
27 of her daughter. He said to her, 'Let the children be satisfied
first; it is not fair to take the children's bread and throw it to the
28 dogs.' 'Sir,' she answered, 'even the dogs under the table eat the
29 children's scraps.' He said to her, 'For saying that, you may go
home content; the unclean spirit has gone out of your daughter.'
30 And when she returned home, she found the child lying in bed;
the spirit had left her.

31 On his return journey from Tyrian territory he went by way of
Sidon to the Sea of Galilee through the territory of the Ten Towns.*b*
32 They brought to him a man who was deaf and had an impediment in
his speech, with the request that he would lay his hand on him.
33 He took the man aside, away from the crowd, put his fingers into
34 his ears, spat, and touched his tongue. Then, looking up to heaven,
he sighed, and said to him, '*Ephphatha*', which means 'Be opened.'
35 With that his ears were opened, and at the same time the impediment
36 was removed and he spoke plainly. Jesus forbade them to tell
anyone; but the more he forbade them, the more they published it.

[a] *Some witnesses here add* (16) If you have ears to hear, then hear. [b] *Greek* Decapolis.

Their astonishment knew no bounds: 'All that he does, he does well,' 37
they said; 'he even makes the deaf hear and the dumb speak.'

THERE WAS another occasion about this time when a huge crowd 8
had collected, and, as they had no food, Jesus called his disciples
and said to them, 'I feel sorry for all these people; they have been 2
with me now for three days and have nothing to eat. If I send them 3
home unfed, they will turn faint on the way; some of them have
come from a distance.' The disciples answered, 'How can anyone 4
provide all these people with bread in this lonely place?' 'How many 5
loaves have you?' he asked; and they answered, 'Seven.' So he 6
ordered the people to sit down on the ground; then he took the seven
loaves, and, after giving thanks to God, he broke the bread and gave
it to his disciples to distribute; and they served it out to the people.
They had also a few small fishes, which he blessed and ordered 7
them to distribute. They all ate to their hearts' content, and seven 8
baskets were filled with the scraps that were left. The people num- 9
bered about four thousand. Then he dismissed them; and, without 10
delay, got into the boat with his disciples and went to the district of
Dalmanutha.[a]
     Then the Pharisees came out and engaged him in discussion. 11
To test him they asked him for a sign from heaven. He sighed deeply 12
to himself and said, 'Why does this generation ask for a sign?
I tell you this: no sign shall be given to this generation.' With that 13
he left them, re-embarked, and went off to the other side of the lake.
     Now they had forgotten to take bread with them; they had no 14
more than one loaf in the boat. He began to warn them: 'Beware,' 15
he said, 'be on your guard against the leaven of the Pharisees and
the leaven of Herod.' They said among themselves, 'It is because 16
we have no bread.' Knowing what was in their minds, he asked 17
them, 'Why do you talk about having no bread? Have you no inkling
yet? Do you still not understand? Are your minds closed? You have 18
eyes: can you not see? You have ears: can you not hear? Have you
forgotten? When I broke the five loaves among five thousand, how 19
many basketfuls of scraps did you pick up?' 'Twelve', they said.
'And how many when I broke the seven loaves among four thou- 20
sand?' They answered, 'Seven.' He said, 'Do you still not under- 21
stand?'

[a] *Some witnesses give* Magedan; *others give* Magdala.

22 They arrived at Bethsaida. There the people brought a blind
23 man to Jesus and begged him to touch him. He took the blind man
by the hand and led him away out of the village. Then he spat on
his eyes, laid his hands upon him, and asked whether he could see
24 anything. The man's sight began to come back, and he said, 'I see
25 men; they look like trees, but they are walking about.' Jesus laid
his hands on his eyes again; he looked hard, and now he was cured
26 so that he saw everything clearly. Then Jesus sent him home,
saying, 'Do not tell anyone in the village.'[a]

27 JESUS and his disciples set out for the villages of Caesarea Philippi.
28 On the way he asked his disciples, 'Who do men say I am?' They
answered, 'Some say John the Baptist, others Elijah, others one
29 of the prophets.' 'And you,' he asked, 'who do you say I am?'
30 Peter replied: 'You are the Messiah.' Then he gave them strict
31 orders not to tell anyone about him; and he began to teach them
that the Son of Man had to undergo great sufferings, and to be
rejected by the elders, chief priests, and doctors of the law; to
32 be put to death, and to rise again three days afterwards. He spoke
about it plainly. At this Peter took him by the arm and began to
33 rebuke him. But Jesus turned round, and, looking at his disciples,
rebuked Peter. 'Away with you, Satan,' he said; 'you think as men
think, not as God thinks.'

34 Then he called the people to him, as well as his disciples, and
said to them, 'Anyone who wishes to be a follower of mine must
leave self behind; he must take up his cross, and come with me.
35 Whoever cares for his own safety is lost; but if a man will let himself
36 be lost for my sake and for the Gospel, that man is safe. What does
a man gain by winning the whole world at the cost of his true self?
37, 38 What can he give to buy that self back? If anyone is ashamed of
me and mine[b] in this wicked and godless age, the Son of Man will
be ashamed of him, when he comes in the glory of his Father and
of the holy angels.'[c]

9   He also said, 'I tell you this: there are some of those standing
here who will not taste death before they have seen the kingdom of
God already come in power.'

2   Six days later Jesus took Peter, James, and John with him

[a] *Some witnesses read* Do not go into the village. [b] *Some witnesses read* me and
my words. [c] *Some witnesses read* Father with the holy angels.

and led them up a high mountain where they were alone; and in
their presence he was transfigured; his clothes became dazzling 3
white, with a whiteness no bleacher on earth could equal. They 4
saw Elijah appear, and Moses with him, and there they were,
conversing with Jesus. Then Peter spoke: 'Rabbi,' he said, 'how 5
good it is that we are here! Shall we make three shelters, one
for you, one for Moses, and one for Elijah?' (For he did not know 6
what to say; they were so terrified.) Then a cloud appeared, casting 7
its shadow over them, and out of the cloud came a voice: 'This is
my Son, my Beloved;*a* listen to him.' And now suddenly, when 8
they looked around, there was nobody to be seen but Jesus alone with
themselves.

On their way down the mountain, he enjoined them not to tell 9
anyone what they had seen until the Son of Man had risen from the
dead. They seized upon those words, and discussed among them- 10
selves what this 'rising from the dead' could mean. And they put 11
a question to him: 'Why do our teachers say that Elijah must be
the first to come?' He replied, 'Yes, Elijah does come first to 12
set everything right. Yet how is it*b* that the scriptures say of the
Son of Man that he is to endure great sufferings and to be treated
with contempt? However, I tell you, Elijah has already come and 13
they have worked their will upon him, as the scriptures say of
him.'

When they came back to the disciples they saw a large crowd 14
surrounding them and lawyers arguing with them. As soon as they 15
saw Jesus the whole crowd were overcome with awe, and they ran
forward to welcome him. He asked them, 'What is this argument 16
about?' A man in the crowd spoke up: 'Master, I brought my son 17
to you. He is possessed by a spirit which makes him speechless.
Whenever it attacks him, it dashes him to the ground, and he foams 18
at the mouth, grinds his teeth, and goes rigid. I asked your disciples to cast it out, but they failed.' Jesus answered: 'What an 19
unbelieving and perverse generation! How long shall I be with you?
How long must I endure you? Bring him to me.' So they brought 20
the boy to him; and as soon as the spirit saw him it threw the boy
into convulsions, and he fell on the ground and rolled about foaming
at the mouth. Jesus asked his father, 'How long has he been like 21

[*a*] Or This is my only Son. [*b*] Or Elijah, you say, comes first to set everything right:
then how is it...

73

22 this?' 'From childhood,' he replied; 'often it has tried to make an
end of him by throwing him into the fire or into water. But if it
23 is at all possible for you, take pity upon us and help us.' 'If it is
possible!' said Jesus. 'Everything is possible to one who has faith.'
24 'I have faith,' cried the boy's father; 'help me where faith falls
25 short.' Jesus saw then that the crowd was closing in upon them,
so he rebuked the unclean spirit. 'Deaf and dumb spirit,' he said,
26 'I command you, come out of him and never go back!' After crying
aloud and racking him fiercely, it came out; and the boy looked
27 like a corpse; in fact, many said, 'He is dead.' But Jesus took his
hand and raised him to his feet, and he stood up.
28   Then Jesus went indoors, and his disciples asked him privately,
29 'Why could not we cast it out?' He said, 'There is no means of
casting out this sort but prayer.'*a*

30 THEY NOW left that district and made a journey through Galilee.
31 Jesus wished it to be kept secret; for he was teaching his disciples,
and telling them, 'The Son of Man is now to be given up into the
power of men, and they will kill him, and three days after being
32 killed, he will rise again.' But they did not understand what he said,
and were afraid to ask.
33   So they came to Capernaum; and when he was indoors, he asked
34 them, 'What were you arguing about on the way?' They were silent,
because on the way they had been discussing who was the greatest.
35 He sat down, called the Twelve, and said to them, 'If anyone wants
to be first, he must make himself last of all and servant of all.'
36 Then he took a child, set him in front of them, and put his arm
37 round him. 'Whoever receives one of these children in my name',
he said, 'receives me; and whoever receives me, receives not me
but the One who sent me.'
38   John said to him, 'Master, we saw a man driving out devils
in your name, and as he was not one of us, we tried to stop him.'
39 Jesus said, 'Do not stop him; no one who does a work of divine
power in my name will be able in the same breath to speak evil
40, 41 of me. For he who is not against us is on our side. I tell you this:
if anyone gives you a cup of water to drink because you are followers
of the Messiah, that man assuredly will not go unrewarded.
42   'As for the man who leads astray one of these little ones who have

[a] *Some witnesses add* and fasting.

74

faith, it would be better for him to be thrown into the sea with
a millstone round his neck. If your hand is your undoing, cut it off; 43
it is better for you to enter into life maimed than to keep both hands
and go to hell and the unquenchable fire.*a* And if it is your foot 45
that leads you astray, cut it off; it is better to enter into life a cripple
than to keep both your feet and be thrown into hell.*b* And if it 47
is your eye, tear it out; it is better to enter into the kingdom of God
with one eye than to keep both eyes and be thrown into hell, where 48
the devouring worm never dies and the fire is not quenched.

'For everyone will be salted with fire.   49

'Salt is a good thing; but if the salt loses its saltness, what will 50
you season it with?

'Have salt in yourselves; and be*c* at peace with one another.'

ON LEAVING those parts he came into the regions of Judaea and 10
Transjordan; and when a crowd gathered round him once again,
he followed his usual practice and taught them. The question was 2
put to him:*d* 'Is it lawful for a man to divorce his wife?' This
was to test him. He asked in return, 'What did Moses command 3
you?' They answered, 'Moses permitted a man to divorce his wife 4
by note of dismissal.' Jesus said to them, 'It was because you were 5
so unteachable that he made this rule for you; but in the beginning, 6
at the creation, God made them male and female. For this reason 7
a man shall leave his father and mother, and be made one with his
wife;*e* and the two shall become one flesh. It follows that they are 8
no longer two individuals: they are one flesh. What God has joined 9
together, man must not separate.'

When they were indoors again the disciples questioned him about 10
this matter; he said to them, 'Whoever divorces his wife and marries 11
another commits adultery against her: so too, if she divorces her 12
husband and marries another, she commits adultery.'

They brought children for him to touch; and the disciples scolded 13
them for it. But when Jesus saw this he was indignant, and said 14
to them, 'Let the children come to me; do not try to stop them;

[a] *Some witnesses add* (44) where the devouring worm never dies and the fire is not
quenched. [b] *Some witnesses add* (46) where the devouring worm never dies and the
fire is not quenched. [c] *Or* Have the salt of fellowship and be...; *or* You have the
salt of fellowship between you; then be... [d] *Some witnesses read* The Pharisees
came forward and asked him the question... [e] *Some witnesses omit* and be made...
wife.

15 for the kingdom of God belongs to such as these. I tell you, whoever does not accept the kingdom of God like a child will never enter it.'

16 And he put his arms round them, laid his hands upon them, and blessed them.

17 As he was starting out on a journey, a stranger ran up, and, kneeling before him, asked, 'Good Master, what must I do to win

18 eternal life?' Jesus said to him, 'Why do you call me good? No

19 one is good except God alone. You know the commandments: "Do not murder; do not commit adultery; do not steal; do not give false evidence; do not defraud; honour your father and mother."'

20 'But, Master,' he replied, 'I have kept all these since I was a boy.'

21 Jesus looked straight at him; his heart warmed to him, and he said, 'One thing you lack: go, sell everything you have, and give to the poor, and you will have riches in heaven; and come, follow

22 me.' At these words his face fell and he went away with a heavy heart; for he was a man of great wealth.

23 Jesus looked round at his disciples and said to them, 'How hard

24 it will be for the wealthy to enter the kingdom of God!' They were amazed that he should say this, but Jesus insisted, 'Children, how

25 hard it is*a* to enter the kingdom of God! It is easier for a camel to pass through the eye of a needle than for a rich man to enter the

26 kingdom of God.' They were more astonished than ever, and said

27 to one another, 'Then who can be saved?' Jesus looked them in the face and said, 'For men it is impossible, but not for God; to God everything is possible.'

28 At this Peter spoke. 'We here', he said, 'have left everything to

29 become your followers.' Jesus said, 'I tell you this: there is no one who has given up home, brothers or sisters, mother, father or

30 children, or land, for my sake and for the Gospel, who will not receive in this age a hundred times as much—houses, brothers and sisters, mothers and children, and land—and persecutions besides;

31 and in the age to come eternal life. But many who are first will be last and the last first.'

[a] *Some witnesses insert* for those who trust in riches.

Challenge to Jerusalem

THEY WERE on the road, going up to Jerusalem, Jesus leading ₃₂ the way; and the disciples were filled with awe; while those who followed behind were afraid. He took the Twelve aside and began to tell them what was to happen to him. 'We are now going ₃₃ to Jerusalem,' he said; 'and the Son of Man will be given up to the chief priests and the doctors of the law; they will condemn him to death and hand him over to the foreign power. He will be mocked ₃₄ and spat upon, flogged and killed; and three days afterwards, he will rise again.'

James and John, the sons of Zebedee, approached him and said, ₃₅ 'Master, we should like you to do us a favour.' 'What is it you ₃₆ want me to do?' he asked. They answered, 'Grant us the right to ₃₇ sit in state with you, one at your right and the other at your left.' Jesus said to them, 'You do not understand what you are asking. ₃₈ Can you drink the cup that I drink, or be baptized with the baptism I am baptized with?' 'We can', they answered. Jesus said, 'The ₃₉ cup that I drink you shall drink, and the baptism I am baptized with shall be your baptism; but to sit at my right or left is not ₄₀ for me to grant; it is for those to whom it has already been assigned.'ᵃ

When the other ten heard this, they were indignant with James ₄₁ and John. Jesus called them to him and said, 'You know that ₄₂ in the world the recognized rulers lord it over their subjects, and their great men make them feel the weight of authority. That is ₄₃ not the way with you; among you, whoever wants to be great must be your servant, and whoever wants to be first must be the willing ₄₄ slave of all. For even the Son of Man did not come to be served but ₄₅ to serve, and to surrender his life as a ransom for many.'

They came to Jericho; and as he was leaving the town, with his ₄₆ disciples and a large crowd, Bartimaeus son of Timaeus, a blind beggar, was seated at the roadside. Hearing that it was Jesus of ₄₇ Nazareth, he began to shout, 'Son of David, Jesus, have pity on me!' Many of the people rounded on him: 'Be quiet', they said; ₄₈ but he shouted all the more, 'Son of David, have pity on me.'

[a] *Some witnesses add* by my Father.

49 Jesus stopped and said, 'Call him'; so they called the blind man
50 and said, 'Take heart; stand up; he is calling you.' At that he
51 threw off his cloak, sprang up, and came to Jesus. Jesus said to
him, 'What do you want me to do for you?' 'Master,' the blind
52 man answered, 'I want my sight back.' Jesus said to him, 'Go;
your faith has cured you.' And at once he recovered his sight and
followed him on the road.

11 THEY WERE now approaching Jerusalem, and when they reached
Bethphage and Bethany, at the Mount of Olives, he sent two of his
2 disciples with these instructions: 'Go to the village opposite, and,
just as you enter, you will find tethered there a colt which no one
3 has yet ridden. Untie it and bring it here. If anyone asks, "Why
are you doing that?", say, "Our Master*a* needs it, and will send it
4 back here without delay."' So they went off, and found the colt
tethered to a door outside in the street. They were untying it
5 when some of the bystanders asked, 'What are you doing, untying
6 that colt?' They answered as Jesus had told them, and were then
7 allowed to take it. So they brought the colt to Jesus and spread
8 their cloaks on it, and he mounted. And people carpeted the road
with their cloaks, while others spread brushwood which they had
9 cut in the fields; and those who went ahead and the others who
came behind shouted, 'Hosanna! Blessings on him who comes in the
10 name of the Lord! Blessings on the coming kingdom of our father
David! Hosanna in the heavens!'
11   He entered Jerusalem and went into the temple, where he looked
at the whole scene; but, as it was now late, he went out to Bethany
with the Twelve.
12   On the following day, after they had left Bethany, he felt hungry,
13 and, noticing in the distance a fig-tree in leaf, he went to see if
he could find anything on it. But when he came there he found
14 nothing but leaves; for it was not the season for figs. He said to the
tree, 'May no one ever again eat fruit from you!' And his disciples
were listening.
15   So they came to Jerusalem, and he went into the temple and began
driving out those who bought and sold in the temple. He upset
the tables of the money-changers and the seats of the dealers in
16 pigeons; and he would not allow anyone to use the temple court

[a] *Or* Its owner.

78

as a thoroughfare for carrying goods. Then he began to teach them, 17 and said, 'Does not Scripture say, "My house shall be called a house of prayer for all the nations"? But you have made it a robbers' cave.' The chief priests and the doctors of the law heard of this and sought 18 some means of making away with him; for they were afraid of him, because the whole crowd was spellbound by his teaching. And when 19 evening came he went out of the city.

Early next morning, as they passed by, they saw that the fig-tree 20 had withered from the roots up; and Peter, recalling what had 21 happened, said to him, 'Rabbi, look, the fig-tree which you cursed has withered.' Jesus answered them, 'Have faith in God. I tell 22, 23 you this: if anyone says to this mountain, "Be lifted from your place and hurled into the sea", and has no inward doubts, but believes that what he says is happening, it will be done for him. I tell 24 you, then, whatever you ask for in prayer, believe that you have received it and it will be yours.

'And when you stand praying, if you have a grievance against 25 anyone, forgive him, so that your Father in heaven may forgive you the wrongs you have done.'[a]

THEY CAME once more to Jerusalem. And as he was walking in 27 the temple court the chief priests, lawyers, and elders came to him and said, 'By what authority are you acting like this? Who 28 gave you authority to act in this way?' Jesus said to them, 'I will 29 ask you one question; and if you give me an answer, I will tell you by what authority I act. The baptism of John: was it from 30 God, or from men? Answer me.' This set them arguing among 31 themselves: 'What shall we say? If we say, "from God", he will say, "Then why did you not believe him?" Shall we say, "from men"?' 32 —but they were afraid of the people, for all held that John was in fact a prophet. So they answered Jesus, 'We do not know.' And 33 Jesus said to them, 'Then neither will I tell you by what authority I act.'

He went on to speak to them in parables: 'A man planted a vine- 12 yard and put a wall round it, hewed out a winepress, and built a watch-tower; then he let it out to vine-growers and went abroad. When the vintage season came, he sent a servant to the tenants 2

[a] *Some witnesses add* (26) But if you do not forgive others, then the wrongs you have done will not be forgiven by your Father in heaven.

3 to collect from them his share of the produce. But they took
4 him, thrashed him, and sent him away empty-handed. Again, he
sent them another servant, whom they beat about the head and
5 treated outrageously. So he sent another, and that one they killed;
and many more besides, of whom they beat some, and killed others.
6 He had now only one left to send, his own dear son.*[a]* In the end
7 he sent him. "They will respect my son", he said. But the tenants
said to one another, "This is the heir; come, let us kill him, and
8 the property will be ours." So they seized him and killed him,
9 and flung his body out of the vineyard. What will the owner of the
vineyard do? He will come and put the tenants to death and give
the vineyard to others.

10 'Can it be that you have never read this text: "The stone which
11 the builders rejected has become the main corner-stone. This is the
Lord's doing, and it is wonderful in our eyes"?'

12 Then they began to look for a way to arrest him, for they saw
that the parable was aimed at them; but they were afraid of popular
feeling, so they left him alone and went away.

13 A NUMBER of Pharisees and men of Herod's party were sent to
14 trap him with a question. They came and said, 'Master, you are
an honest man, we know, and truckle to no man, whoever he may
be; you teach in all honesty the way of life that God requires.
Are we or are we not permitted to pay taxes to the Roman Emperor?
15 Shall we pay or not?' He saw how crafty their question was, and
said, 'Why are you trying to catch me out? Fetch me a silver
16 piece, and let me look at it.' They brought one, and he said to
them, 'Whose head is this, and whose inscription?' 'Caesar's',
17 they replied. Then Jesus said, 'Pay Caesar what is due to Caesar,
and pay God what is due to God.' And they heard him with
astonishment.

18 Next Sadducees came to him. (It is they who say that there
19 is no resurrection.) Their question was this: 'Master, Moses laid
it down for us that if there are brothers, and one dies leaving
a wife but no child, then the next should marry the widow and
20 carry on his brother's family. Now there were seven brothers.
21 The first took a wife and died without issue. Then the second
married her, and he too died without issue. So did the third.

[a] *Or* his only son.

Eventually the seven of them died, all without issue. Finally the 22 woman died. At the resurrection, when they come back to life, 23 whose wife will she be, since all seven had married her?' Jesus 24 said to them, 'You are mistaken, and surely this is the reason: you do not know either the scriptures or the power of God. When 25 they rise from the dead, men and women do not marry; they are like angels in heaven.

'Now about the resurrection of the dead, have you never read 26 in the Book of Moses, in the story of the burning bush, how God spoke to him and said, "I am the God of Abraham, the God of Isaac, and the God of Jacob"? God is not God of the dead but of 27 the living. You are greatly mistaken.'

Then one of the lawyers, who had been listening to these discus- 28 sions and had noted how well he answered, came forward and asked him, 'Which commandment is first of all?' Jesus answered, 29 'The first is, "Hear, O Israel: the Lord your God is the only Lord; love the Lord your God with all your heart, with all your 30 soul, with all your mind, and with all your strength." The second 31 is this: "Love your neighbour as yourself." There is no other commandment greater than these.' The lawyer said to him, 'Well 32 said, Master. You are right in saying that God is one and beside him there is no other. And to love him with all your heart, all 33 your understanding, and all your strength, and to love your neighbour as yourself—that is far more than any burnt offerings or sacrifices.' When Jesus saw how sensibly he answered, he said to 34 him, 'You are not far from the kingdom of God.'

After that nobody ventured to put any more questions to him; and Jesus went on to say, as he taught in the temple, 'How can 35 the teachers of the law maintain that the Messiah is "Son of David"? David himself said, when inspired by the Holy Spirit, 36 "The Lord said to my Lord, 'Sit at my right hand until I make your enemies your footstool.'" David himself calls him "Lord"; 37 how can he also be David's son?'

There was a great crowd and they listened eagerly.[a] He said 38 as he taught them, 'Beware of the doctors of the law, who love to walk up and down in long robes, receiving respectful greetings in the street; and to have the chief seats in synagogues, and places 39 of honour at feasts. These are the men who eat up the property of 40

[a] Or The mass of the people listened eagerly.

81

widows, while they say long prayers for appearance' sake, and they will receive the severest sentence.'[a]

41 Once he was standing opposite the temple treasury, watching as people dropped their money into the chest. Many rich people
42 were giving large sums. Presently there came a poor widow who
43 dropped in two tiny coins, together worth a farthing. He called his disciples to him. 'I tell you this,' he said: 'this widow has
44 given more than any of the others; for those others who have given had more than enough, but she, with less than enough, has given all that she had to live on.'

13 AS HE WAS leaving the temple, one of his disciples exclaimed,
2   'Look, Master, what huge stones! What fine buildings!' Jesus said to him, 'You see these great buildings? Not one stone will be left upon another; all will be thrown down.'
3   When he was sitting on the Mount of Olives facing the temple he was questioned privately by Peter, James, John, and Andrew.
4   'Tell us,' they said, 'when will this happen? What will be the sign when the fulfilment of all this is at hand?'
5, 6   Jesus began: 'Take care that no one misleads you. Many will come claiming my name, and saying, "I am he"; and many will be misled by them.
7   'When you hear the noise of battle near at hand and the news of battles far away, do not be alarmed. Such things are bound
8   to happen; but the end is still to come. For nation will make war upon nation, kingdom upon kingdom; there will be earthquakes in many places; there will be famines. With these things the birth-pangs of the new age begin.
9   'As for you, be on your guard. You will be handed over to the courts. You will be flogged in synagogues. You will be summoned to appear before governors and kings on my account to testify
10 in their presence. But before the end the Gospel must be pro-
11 claimed to all nations. So when you are arrested and taken away, do not worry beforehand about what you will say, but when the time comes say whatever is given you to say; for it will not be
12 you that speak, but the Holy Spirit. Brother will betray brother to death, and the father his child; children will turn against their

[a] *Or* As for those who eat up the property of widows, while they say long prayers for appearance' sake, they will have an even sterner judgement to face.

parents and send them to their death. All will hate you for your 13
allegiance to me; but the man who holds out to the end will be
saved.

'But when you see "the abomination of desolation" usurping 14
a place which is not his (let the reader understand), then those
who are in Judaea must take to the hills. If a man is on the roof, 15
he must not come down into the house to fetch anything out; if in 16
the field, he must not turn back for his cloak. Alas for women 17
with child in those days, and for those who have children at the
breast! Pray that it may not come in winter. For those days will 18, 19
bring distress such as never has been until now since the beginning
of the world which God created—and will never be again. If the 20
Lord had not cut short that time of troubles, no living thing could
survive. However, for the sake of his own, whom he has chosen,
he has cut short the time.

'Then, if anyone says to you, "Look, here is the Messiah", or, 21
"Look, there he is", do not believe it. Impostors will come claiming 22
to be messiahs or prophets, and they will produce signs and wonders
to mislead God's chosen, if such a thing were possible. But you 23
be on your guard; I have forewarned you of it all.

'But in those days, after that distress, the sun will be darkened, 24
the moon will not give her light; the stars will come falling from 25
the sky, the celestial powers will be shaken. Then they will see 26
the Son of Man coming in the clouds with great power and glory,
and he will send out the angels and gather his chosen from the 27
four winds, from the farthest bounds of earth to the farthest bounds
of heaven.

'Learn a lesson from the fig-tree. When its tender shoots appear 28
and are breaking into leaf, you know that summer is near. In the 29
same way, when you see all this happening, you may know that the
end is near,*a* at the very door. I tell you this: the present generation 30
will live to see it all. Heaven and earth will pass away; my words 31
will never pass away.

'But about that day or that hour no one knows, not even the angels 32
in heaven, not even the Son; only the Father.

'Be alert, be wakeful.*b* You do not know when the moment comes. 33
It is like a man away from home: he has left his house and put 34
his servants in charge, each with his own work to do, and he has

[a] *Or* that he is near. [b] *Some witnesses add* and pray.

83

35 ordered the door-keeper to stay awake. Keep awake, then, for you
do not know when the master of the house is coming. Evening or
36 midnight, cock-crow or early dawn—if he comes suddenly, he must
37 not find you asleep. And what I say to you, I say to everyone: Keep
awake.'

The Final Conflict

14 NOW THE FESTIVAL of Passover and Unleavened Bread was
only two days off; and the chief priests and the doctors of the
law were trying to devise some cunning plan to seize him and put
2 him to death. 'It must not be during the festival,' they said, 'or
we should have rioting among the people.'

3 Jesus was at Bethany, in the house of Simon the leper. As he
sat at table, a woman came in carrying a small bottle of very costly
perfume, oil of pure nard. She broke it open and poured the oil
4 over his head. Some of those present said to one another angrily,
5 'Why this waste? The perfume might have been sold for thirty
pounds*a* and the money given to the poor'; and they turned upon
6 her with fury. But Jesus said, 'Let her alone. Why must you make
7 trouble for her? It is a fine thing she has done for me. You have
the poor among you always, and you can help them whenever you
8 like; but you will not always have me. She has done what lay in
her power; she is beforehand with anointing my body for burial.
9 I tell you this: wherever in all the world the Gospel is proclaimed,
what she has done will be told as her memorial.'

10 Then Judas Iscariot, one of the Twelve, went to the chief priests
11 to betray him to them. When they heard what he had come for,
they were greatly pleased, and promised him money; and he began
to look for a good opportunity to betray him.

12 NOW ON the first day of Unleavened Bread, when the Passover lambs
were being slaughtered, his disciples said to him, 'Where would
13 you like us to go and prepare for your Passover supper?' So he
sent out two of his disciples with these instructions: 'Go into the
city, and a man will meet you carrying a jar of water. Follow him,
14 and when he enters a house give this message to the householder:

[a] *Literally* 300 denarii; *some witnesses read* more than 300 denarii.

"The Master says, 'Where is the room reserved for me to eat the Passover with my disciples?'" He will show you a large room up- 15 stairs, set out in readiness. Make the preparations for us there.' Then 16 the disciples went off, and when they came into the city they found everything just as he had told them. So they prepared for Passover.

In the evening he came to the house with the Twelve. As they 17, 18 sat at supper Jesus said, 'I tell you this: one of you will betray me— one who is eating with me.' At this they were dismayed; and one 19 by one they said to him, 'Not I, surely?' 'It is one of the Twelve', 20 he said, 'who is dipping into the same bowl with me. The Son of 21 Man is going the way appointed for him in the scriptures; but alas for that man by whom the Son of Man is betrayed! It would be better for that man if he had never been born.'

During supper he took bread, and having said the blessing he 22 broke it and gave it to them, with the words: 'Take this; this is my body.' Then he took a cup, and having offered thanks to God 23 he gave it to them; and they all drank from it. And he said, 'This 24 is my blood of the covenant, shed for many. I tell you this: never 25 again shall I drink from the fruit of the vine until that day when I drink it new in the kingdom of God.'

After singing the Passover Hymn, they went out to the Mount 26 of Olives. And Jesus said, 'You will all fall from your faith; for 27 it stands written: "I will strike the shepherd down and the sheep will be scattered." Nevertheless, after I am raised again I will go 28 on before you into Galilee.' Peter answered, 'Everyone else may 29 fall away, but I will not.' Jesus said, 'I tell you this: today, this 30 very night, before the cock crows twice, you yourself will disown me three times.' But he insisted and repeated: 'Even if I must die 31 with you, I will never disown you.' And they all said the same.

WHEN THEY REACHED a place called Gethsemane, he said to his 32 disciples, 'Sit here while I pray.' And he took Peter and James 33 and John with him. Horror and dismay came over him, and he said 34 to them, 'My heart is ready to break with grief; stop here, and stay awake.' Then he went forward a little, threw himself on the 35 ground, and prayed that, if it were possible, this hour might pass him by. 'Abba, Father,' he said, 'all things are possible to thee; 36 take this cup away from me. Yet not what I will, but what thou wilt.'

37 He came back and found them asleep; and he said to Peter,
'Asleep, Simon? Were you not able to keep awake for one hour?
38 Stay awake, all of you; and pray that you may be spared the test:
39 the spirit is willing, but the flesh is weak.' Once more he went
40 away and prayed.*ᵃ* On his return he found them asleep again, for
their eyes were heavy; and they did not know how to answer him.
41 The third time he came and said to them, 'Still sleeping? Still
taking your ease? Enough!*ᵇ* The hour has come. The Son of Man
42 is betrayed to sinful men. Up, let us go forward! My betrayer is
upon us.'

43 Suddenly, while he was still speaking, Judas, one of the Twelve,
appeared, and with him was a crowd armed with swords and
44 cudgels, sent by the chief priests, lawyers, and elders. Now the
traitor had agreed with them upon a signal: 'The one I kiss is
45 your man; seize him and get him safely away.' When he reached
the spot, he stepped forward at once and said to Jesus, 'Rabbi',
46 and kissed him. Then they seized him and held him fast.
47 One of the party*ᶜ* drew his sword, and struck at the High Priest's
48 servant, cutting off his ear. Then Jesus spoke: 'Do you take me
for a bandit, that you have come out with swords and cudgels
49 to arrest me? Day after day I was within your reach as I taught in
the temple, and you did not lay hands on me. But let the scriptures
50 be fulfilled.' Then the disciples all deserted him and ran away.
51 Among those following was a young man with nothing on but
52 a linen cloth. They tried to seize him; but he slipped out of the
linen cloth and ran away naked.

53 THEN THEY LED Jesus away to the High Priest's house, where
the chief priests, elders, and doctors of the law were all assembling.
54 Peter followed him at a distance right into the High Priest's courtyard; and there he remained, sitting among the attendants, warming
himself at the fire.
55 The chief priests and the whole Council tried to find some evidence against Jesus to warrant a death-sentence, but failed to find
56 any. Many gave false evidence against him, but their statements
57 did not tally. Some stood up and gave this false evidence against
58 him: 'We heard him say, "I will throw down this temple, made

[a] *Some witnesses add* using the same words. [b] *The Greek is obscure; a possible meaning
is* 'The money has been paid', 'The account is settled.' [c] *Or of the bystanders.*

with human hands, and in three days I will build another, not made with hands."' But even on this point their evidence did 59 not agree.

Then the High Priest stood up in his place and questioned Jesus: 60 'Have you no answer to the charges that these witnesses bring against you?' But he kept silence; he made no reply. 61

Again the High Priest questioned him: 'Are you the Messiah, the Son of the Blessed One?' Jesus said, 'I am; and you will see the 62 Son of Man seated on the right hand of God*a* and coming with the clouds of heaven.' Then the High Priest tore his robes and said, 63 'Need we call further witnesses? You have heard the blasphemy. 64 What is your opinion?' Their judgement was unanimous: that he was guilty and should be put to death.

Some began to spit on him, blindfolded him, and struck him with 65 their fists, crying out, 'Prophesy!'*b* And the High Priest's men set upon him with blows.

Meanwhile Peter was still in the courtyard downstairs. One of 66 the High Priest's serving-maids came by and saw him there warming 67 himself. She looked into his face and said, 'You were there too, with this man from Nazareth, this Jesus.' But he denied it: 'I know 68 nothing,' he said; 'I do not understand what you mean.' Then he went outside into the porch;*c* and the maid saw him there again 69 and began to say to the bystanders, 'He is one of them'; and again 70 he denied it.

Again, a little later, the bystanders said to Peter, 'Surely you are one of them. You must be; you are a Galilean.' At this he broke 71 out into curses, and with an oath he said, 'I do not know this man you speak of.' Then the cock crew a second time; and Peter remem- 72 bered how Jesus had said to him, 'Before the cock crows twice you will disown me three times.' And he burst into tears.

WHEN MORNING came the chief priests, having made their plan 15 with the elders and lawyers and all the Council, put Jesus in chains; then they led him away and handed him over to Pilate. Pilate 2 asked him, 'Are you the king of the Jews?' He replied, 'The words are yours.'*d* And the chief priests brought many charges against 3 him. Pilate questioned him again: 'Have you nothing to say in your 4

[a] *Literally* of the Power. [b] *Some witnesses add* Who hit you? *as in Matthew and Luke.* [c] *Some witnesses insert* and the cock crew. [d] *Or* It is as you say.

defence? You see how many charges they are bringing against you.'
5 But, to Pilate's astonishment, Jesus made no further reply.
6 At the festival season the Governor used to release one prisoner
7 at the people's request. As it happened, the man known as Barabbas
was then in custody with the rebels who had committed murder
8 in the rising. When the crowd appeared*a* asking for the usual favour,
9 Pilate replied, 'Do you wish me to release for you the king of the
10 Jews?' For he knew it was out of spite that they had brought Jesus
11 before him. But the chief priests incited the crowd to ask him to
12 release Barabbas rather than Jesus. Pilate spoke to them again:
13 'Then what shall I do with the man you call king of the Jews?' They
14 shouted back, 'Crucify him!' 'Why, what harm has he done?'
15 Pilate asked. They shouted all the louder, 'Crucify him!' So Pilate,
in his desire to satisfy the mob, released Barabbas to them; and he
had Jesus flogged and handed him over to be crucified.
16 Then the soldiers took him inside the courtyard (the Governor's
17 headquarters*b*) and called together the whole company. They dressed
him in purple, and having plaited a crown of thorns, placed it
18 on his head. Then they began to salute him with, 'Hail, King of the
19 Jews!' They beat him about the head with a cane and spat upon
20 him, and then knelt and paid mock homage to him. When they had
finished their mockery, they stripped him of the purple and dressed
him in his own clothes.

21 THEN THEY TOOK him out to crucify him. A man called Simon,
from Cyrene, the father of Alexander and Rufus, was passing by
on his way in from the country, and they pressed him into service
to carry his cross.
22 They brought him to the place called Golgotha, which means
23 'Place of a skull'. He was offered drugged wine, but he would not
24 take it. Then they fastened him to the cross. They divided his
clothes among them, casting lots to decide what each should
have.
25, 26 The hour of the crucifixion was nine in the morning, and the
inscription giving the charge against him read, 'The king of the
27 Jews.' Two bandits were crucified with him, one on his right and
the other on his left.*c*

[a] *Some witnesses read* shouted. [b] *Greek* praetorium. [c] *Some witnesses add* (28)
Thus that text of Scripture came true which says, 'He was reckoned among criminals.'

The passers-by hurled abuse at him: 'Aha!' they cried, wagging 29
their heads, 'you would pull the temple down, would you, and
build it in three days? Come down from the cross and save your- 30
self!' So too the chief priests and the doctors of the law jested 31
with one another: 'He saved others,' they said, 'but he cannot
save himself. Let the Messiah, the king of Israel, come down 32
now from the cross. If we see that, we shall believe.' Even those
who were crucified with him taunted him.

At midday darkness fell over the whole land, which lasted till 33
three in the afternoon; and at three Jesus cried aloud, '*Eli, Eli, lema* 34
sabachthani?', which means, 'My God, my God, why hast thou
forsaken me?'*ᵃ* Some of the passers-by, on hearing this, said, 'Hark, 35
he is calling Elijah.' A man came running with a sponge, soaked 36
in sour wine, on the end of a cane, and held it to his lips. 'Let us
see', he said, 'if Elijah is coming to take him down.' Then Jesus 37
gave a loud cry and died. And the curtain of the temple was torn 38
in two from top to bottom. And when the centurion who was 39
standing opposite him saw how he died,*ᵇ* he said, 'Truly this man
was a son of God.'

A NUMBER of women were also present, watching from a distance. 40
Among them were Mary of Magdala, Mary the mother of James the
younger and of Joseph, and Salome, who had all followed him and 41
waited on him when he was in Galilee, and there were several
others who had come up to Jerusalem with him.

By this time evening had come; and as it was Preparation-day 42
(that is, the day before the Sabbath), Joseph of Arimathaea, a 43
respected member of the Council, a man who was eagerly awaiting
the kingdom of God, bravely went in to Pilate and asked for the
body of Jesus. Pilate was surprised to hear that he was already 44
dead; so he sent for the centurion and asked him whether it was
long since he died. And when he heard the centurion's report, he 45
gave Joseph leave to take the dead body. So Joseph bought a linen 46
sheet, took him down from the cross, and wrapped him in the sheet.
Then he laid him in a tomb cut out of the rock, and rolled a stone
against the entrance. And Mary of Magdala and Mary the mother 47
of Joseph were watching and saw where he was laid.

[a] *Some witnesses read* My God, my God, why hast thou shamed me? [b] *Some*
witnesses read saw that he died with a cry.

16   When the Sabbath was over, Mary of Magdala, Mary the mother
     of James, and Salome bought*a* aromatic oils intending to go and
2   anoint him; and very early on the Sunday morning, just after
3   sunrise, they came to the tomb. They were wondering among them-
     selves who would roll away the stone for them from the entrance to
4   the tomb, when they looked up and saw that the stone, huge as it
5   was, had been rolled back already. They went into the tomb, where
     they saw a youth sitting on the right-hand side, wearing a white
6   robe; and they were dumbfounded. But he said to them, 'Fear
     nothing; you are looking for Jesus of Nazareth, who was crucified.
     He has risen; he is not here; look, there is the place where they
7   laid him. But go and give this message to his disciples and Peter:
     "He will go on before you into Galilee and you will see him there,
8   as he told you."' Then they went out and ran away from the tomb,
     beside themselves with terror. They said nothing to anybody, for
     they were afraid.*b*

     And they delivered all these instructions briefly to Peter and his
     companions. Afterwards Jesus himself sent out by them from east
     to west the sacred and imperishable message of eternal salvation.*c*

9   When he had risen from the dead early on Sunday morning he
     appeared first to Mary of Magdala, from whom he had formerly cast
10   out seven devils. She went and carried the news to his mourning
11   and sorrowful followers, but when they were told that he was
     alive and that she had seen him they did not believe it.
12   Later he appeared in a different guise to two of them as they
13   were walking, on their way into the country. These also went and
     took the news to the others, but again no one believed them.
14   Afterwards while the Eleven were at table he appeared to them
     and reproached them for their incredulity and dullness, because
     they had not believed those who had seen him risen from the dead.
15   Then he said to them: 'Go forth to every part of the world, and
16   proclaim the Good News to the whole creation. Those who believe
     it and receive baptism will find salvation; those who do not believe
17   will be condemned. Faith will bring with it these miracles: believers

[a] *Some witnesses omit* When the Sabbath...Salome, *reading* And they went and
bought... [b] *At this point some of the most ancient witnesses bring the book to a close.*
[c] *Some witnesses add this paragraph, which in one of them is the conclusion of the book.*

will cast out devils in my name and speak in strange tongues; if 18
they handle snakes or drink any deadly poison, they will come to
no harm; and the sick on whom they lay their hands will recover.'

So after talking with them the Lord Jesus was taken up into 19
heaven, and he took his seat at the right hand of God; but they 20
went out to make their proclamation everywhere, and the Lord
worked with them and confirmed their words by the miracles that
followed.[a]

[a] *Some witnesses give verses 9–20 either instead of, or in addition to, the paragraph*
And they delivered...eternal salvation (*here printed before verse 9*), *and so bring the*
book to a close. Others insert further additional matter.

THE
GOSPEL ACCORDING TO
LUKE

1 THE AUTHOR TO THEOPHILUS: Many writers
have undertaken to draw up an account of the events that
2 have happened among us, following the traditions handed
down to us by the original eyewitnesses and servants of the Gospel.
3 And so I in my turn, your Excellency, as one who has gone over
the whole course of these events in detail, have decided to write a
4 connected narrative for you, so as to give you authentic knowledge
about the matters of which you have been informed.

The Coming of the Messiah

5 IN THE DAYS of Herod king of Judaea there was a priest named
Zechariah, of the division of the priesthood called after Abijah.
6 His wife also was of priestly descent; her name was Elizabeth. Both
of them were upright and devout, blamelessly observing all the com-
7 mandments and ordinances of the Lord. But they had no children,
for Elizabeth was barren, and both were well on in years.
8   Once, when it was the turn of his division and he was there to
9 take part in divine service, it fell to his lot, by priestly custom, to
10 enter the sanctuary of the Lord and offer the incense; and the whole
congregation was at prayer outside. It was the hour of the incense-
11 offering. There appeared to him an angel of the Lord, standing
12 on the right of the altar of incense. At this sight, Zechariah was
13 startled, and fear overcame him. But the angel said to him, 'Do
not be afraid, Zechariah; your prayer has been heard: your wife
14 Elizabeth will bear you a son, and you shall name him John. Your
15 heart will thrill with joy and many will be glad that he was born; for
he will be great in the eyes of the Lord. He shall never touch wine
or strong drink. From his very birth he will be filled with the Holy
16 Spirit; and he will bring back many Israelites to the Lord their God.

He will go before him as forerunner,*a* possessed by the spirit and 17
power of Elijah, to reconcile father and child, to convert the rebel-
lious to the ways of the righteous, to prepare a people that shall be
fit for the Lord.'

Zechariah said to the angel, 'How can I be sure of this? I am an 18
old man and my wife is well on in years.'

The angel replied, 'I am Gabriel; I stand in attendance upon 19
God, and I have been sent to speak to you and bring you this good
news. But now listen: you will lose your powers of speech, and 20
remain silent until the day when these things happen to you, because
you have not believed me, though at their proper time my words
will be proved true.'

Meanwhile the people were waiting for Zechariah, surprised that 21
he was staying so long inside. When he did come out he could not 22
speak to them, and they realized that he had had a vision in the
sanctuary. He stood there making signs to them, and remained dumb.

When his period of duty was completed Zechariah returned home. 23
After this his wife Elizabeth conceived, and for five months she 24
lived in seclusion, thinking, 'This is the Lord's doing; now at last 25
he has deigned to take away my reproach among men.'

In the sixth month the angel Gabriel was sent from God to a town 26
in Galilee called Nazareth, with a message for a girl betrothed to 27
a man named Joseph, a descendant of David; the girl's name was
Mary. The angel went in and said to her, 'Greetings, most favoured 28
one! The Lord is with you.' But she was deeply troubled by what 29
he said and wondered what this greeting might mean. Then the 30
angel said to her, 'Do not be afraid, Mary, for God has been
gracious to you; you shall conceive and bear a son, and you shall 31
give him the name Jesus. He will be great; he will bear the title 32
"Son of the Most High"; the Lord God will give him the throne of
his ancestor David, and he will be king over Israel*b* for ever; his 33
reign shall never end.' 'How can this be,' said Mary, 'when I have 34
no husband?' The angel answered, 'The Holy Spirit will come upon 35
you, and the power of the Most High will overshadow you; and for
that reason the holy child to be born will be called "Son of God".*c*
Moreover your kinswoman Elizabeth has herself conceived a son in 36
her old age; and she who is reputed barren is now in her sixth

[*a*] *Or* In his sight he will go forth. [*b*] *Literally* the house of Jacob. [*c*] *Or* the child
to be born will be called holy, "Son of God".

37, 38 month, for God's promises can never fail.'*a* 'Here am I,' said Mary;
'I am the Lord's servant; as you have spoken, so be it.' Then the
angel left her.

39 About this time Mary set out and went straight to a town in the
40 uplands of Judah. She went into Zechariah's house and greeted
41 Elizabeth. And when Elizabeth heard Mary's greeting, the baby
stirred in her womb. Then Elizabeth was filled with the Holy Spirit
42 and cried aloud, 'God's blessing is on you above all women, and his
43 blessing is on the fruit of your womb. Who am I, that the mother
44 of my Lord should visit me? I tell you, when your greeting sounded
45 in my ears, the baby in my womb leapt for joy. How happy is she
who has had faith that the Lord's promise would be fulfilled!'

46 And Mary*b* said:

'Tell out, my soul, the greatness of the Lord,
47 rejoice, rejoice, my spirit, in God my saviour;
48 so tenderly has he looked upon his servant,
humble as she is.
For, from this day forth,
all generations will count me blessed,
49 so wonderfully has he dealt with me,
the Lord, the Mighty One.

His name is Holy;
50 his mercy sure from generation to generation
toward those who fear him;
51 the deeds his own right arm has done
disclose his might:
the arrogant of heart and mind he has put to rout,
52 he has torn imperial powers from their thrones,
but the humble have been lifted high.
53 The hungry he has satisfied with good things,
the rich sent empty away.

54 He has ranged himself at the side of Israel his servant;
55 firm in his promise to our forefathers,
he has not forgotten to show mercy to Abraham
and his children's children, for ever.'

56 Mary stayed with her about three months and then returned home.

[a] *Some witnesses read* for with God nothing will prove impossible. [b] *So the majority
of ancient witnesses; some read* Elizabeth; *the original may have had no name.*

NOW THE TIME came for Elizabeth's child to be born, and she gave 57
birth to a son. When her neighbours and relatives heard what great 58
favour the Lord had shown her, they were as delighted as she was.
Then on the eighth day they came to circumcise the child; and they 59
were going to name him Zechariah after his father. But his mother 60
spoke up and said, 'No! he is to be called John.' 'But', they said, 61
'there is nobody in your family who has that name.' They inquired 62
of his father by signs what he would like him to be called. He asked 63
for a writing-tablet and to the astonishment of all wrote down, 'His
name is John.' Immediately his lips and tongue were freed and he 64
began to speak, praising God. All the neighbours were struck with 65
awe, and everywhere in the uplands of Judaea the whole story
became common talk. All who heard it were deeply impressed and 66
said, 'What will this child become?' For indeed the hand of the
Lord was upon him.ᵃ

And Zechariah his father was filled with the Holy Spirit and 67
uttered this prophecy:

'Praise to the God of Israel!   68
For he has turned to his people, saved them and set them free,
and has raised up a deliverer of victorious power   69
from the house of his servant David.

So he promised: age after age he proclaimed   70
by the lips of his holy prophets,
that he would deliver us from our enemies,   71
out of the hands of all who hate us;
that he would deal mercifully with our fathers,   72
calling to mind his solemn covenant.

Such was the oath he swore to our father Abraham,   73
to rescue us from enemy hands,   74
and grant us, free from fear, to worship him
with a holy worship, with uprightness of heart,   75
in his presence, our whole life long.

And you, my child, you shall be called Prophet of the Highest, 76
for you will be the Lord's forerunner, to prepare his way
and lead his people to salvation through knowledge of him, 77
by the forgiveness of their sins:

[a] *Some witnesses read* 'What will this child become, for indeed the hand of the Lord is upon him?'

78 for in the tender compassion of our God
the morning sun from heaven will rise*ᵃ* upon us,
79 to shine on those who live in darkness, under the cloud of death,
and to guide our feet into the way of peace.'

80 As the child grew up he became strong in spirit; he lived out in
the wilds until the day when he appeared publicly before Israel.

2 IN THOSE DAYS a decree was issued by the Emperor Augustus for a
2 general registration throughout the Roman world. This was the first
registration of its kind; it took place when Quirinius*ᵇ* was governor
3 of Syria. For this purpose everyone made his way to his own town;
4 and so Joseph went up to Judaea from the town of Nazareth in
5 Galilee, to be registered at the city of David, called Bethlehem,
because he was of the house of David by descent; and with him went
6 Mary who was betrothed to him. She was pregnant, and while they
7 were there the time came for her child to be born, and she gave birth
to a son, her first-born. She wrapped him round, and laid him in a
manger, because there was no room for them to lodge in the house.
8 Now in this same district there were shepherds out in the fields,
9 keeping watch through the night over their flock, when suddenly
there stood before them an angel of the Lord, and the splendour of
10 the Lord shone round them. They were terror-struck, but the angel
said, 'Do not be afraid; I have good news for you: there is great joy
11 coming to the whole people. Today in the city of David a deliverer
12 has been born to you—the Messiah, the Lord.*ᶜ* And this is your
13 sign: you will find a baby lying all wrapped up, in a manger.' All
at once there was with the angel a great company of the heavenly
host, singing the praises of God:

14   'Glory to God in highest heaven,
And on earth his peace for men on whom his favour rests.'*ᵈ*

15 After the angels had left them and gone into heaven the shepherds
said to one another, 'Come, we must go straight to Bethlehem and
see this thing that has happened, which the Lord has made known
16 to us.' So they went with all speed and found their way to Mary
17 and Joseph; and the baby was lying in the manger. When they saw

[*a*] *Some witnesses read* has risen. [*b*] *Or* This was the first registration carried out while
Quirinius... [*c*] *Some witnesses read* to you—the Lord's Messiah. [*d*] *Some witnesses
read* And on earth his peace, his favour towards men.

him, they recounted what they had been told about this child; and 18
all who heard were astonished at what the shepherds said. But 19
Mary treasured up all these things and pondered over them. Mean- 20
while the shepherds returned glorifying and praising God for what
they had heard and seen; it had all happened as they had been told.

Eight days later the time came to circumcise him, and he was 21
given the name Jesus, the name given by the angel before he was
conceived.

Then, after their purification had been completed in accordance 22
with the Law of Moses, they brought him up to Jerusalem to present
him to the Lord (as prescribed in the law of the Lord: 'Every first- 23
born male shall be deemed to belong to the Lord'), and also to make 24
the offering as stated in the law of the Lord: 'A pair of turtle doves
or two young pigeons.'

There was at that time in Jerusalem a man called Simeon. This 25
man was upright and devout, one who watched and waited for the
restoration of Israel, and the Holy Spirit was upon him. It had been 26
disclosed to him by the Holy Spirit that he would not see death until
he had seen the Lord's Messiah. Guided by the Spirit he came into 27
the temple; and when the parents brought in the child Jesus to do
for him what was customary under the Law, he took him in his 28
arms, praised God, and said:

'This day, Master, thou givest thy servant his discharge in peace; 29
    now thy promise is fulfilled.
For I have seen with my own eyes 30
the deliverance which thou hast made ready in full view of all the 31
    nations:
A light that will be a revelation to the heathen, 32
    and glory to thy people Israel.'

The child's father and mother were full of wonder at what was 33
being said about him. Simeon blessed them and said to Mary his 34
mother, 'This child is destined to be a sign which men reject; and 35
you too shall be pierced to the heart. Many in Israel will stand or
fall*a* because of him, and thus the secret thoughts of many will be
laid bare.'

There was also a prophetess, Anna the daughter of Phanuel, of 36
the tribe of Asher. She was a very old woman, who had lived seven

[a] *Or* Many in Israel will fall and rise again...

37 years with her husband after she was first married, and then alone as a widow to the age of eighty-four.*ª* She never left the temple,
38 but worshipped day and night, fasting and praying. Coming up at that very moment, she returned thanks to God; and she talked about the child to all who were looking for the liberation of Jerusalem.
39   When they had done everything prescribed in the law of the
40 Lord, they returned to Galilee to their own town of Nazareth. The child grew big and strong and full of wisdom; and God's favour was upon him.
41   Now it was the practice of his parents to go to Jerusalem every
42 year for the Passover festival; and when he was twelve, they made
43 the pilgrimage as usual. When the festive season was over and they started for home, the boy Jesus stayed behind in Jerusalem. His
44 parents did not know of this; but thinking that he was with the party they journeyed on for a whole day, and only then did they
45 begin looking for him among their friends and relations. As they
46 could not find him they returned to Jerusalem to look for him; and after three days they found him sitting in the temple surrounded
47 by the teachers, listening to them and putting questions; and all who heard him were amazed at his intelligence and the answers he
48 gave. His parents were astonished to see him there, and his mother said to him, 'My son, why have you treated us like this? Your father
49 and I have been searching for you in great anxiety.' 'What made you search?' he said. 'Did you not know that I was bound to be in
50 my Father's house?' But they did not understand what he meant.
51 Then he went back with them to Nazareth, and continued to be under their authority; his mother treasured up all these things in
52 her heart. As Jesus grew up he advanced in wisdom and in favour with God and men.

3 IN THE FIFTEENTH year of the Emperor Tiberius, when Pontius Pilate was governor of Judaea, when Herod was prince of Galilee, his brother Philip prince of Ituraea and Trachonitis, and Lysanias
2 prince of Abilene, during the high-priesthood of Annas and Caiaphas, the word of God came to John son of Zechariah in the wilderness.
3 And he went all over the Jordan valley proclaiming a baptism in
4 token of repentance for the forgiveness of sins, as it is written in the book of the prophecies of Isaiah:

[a] *Or* widow for another eighty-four years.

'A voice crying aloud in the wilderness,
"Prepare a way for the Lord;
Clear a straight path for him.
Every ravine shall be filled in,   5
And every mountain and hill levelled;
The corners shall be straightened,
And the rough ways made smooth;
And all mankind shall see God's deliverance."'   6

Crowds of people came out to be baptized by him, and he said   7
to them: 'You vipers' brood! Who warned you to escape from the
coming retribution? Then prove your repentance by the fruit it 8
bears; and do not begin saying to yourselves, "We have Abraham
for our father." I tell you that God can make children for Abraham
out of these stones here. Already the axe is laid to the roots of the 9
trees; and every tree that fails to produce good fruit is cut down and
thrown on the fire.'

The people asked him, 'Then what are we to do?' He replied,   10, 11
'The man with two shirts must share with him who has none, and
anyone who has food must do the same.' Among those who came   12
to be baptized were tax-gatherers, and they said to him, 'Master,
what are we to do?' He told them, 'Exact no more than the assess- 13
ment.' Soldiers on service also asked him, 'And what of us?' To   14
them he said, 'No bullying; no blackmail; make do with your pay!'

The people were on the tiptoe of expectation, all wondering about 15
John, whether perhaps he was the Messiah, but he spoke out and   16
said to them all, 'I baptize you with water; but there is one to come
who is mightier than I. I am not fit to unfasten his shoes. He will
baptize you with the Holy Spirit and with fire. His shovel is ready in 17
his hand, to winnow his threshing-floor and gather the wheat into his
granary; but he will burn the chaff on a fire that can never go out.'

In this and many other ways he made his appeal to the people 18
and announced the good news. But Prince Herod, when he was   19
rebuked by him over the affair of his brother's wife Herodias and for
his other misdeeds, crowned them all by shutting John up in prison. 20

DURING a general baptism of the people, when Jesus too had   21
been baptized and was praying, heaven opened and the Holy Spirit   22
descended on him in bodily form like a dove; and there came a voice

99

from heaven, 'Thou art my Son, my Beloved;[a] on thee my favour rests.'[b]

23   When Jesus began his work he was about thirty years old, the
24 son, as people thought, of Joseph, son of Heli, son of Matthat, son
25 of Levi, son of Melchi, son of Jannai, son of Joseph, son of Mattathiah, son of Amos, son of Nahum, son of Esli, son of Naggai,
26 son of Maath, son of Mattathiah, son of Semein, son of Josech, son
27 of Joda, son of Johanan, son of Rhesa, son of Zerubbabel, son of
28 Shealtiel, son of Neri, son of Melchi, son of Addi, son of Cosam,
29 son of Elmadam, son of Er, son of Joshua, son of Eliezer, son of
30 Jorim, son of Matthat, son of Levi, son of Symeon, son of Judah,
31 son of Joseph, son of Jonam, son of Eliakim, son of Melea, son of
32 Menna, son of Mattatha, son of Nathan, son of David, son of Jesse,
33 son of Obed, son of Boaz, son of Salmon, son of Nahshon, son of
Amminadab,[c] son of Arni,[d] son of Hezron, son of Perez, son of
34 Judah, son of Jacob, son of Isaac, son of Abraham, son of Terah,
35 son of Nahor, son of Serug, son of Reu, son of Peleg, son of Eber,
36 son of Shelah, son of Cainan, son of Arpachshad, son of Shem,
37 son of Noah, son of Lamech, son of Methuselah, son of Enoch, son
38 of Jared, son of Mahalaleel, son of Cainan, son of Enosh, son of
Seth, son of Adam, son of God.

4 1, 2   Full of the Holy Spirit, Jesus returned from the Jordan, and for
forty days was led by the Spirit up and down the wilderness and
tempted by the devil.

All that time he had nothing to eat, and at the end of it he was
3 famished. The devil said to him, 'If you are the Son of God, tell
4 this stone to become bread.' Jesus answered, 'Scripture says, "Man
cannot live on bread alone."'

5   Next the devil led him up and showed him in a flash all the
6 kingdoms of the world. 'All this dominion will I give to you,' he
said, 'and the glory that goes with it; for it has been put in my hands
7 and I can give it to anyone I choose. You have only to do homage to
8 me and it shall all be yours.' Jesus answered him, 'Scripture says,
"You shall do homage to the Lord your God and worship him alone."'

9   The devil took him to Jerusalem and set him on the parapet of
the temple. 'If you are the Son of God,' he said, 'throw yourself

---

[a] *Or* Thou art my only Son. [b] *Some witnesses read* My Son art thou; this day I have
begotten thee. [c] *Some witnesses add* son of Admin. [d] *Some witnesses read* Aram;
Ruth 4. 19 & 1 Chronicles 2. 9 have Ram.

down; for Scripture says, "He will give his angels orders to take care 10
of you", and again, "They will support you in their arms for fear 11
you should strike your foot against a stone."' Jesus answered him, 12
'It has been said, "You are not to test the Lord your God."'

So, having come to the end of all his temptations, the devil 13
departed, biding his time.

In Galilee: Success and Opposition

THEN JESUS, armed with the power of the Spirit, returned to 14
Galilee; and reports about him spread through the whole country-
side. He taught in their synagogues and all men sang his praises. 15

So he came to Nazareth, where he had been brought up, and went 16
to synagogue on the Sabbath day as he regularly did. He stood up
to read the lesson and was handed the scroll of the prophet Isaiah. 17
He opened the scroll and found the passage which says,

'The spirit of the Lord is upon me because he has anointed me;   18
He has sent me to announce good news to the poor,
To proclaim release for prisoners and recovery of sight for the blind;
To let the broken victims go free,
To proclaim the year of the Lord's favour.'   19

He rolled up the scroll, gave it back to the attendant, and sat down; 20
and all eyes in the synagogue were fixed on him.

He began to speak: 'Today', he said, 'in your very hearing this 21
text has come true.'[a] There was a general stir of admiration; they 22
were surprised that words of such grace should fall from his lips.
'Is not this Joseph's son?' they asked. Then Jesus said, 'No doubt 23
you will quote the proverb to me, "Physician, heal yourself!", and
say, "We have heard of all your doings at Capernaum; do the same
here in your own home town." I tell you this,' he went on: 'no 24
prophet is recognized in his own country. There were many widows 25
in Israel, you may be sure, in Elijah's time, when for three years and
six months the skies never opened, and famine lay hard over the
whole country; yet it was to none of those that Elijah was sent, but 26
to a widow at Sarepta in the territory of Sidon. Again, in the time 27

[a] *Or* 'Today', he said, 'this text which you have just heard has come true.'

of the prophet Elisha there were many lepers in Israel, and not

28 one of them was healed, but only Naaman, the Syrian.' At these

29 words the whole congregation were infuriated. They leapt up, threw him out of the town, and took him to the brow of the hill on which

30 it was built, meaning to hurl him over the edge. But he walked straight through them all, and went away.

31   Coming down to Capernaum, a town in Galilee, he taught the

32 people on the Sabbath, and they were astounded at his teaching,

33 for what he said had the note of authority. Now there was a man in the synagogue possessed by a devil, an unclean spirit. He

34 shrieked at the top of his voice, 'What do you want with us, Jesus of Nazareth? Have you*a* come to destroy us? I know who you

35 are—the Holy One of God.' Jesus rebuked him: 'Be silent', he said, 'and come out of him.' Then the devil, after throwing the man down in front of the people, left him without doing him any injury.

36 Amazement fell on them all and they said to one another: 'What is there in this man's words? He gives orders to the unclean spirits

37 with authority and power, and out they go.' So the news spread, and he was the talk of the whole district.

38   On leaving the synagogue he went to Simon's house. Simon's mother-in-law was in the grip of a high fever; and they asked him

39 to help her. He came and stood over her and rebuked the fever. It left her, and she got up at once and waited on them.

40   At sunset all who had friends suffering from one disease or another brought them to him; and he laid his hands on them one by one

41 and cured them. Devils also came out of many of them, shouting, 'You are the Son of God.' But he rebuked them and forbade them to speak, because they knew that he was the Messiah.

42   When day broke he went out and made his way to a lonely spot. But the people went in search of him, and when they came to where

43 he was they pressed him not to leave them. But he said, 'I must give the good news of the kingdom of God to the other towns also, for

44 that is what I was sent to do.' So he proclaimed the Gospel in the synagogues of Judaea.*b*

5   One day as he stood by the Lake of Gennesaret, and the people

2 crowded upon him to listen to the word of God, he noticed two boats lying at the water's edge; the fishermen had come ashore

[a] *Or* You have. [b] *Or* the Jewish synagogues; *some witnesses read* the synagogues of Galilee.

and were washing their nets. He got into one of the boats, which 3
belonged to Simon, and asked him to put out a little way from
the shore; then he went on teaching the crowds from his seat in
the boat. When he had finished speaking, he said to Simon, 'Put 4
out into deep water and let down your nets for a catch.' Simon 5
answered, 'Master, we were hard at work all night and caught
nothing at all; but if you say so, I will let down the nets.' They did 6
so and made a big haul of fish; and their nets began to split. So they 7
signalled to their partners in the other boat to come and help them.
This they did, and loaded both boats to the point of sinking. When 8
Simon saw what had happened he fell at Jesus's knees and said,
'Go, Lord, leave me, sinner that I am!' For he and all his com- 9
panions were amazed at the catch they had made; so too were his 10
partners James and John, Zebedee's sons. 'Do not be afraid,' said
Jesus to Simon; 'from now on you will be catching men.' As soon 11
as they had brought the boats to land, they left everything and
followed him.

He was once in a certain town where there happened to be a man 12
covered with leprosy; seeing Jesus, he bowed to the ground and
begged his help. 'Sir,' he said, 'if only you will, you can cleanse
me.' Jesus stretched out his hand, touched him, and said, 'Indeed 13
I will; be clean again.' The leprosy left him immediately. Jesus 14
then ordered him not to tell anybody. 'But go,' he said, 'show
yourself to the priest, and make the offering laid down by Moses
for your cleansing; that will certify the cure.' But the talk about 15
him spread all the more; great crowds gathered to hear him and
to be cured of their ailments. And from time to time he would 16
withdraw to lonely places for prayer.

One day he was teaching, and Pharisees and teachers of the law 17
were sitting round. People had come from every village of Galilee
and from Judaea and Jerusalem,[a] and the power of God was with
him to heal the sick. Some men appeared carrying a paralysed man 18
on a bed. They tried to bring him in and set him down in front of
Jesus, but finding no way to do so because of the crowd, they went 19
up on to the roof and let him down through the tiling, bed and all,
into the middle of the company in front of Jesus. When Jesus saw 20
their faith, he said, 'Man, your sins are forgiven you.'

[a] *Some witnesses read* and Pharisees and teachers of the law, who had come from every
village of Galilee and from Judaea and Jerusalem, were sitting round.

21 The lawyers and the Pharisees began saying to themselves, 'Who is this fellow with his blasphemous talk? Who but God alone can 22 forgive sins?' But Jesus knew their thoughts and answered them: 23 'Why do you harbour thoughts like these? Is it easier to say, "Your 24 sins are forgiven you", or to say, "Stand up and walk"? But to convince you that the Son of Man has the right on earth to forgive sins' —he turned to the paralysed man—'I say to you, stand up, take your 25 bed, and go home.' And at once he rose to his feet before their eyes, took up the bed he had been lying on, and went home praising God. 26 They were all lost in amazement and praised God; filled with awe they said, 'You would never believe the things we have seen today.'

27 Later, when he went out, he saw a tax-gatherer, Levi by name, 28 at his seat in the custom-house. He said to him, 'Follow me'; and he rose to his feet, left everything behind, and followed him.

29 Afterwards Levi held a big reception in his house for Jesus; 30 among the guests was a large party of tax-gatherers and others. The Pharisees and the lawyers of their sect complained to his disciples: 'Why do you eat and drink', they said, 'with tax-gatherers and 31 sinners?' Jesus answered them: 'It is not the healthy that need a 32 doctor, but the sick; I have not come to invite virtuous people, but to call sinners to repentance.'

33 Then they said to him, 'John's disciples are much given to fasting and the practice of prayer, and so are the disciples of the 34 Pharisees; but yours eat and drink.' Jesus replied, 'Can you make the bridegroom's friends fast while the bridegroom is with them? 35 But a time will come: the bridegroom will be taken away from them, and that will be the time for them to fast.'

36 He told them this parable also: 'No one tears a piece from a new cloak to patch an old one; if he does, he will have made a hole in the 37 new cloak, and the patch from the new will not match the old. Nor does anyone put new wine into old wine-skins; if he does, the new wine will burst the skins, the wine will be wasted, and the skins 38, 39 ruined. Fresh skins for new wine! And no one after drinking old wine wants new; for he says, "The old wine is good."'

6 One Sabbath he was going through the cornfields, and his disciples were plucking the ears of corn, rubbing them in their hands, and 2 eating them. Some of the Pharisees said, 'Why are you doing what 3 is forbidden on the Sabbath?' Jesus answered, 'So you have not 4 read what David did when he and his men were hungry? He went

into the House of God and took the consecrated loaves to eat and
gave them to his men, though priests alone are allowed to eat them,
and no one else.' He also said, 'The Son of Man is sovereign even 5
over the Sabbath.'

On another Sabbath he had gone to synagogue and was teaching. 6
There happened to be a man in the congregation whose right arm
was withered; and the lawyers and the Pharisees were on the watch 7
to see whether Jesus would cure him on the Sabbath, so that they
could find a charge to bring against him. But he knew what was in 8
their minds and said to the man with the withered arm, 'Get up
and stand out here.' So he got up and stood there. Then Jesus said 9
to them, 'I put the question to you: is it permitted to do good or
to do evil on the Sabbath, to save life or to destroy it?' He looked 10
round at them all and then said to the man, 'Stretch out your arm.'
He did so, and his arm was restored. But they were beside them- 11
selves with anger, and began to discuss among themselves what they
could do to Jesus.

During this time he went out one day into the hills to pray, and 12
spent the night in prayer to God. When day broke he called his dis- 13
ciples to him, and from among them he chose twelve and named them
Apostles: Simon, to whom he gave the name of Peter, and Andrew 14
his brother, James and John, Philip and Bartholomew, Matthew 15
and Thomas, James son of Alphaeus, and Simon who was called the
Zealot, Judas son of James, and Judas Iscariot who turned traitor. 16

He came down the hill with them and took his stand on level 17
ground. There was a large concourse of his disciples and great
numbers of people from Jerusalem and Judaea and from the seaboard
of Tyre and Sidon, who had come to listen to him, and to be cured
of their diseases. Those who were troubled with unclean spirits were 18
cured; and everyone in the crowd was trying to touch him, because 19
power went out from him and cured them all.

THEN TURNING to his disciples he began to speak: 20
'How blest are you who are poor; the kingdom of God is yours.
'How blest are you who now go hungry; your hunger shall be 21
satisfied.
'How blest are you who weep now; you shall laugh.
'How blest you are when men hate you, when they outlaw you and 22
insult you, and ban your very name as infamous, because of the Son

23 of Man. On that day be glad and dance for joy; for assuredly you have a rich reward in heaven; in just the same way did their fathers treat the prophets.

24 'But alas for you who are rich; you have had your time of happiness.

25 'Alas for you who are well-fed now; you shall go hungry.
'Alas for you who laugh now; you shall mourn and weep.

26 'Alas for you when all speak well of you; just so did their fathers treat the false prophets.

27 'But to you who hear me I say:

28 'Love your enemies; do good to those who hate you; bless those

29 who curse you; pray for those who treat you spitefully. When a man hits you on the cheek, offer him the other cheek too; when a man

30 takes your coat, let him have your shirt as well. Give to everyone who asks you; when a man takes what is yours, do not demand it

31 back. Treat others as you would like them to treat you.

32 'If you love only those who love you, what credit is that to you?

33 Even sinners love those who love them. Again, if you do good only to those who do good to you, what credit is that to you? Even sinners

34 do as much. And if you lend only where you expect to be repaid, what credit is that to you? Even sinners lend to each other if they

35 are to be repaid in full. But you must love your enemies and do good; and lend without expecting any return;[a] and you will have a rich reward: you will be sons of the Most High, because he himself

36 is kind to the ungrateful and wicked. Be compassionate as your Father is compassionate.

37 'Pass no judgement, and you will not be judged; do not condemn, and you will not be condemned; acquit, and you will be acquitted;

38 give, and gifts will be given you. Good measure, pressed down, shaken together, and running over, will be poured into your lap; for whatever measure you deal out to others will be dealt to you in return.'

39 He also offered them a parable: 'Can one blind man be guide to

40 another? Will they not both fall into the ditch? A pupil is not superior to his teacher; but everyone, when his training is complete, will reach his teacher's level.

41 'Why do you look at the speck of sawdust in your brother's eye,

42 with never a thought for the great plank in your own? How can you

[a] *Or* without ever giving up hope; *some witnesses read* without giving up hope of anyone.

say to your brother, "My dear brother, let me take the speck out of your eye", when you are blind to the plank in your own? You hypocrite! First take the plank out of your own eye, and then you will see clearly to take the speck out of your brother's.

'There is no such thing as a good tree producing worthless fruit, 43 nor yet a worthless tree producing good fruit. For each tree is known 44 by its own fruit: you do not gather figs from thistles, and you do not pick grapes from brambles. A good man produces good from the 45 store of good within himself; and an evil man from evil within produces evil. For the words that the mouth utters come from the overflowing of the heart.

'Why do you keep calling me "Lord, Lord"—and never do what 46 I tell you? Everyone who comes to me and hears what I say, and 47 acts upon it—I will show you what he is like. He is like a man who, 48 in building his house, dug deep and laid the foundations on rock. When the flood came, the river burst upon that house, but could not shift it, because it had been soundly built. But he who hears 49 and does not act is like a man who built his house on the soil without foundations. As soon as the river burst upon it, the house collapsed, and fell with a great crash.'

WHEN HE HAD finished addressing the people, he went to Caper- 7 naum. A centurion there had a servant whom he valued highly; 2 this servant was ill and near to death. Hearing about Jesus, he sent 3 some Jewish elders with the request that he would come and save his servant's life. They approached Jesus and pressed their petition 4 earnestly: 'He deserves this favour from you,' they said, 'for he 5 is a friend of our nation and it is he who built us our synagogue.' Jesus went with them; but when he was not far from the house, the 6 centurion sent friends with this message: 'Do not trouble further, sir; it is not for me to have you under my roof, and that is why I 7 did not presume to approach you in person. But say the word and my servant will be cured. I know, for in my position I am myself 8 under orders, with soldiers under me. I say to one, "Go", and he goes; to another, "Come here", and he comes; and to my servant, "Do this", and he does it.' When Jesus heard this, he admired the man, 9 and, turning to the crowd that was following him, he said, 'I tell you, nowhere, even in Israel, have I found faith like this.' And the 10 messengers returned to the house and found the servant in good health.

11 Afterwards*ᵃ* Jesus went to a town called Nain, accompanied by
12 his disciples and a large crowd. As he approached the gate of the
town he met a funeral. The dead man was the only son of his
widowed mother; and many of the townspeople were there with her.
13 When the Lord saw her his heart went out to her, and he said,
14 'Weep no more.' With that he stepped forward and laid his hand
on the bier; and the bearers halted. Then he spoke: 'Young man,
15 rise up!' The dead man sat up and began to talk; and Jesus gave him
16 back to his mother. Deep awe fell upon them all, and they praised
God. 'A great prophet has arisen among us', they said, and again,
17 'God has shown his care for his people.' The story of what he had
done ran through all parts of Judaea and the whole neighbourhood.
18, 19 John too was informed of all this by his disciples. Summoning
two of their number he sent them to the Lord with this message:
'Are you the one who is to come, or are we to expect some other?'
20 The messengers made their way to Jesus and said, 'John the Baptist
has sent us to you: he asks, "Are you the one who is to come, or are
21 we to expect some other?"' There and then he cured many sufferers
from diseases, plagues, and evil spirits; and on many blind people he
22 bestowed sight. Then he gave them his answer: 'Go', he said, 'and
tell John what you have seen and heard: how the blind recover their
sight, the lame walk, the lepers are clean, the deaf hear, the dead are
23 raised to life, the poor are hearing the good news—and happy is the
man who does not find me a stumbling-block.'
24 After John's messengers had left, Jesus began to speak about him
to the crowds: 'What was the spectacle that drew you to the wilder-
25 ness? A reed-bed swept by the wind? No? Then what did you go
out to see? A man dressed in silks and satins? Surely you must look
26 in palaces for grand clothes and luxury. But what did you go out
27 to see? A prophet? Yes indeed, and far more than a prophet. He is
the man of whom Scripture says,

> "Here is my herald, whom I send on ahead of you,
> And he will prepare your way before you."

28 I tell you, there is not a mother's son greater than John, and yet the
least in the kingdom of God is greater than he.'
29 When they heard him, all the people, including the tax-gatherers,
30 praised God, for they had accepted John's baptism; but the Pharisees

[a] *Some witnesses read* On the next day.

and lawyers, who refused his baptism, had rejected[a] God's purpose
for themselves.

'How can I describe the people of this generation? What are they ³¹
like? They are like children sitting in the market-place and shouting ³²
at each other,

> "We piped for you and you would not dance."
> "We wept and wailed, and you would not mourn."

For John the Baptist came neither eating bread nor drinking wine, ³³
and you say, "He is possessed." The Son of Man came eating and ³⁴
drinking, and you say, "Look at him! a glutton and a drinker, a friend
of tax-gatherers and sinners!" And yet God's wisdom is proved ³⁵
right by all who are her children.'

One of the Pharisees invited him to dinner; he went to the ³⁶
Pharisee's house and took his place at table. A woman who was ³⁷
living an immoral life in the town had learned that Jesus was dining
in the Pharisee's house and had brought oil of myrrh in a small flask.
She took her place behind him, by his feet, weeping. His feet were ³⁸
wetted with her tears and she wiped them with her hair, kissing
them and anointing them with the myrrh. When his host the ³⁹
Pharisee saw this he said to himself, 'If this fellow were a real
prophet, he would know who this woman is that touches him, and
what sort of woman she is, a sinner.' Jesus took him up and said, ⁴⁰
'Simon, I have something to say to you.' 'Speak on, Master', said
he. 'Two men were in debt to a money-lender: one owed him five ⁴¹
hundred silver pieces, the other fifty. As neither had anything to pay ⁴²
with he let them both off. Now, which will love him most?' Simon ⁴³
replied, 'I should think the one that was let off most.' 'You are
right', said Jesus. Then turning to the woman, he said to Simon, ⁴⁴
'You see this woman? I came to your house: you provided no water
for my feet; but this woman has made my feet wet with her tears
and wiped them with her hair. You gave me no kiss; but she has ⁴⁵
been kissing my feet ever since I came in. You did not anoint my ⁴⁶
head with oil; but she has anointed my feet with myrrh. And so, ⁴⁷
I tell you, her great love proves that her many sins have been forgiven; where little has been forgiven, little love is shown.' Then he ⁴⁸

[a] *Or* '...greater than he. And all the people, including the tax-gatherers, when they
heard him, accepted John's baptism and acknowledged the righteous dealing of God;
but the Pharisees and lawyers, by refusing his baptism, rejected...'

49 said to her, 'Your sins are forgiven.' The other guests began to
50 ask themselves, 'Who is this, that he can forgive sins?' But he said
to the woman, 'Your faith has saved you; go in peace.'

8 AFTER THIS he went journeying from town to town and village
to village, proclaiming the good news of the kingdom of God. With
2 him were the Twelve and a number of women who had been set
free from evil spirits and infirmities: Mary, known as Mary of
3 Magdala, from whom seven devils had come out, Joanna, the wife
of Chuza a steward of Herod's, Susanna, and many others. These
women provided for them out of their own resources.
4 People were now gathering in large numbers, and as they made
their way to him from one town after another, he said in a parable:
5 'A sower went out to sow his seed. And as he sowed, some seed
fell along the footpath, where it was trampled on, and the birds
6 ate it up. Some seed fell on rock and, after coming up, withered
7 for lack of moisture. Some seed fell in among thistles, and the
8 thistles grew up with it and choked it. And some of the seed fell
into good soil, and grew, and yielded a hundredfold.' As he said
this he called out, 'If you have ears to hear, then hear.'
9, 10 His disciples asked him what this parable meant, and he said,
'It has been granted to you to know the secrets of the kingdom of
God; but the others have only parables, in order that they may
look but see nothing, hear but understand nothing.
11 'This is what the parable means. The seed is the word of God.
12 Those along the footpath are the men who hear it, and then the
devil comes and carries off the word from their hearts for fear they
13 should believe and be saved. The seed sown on rock stands for those
who receive the word with joy when they hear it, but have no root;
they are believers for a while, but in the time of testing they desert.
14 That which fell among thistles represents those who hear, but their
further growth is choked by cares and wealth and the pleasures of
15 life, and they bring nothing to maturity. But the seed in good
soil represents those who bring a good and honest heart to the
hearing of the word, hold it fast, and by their perseverance yield a
harvest.
16 'Nobody lights a lamp and then covers it with a basin or puts it
under the bed. On the contrary, he puts it on a lamp-stand so that
17 those who come in may see the light. For there is nothing hidden

that will not become public, nothing under cover that will not be
made known and brought into the open.

'Take care, then, how you listen; for the man who has will be 18
given more, and the man who has not will forfeit even what he thinks
he has.'

His mother and his brothers arrived but could not get to him 19
for the crowd. He was told, 'Your mother and brothers are standing 20
outside, and they want to see you.' He replied, 'My mother and 21
my brothers—they are those who hear the word of God and act
upon it.'

One day he got into a boat with his disciples and said to them, 22
'Let us cross over to the other side of the lake.' So they put out;
and as they sailed along he went to sleep. Then a heavy squall 23
struck the lake; they began to ship water and were in grave danger.
They went to him, and roused him, crying, 'Master, Master, we 24
are sinking!' He awoke, and rebuked the wind and the turbulent
waters. The storm subsided and all was calm. 'Where is your faith?' 25
he asked. In fear and astonishment they said to one another, 'Who
can this be? He gives his orders to wind and waves, and they obey
him.'

So they landed in the country of the Gergesenes,[a] which is oppo- 26
site Galilee. As he stepped ashore he was met by a man from the 27
town who was possessed by devils. For a long time he had neither
worn clothes nor lived in a house, but stayed among the tombs.
When he saw Jesus he cried out, and fell at his feet shouting, 28
'What do you want with me, Jesus, son of the Most High God?
I implore you, do not torment me.'

For Jesus was already ordering the unclean spirit to come out 29
of the man. Many a time it had seized him, and then, for safety's
sake, they would secure him with chains and fetters; but each time
he broke loose, and with the devil in charge made off to the solitary
places.

Jesus asked him, 'What is your name?' 'Legion', he replied. 30
This was because so many devils had taken possession of him. And 31
they begged him not to banish them to the Abyss.

There happened to be a large herd of pigs nearby, feeding on 32
the hill; and the spirits begged him to let them go into these pigs.
He gave them leave; the devils came out of the man and went into 33

[a] *Some witnesses read* Gerasenes; *others read* Gadarenes.

the pigs, and the herd rushed over the edge into the lake and were drowned.

34 The men in charge of them saw what had happened, and, taking to their heels, they carried the news to the town and country-side;

35 and the people came out to see for themselves. When they came to Jesus, and found the man from whom the devils had gone out sitting

36 at his feet clothed and in his right mind, they were afraid. The spec-

37 tators told them how the madman had been cured. Then the whole population of the Gergesene[a] district asked him to go, for they were in the grip of a great fear. So he got into the boat and returned.

38 The man from whom the devils had gone out begged leave to go

39 with him; but Jesus sent him away: 'Go back home,' he said, 'and tell them everything that God has done for you.' The man went all over the town spreading the news of what Jesus had done for him.

40 When Jesus returned, the people welcomed him, for they were

41 all expecting him. Then a man appeared—Jairus was his name and he was president of the synagogue. Throwing himself down at Jesus's

42 feet he begged him to come to his house, because he had an only daughter, about twelve years old, who was dying. And while Jesus was on his way he could hardly breathe for the crowds.

43 Among them was a woman who had suffered from haemorrhages

44 for twelve years; and[b] nobody had been able to cure her. She came up from behind and touched the edge of[c] his cloak, and at

45 once her haemorrhage stopped. Jesus said, 'Who was it that touched me?' All disclaimed it, and Peter and his companions said, 'Master,

46 the crowds are hemming you in and pressing upon you!' But Jesus said, 'Someone did touch me, for I felt that power had gone out

47 from me.' Then the woman, seeing that she was detected, came trembling and fell at his feet. Before all the people she explained

48 why she had touched him and how she had been instantly cured. He said to her, 'My daughter, your faith has cured you. Go in peace.'

49 While he was still speaking, a man came from the president's house with the message, 'Your daughter is dead; trouble the Rabbi

50 no further.' But Jesus heard, and interposed. 'Do not be afraid,'

51 he said; 'only show faith and she will be well again.' On arrival at the house he allowed no one to go in with him except Peter,

52 John, and James, and the child's father and mother. And all were

[a] *Some witnesses read* Gerasene; *others read* Gadarene.   [b] *Some witnesses add* though she had spent all she had on doctors.   [c] *Some witnesses omit* the edge of.

weeping and lamenting for her. He said, 'Weep no more; she is not dead: she is asleep.' But they only laughed at him, well knowing 53 that she was dead. But Jesus took hold of her hand and called her: 54 'Get up, my child.' Her spirit returned, she stood up immediately, 55 and he told them to give her something to eat. Her parents were 56 astounded; but he forbade them to tell anyone what had happened.

HE NOW called the Twelve together and gave them power and 9 authority to overcome all the devils and to cure diseases, and sent 2 them to proclaim the kingdom of God and to heal. 'Take nothing 3 for the journey,' he told them, 'neither stick nor pack, neither bread nor money; nor are you each to have a second coat. When you are 4 admitted to a house, stay there, and go on from there. As for those 5 who will not receive you, when you leave their town shake the dust off your feet as a warning to them.' So they set out and travelled 6 from village to village, and everywhere they told the good news and healed the sick.

Now Prince Herod heard of all that was happening, and did not 7 know what to make of it; for some were saying that John had been raised from the dead, others that Elijah had appeared, others again 8 that one of the old prophets had come back to life. Herod said, 9 'As for John, I beheaded him myself; but who is this I hear such talk about?' And he was anxious to see him.

On their return the apostles told Jesus all they had done; and 10 he took them with him and withdrew privately to a town called Bethsaida. But the crowds found out and followed him. He wel- 11 comed them, and spoke to them about the kingdom of God, and cured those who were in need of healing. When evening was drawing 12 on, the Twelve approached him and said, 'Send these people away; then they can go into the villages and farms round about to find food and lodging; for we are in a lonely place here.' 'Give them some- 13 thing to eat yourselves', he replied. But they said, 'All we have is five loaves and two fishes, nothing more—unless perhaps we our- selves are to go and buy provisions for all this company.' (There 14 were about five thousand men.) He said to his disciples, 'Make them sit down in groups of fifty or so.' They did so and got them all 15 seated. Then, taking the five loaves and the two fishes, he looked 16 up to heaven, said the blessing over them, broke them, and gave them to the disciples to distribute to the people. They all ate to their 17 hearts' content; and when the scraps they left were picked up, they filled twelve great baskets.

18 One day when he was praying alone in the presence of his dis-
19 ciples, he asked them, 'Who do the people say I am?' They answered, 'Some say John the Baptist, others Elijah, others that one of the
20 old prophets has come back to life.' 'And you,' he said, 'who do
21 you say I am?' Peter answered, 'God's Messiah.' Then he gave
22 them strict orders not to tell this to anyone. And he said, 'The Son of Man has to undergo great sufferings, and to be rejected by the elders, chief priests, and doctors of the law, to be put to death and to be raised again on the third day.'

23 And to all he said, 'If anyone wishes to be a follower of mine, he must leave self behind; day after day he must take up his cross,
24 and come with me. Whoever cares for his own safety is lost; but if a man will let himself be lost for my sake, that man is safe.
25 What will a man gain by winning the whole world, at the cost of his
26 true self? For whoever is ashamed of me and mine,*a* the Son of Man will be ashamed of him, when he comes in his glory and the
27 glory of the Father and the holy angels. And I tell you this: there are some of those standing here who will not taste death before they have seen the kingdom of God.'

28 About eight days after this conversation he took Peter, John, and
29 James with him and went up into the hills to pray. And while he was praying the appearance of his face changed and his clothes
30 became dazzling white. Suddenly there were two men talking with
31 him; these were Moses and Elijah, who appeared in glory and spoke
32 of his departure, the destiny he was to fulfil in Jerusalem. Meanwhile Peter and his companions had been in a deep sleep; but when they awoke, they saw his glory and the two men who stood beside
33 him. And as these were moving away from Jesus, Peter said to him, 'Master, how good it is that we are here! Shall we make three shelters, one for you, one for Moses, and one for Elijah?'; but he spoke
34 without knowing what he was saying. The words were still on his lips, when there came a cloud which cast a shadow over them; they
35 were afraid as they entered the cloud, and from it came a voice:
36 'This is my Son, my Chosen; listen to him.' When the voice had spoken, Jesus was seen to be alone. The disciples kept silence and at that time told nobody anything of what they had seen.

[*a*] *Some witnesses read* me and my words.

Next day when they came down from the hills he was met by 37
a large crowd. All at once there was a shout from a man in the crowd: 38
'Master, look at my son, I implore you, my only child. From time 39
to time a spirit seizes him, gives a sudden scream, and throws him
into convulsions with foaming at the mouth, and it keeps on mauling
him and will hardly let him go. I asked your disciples to cast it 40
out, but they could not.' Jesus answered, 'What an unbelieving 41
and perverse generation! How long shall I be with you and endure
you all? Bring your son here.' But before the boy could reach him 42
the devil dashed him to the ground and threw him into convulsions.
Jesus rebuked the unclean spirit, cured the boy, and gave him back
to his father. And they were all struck with awe at the majesty of 43
God.

Amid the general wonder and admiration at all he was doing,
Jesus said to his disciples, 'What I now say is for you: ponder my 44
words. The Son of Man is going to be given up into the power of
men.' But they did not understand what he said; it had been hidden 45
from them so that they should not*ª* perceive its drift; and they were
afraid to ask him what it meant.

A dispute arose among them: which of them was the greatest? 46
Jesus knew what was passing in their minds, so he took a child by 47
the hand and stood him at his side, and said, 'Whoever receives this 48
child in my name receives me; and whoever receives me receives the
One who sent me. For the least among you all—he is the greatest.'

'Master,' said John, 'we saw a man casting out devils in your name, 49
but as he is not one of us we tried to stop him.' Jesus said to him, 50
'Do not stop him, for he who is not against you is on your side.'

Journeys and Encounters

A S THE TIME approached when he was to be taken up to heaven, he 51
set his face resolutely towards Jerusalem, and sent messengers 52
ahead. They set out and went into a Samaritan village to make
arrangements for him; but the villagers would not have him because 53
he was making for Jerusalem. When the disciples James and John 54
saw this they said, 'Lord, may we call down fire from heaven to

[a] *Or* it was so obscure to them that they could not...

115

55, 56 burn them up^{*a*}?' But he turned and rebuked them,^{*b*} and they went
on to another village.

57   As they were going along the road a man said to him, 'I will
58 follow you wherever you go.' Jesus answered, 'Foxes have their
holes, the birds their roosts; but the Son of Man has nowhere to
59 lay his head.' To another he said, 'Follow me', but the man replied,
60 'Let me go and bury my father first.' Jesus said, 'Leave the dead
to bury their dead; you must go and announce the kingdom of
God.'

61   Yet another said, 'I will follow you, sir; but let me first say good-
62 bye to my people at home.' To him Jesus said, 'No one who sets
his hand to the plough and then keeps looking back^{*c*} is fit for the
kingdom of God.'

10   After this the Lord appointed a further seventy-two^{*d*} and sent
them on ahead in pairs to every town and place he was going to
2 visit himself. He said to them: 'The crop is heavy, but labourers
are scarce; you must therefore beg the owner to send labourers to
3 harvest his crop. Be on your way. And look, I am sending you like
4 lambs among wolves. Carry no purse or pack, and travel barefoot.
5 Exchange no greetings on the road. When you go into a house, let
6 your first words be, "Peace to this house." If there is a man of
peace there, your peace will rest upon him; if not, it will return
7 and rest upon you. Stay in that one house, sharing their food and
drink; for the worker earns his pay. Do not move from house to house.
8 When you come into a town and they make you welcome, eat the
9 food provided for you; heal the sick there, and say, "The kingdom
10 of God has come close to you." When you enter a town and they
11 do not make you welcome, go out into its streets and say, "The
very dust of your town that clings to our feet we wipe off to your
shame. Only take note of this: the kingdom of God has come close."
12 I tell you, it will be more bearable for Sodom on the great Day than
for that town.

13   Alas for you, Chorazin! Alas for you, Bethsaida! If the miracles
that were performed in you had been performed in Tyre and Sidon,
they would have repented long ago, sitting in sackcloth and ashes.

[*a*] *Some witnesses add* as Elijah did. [*b*] *Some witnesses insert* 'You do not know', he said,
'to what spirit you belong; (56) for the Son of Man did not come to destroy men's
lives but to save them.' [*c*] *Some witnesses read* No one who looks back as he sets hand
to the plough... [*d*] *Some witnesses read* seventy.

But it will be more bearable for Tyre and Sidon at the Judgement 14
than for you. And as for you, Capernaum, will you be exalted to the 15
skies? No, brought down to the depths!

'Whoever listens to you listens to me; whoever rejects you rejects 16
me. And whoever rejects me rejects the One who sent me.'

The seventy-two*a* came back jubilant. 'In your name, Lord,' 17
they said, 'even the devils submit to us.' He replied, 'I watched 18
how Satan fell, like lightning, out of the sky. And now you see 19
that I have given you the power to tread underfoot snakes and
scorpions and all the forces of the enemy, and nothing will ever
harm you.*b* Nevertheless, what you should rejoice over is not that 20
the spirits submit to you, but that your names are enrolled in
heaven.'

At that moment Jesus exulted in the Holy*c* Spirit and said, 'I 21
thank thee, Father, Lord of heaven and earth, for hiding these things
from the learned and wise, and revealing them to the simple. Yes,
Father, such*d* was thy choice.' Then turning to his disciples he 22
said,*e* 'Everything is entrusted to me by my Father; and no one
knows who the Son is but the Father, or who the Father is but the
Son, and those to whom the Son may choose to reveal him.'

Turning to his disciples in private he said, 'Happy the eyes that 23
see what you are seeing! I tell you, many prophets and kings 24
wished to see what you now see, yet never saw it; to hear what you
hear, yet never heard it.'

ON ONE occasion a lawyer came forward to put this test question 25
to him: 'Master, what must I do to inherit eternal life?' Jesus said, 26
'What is written in the Law? What is your reading of it?' He replied, 27
'Love the Lord your God with all your heart, with all your soul,
with all your strength, and with all your mind; and your neighbour
as yourself.' 'That is the right answer,' said Jesus; 'do that and you 28
will live.'

But he wanted to vindicate himself, so he said to Jesus, 'And who 29
is my neighbour?' Jesus replied, 'A man was on his way from Jeru- 30
salem down to Jericho when he fell in with robbers, who stripped
him, beat him, and went off leaving him half dead. It so happened 31

[*a*] *Some witnesses read* seventy. [*b*] *Or* and he will have no way at all to harm you.
[*c*] *Some witnesses omit* Holy. [*d*] *Or* Yes, I thank thee, Father, that such... [*e*] *Some
witnesses omit* Then...he said.

that a priest was going down by the same road; but when he saw
32 him, he went past on the other side. So too a Levite came to the
33 place, and when he saw him went past on the other side. But a
Samaritan who was making the journey came upon him, and when
34 he saw him was moved to pity. He went up and bandaged his
wounds, bathing them with oil and wine. Then he lifted him on to
his own beast, brought him to an inn, and looked after him there.
35 Next day he produced two silver pieces and gave them to the inn-
keeper, and said, "Look after him; and if you spend any more, I will
36 repay you on my way back." Which of these three do you think
was neighbour to the man who fell into the hands of the robbers?'
37 He answered, 'The one who showed him kindness.' Jesus said,
'Go and do as he did.'

38   While they were on their way Jesus came to a village where a
39 woman named Martha made him welcome in her home. She had
a sister, Mary, who seated herself at the Lord's feet and stayed there
40 listening to his words. Now Martha was distracted by her many
tasks, so she came to him and said, 'Lord, do you not care that my
sister has left me to get on with the work by myself? Tell her to
41 come and lend a hand.' But the Lord answered, 'Martha, Martha,
42 you are fretting and fussing about so many things; but one thing
is necessary.*a* The part that Mary has chosen is best; and it shall
not be taken away from her.'

11   Once, in a certain place, Jesus was at prayer. When he ceased,
one of his disciples said, 'Lord, teach us to pray, as John taught his
2 disciples.' He answered, 'When you pray, say,

"Father,*b* thy name be hallowed;
Thy kingdom come.*c*
3   Give us each day our daily bread.*d*
4   And forgive us our sins,
For we too forgive all who have done us wrong.
And do not bring us to the test."*e*

5   He added, 'Suppose one of you has a friend who comes to him
in the middle of the night and says, "My friend, lend me three

[a] *Some witnesses read* but few things are necessary, or rather, one alone; *others omit* you are fretting…necessary. [b] *Some witnesses read* Our Father in heaven. [c] *One witness reads* Thy kingdom come upon us; *some others have* Thy Holy Spirit come upon us and cleanse us; *some insert* Thy will be done, On earth as in heaven. [d] *Or* our bread for the morrow. [e] *Some witnesses add* But save us from the evil one.

loaves, for a friend of mine on a journey has turned up at my house, 6
and I have nothing to offer him"; and he replies from inside, "Do not 7
bother me. The door is shut for the night; my children and I have
gone to bed; and I cannot get up and give you what you want."
I tell you that even if he will not provide for him out of friendship, 8
the very shamelessness of the request will make him get up and give
him all he needs. And so I say to you, ask, and you will receive; 9
seek, and you will find; knock, and the door will be opened. For 10
everyone who asks receives, he who seeks finds, and to him who
knocks, the door will be opened.

'Is there a father among you who will offer his son*a* a snake when 11
he asks for fish, or a scorpion when he asks for an egg? If you, then, 12, 13
bad as you are, know how to give your children what is good for
them, how much more will the heavenly Father give the Holy
Spirit*b* to those who ask him!'

HE WAS driving out a devil which was dumb; and when the devil 14
had come out, the dumb man began to speak. The people were
astonished, but some of them said, 'It is by Beelzebub prince of 15
devils that he drives the devils out.' Others, by way of a test, 16
demanded of him a sign from heaven. But he knew what was in 17
their minds, and said, 'Every kingdom divided against itself goes
to ruin, and a divided household falls. Equally if Satan is divided 18
against himself, how can his kingdom stand?—since, as you would
have it, I drive out the devils by Beelzebub. If it is by Beelzebub that 19
I cast out devils, by whom do your own people drive them out?
If this is your argument, they themselves will refute you. But if it 20
is by the finger of God that I drive out the devils, then be sure the
kingdom of God has already come upon you.

'When a strong man fully armed is on guard over his castle his 21
possessions are safe. But when someone stronger comes upon him 22
and overpowers him, he carries off the arms and armour on which
the man had relied and divides the plunder.

'He who is not with me is against me, and he who does not 23
gather with me scatters.*c*

'When an unclean spirit comes out of a man it wanders over the 24
deserts seeking a resting-place; and finding none, it says, "I will

[a] *Some witnesses insert* a stone when he asks for bread, or... [b] *Some witnesses read*
a good gift; *some others read* good things. [c] *Some witnesses add* me.

25 go back to the home I left." So it returns and finds the house*a* swept
26 clean, and tidy. Off it goes and collects seven other spirits more
wicked than itself, and they all come in and settle down; and in the
end the man's plight is worse than before.'
27 While he was speaking thus, a woman in the crowd called out,
'Happy the womb that carried you and the breasts that suckled you!'
28 He rejoined, 'No, happy are those who hear the word of God and
keep it.'
29 With the crowds swarming round him he went on to say: 'This
is a wicked generation. It demands a sign, and the only sign that
30 will be given to it is the sign of Jonah. For just as Jonah was a sign
to the Ninevites, so will the Son of Man be to this generation.
31 At the Judgement, when the men of this generation are on trial,
the Queen of the South will appear against*b* them and ensure their
condemnation, for she came from the ends of the earth to hear the
wisdom of Solomon; and what is here is greater than Solomon.
32 The men of Nineveh will appear at the Judgement when the men
of this generation are on trial, and ensure*c* their condemnation,
for they repented at the preaching of Jonah; and what is here is
greater than Jonah.
33 'No one lights a lamp and puts it in a cellar,*d* but rather on the
34 lamp-stand so that those who enter may see the light. The lamp
of your body is the eye. When your eyes are sound, you have light
for your whole body; but when the eyes are bad, you are in darkness.
35, 36 See to it then that the light you have is not darkness. If you have
light for your whole body with no trace of darkness, it will all be
as bright as when a lamp flashes its rays upon you.'

37 WHEN HE HAD finished speaking, a Pharisee invited him to dinner.
38 He came in and sat down. The Pharisee noticed with surprise that
39 he had not begun by washing before the meal. But the Lord said
to him, 'You Pharisees! You clean the outside of cup and plate;
40 but inside you there is nothing but greed and wickedness. You
41 fools! Did not he who made the outside make the inside too? But
let what is in the cup*e* be given in charity, and all is clean.

[*a*] *Some witnesses insert* unoccupied. [*b*] *Or* will be raised to life together with...
[*c*] *Or* At the Judgement the men of Nineveh will rise again together with the men
of this generation and will ensure... [*d*] *Some witnesses insert* or under the meal-tub.
[*e*] *Or* what you can afford.

'Alas for you Pharisees! You pay tithes of mint and rue and every 42
garden-herb, but have no care for justice and the love of God. It is
these you should have practised, without neglecting the others.[a]

'Alas for you Pharisees! You love the seats of honour in syna- 43
gogues, and salutations in the market-places.

'Alas, alas, you are like unmarked graves over which men may 44
walk without knowing it.'

In reply to this one of the lawyers said, 'Master, when you say 45
things like this you are insulting us too.' Jesus rejoined: 'Yes, you 46
lawyers, it is no better with you! For you load men with intolerable
burdens, and will not put a single finger to the load.

'Alas, you build the tombs of the prophets whom your fathers 47
murdered, and so testify that you approve of the deeds your fathers 48
did; they committed the murders and you provide the tombs.

'This is why the Wisdom of God said, "I will send them prophets 49
and messengers; and some of these they will persecute and kill";
so that this generation will have to answer for the blood of all the 50
prophets shed since the foundation of the world; from the blood 51
of Abel to the blood of Zechariah who perished between the altar
and the sanctuary. I tell you, this generation will have to answer for
it all.

'Alas for you lawyers! You have taken away the key of knowledge. 52
You did not go in yourselves, and those who were on their way in,
you stopped.'

After he had left the house, the lawyers and Pharisees began to 53
assail him fiercely and to ply him with a host of questions, laying 54
snares to catch him with his own words.

MEANWHILE, when a crowd of many thousands had gathered, 12
packed so close that they were treading on one another, he began
to speak first to his disciples: 'Beware of the leaven of the Pharisees;
I mean their hypocrisy. There is nothing covered up that will not 2
be uncovered, nothing hidden that will not be made known. You 3
may take it, then, that everything you have said in the dark will
be heard in broad daylight, and what you have whispered behind
closed doors will be shouted from the house-tops.

'To you who are my friends I say: Do not fear those who kill 4
the body and after that have nothing more they can do. I will warn 5

[a] *Some witnesses omit* It is...others.

121

you whom to fear: fear him who, after he has killed, has authority
to cast into hell. Believe me, he is the one to fear.

6   'Are not sparrows five for twopence? And yet not one of them is
7   overlooked by God. More than that, even the hairs of your head
have all been counted. Have no fear; you are worth more than any
number of sparrows.

8   'I tell you this: everyone who acknowledges me before men, the
9   Son of Man will acknowledge before the angels of God; but he
who disowns me before men will be disowned before the angels
of God.

10   'Anyone who speaks a word against the Son of Man will receive
forgiveness; but for him who slanders the Holy Spirit there will be
no forgiveness.

11   'When you are brought before synagogues and state authorities,
do not begin worrying about how you will conduct your defence or
12   what you will say. For when the time comes the Holy Spirit will
instruct you what to say.'

13   A man in the crowd said to him, 'Master, tell my brother to
14   divide the family property with me.' He replied, 'My good man,
15   who set me over you to judge or arbitrate?'ᵃ Then he said to the
people, 'Beware! Be on your guard against greed of every kind, for
even when a man has more than enough, his wealth does not give
16   him life.' And he told them this parable: 'There was a rich man
17   whose land yielded heavy crops. He debated with himself: "What
18   am I to do? I have not the space to store my produce. This is what
I will do," said he: "I will pull down my storehouses and build them
19   bigger. I will collect in them all my corn and other goods, and then
say to myself, 'Man, you have plenty of good things laid by, enough
20   for many years: take life easy, eat, drink, and enjoy yourself.'" But
God said to him, "You fool, this very night you must surrender your
21   life; you have made your money—who will get it now?" That is how
it is with the man who amasses wealth for himself and remains
a pauper in the sight of God.ᵇ

22   'Therefore', he said to his disciples, 'I bid you put away anxious
thoughts about food to keep you alive and clothes to cover your
23, 24   body. Life is more than food, the body more than clothes. Think
of the ravens: they neither sow nor reap; they have no storehouse

[a] *Some witnesses omit* or arbitrate. [b] *Some witnesses omit* That...God; *others add
at the end* When he said this he cried out, 'If you have ears to hear, then hear.'

or barn; yet God feeds them. You are worth far more than the birds! Is there a man among you who by anxious thought can add a foot 25 to his height*^a*? If, then, you cannot do even a very little thing, why 26 are you anxious about the rest?

'Think of the lilies: they neither spin nor weave;*^b* yet I tell you, 27 even Solomon in all his splendour was not attired like one of these. But if that is how God clothes the grass, which is growing in the field 28 today, and tomorrow is thrown on the stove, how much more will he clothe you! How little faith you have! And so you are not to set 29 your mind on food and drink; you are not to worry. For all these 30 are things for the heathen to run after; but you have a Father who knows that you need them. No, set your mind upon his kingdom, and 31 all the rest will come to you as well.

'Have no fear, little flock; for your Father has chosen to give you 32 the Kingdom. Sell your possessions and give in charity. Provide for 33 yourselves purses that do not wear out, and never-failing wealth in heaven, where no thief can get near it, no moth destroy it. For where 34 your wealth is, there will your heart be also.

'Be ready for action, with belts fastened and lamps alight. Be like 35, 36 men who wait for their master's return from a wedding-party, ready to let him in the moment he arrives and knocks. Happy are those 37 servants whom the master finds on the alert when he comes. I tell you this: he will buckle his belt, seat them at table, and come and wait on them. Even if it is the middle of the night or before dawn 38 when he comes, happy they if he finds them alert. And remember, 39 if the householder had known what time the burglar was coming he would not have let his house be broken into. Hold yourselves 40 ready, then, because the Son of Man is coming at the time you least expect him.'

Peter said, 'Lord, do you intend this parable specially for us or 41 is it for everyone?' The Lord said, 'Well, who is the trusty and 42 sensible man whom his master will appoint as his steward, to manage his servants and issue their rations at the proper time? Happy that 43 servant who is found at his task when his master comes! I tell you 44 this: he will be put in charge of all his master's property. But if 45 that servant says to himself, "The master is a long time coming", and begins to bully the menservants and maids, and eat and drink and get drunk; then the master will arrive on a day that servant 46

[a] *Or* a day to his life. [b] *Many witnesses read* they grow, they do not toil or spin.

does not expect, at a time he does not know, and will cut him in pieces. Thus he will find his place among the faithless.

47 'The servant who knew his master's wishes, yet made no attempt
48 to carry them out, will be flogged severely. But one who did not know them and earned a beating will be flogged less severely. Where a man has been given much, much will be expected of him; and the more a man has had entrusted to him the more he will be required to repay.

49 'I have come to set fire to the earth, and how I wish it were already
50 kindled! I have a baptism to undergo, and how hampered I am until
51 the ordeal is over! Do you suppose I came to establish peace on
52 earth? No indeed, I have come to bring division. For from now on, five members of a family will be divided, three against two and
53 two against three; father against son and son against father, mother against daughter and daughter against mother, mother against son's wife and son's wife against her mother-in-law.'

54 He also said to the people, 'When you see cloud banking up in the west, you say at once, "It is going to rain", and rain it does.
55 And when the wind is from the south, you say, "There will be a heat-
56 wave", and there is. What hypocrites you are! You know how to interpret the appearance of earth and sky; how is it you cannot interpret this fateful hour?

57 'And why can you not judge for yourselves what is the right course?
58 While you are going with your opponent to court, make an effort to settle with him while you are still on the way; otherwise he may drag you before the judge, and the judge hand you over to the
59 constable, and the constable put you in jail. I tell you, you will not come out till you have paid the last farthing.'

13 AT THAT very time there were some people present who told him about the Galileans whose blood Pilate had mixed with their sacri-
2 fices. He answered them: 'Do you imagine that, because these Galileans suffered this fate, they must have been greater sinners
3 than anyone else in Galilee? I tell you they were not; but unless you
4 repent, you will all of you come to the same end. Or the eighteen people who were killed when the tower fell on them at Siloam—do you imagine they were more guilty than all the other people living
5 in Jerusalem? I tell you they were not; but unless you repent, you will all of you come to the same end.'

He told them this parable: 'A man had a fig-tree growing in his 6
vineyard; and he came looking for fruit on it, but found none. So he 7
said to the vine-dresser, "Look here! For the last three years I have
come looking for fruit on this fig-tree without finding any. Cut it
down. Why should it go on using up the soil?" But he replied, "Leave 8
it, sir, this one year while I dig round it and manure it. And if it 9
bears next season, well and good; if not, you shall have it down."'

One Sabbath he was teaching in a synagogue, and there was a 10, 11
woman there possessed by a spirit that had crippled her for eighteen
years. She was bent double and quite unable to stand up straight.
When Jesus saw her he called her and said, 'You are rid of your 12
trouble.' Then he laid his hands on her, and at once she straightened 13
up and began to praise God. But the president of the synagogue, 14
indignant with Jesus for healing on the Sabbath, intervened and
said to the congregation, 'There are six working-days: come and
be cured on one of them, and not on the Sabbath.' The Lord gave 15
him his answer: 'What hypocrites you are!' he said. 'Is there a single
one of you who does not loose his ox or his donkey from the manger
and take it out to water on the Sabbath? And here is this woman, 16
a daughter of Abraham, who has been kept prisoner by Satan for
eighteen long years: was it wrong for her to be freed from her bonds
on the Sabbath?' At these words all his opponents were covered with 17
confusion, while the mass of the people were delighted at all the
wonderful things he was doing.

'What is the kingdom of God like?' he continued. 'What shall 18
I compare it with? It is like a mustard-seed which a man took and 19
sowed in his garden; and it grew to be a tree and the birds came to
roost among its branches.'

Again he said, 'What shall I compare the kingdom of God with? 20
It is like yeast which a woman took and mixed with half a hundred- 21
weight of flour till it was all leavened.'

HE CONTINUED his journey through towns and villages, teaching 22
as he made his way towards Jerusalem. Someone asked him, 'Sir, 23
are only a few to be saved?' His answer was: 'Struggle to get in 24
through the narrow door; for I tell you that many will try to enter
and not be able.

'When once the master of the house has got up and locked the 25
door, you may stand outside and knock, and say, "Sir, let us in!",

but he will only answer, "I do not know where you come from."
26 Then you will begin to say, "We sat at table with you and you taught
27 in our streets." But he will repeat, "I tell you, I do not know where
you come from. Out of my sight, all of you, you and your wicked
28 ways!" There will be wailing and grinding of teeth there, when you
see Abraham, Isaac, and Jacob, and all the prophets, in the kingdom
29 of God, and yourselves thrown out. From east and west people
will come, from north and south, for the feast in the kingdom of
30 God. Yes, and some who are now last will be first, and some who
are first will be last.'

31   At that time a number of Pharisees came to him and said, 'You
should leave this place and go on your way; Herod is out to kill you.'
32 He replied, 'Go and tell that fox, "Listen: today and tomorrow I
shall be casting out devils and working cures; on the third day I
33 reach my goal." However, I must be on my way today and tomorrow
and the next day, because it is unthinkable for a prophet to meet his
death anywhere but in Jerusalem.

34   'O Jerusalem, Jerusalem, the city that murders the prophets and
stones the messengers sent to her! How often have I longed to
gather your children, as a hen gathers her brood under her wings;
35 but you would not let me. Look, look! there is your temple, forsaken
by God. And I tell you, you shall never see me until the time comes
when you say, "Blessings on him who comes in the name of the
Lord!"'

14 ONE SABBATH he went to have a meal in the house of a leading
2 Pharisee; and they were watching him closely. There, in front of
3 him, was a man suffering from dropsy. Jesus asked the lawyers
and the Pharisees: 'Is it permitted to cure people on the Sabbath
4 or not?' They said nothing. So he took the man, cured him, and
5 sent him away. Then he turned to them and said, 'If one of you
has a donkey[a] or an ox and it falls into a well, will he hesitate to
6 haul it up on the Sabbath day?' To this they could find no reply.

7   When he noticed how the guests were trying to secure the places
8 of honour, he spoke to them in a parable: 'When you are asked by
someone to a wedding-feast, do not sit down in the place of honour.
It may be that some person more distinguished than yourself has
9 been invited; and the host will come and say to you, "Give this man

[a] *Some ancient witnesses read* son.

126

your seat." Then you will look foolish as you begin to take the lowest place. No, when you receive an invitation, go and sit down in the 10 lowest place, so that when your host comes he will say, "Come up higher, my friend." Then all your fellow-guests will see the respect in which you are held. For everyone who exalts himself will be 11 humbled; and whoever humbles himself will be exalted.'

Then he said to his host, 'When you give a lunch or dinner party, 12 do not invite your friends, your brothers or other relations, or your rich neighbours; they will only ask you back again and so you will be repaid. But when you give a party, ask the poor, the crippled, 13 the lame, and the blind; and so find happiness. For they have no 14 means of repaying you; but you will be repaid on the day when good men rise from the dead.'

One of the company, after hearing all this, said to him, 'Happy 15 the man who shall sit at the feast in the kingdom of God!' Jesus 16 answered, 'A man was giving a big dinner party and had sent out many invitations. At dinner-time he sent his servant with a message 17 for his guests, "Please come, everything is now ready." They began 18 one and all to excuse themselves. The first said, "I have bought a piece of land, and I must go and look over it; please accept my apologies." The second said, "I have bought five yoke of oxen, and 19 I am on my way to try them out; please accept my apologies." The 20 next said, "I have just got married and for that reason I cannot come." When the servant came back he reported this to his master. The 21 master of the house was angry and said to him, "Go out quickly into the streets and alleys of the town, and bring me in the poor, the crippled, the blind, and the lame." The servant said, "Sir, your 22 orders have been carried out and there is still room." The master 23 replied, "Go out on to the highways and along the hedgerows and make them come in; I want my house to be full. I tell you that not 24 one of those who were invited shall taste my banquet."'

Once when great crowds were accompanying him, he turned to 25 them and said: 'If anyone comes to me and does not hate his father 26 and mother, wife and children, brothers and sisters, even his own life, he cannot be a disciple of mine. No one who does not carry his 27 cross and come with me can be a disciple of mine. Would any of you 28 think of building a tower without first sitting down and calculating the cost, to see whether he could afford to finish it? Otherwise, if 29 he has laid its foundation and then is not able to complete it, all the

30 onlookers will laugh at him. "There is the man", they will say, "who
31 started to build and could not finish." Or what king will march to
battle against another king, without first sitting down to consider
whether with ten thousand men he can face an enemy coming to
32 meet him with twenty thousand? If he cannot, then, long before the
33 enemy approaches, he sends envoys, and asks for terms. So also
none of you can be a disciple of mine without taking leave of all his
possessions.
34   'Salt is a good thing; but if salt itself becomes tasteless, what will
35 you use to season it? It is useless either on the land or on the dung-
heap: it can only be thrown away. If you have ears to hear with,
hear.'

15 ANOTHER TIME, the tax-gatherers and other bad characters were
2 all crowding in to listen to him; and the Pharisees and the doctors
of the law began grumbling among themselves: 'This fellow', they
3 said, 'welcomes sinners and eats with them.' He answered them
4 with this parable: 'If one of you has a hundred sheep and loses one
of them, does he not leave the ninety-nine in the open pasture and
5 go after the missing one until he has found it? How delighted he is
6 then! He lifts it on to his shoulders, and home he goes to call his
friends and neighbours together. "Rejoice with me!" he cries. "I
7 have found my lost sheep." In the same way, I tell you, there will be
greater joy in heaven over one sinner who repents than over ninety-
nine righteous people who do not need to repent.
8   'Or again, if a woman has ten silver pieces and loses one of them,
does she not light the lamp, sweep out the house, and look in every
9 corner till she has found it? And when she has, she calls her friends
and neighbours together, and says, "Rejoice with me! I have found
10 the piece that I lost." In the same way, I tell you, there is joy among
the angels of God over one sinner who repents.'
11, 12   Again he said: 'There was once a man who had two sons; and
the younger said to his father, "Father, give me my share of the
13 property." So he divided his estate between them. A few days later
the younger son turned the whole of his share into cash and left home
for a distant country, where he squandered it in reckless living.
14 He had spent it all, when a severe famine fell upon that country and
15 he began to feel the pinch. So he went and attached himself to one
of the local landowners, who sent him on to his farm to mind the

pigs. He would have been glad to fill his belly with*ª* the pods that   16
the pigs were eating; and no one gave him anything. Then he came   17
to his senses and said, "How many of my father's paid servants
have more food than they can eat, and here am I, starving to death!
I will set off and go to my father, and say to him, 'Father, I have   18
sinned, against God and against you; I am no longer fit to be   19
called your son; treat me as one of your paid servants.'" So he set   20
out for his father's house. But while he was still a long way off
his father saw him, and his heart went out to him. He ran to meet
him, flung his arms round him, and kissed him. The son said,   21
"Father, I have sinned, against God and against you; I am no longer
fit to be called your son."*ᵇ* But the father said to his servants,   22
"Quick! fetch a robe, my best one, and put it on him; put a ring
on his finger and shoes on his feet. Bring the fatted calf and kill it,   23
and let us have a feast to celebrate the day. For this son of mine was   24
dead and has come back to life; he was lost and is found." And the
festivities began.

'Now the elder son was out on the farm; and on his way back,   25
as he approached the house, he heard music and dancing. He called   26
one of the servants and asked what it meant. The servant told him,   27
"Your brother has come home, and your father has killed the fatted
calf because he has him back safe and sound." But he was angry and   28
refused to go in. His father came out and pleaded with him; but   29
he retorted, "You know how I have slaved for you all these years;
I never once disobeyed your orders; and you never gave me so much
as a kid, for a feast with my friends. But now that this son of yours   30
turns up, after running through your money with his women, you
kill the fatted calf for him." "My boy," said the father, "you are   31
always with me, and everything I have is yours. How could we help   32
celebrating this happy day? Your brother here was dead and has
come back to life, was lost and is found."'

He said to his disciples, 'There was a rich man who had a bailiff,   16
and he received complaints that this man was squandering the
property. So he sent for him, and said, "What is this that I hear?   2
Produce your accounts, for you cannot be manager here any longer."
The bailiff said to himself, "What am I to do now that my employer   3
is dismissing me? I am not strong enough to dig, and too proud to

[a] *Some witnesses read* to have his fill of... [b] *Some witnesses add* treat me as one of
your paid servants.

4 beg. I know what I must do, to make sure that, when I have to
5 leave, there will be people to give me house and home." He summoned his master's debtors one by one. To the first he said, "How
6 much do you owe my master?" He replied, "A thousand gallons
of olive oil." He said, "Here is your account. Sit down and make it
7 five hundred; and be quick about it." Then he said to another,
"And you, how much do you owe?" He said, "A thousand bushels of
wheat", and was told, "Take your account and make it eight hundred."
8 And the master applauded the dishonest bailiff for acting so astutely.
For the worldly are more astute than the other-worldly in dealing
with their own kind.
9   'So I say to you, use your worldly wealth to win friends for yourselves, so that when money is a thing of the past you may be received
into an eternal home.
10   'The man who can be trusted in little things can be trusted also
in great; and the man who is dishonest in little things is dishonest
11 also in great things. If, then, you have not proved trustworthy with
the wealth of this world, who will trust you with the wealth that is
12 real? And if you have proved untrustworthy with what belongs to
another, who will give you what is your own?
13   'No servant can be the slave of two masters; for either he will
hate the first and love the second, or he will be devoted to the first
and think nothing of the second. You cannot serve God and Money.'
14   The Pharisees, who loved money, heard all this and scoffed at
15 him. He said to them, 'You are the people who impress your fellow-
men with your righteousness; but God sees through you; for what
sets itself up to be admired by men is detestable in the sight of God.
16   'Until John, it was the Law and the prophets: since then, there
is the good news of the kingdom of God, and everyone forces his
way in.
17   'It is easier for heaven and earth to come to an end than for one
dot or stroke of the Law to lose its force.
18   'A man who divorces his wife and marries another commits
adultery; and anyone who marries a woman divorced from her
husband commits adultery.
19   'There was once a rich man, who dressed in purple and the finest
20 linen, and feasted in great magnificence every day. At his gate,
21 covered with sores, lay a poor man named Lazarus, who would
have been glad to satisfy his hunger with the scraps from the rich

man's table. Even the dogs used to come and lick his sores. One ₂₂
day the poor man died and was carried away by the angels to be
with Abraham. The rich man also died and was buried, and in Hades, ₂₃
where he was in torment, he looked up; and there, far away, was
Abraham with Lazarus close beside him. "Abraham, my father," ₂₄
he called out, "take pity on me! Send Lazarus to dip the tip of his
finger in water, to cool my tongue, for I am in agony in this fire."
But Abraham said, "Remember, my child, that all the good things ₂₅
fell to you while you were alive, and all the bad to Lazarus; now
he has his consolation here and it is you who are in agony. But that ₂₆
is not all: there is a great chasm fixed between us; no one from our
side who wants to reach you can cross it, and none may pass from
your side to us." "Then, father," he replied, "will you send him to ₂₇
my father's house, where I have five brothers, to warn them, so ₂₈
that they too may not come to this place of torment?" But Abraham ₂₉
said, "They have Moses and the prophets; let them listen to them."
"No, father Abraham," he replied, "but if someone from the dead ₃₀
visits them, they will repent." Abraham answered, "If they do not ₃₁
listen to Moses and the prophets they will pay no heed even if
someone should rise from the dead."'

HE SAID to his disciples, 'Causes of stumbling are bound to arise; 17
but woe betide the man through whom they come. It would be ₂
better for him to be thrown into the sea with a millstone round his
neck than to cause one of these little ones to stumble. Keep watch ₃
on yourselves.

'If your brother wrongs you, rebuke him; and if he repents,
forgive him. Even if he wrongs you seven times in a day and comes ₄
back to you seven times saying, "I am sorry", you are to forgive
him.'

The apostles said to the Lord, 'Increase our faith'; and the Lord ₅,₆
replied, 'If you had faith no bigger even than a mustard-seed, you
could say to this sycamore-tree, "Be rooted up and replanted in
the sea"; and it would at once obey you.

'Suppose one of you has a servant ploughing or minding sheep. ₇
When he comes back from the fields, will the master say, "Come
along at once and sit down"? Will he not rather say, "Prepare my ₈
supper, buckle your belt, and then wait on me while I have my meal;
you can have yours afterwards"? Is he grateful to the servant for ₉

131

10 carrying out his orders? So with you: when you have carried out all your orders, you should say, "We are servants and deserve no credit; we have only done our duty."'

11 In the course of his journey to Jerusalem he was travelling through
12 the borderlands of Samaria and Galilee. As he was entering a village he was met by ten men with leprosy. They stood some way off
13, 14 and called out to him, 'Jesus, Master, take pity on us.' When he saw them he said, 'Go and show yourselves to the priests'; and while
15 they were on their way, they were made clean. One of them, finding
16 himself cured, turned back praising God aloud. He threw himself down at Jesus's feet and thanked him. And he was a Samaritan.
17 At this Jesus said: 'Were not all ten cleansed? The other nine,
18 where are they? Could none be found to come back and give praise
19 to God except this foreigner?' And he said to the man, 'Stand up and go on your way; your faith has cured you.'

20 THE PHARISEES asked him, 'When will the kingdom of God come?' He said, 'You cannot tell by observation when the kingdom of God
21 comes. There will be no saying, "Look, here it is!" or "there it is!"; for in fact the kingdom of God is among you.'*ᵃ*
22 He said to the disciples, 'The time will come when you will long to see one of the days of the Son of Man, but you will not see it.
23 They will say to you, "Look! There!" and "Look! Here!" Do not
24 go running off in pursuit. For like the lightning-flash that lights up the earth from end to end, will the Son of Man be when his day
25 comes. But first he must endure much suffering and be repudiated by this generation.
26 'As things were in Noah's days, so will they be in the days of the
27 Son of Man. They ate and drank and married, until the day that Noah went into the ark and the flood came and made an end of them
28 all. As things were in Lot's days, also: they ate and drank; they
29 bought and sold; they planted and built; but the day that Lot went out from Sodom, it rained fire and sulphur from heaven and made
30 an end of them all—it will be like that on the day when the Son of Man is revealed.
31 'On that day the man who is on the roof and his belongings in the house must not come down to pick them up; he, too, who is in the

[a] *Or* for in fact the kingdom of God is within you, *or* for in fact the kingdom of God is within your grasp, *or* for suddenly the kingdom of God will be among you.

fields must not go back. Remember Lot's wife. Whoever seeks to 32, 33
save his life will lose it; and whoever loses it will save it, and live.

'I tell you, on that night there will be two men in one bed: one 34
will be taken, the other left. There will be two women together 35
grinding corn: one will be taken, the other left.'ᵃ When they heard 37
this they asked, 'Where, Lord?' He said, 'Where the corpse is,
there the vultures will gather.'

HE SPOKE to them in a parable to show that they should keep on 18
praying and never lose heart: 'There was once a judge who cared 2
nothing for God or man, and in the same town there was a widow 3
who constantly came before him demanding justice against her
opponent. For a long time he refused; but in the end he said to 4
himself, "True, I care nothing for God or man; but this widow is so 5
great a nuisance that I will see her righted before she wears me out
with her persistence."' The Lord said, 'You hear what the unjust 6
judge says; and will not God vindicate his chosen, who cry out 7
to him day and night, while he listens patiently to themᵇ? I tell you, 8
he will vindicate them soon enough. But when the Son of Man
comes, will he find faith on earth?'

And here is another parable that he told. It was aimed at those 9
who were sure of their own goodness and looked down on everyone
else. 'Two men went up to the temple to pray, one a Pharisee and 10
the other a tax-gatherer. The Pharisee stood up and prayed thus:ᶜ 11
"I thank thee, O God, that I am not like the rest of men, greedy,
dishonest, adulterous; or, for that matter, like this tax-gatherer.
I fast twice a week; I pay tithes on all that I get." But the other kept 12, 13
his distance and would not even raise his eyes to heaven, but beat
upon his breast, saying, "O God, have mercy on me, sinner that
I am." It was this man, I tell you, and not the other, who went 14
home acquitted of his sins. For everyone who exalts himself will
be humbled; and whoever humbles himself will be exalted.'

They even brought babies for him to touch; but when the dis- 15
ciples saw them they scolded them for it. But Jesus called for the 16
children and said, 'Let the little ones come to me; do not try to
stop them; for the kingdom of God belongs to such as these. I tell 17

[a] *Some witnesses add* (36) two men in the fields: one will be taken, the other left.
[b] *Or* delays to help them. [c] *Some witnesses read* stood up by himself and prayed
thus; *others read* stood up and prayed thus privately.

you that whoever does not accept the kingdom of God like a child will never enter it.'

18 A man of the ruling class put this question to him: 'Good Master,
19 what must I do to win eternal life?' Jesus said to him, 'Why do you
20 call me good? No one is good except God alone. You know the commandments: "Do not commit adultery; do not murder; do not steal; do not give false evidence; honour your father and mother."'
21, 22 The man answered, 'I have kept all these since I was a boy.' On hearing this Jesus said, 'There is still one thing lacking: sell everything you have and distribute to the poor, and you will have riches
23 in heaven; and come, follow me.' At these words his heart sank;
24 for he was a very rich man. When Jesus saw it he said, 'How hard
25 it is for the wealthy to enter the kingdom of God! It is easier for a camel to go through the eye of a needle than for a rich man to enter
26 the kingdom of God.' Those who heard asked, 'Then who can be
27 saved?' He answered, 'What is impossible for men is possible for God.'
28 Peter said, 'Here are we who gave up our belongings to become
29 your followers.' Jesus said, 'I tell you this: there is no one who has given up home, or wife, brothers, parents, or children, for the sake
30 of the kingdom of God, who will not be repaid many times over in this age, and in the age to come have eternal life.'

Challenge to Jerusalem

31 HE TOOK the Twelve aside and said, 'We are now going up to Jerusalem; and all that was written by the prophets will come
32 true for the Son of Man. He will be handed over to the foreign
33 power. He will be mocked, maltreated, and spat upon. They will flog him and kill him. And on the third day he will rise again.'
34 But they understood nothing of all this; they did not grasp what he was talking about; its meaning was concealed from them.
35 As he approached Jericho a blind man sat at the roadside begging.
36, 37 Hearing a crowd going past, he asked what was happening. They
38 told him, 'Jesus of Nazareth is passing by.' Then he shouted out,
39 'Jesus, Son of David, have pity on me.' The people in front told him sharply to hold his tongue; but he called out all the more, 'Son of

David, have pity on me.' Jesus stopped and ordered the man to be 40
brought to him. When he came up he asked him, 'What do you 41
want me to do for you?' 'Sir, I want my sight back', he answered.
Jesus said to him, 'Have back your sight; your faith has cured you.' 42
He recovered his sight instantly; and he followed Jesus, praising 43
God. And all the people gave praise to God for what they had
seen.

Entering Jericho he made his way through the city. There was 19 1, 2
a man there named Zacchaeus; he was superintendent of taxes and
very rich. He was eager to see what Jesus looked like; but, being 3
a little man, he could not see him for the crowd. So he ran on ahead 4
and climbed a sycamore-tree in order to see him, for he was to pass
that way. When Jesus came to the place, he looked up and said, 5
'Zacchaeus, be quick and come down; I must come and stay with
you today.' He climbed down as fast as he could and welcomed him 6
gladly. At this there was a general murmur of disapproval. 'He 7
has gone in', they said, 'to be the guest of a sinner.' But Zacchaeus 8
stood there and said to the Lord, 'Here and now, sir, I give half
my possessions to charity; and if I have cheated anyone, I am ready
to repay him four times over.' Jesus said to him, 'Salvation has come 9
to this house today!—for this man too is a son of Abraham, and the 10
Son of Man has come to seek and save what is lost.'

While they were listening to this, he went on to tell them a parable, 11
because he was now close to Jerusalem and they thought the reign of
God might dawn at any moment. He said, 'A man of noble birth 12
went on a long journey abroad, to be appointed king and then return.
But first he called ten of his servants and gave them a pound each, 13
saying, "Trade with this while I am away." His fellow-citizens hated 14
him, and they sent a delegation on his heels to say, "We do not want
this man as our king." However, back he came as king, and sent for 15
the servants to whom he had given the money, to see what profit
each had made. The first came and said, "Your pound, sir, has made 16
ten more." "Well done," he replied; "you are a good servant. You 17
have shown yourself trustworthy in a very small matter, and you
shall have charge of ten cities." The second came and said, "Your 18
pound, sir, has made five more"; and he also was told, "You too, take 19
charge of five cities." The third came and said, "Here is your pound, 20
sir; I kept it put away in a handkerchief. I was afraid of you, 21
because you are a hard man: you draw out what you never put in

22 and reap what you did not sow." "You rascal!" he replied; "I will judge you by your own words. You knew, did you, that I am a hard man, that I draw out what I never put in, and reap what I did not
23 sow? Then why did you not put my money on deposit, and I could
24 have claimed it with interest when I came back?" Turning to his attendants he said, "Take the pound from him and give it to the man
25, 26 with ten." "But, sir," they replied, "he has ten already." "I tell you," he went on, "the man who has will always be given more; but the
27 man who has not will forfeit even what he has. But as for those enemies of mine who did not want me for their king, bring them here and slaughter them in my presence." '

28 WITH THAT Jesus went forward and began the ascent to Jerusalem.
29 As he approached Bethphage and Bethany at the hill called Olivet,
30 he sent two of the disciples with these instructions: 'Go to the village opposite; as you enter it you will find tethered there a
31 colt which no one has yet ridden. Untie it and bring it here. If anyone asks why you are untying it, say, "Our Master needs it." '
32 The two went on their errand and found it as he had told them;
33 and while they were untying the colt, its owners asked, 'Why are
34 you untying that colt?' They answered, 'The Master needs it.'
35 So they brought the colt to Jesus.
   Then they threw their cloaks on the colt, for Jesus to mount,
36 and they carpeted the road with them as he went on his way.
37 And now, as he approached the descent from the Mount of Olives, the whole company of his disciples in their joy began to sing aloud the praises of God for all the things they had seen:

38   'Blessings on him who comes as king in the name of the Lord!
      Peace in heaven, glory in highest heaven!'

39   Some Pharisees who were in the crowd said to him, 'Master,
40 reprimand your disciples.' He answered, 'I tell you, if my disciples keep silence the stones will shout aloud.'
41, 42   When he came in sight of the city, he wept over it and said, 'If only you had known, on this great day, the way that leads to
43 peace! But no; it is hidden from your sight. For a time will come upon you, when your enemies will set up siege-works against you;
44 they will encircle you and hem you in at every point; they will bring you to the ground, you and your children within your walls, and

not leave you one stone standing on another, because you did not
recognize God's moment when it came.'

Then he went into the temple and began driving out the traders, 45
with these words: 'Scripture says, "My house shall be a house of 46
prayer"; but you have made it a robbers' cave.'

Day by day he taught in the temple. And the chief priests and 47
lawyers were bent on making an end of him, with the support of
the leading citizens, but found they were helpless, because the people 48
all hung upon his words.

ONE DAY, as he was teaching the people in the temple and telling 20
them the good news, the priests and lawyers, and the elders with
them, came upon him and accosted him. 'Tell us', they said, 'by 2
what authority you are acting like this; who gave you this authority?'
He answered them, 'I have a question to ask you too: tell me, 3
was the baptism of John from God or from men?' This set them 4, 5
arguing among themselves: 'If we say, "from God", he will say,
"Why did you not believe him?" And if we say, "from men", the 6
people will all stone us, for they are convinced that John was a
prophet.' So they replied that they could not tell. And Jesus said 7, 8
to them, 'Neither will I tell you by what authority I act.'

He went on to tell the people this parable: 'A man planted a 9
vineyard, let it out to vine-growers, and went abroad for a long time.
When the season came, he sent a servant to the tenants to collect 10
from them his share of the produce; but the tenants thrashed him
and sent him away empty-handed. He tried again and sent a second 11
servant; but he also was thrashed, outrageously treated, and sent
away empty-handed. He tried once more with a third; this one too 12
they wounded and flung out. Then the owner of the vineyard said, 13
"What am I to do? I will send my own dear son;*a* perhaps they will
respect him." But when the tenants saw him they talked it over 14
together. "This is the heir," they said; "let us kill him so that the
property may come to us." So they flung him out of the vineyard 15
and killed him. What then will the owner of the vineyard do to them?
He will come and put these tenants to death and let the vineyard to 16
others.'

When they heard this, they said, 'God forbid!' But he looked 17
straight at them and said, 'Then what does this text of Scripture

[a] *Or* my only son.

137

mean: "The stone which the builders rejected has become the main
18 corner-stone"? Any man who falls on that stone will be dashed to
pieces; and if it falls on a man he will be crushed by it.'
19   The lawyers and chief priests wanted to lay hands on him there
and then, for they saw that this parable was aimed at them; but
20 they were afraid of the people. So they watched their opportunity
and sent secret agents in the guise of honest men, to seize upon
some word of his as a pretext for handing him over to the authority
21 and jurisdiction of the Governor. They put a question to him:
'Master,' they said, 'we know that what you speak and teach is
sound; you pay deference to no one, but teach in all honesty the
22 way of life that God requires. Are we or are we not permitted to
23 pay taxes to the Roman Emperor?' He saw through their trick and
24 said, 'Show me a silver piece. Whose head does it bear, and whose
25 inscription?' 'Caesar's', they replied. 'Very well then,' he said,
'pay Caesar what is due to Caesar, and pay God what is due to
26 God.' Thus their attempt to catch him out in public failed, and,
astonished by his reply, they fell silent.
27   Then some Sadducees came forward. They are the people who
28 deny that there is a resurrection. Their question was this: 'Master,
Moses laid it down for us that if there are brothers, and one dies
leaving a wife but no child, then the next should marry the widow
29 and carry on his brother's family. Now, there were seven brothers:
30 the first took a wife and died childless; then the second married her,
31 then the third. In this way the seven of them died leaving no
32, 33 children. Afterwards the woman also died. At the resurrection
34 whose wife is she to be, since all seven had married her?' Jesus said
35 to them, 'The men and women of this world marry; but those who
have been judged worthy of a place in the other world and of the
36 resurrection from the dead, do not marry, for they are not subject
to death any longer. They are like angels; they are sons of God,
37 because they share in the resurrection. That the dead are raised
to life again is shown by Moses himself in the story of the burning
bush, when he calls the Lord, "the God of Abraham, Isaac, and
38 Jacob". God is not God of the dead but of the living; for him all
are[a] alive.'
39, 40   At this some of the lawyers said, 'Well spoken, Master.' For there
was no further question that they ventured to put to him.

[a] *Or* they are all.

138

He said to them, 'How can they say that the Messiah is son of 41
David? For David himself says in the Book of Psalms: "The Lord 42
said to my Lord, 'Sit at my right hand until I make your enemies 43
your footstool.'" Thus David calls him "Lord"; how then can he be 44
David's son?'

In the hearing of all the people Jesus said to his disciples: 'Beware 45, 46
of the lawyers who love to walk up and down in long robes, and have
a great liking for respectful greetings in the street, the chief seats
in our synagogues, and places of honour at feasts. These are the men 47
who eat up the property of widows, while they say long prayers for
appearance' sake; and they will receive the severest sentence.'

He looked up and saw the rich people dropping their gifts into 21
the chest of the temple treasury; and he noticed a poor widow 2
putting in two tiny coins. 'I tell you this,' he said: 'this poor widow 3
has given more than any of them; for those others who have given 4
had more than enough, but she, with less than enough, has given
all she had to live on.'

SOME PEOPLE were talking about the temple and the fine stones 5
and votive offerings with which it was adorned. He said, 'These 6
things which you are gazing at—the time will come when not one
stone of them will be left upon another: all will be thrown down.'
'Master,' they asked, 'when will it all come about? What will be 7
the sign when it is due to happen?'

He said, 'Take care that you are not misled. For many will come 8
claiming my name and saying, "I am he", and, "The Day is upon us."
Do not follow them. And when you hear of wars and insurrections, 9
do not fall into a panic. These things are bound to happen first;
but the end does not follow immediately. Nation will make war 10
upon nation, kingdom upon kingdom; there will be great earth- 11
quakes, and famines and plagues in many places; in the sky terrors
and great portents.

'But before all this happens they will set upon you and persecute 12
you. You will be brought before synagogues and put in prison;
you will be haled before kings and governors for your allegiance
to me. This will be your opportunity to testify; so make up your 13, 14
minds not to prepare your defence beforehand, because I myself 15
will give you power of utterance and a wisdom which no opponent
will be able to resist or refute. Even your parents and brothers, 16

your relations and friends, will betray you. Some of you will be put

17 to death; and you will be hated by all for your allegiance to me.

18, 19 But not a hair of your head shall be lost. By standing firm you will win true life for yourselves.

20 'But when you see Jerusalem encircled by armies, then you may

21 be sure that her destruction is near. Then those who are in Judaea must take to the hills; those who are in the city itself must leave it,

22 and those who are out in the country must not enter; because this is the time of retribution, when all that stands written is to be

23 fulfilled. Alas for women who are with child in those days, or have children at the breast! For there will be great distress in the land

24 and a terrible judgement upon this people. They will fall at the sword's point; they will be carried captive into all countries; and Jerusalem will be trampled down by foreigners until their day has run its course.

25 'Portents will appear in sun, moon, and stars. On earth nations will stand helpless, not knowing which way to turn from the roar

26 and surge of the sea; men will faint with terror at the thought of all that is coming upon the world; for the celestial powers will be

27 shaken. And then they will see the Son of Man coming on a cloud

28 with great power and glory. When all this begins to happen, stand upright and hold your heads high, because your liberation is near.'

29 He told them this parable: 'Look at the fig-tree, or any other

30 tree. As soon as it buds, you can see for yourselves that summer is

31 near. In the same way when you see all this happening, you may be sure that the kingdom of God is near.

32 'I tell you this: the present generation will live to see it all.

33 Heaven and earth will pass away; my words will never pass away.

34 'Keep a watch on yourselves; do not let your minds be dulled by dissipation and drunkenness and worldly cares so that the great Day

35 closes upon you suddenly like a trap; for that day will come on all

36 men, wherever they are, the whole world over. Be on the alert, praying at all times for strength to pass safely through all these imminent troubles and to stand in the presence of the Son of Man.'

37 His days were given to teaching in the temple; and then he would

38 leave the city and spend the night on the hill called Olivet. And in the early morning the people flocked to listen to him in the temple.[a]

[a] *Some witnesses here insert the passage printed on p. 193.*

The Final Conflict

NOW THE FESTIVAL of Unleavened Bread, known as Passover, 22
was approaching, and the chief priests and the doctors of the 2
law were trying to devise some means of doing away with him; for
they were afraid of the people.

Then Satan entered into Judas Iscariot, who was one of the 3
Twelve; and Judas went to the chief priests and officers of the 4
temple police to discuss ways and means of putting Jesus into their
power. They were greatly pleased and undertook to pay him a sum 5
of money. He agreed, and began to look out for an opportunity to 6
betray him to them without collecting a crowd.

Then came the day of Unleavened Bread, on which the Passover 7
victim had to be slaughtered, and Jesus sent Peter and John with 8
these instructions: 'Go and prepare for our Passover supper.'
'Where would you like us to make the preparations?' they asked. 9
He replied, 'As soon as you set foot in the city a man will meet you 10
carrying a jar of water. Follow him into the house that he enters
and give this message to the householder: "The Master says, 'Where 11
is the room in which I may eat the Passover with my disciples?'" He 12
will show you a large room upstairs all set out: make the preparations
there.' They went and found everything as he had said. So they 13
prepared for Passover.

When the time came he took his place at table, and the apostles with 14
him; and he said to them, 'How I have longed[a] to eat this Passover 15
with you before my death! For I tell you, never again shall I[b] eat 16
it until the time when it finds its fulfilment in the kingdom of God.'

Then he took a cup, and after giving thanks he said, 'Take this 17
and share it among yourselves; for I tell you, from this moment I 18
shall drink from the fruit of the vine no more until the time when
the kingdom of God comes.' And he took bread, gave thanks, 19
and broke it; and he gave it to them, with the words: 'This is my
body.'[c]

[a] Or said to them, 'I longed...' [b] Some witnesses read For I tell you, I shall not...
[c] Some witnesses add, in whole or in part, and with various arrangements, the following:
'which is given for you; do this as a memorial of me.' (20) In the same way he took
the cup after supper, and said, 'This cup, poured out for you, is the new covenant
sealed by my blood.'

21 'But mark this—my betrayer is here, his hand with mine on the
22 table. For the Son of Man is going his appointed way; but alas for
23 that man by whom he is betrayed!' At this they began to ask among
themselves which of them it could possibly be who was to do this
thing.
24   Then a jealous dispute broke out: who among them should rank
25 highest? But he said, 'In the world, kings lord it over their subjects;
26 and those in authority are called their country's "Benefactors". Not
so with you: on the contrary, the highest among you must bear
27 himself like the youngest, the chief of you like a servant. For who
is greater—the one who sits at table or the servant who waits on
him? Surely the one who sits at table. Yet here am I among you
like a servant.
28   'You are the men who have stood firmly by me in my times of
29 trial; and now I vest in you the kingship which my Father vested
30 in me; you shall eat and drink at my table in my kingdom and sit*
on thrones as judges of the twelve tribes of Israel.
31   'Simon, Simon, take heed: Satan has been given leave to sift all
32 of you like wheat; but for you I have prayed that your faith may not
fail; and when you have come to yourself, you must lend strength
33 to your brothers.' 'Lord,' he replied, 'I am ready to go with you
34 to prison and death.' Jesus said, 'I tell you, Peter, the cock will
not crow tonight until you have three times over denied that you
know me.'
35   He said to them, 'When I sent you out barefoot without purse or
36 pack, were you ever short of anything?' 'No', they answered. 'It
is different now,' he said; 'whoever has a purse had better take it
with him, and his pack too; and if he has no sword, let him sell his
37 cloak to buy one. For Scripture says, "And he was counted among
the outlaws", and these words, I tell you, must find fulfilment in
38 me; indeed, all that is written of me is being fulfilled.' 'Look,
Lord,' they said, 'we have two swords here.' 'Enough, enough!'
he replied.

39 THEN HE WENT out and made his way as usual to the Mount of
40 Olives, accompanied by the disciples. When he reached the place
he said to them, 'Pray that you may be spared the hour of testing.'

[a] *Or* trial; and as my Father gave me the right to reign, so I give you the right to
eat and to drink...and to sit...

He himself withdrew from them about a stone's throw, knelt down, 41
and began to pray: 'Father, if it be thy will, take this cup away 42
from me. Yet not my will but thine be done.'

And now there appeared to him an angel from heaven bringing 43
him strength, and in anguish of spirit he prayed the more urgently; 44
and his sweat was like clots of blood falling to the ground.[a]

When he rose from prayer and came to the disciples he found 45
them asleep, worn out by grief. 'Why are you sleeping?' he said. 46
'Rise and pray that you may be spared the test.'

WHILE HE WAS still speaking a crowd appeared with the man called 47
Judas, one of the Twelve, at their head. He came up to Jesus to
kiss him; but Jesus said, 'Judas, would you betray the Son of Man 48
with a kiss?'

When his followers saw what was coming, they said, 'Lord, shall 49
we use our swords?' And one of them struck at the High Priest's 50
servant, cutting off his right ear. But Jesus answered, 'Let them 51
have their way.' Then he touched the man's ear and healed
him.[b]

Turning to the chief priests, the officers of the temple police, 52
and the elders, who had come to seize him, he said, 'Do you take
me for a bandit, that you have come out with swords and cudgels
to arrest me? Day after day, when I was in the temple with you, 53
you kept your hands off me. But this is your moment—the hour
when darkness reigns.'

Then they arrested him and led him away. They brought him to 54
the High Priest's house, and Peter followed at a distance. They lit 55
a fire in the middle of the courtyard and sat round it, and Peter sat
among them. A serving-maid who saw him sitting in the firelight 56
stared at him and said, 'This man was with him too.' But he denied 57
it: 'Woman,' he said, 'I do not know him.' A little later someone 58
else noticed him and said, 'You also are one of them.' But Peter
said to him, 'No, I am not.' About an hour passed and another 59
spoke more strongly still: 'Of course this fellow was with him.
He must have been; he is a Galilean.' But Peter said, 'Man, I do 60
not know what you are talking about.' At that moment, while he
was still speaking, a cock crew; and the Lord turned and looked 61

[a] *Some witnesses omit* And now...ground. [b] *Or* 'Let me do as much as this', and
touching the man's ear, he healed him.

straight at Peter. And Peter remembered the Lord's words, 'Tonight before the cock crows you will disown me three times.'*a*

63 The men who were guarding Jesus mocked at him. They beat
64 him, they blindfolded him, and they kept asking him, 'Now, prophet,
65 who hit you? Tell us that.' And so they went on heaping insults upon him.

66 WHEN DAY broke, the elders of the nation, chief priests, and doctors of the law assembled, and he was brought before their Council.
67 'Tell us,' they said, 'are you the Messiah?' 'If I tell you,' he replied,
68 'you will not believe me; and if I ask questions, you will not answer.
69 But from now on, the Son of Man will be seated at the right hand
70 of Almighty God.'*b* 'You are the Son of God, then?' they all said,
71 and he replied, 'It is you who say I am.'*c* They said, 'Need we call further witnesses? We have heard it ourselves from his own lips.'
23 With that the whole assembly rose, and they brought him before
2 Pilate. They opened the case against him by saying, 'We found this man subverting our nation, opposing the payment of taxes to Caesar,
3 and claiming to be Messiah, a king.'*d* Pilate asked him, 'Are you
4 the king of the Jews?' He replied, 'The words are yours.'*e* Pilate then said to the chief priests and the crowd, 'I find no case for this
5 man to answer.' But they insisted: 'His teaching is causing disaffection among the people all through Judaea. It started from Galilee and has spread as far as this city.'
6, 7 When Pilate heard this, he asked if the man was a Galilean, and on learning that he belonged to Herod's jurisdiction he remitted the
8 case to him, for Herod was also in Jerusalem at that time. When Herod saw Jesus he was greatly pleased; having heard about him, he had long been wanting to see him, and had been hoping to see
9 some miracle performed by him. He questioned him at some length
10 without getting any reply; but the chief priests and lawyers appeared
11 and pressed the case against him vigorously. Then Herod and his troops treated him with contempt and ridicule, and sent him back
12 to Pilate dressed in a gorgeous robe. That same day Herod and Pilate became friends: till then there had been a standing feud between them.

[*a*] *Some witnesses add* (62) He went outside, and wept bitterly, *as in Matthew 26. 75.*
[*b*] *Literally* of the Power of God. [*c*] *Or* You are right, for I am. [*d*] *Or* to be an anointed king. [*e*] *Or* It is as you say.

Pilate now called together the chief priests, councillors, and people, 13
and said to them, 'You brought this man before me on a charge of 14
subversion. But, as you see, I have myself examined him in your
presence and found nothing in him to support your charges. No 15
more did Herod, for he has referred him back to us. Clearly he has
done nothing to deserve death. I therefore propose to let him off 16
with a flogging.' But[a] there was a general outcry, 'Away with him! 18
Give us Barabbas.' (This man had been put in prison for a rising 19
that had taken place in the city, and for murder.) Pilate addressed 20
them again, in his desire to release Jesus, but they shouted back, 21
'Crucify him, crucify him!' For the third time he spoke to them: 22
'Why, what wrong has he done? I have not found him guilty of
any capital offence. I will therefore let him off with a flogging.' But 23
they insisted on their demand, shouting that Jesus should be crucified.
Their shouts prevailed and Pilate decided that they should have 24
their way. He released the man they asked for, the man who had 25
been put in prison for insurrection and murder, and gave Jesus up
to their will.

As they led him away to execution they seized upon a man called 26
Simon, from Cyrene, on his way in from the country, put the cross
on his back, and made him walk behind Jesus carrying it.

Great numbers of people followed, many women among them, 27
who mourned and lamented over him. Jesus turned to them and 28
said, 'Daughters of Jerusalem, do not weep for me; no, weep for
yourselves and your children. For the days are surely coming when 29
they will say, "Happy are the barren, the wombs that never bore a
child, the breasts that never fed one." Then they will start saying 30
to the mountains, "Fall on us", and to the hills, "Cover us." For if 31
these things are done when the wood is green, what will happen
when it is dry?'

There were two others with him, criminals who were being led 32
away to execution; and when they reached the place called The 33
Skull, they crucified him there, and the criminals with him, one on
his right and the other on his left. Jesus said, 'Father, forgive them; 34
they do not know what they are doing.'[b]

They divided his clothes among them by casting lots. The people 35

[a] *Some witnesses read* (17) At festival time he was obliged to release one person for
them; (18) and now... [b] *Some witnesses omit* Jesus said, 'Father...doing.'

stood looking on, and their rulers jeered at him: 'He saved others: now let him save himself, if this is God's Anointed, his Chosen.'
36 The soldiers joined in the mockery and came forward offering him
37 their sour wine. 'If you are the king of the Jews,' they said, 'save
38 yourself.' There was an inscription above his head which ran: 'This is the king of the Jews.'
39 One of the criminals who hung there with him taunted him: 'Are
40 not you the Messiah? Save yourself, and us.' But the other answered sharply, 'Have you no fear of God? You are under the same sen-
41 tence as he. For us it is plain justice; we are paying the price for
42 our misdeeds; but this man has done nothing wrong.' And he said,
43 'Jesus, remember me when you come to your throne.'*a* He answered, 'I tell you this: today you shall be with me in Paradise.'
44 By now it was about midday and there came a darkness over the
45 whole land, which lasted until three in the afternoon; the sun was
46 in eclipse. And the curtain of the temple was torn in two. Then Jesus gave a loud cry and said, 'Father, into thy hands I commit
47 my spirit'; and with these words he died. The centurion saw it all, and gave praise to God. 'Beyond all doubt', he said, 'this man was innocent.'
48 The crowd who had assembled for the spectacle, when they saw what had happened, went home beating their breasts.

49 HIS FRIENDS had all been standing at a distance; the women who had accompanied him from Galilee stood with them and watched it all.
50 Now there was a man called Joseph, a member of the Council,
51 a good, upright man, who had dissented from their policy and the action they had taken. He came from the Jewish town of Arima-thaea, and he was one who looked forward to the kingdom of God.
52 This man now approached Pilate and asked for the body of Jesus.
53 Taking it down from the cross, he wrapped it in a linen sheet, and laid it in a tomb cut out of the rock, in which no one had been laid
54 before. It was Friday, and the Sabbath was about to begin.
55 The women who had accompanied him from Galilee followed; they took note of the tomb and observed how his body was laid.
56 Then they went home and prepared spices and perfumes; and on
24 the Sabbath they rested in obedience to the commandment. But

[a] *Some witnesses read* come in royal power.

on the Sunday morning very early they came to the tomb bringing
the spices they had prepared. Finding that the stone had been 2
rolled away from the tomb, they went inside; but the body was not 3
to be found. While they stood utterly at a loss, all of a sudden two 4
men in dazzling garments were at their side. They were terrified, 5
and stood with eyes cast down, but the men said, 'Why search
among the dead for one who lives?*a* Remember what he told you 6
while he was still in Galilee, about the Son of Man: how he must 7
be given up into the power of sinful men and be crucified, and must
rise again on the third day.' Then they recalled his words and, 8,9
returning from the tomb, they reported all this to the Eleven and
all the others.

The women were Mary of Magdala, Joanna, and Mary the 10
mother*b* of James, and they, with the other women, told the
apostles. But the story appeared to them to be nonsense, and they 11
would not believe them.*c*

THAT SAME DAY two of them were on their way to a village called 13
Emmaus, which lay about seven miles from Jerusalem, and they 14
were talking together about all these happenings. As they talked 15
and discussed it with one another, Jesus himself came up and walked
along with them; but something held their eyes from seeing who it 16
was. He asked them, 'What is it you are debating as you walk?' 17
They halted, their faces full of gloom, and one, called Cleopas, 18
answered, 'Are you the only person staying in Jerusalem not to
know*d* what has happened there in the last few days?' 'What do 19
you mean?' he said. 'All this about Jesus of Nazareth,' they replied,
'a prophet powerful in speech and action before God and the whole
people; how our chief priests and rulers handed him over to be 20
sentenced to death, and crucified him. But we had been hoping that 21
he was the man to liberate Israel. What is more, this is the third
day since it happened, and now some women of our company have 22
astounded us: they went early to the tomb, but failed to find his 23
body, and returned with a story that they had seen a vision of angels
who told them he was alive. So some of our people went to the 24

[*a*] *Some witnesses insert* He is not here: he has risen. [*b*] *Or* wife, *or* daughter. [*c*] *Some
witnesses add* (12) Peter, however, got up and ran to the tomb, and, peering in, saw
the wrappings and nothing more; and he went home amazed at what had happened.
[*d*] *Or* Have you been staying by yourself in Jerusalem, that you do not know...

tomb and found things just as the women had said; but him they did not see.'

25 'How dull you are!' he answered. 'How slow to believe all that
26 the prophets said! Was the Messiah not bound to suffer thus before
27 entering upon his glory?' Then he began with Moses and all the prophets, and explained to them the passages which referred to himself in every part of the scriptures.

28 By this time they had reached the village to which they were
29 going, and he made as if to continue his journey, but they pressed him: 'Stay with us, for evening draws on, and the day is almost
30 over.' So he went in to stay with them. And when he had sat down with them at table, he took bread and said the blessing; he broke
31 the bread, and offered it to them. Then their eyes were opened, and
32 they recognized him; and he vanished from their sight. They said to one another, 'Did we not feel our hearts on fire as he talked with us on the road and explained the scriptures to us?'

33 Without a moment's delay they set out and returned to Jerusalem. There they found that the Eleven and the rest of the company had
34 assembled, and were saying, 'It is true: the Lord has risen; he has
35 appeared to Simon.' Then they gave their account of the events of their journey and told how he had been recognized by them at the breaking of the bread.

36 As they were talking about all this, there he was, standing among
37 them.*ᵃ* Startled and terrified, they thought they were seeing a ghost.
38 But he said, 'Why are you so perturbed? Why do questionings arise
39 in your minds? Look at my hands and feet. It is I myself. Touch me and see; no ghost has flesh and bones as you can see that I have.'*ᵇ*
41 They were still unconvinced, still wondering, for it seemed too good to be true. So he asked them, 'Have you anything here to eat?'
42, 43 They offered him a piece of fish they had cooked, which he took and ate before their eyes.

44 And he said to them, 'This is what I meant by saying, while I was still with you, that everything written about me in the Law of Moses and in the prophets and psalms was bound to be fulfilled.'
45, 46 Then he opened their minds to understand the scriptures. 'This', he said, 'is what is written: that the Messiah is to suffer death
47 and to rise from the dead on the third day, and that in his name

[*a*] *Some witnesses insert* And he said to them, 'Peace be with you!' [*b*] *Some witnesses insert* (40) After saying this he showed them his hands and feet.

repentance bringing the forgiveness of sins is to be proclaimed to all nations. Begin from Jerusalem: it is you who are the witnesses 48 to all this. And mark this: I am sending upon you my Father's 49 promised gift; so stay here in this city until you are armed with the power from above.'

Then he led them out as far as Bethany, and blessed them with 50 uplifted hands; and in the act of blessing he parted from them.*a* 51 And they*b* returned to Jerusalem with great joy, and spent all their 52, 53 time in the temple praising God.

[a] *Some witnesses add* and was carried up into heaven. [b] *Some witnesses insert* worshipped him and...

THE
GOSPEL ACCORDING TO
JOHN

The Coming of Christ

1 WHEN ALL THINGS began, the Word already was.*ᵃ*
The Word dwelt with God, and what God was, the
2 Word was. The Word, then, was with God at the begin-
3 ning, and through him all things came to be; no single thing was
4 created without him. All that came to be was alive with his life,*ᵇ*
5 and that life was the light of men. The light shines on in the dark,
and the darkness has never quenched it.

6,7 There appeared a man named John, sent from God; he came as
a witness to testify to the light, that all might become believers
8 through him. He was not himself the light; he came to bear witness
9 to the light. The real light which enlightens every man was even
then coming into the world.*ᶜ*

10 He was in the world;*ᵈ* but the world, though it owed its being to
11 him, did not recognize him. He entered his own realm, and his own
12 would not receive him. But to all who did receive him, to those
who have yielded him their allegiance, he gave the right to become
13 children of God, not born of any human stock, or by the fleshly
14 desire of a human father, but the offspring of God himself. So
the Word became flesh; he came to dwell among us, and we saw
his glory, such glory as befits the Father's only Son, full of grace
and truth.

15 Here is John's testimony to him: he cried aloud, 'This is the man
I meant when I said, "He comes after me, but takes rank before me";
for before I was born, he already was.'

16,17 Out of his full store we have all received grace upon grace; for
while the Law was given through Moses, grace and truth came

[a] *Or* The Word was at the creation. [b] *Or* no single created thing came into being
without him. There was life in him... [c] *Or* The light was in being, light absolute,
enlightening every man born into the world. [d] *Or* The Word, then, was in the
world.

through Jesus Christ. No one has ever seen God; but God's only 18
Son, he who is nearest to the Father's heart, he has made him
known.*

THIS IS the testimony which John gave when the Jews of Jerusalem 19
sent a deputation of priests and Levites to ask him who he was.
He confessed without reserve and avowed, 'I am not the Messiah.' 20
'What then? Are you Elijah?' 'No', he replied. 'Are you the prophet 21
we await?' He answered 'No.' 'Then who are you?' they asked. 22
'We must give an answer to those who sent us. What account do
you give of yourself?' He answered in the words of the prophet 23
Isaiah: 'I am a voice crying aloud in the wilderness, "Make the
Lord's highway straight."'
  Some Pharisees who were in the deputation asked him, 'If you 24, 25
are not the Messiah, nor Elijah, nor the prophet, why then are you
baptizing?' 'I baptize in water,' John replied, 'but among you, 26
though you do not know him, stands the one who is to come after 27
me. I am not good enough to unfasten his shoes.' This took place 28
at Bethany beyond Jordan, where John was baptizing.
  The next day he saw Jesus coming towards him. 'Look,' he said, 29
'there is the Lamb of God; it is he who takes away the sin of the
world. This is he of whom I spoke when I said, "After me a man is 30
coming who takes rank before me"; for before I was born, he already
was. I myself did not know who he was; but the very reason 31
why I came, baptizing in water, was that he might be revealed to
Israel.'
  John testified further: 'I saw the Spirit coming down from heaven 32
like a dove and resting upon him. I did not know him, but he who 33
sent me to baptize in water had told me, "When you see the Spirit
coming down upon someone and resting upon him you will know
that this is he who is to baptize in Holy Spirit." I saw it myself, and 34
I have borne witness. This is God's Chosen One.'*
  The next day again John was standing with two of his disciples 35
when Jesus passed by. John looked towards him and said, 'There is 36
the Lamb of God.' The two disciples heard him say this, and fol- 37
lowed Jesus. When he turned and saw them following him, he asked, 38

[a] *Some witnesses read* but the only one, the one nearest to the Father's heart, has made
him known; *others read* but the only one, himself God, the nearest to the Father's
heart, has made him known. [b] *Some witnesses read* This is the Son of God.

'What are you looking for?' They said, 'Rabbi' (which means a
39 teacher), 'where are you staying?' 'Come and see', he replied. So
they went and saw where he was staying, and spent the rest of the
day with him. It was then about four in the afternoon.
40   One of the two who followed Jesus after hearing what John said
41 was Andrew, Simon Peter's brother. The first thing he did was to
find*a* his brother Simon. He said to him, 'We have found the Mes-
42 siah' (which is the Hebrew for 'Christ'). He brought Simon to
Jesus, who looked him in the face, and said, 'You are Simon, son
of John. You shall be called Cephas' (that is, Peter, the Rock).
43   The next day Jesus decided to leave for Galilee. He met Philip,
44 who, like Andrew and Peter, came from Bethsaida, and said to him,
45 'Follow me.' Philip went to find Nathanael, and told him, 'We
have met the man spoken of by Moses in the Law, and by the
46 prophets: it is Jesus son of Joseph, from Nazareth.' 'Nazareth!'
Nathanael exclaimed; 'can anything good come from Nazareth?'
47 Philip said, 'Come and see.' When Jesus saw Nathanael coming, he
said, 'Here is an Israelite worthy of the name; there is nothing false
48 in him.' Nathanael asked him, 'How do you come to know me?'
Jesus replied, 'I saw you under the fig-tree before Philip spoke
49 to you.' 'Rabbi,' said Nathanael, 'you are the Son of God; you
50 are king of Israel.' Jesus answered, 'Is this the ground of your faith,
that I told you I saw you under the fig-tree? You shall see greater
51 things than that.' Then he added, 'In truth, in very truth I tell you
all, you shall see heaven wide open, and God's angels ascending and
descending upon the Son of Man.'

Christ the Giver of Life

2 ON THE THIRD DAY there was a wedding at Cana-in-Galilee.
2   The mother of Jesus was there, and Jesus and his disciples
3 were guests also. The wine gave out, so Jesus's mother said to him,
4 'They have no wine left.' He answered, 'Your concern, mother,
5 is not mine. My hour has not yet come.' His mother said to the
6 servants, 'Do whatever he tells you.' There were six stone water-jars
standing near, of the kind used for Jewish rites of purification; each

[a] *Some witnesses read* In the morning he found...

held from twenty to thirty gallons. Jesus said to the servants, 'Fill 7
the jars with water', and they filled them to the brim. 'Now draw 8
some off', he ordered, 'and take it to the steward of the feast'; and
they did so. The steward tasted the water now turned into wine, not 9
knowing its source; though the servants who had drawn the water
knew. He hailed the bridegroom and said, 'Everyone serves the 10
best wine first, and waits until the guests have drunk freely before
serving the poorer sort; but you have kept the best wine till now.'
    This deed at Cana-in-Galilee is the first of the signs by which 11
Jesus revealed his glory and led his disciples to believe in him.

AFTER THIS he went down to Capernaum in company with his 12
mother, his brothers, and his disciples, but they did not stay there
long. As it was near the time of the Jewish Passover, Jesus went up 13
to Jerusalem. There he found in the temple the dealers in cattle, 14
sheep, and pigeons, and the money-changers seated at their tables.
Jesus made a whip of cords and drove them out of the temple, sheep, 15
cattle, and all. He upset the tables of the money-changers, scattering
their coins. Then he turned on the dealers in pigeons: 'Take them 16
out,' he said; 'you must not turn my Father's house into a market.'
His disciples recalled the words of Scripture, 'Zeal for thy house 17
shall destroy me.' The Jews challenged Jesus: 'What sign', they 18
asked, 'can you show as authority for your action?' 'Destroy this 19
temple,' Jesus replied, 'and in three days I will raise it again.'
They said, 'It has taken forty-six years to build this temple. Are 20
you going to raise it again in three days?' But the temple he was 21
speaking of was his body. After his resurrection his disciples recalled 22
what he had said, and they believed the Scripture and the words
that Jesus had spoken.

WHILE HE WAS in Jerusalem for Passover many gave their allegiance 23
to him when they saw the signs that he performed. But Jesus for 24
his part would not trust himself to them. He knew men so well, all
of them, that he needed no evidence from others about a man, for 25
he himself could tell what was in a man.

THERE WAS one of the Pharisees named Nicodemus, a member of 3
the Jewish Council, who came to Jesus by night. 'Rabbi,' he said, 2
'we know that you are a teacher sent by God; no one could perform

3 these signs of yours unless God were with him.' Jesus answered,
'In truth, in very truth I tell you, unless a man has been born over
4 again he cannot see the kingdom of God.' 'But how is it possible',
said Nicodemus, 'for a man to be born when he is old? Can he enter
5 his mother's womb a second time and be born?' Jesus answered,
'In truth I tell you, no one can enter the kingdom of God without
6 being born from water and spirit. Flesh can give birth only to flesh;
7 it is spirit that gives birth to spirit. You ought not to be astonished,
8 then, when I tell you that you must be born over again. The wind*a*
blows where it wills; you hear the sound of it, but you do not know
where it comes from, or where it is going. So with everyone who is
born from spirit*a*.'
9, 10   Nicodemus replied, 'How is this possible?' 'What!' said Jesus.
11 'Is this famous teacher of Israel ignorant of such things? In very
truth I tell you, we speak of what we know, and testify to what we
12 have seen, and yet you all reject our testimony. If you disbelieve me
when I talk to you about things on earth, how are you to believe
if I should talk about the things of heaven?
13   'No one ever went up into heaven except the one who came down
14 from heaven, the Son of Man whose home is in heaven.*b* This Son
of Man must be lifted up as the serpent was lifted up by Moses in
15 the wilderness, so that everyone who has faith in him may in him
possess eternal life.
16   'God loved the world so much that he gave his only Son, that
everyone who has faith in him may not die but have eternal life.
17 It was not to judge the world that God sent his Son into the world,
but that through him the world might be saved.
18   'The man who puts his faith in him does not come under judgement; but the unbeliever has already been judged in that he has
19 not given his allegiance to God's only Son. Here lies the test: the
light has come into the world, but men preferred darkness to light
20 because their deeds were evil. Bad men all hate the light and avoid
21 it, for fear their practices should be shown up. The honest man comes
to the light so that it may be clearly seen that God is in all he does.'

22 AFTER THIS, Jesus went into Judaea with his disciples, stayed
23 there with them, and baptized. John too was baptizing at Aenon,

[a] *A single Greek word with both meanings.* [b] *Some witnesses omit* whose home is in
heaven.

near to Salim, because water was plentiful in that region; and
people were constantly coming for baptism. This was before John's 24
imprisonment.

Some of John's disciples had fallen into a dispute with Jews about 25
purification; so they came to him and said, 'Rabbi, there was a man 26
with you on the other side of the Jordan, to whom you bore your
witness. Here he is, baptizing, and crowds are flocking to him.'
John's answer was: 'A man can have only what God gives him. 27
You yourselves can testify that I said, "I am not the Messiah; I 28
have been sent as his forerunner." It is the bridegroom to whom 29
the bride belongs. The bridegroom's friend, who stands by and
listens to him, is overjoyed at hearing the bridegroom's voice. This
joy, this perfect joy, is now mine. As he grows greater, I must grow 30
less.'

He who comes from above is above all others; he who is from the 31
earth belongs to the earth and uses earthly speech. He who comes
from heaven*a* bears witness to what he has seen and heard, yet 32
no one accepts his witness. To accept his witness is to attest that 33
God speaks true; for he whom God sent utters the words of God, 34
so measureless is God's gift of the Spirit. The Father loves the 35
Son and has entrusted him with all authority. He who puts his 36
faith in the Son has hold of eternal life, but he who disobeys the Son
shall not see that life; God's wrath rests upon him.

A REPORT now reached the Pharisees: 'Jesus is winning and bap- 4
tizing more disciples than John'; although, in fact, it was only the 2
disciples who were baptizing and not Jesus himself. When Jesus
learned this, he left Judaea and set out once more for Galilee. 3
He had to pass through Samaria, and on his way came to a Samaritan 4, 5
town called Sychar, near the plot of ground which Jacob gave to
his son Joseph and the spring called Jacob's well. It was about noon, 6
and Jesus, tired after his journey, sat down by the well.

The disciples had gone away to the town to buy food. Meanwhile 8, 7
a Samaritan woman came to draw water. Jesus said to her, 'Give me
a drink.' The Samaritan woman said, 'What! You, a Jew, ask a drink 9
of me, a Samaritan woman?' (Jews and Samaritans, it should be
noted, do not use vessels in common.*b*) Jesus answered her, 'If only 10

[a] *Some witnesses insert* is above all and... [b] *Or* Jews, it should be noted, are not on
familiar terms with Samaritans; *some witnesses omit these words.*

you knew what God gives, and who it is that is asking you for a drink, you would have asked him and he would have given you living water.'

11 'Sir,' the woman said, 'you have no bucket and this well is deep.
12 How can you give me "living water"? Are you a greater man than Jacob our ancestor, who gave us the well, and drank from it himself,
13 he and his sons, and his cattle too?' Jesus said, 'Everyone who drinks
14 this water will be thirsty again, but whoever drinks the water that I shall give him will never suffer thirst any more. The water that I shall give him will be an inner spring always welling up for eternal
15 life.' 'Sir,' said the woman, 'give me that water, and then I shall not be thirsty, nor have to come all this way to draw.'

16 Jesus replied, 'Go home, call your husband and come back.'
17 She answered, 'I have no husband.' 'You are right', said Jesus,
18 'in saying that you have no husband, for, although you have had five husbands, the man with whom you are now living is not your
19 husband; you told me the truth there.' 'Sir,' she replied, 'I can see
20 that you are a prophet. Our fathers worshipped on this mountain, but you Jews say that the temple where God should be worshipped
21 is in Jerusalem.' 'Believe me,' said Jesus, 'the time is coming when you will worship the Father neither on this mountain, nor in
22 Jerusalem. You Samaritans worship without knowing what you worship, while we worship what we know. It is from the Jews that
23 salvation comes. But the time approaches, indeed it is already here, when those who are real worshippers will worship the Father in spirit and in truth. Such are the worshippers whom the Father
24 wants. God is spirit, and those who worship him must worship in
25 spirit and in truth.' The woman answered, 'I know that Messiah' (that is Christ) 'is coming. When he comes he will tell us every-
26 thing.' Jesus said, 'I am he, I who am speaking to you now.'

27 At that moment his disciples returned, and were astonished to find him talking with a woman; but none of them said, 'What do you
28 want?' or, 'Why are you talking with her?' The woman put down her water-jar and went away to the town, where she said to the
29 people, 'Come and see a man who has told me everything I ever did.
30 Could this be the Messiah?' They came out of the town and made their way towards him.

31 Meanwhile the disciples were urging him, 'Rabbi, have something
32 to eat.' But he said, 'I have food to eat of which you know nothing.'
33 At this the disciples said to one another, 'Can someone have brought

him food?' But Jesus said, 'It is meat and drink for me to do the will 34
of him who sent me until I have finished his work.

'Do you not say, "Four months more and then comes harvest"? 35
But look, I tell you, look round on the fields; they are already white,
ripe for harvest. The reaper is drawing his pay and gathering a crop 36
for eternal life, so that sower and reaper may rejoice together.
That is how the saying comes true: "One sows, and another reaps." 37
I sent you to reap a crop for which you have not toiled. Others toiled 38
and you have come in for the harvest of their toil.'

Many Samaritans of that town came to believe in him because 39
of the woman's testimony: 'He told me everything I ever did.'
So when these Samaritans had come to him they pressed him to stay 40
with them; and he stayed there two days. Many more became 41
believers because of what they heard from his own lips. They told 42
the woman, 'It is no longer because of what you said that we believe,
for we have heard him ourselves; and we know that this is in truth
the Saviour of the world.'

WHEN the two days were over he set out for Galilee; for Jesus 43, 44
himself declared that a prophet is without honour in his own
country. On his arrival in Galilee the Galileans gave him a welcome, 45
because they had seen all that he did at the festival in Jerusalem;
they had been at the festival themselves.

Once again he visited Cana-in-Galilee, where he had turned the 46
water into wine. An officer in the royal service was there, whose
son was lying ill at Capernaum. When he heard that Jesus had come 47
from Judaea into Galilee, he came to him and begged him to go
down and cure his son, who was at the point of death. Jesus said 48
to him, 'Will none of you ever believe without seeing signs and
portents?' The officer pleaded with him, 'Sir, come down before my 49
boy dies.' Then Jesus said, 'Return home; your son will live.' The man 50
believed what Jesus said and started for home. When he was on his 51
way down his servants met him with the news, 'Your boy is going
to live.' So he asked them what time it was when he got better. 52
They said, 'Yesterday at one in the afternoon the fever left him.' The 53
father noted that this was the exact time when Jesus had said to him,
'Your son will live', and he and all his household became believers.

This was now the second sign which Jesus performed after coming 54
down from Judaea into Galilee.

5 LATER ON Jesus went up to Jerusalem for one of the Jewish
2 festivals.*ᵃ* Now at the Sheep-Pool in Jerusalem there is a place with
   five colonnades. Its name in the language of the Jews is Bethesda.
3 In these colonnades there lay a crowd of sick people, blind, lame,
5 and paralysed.*ᵇ* Among them was a man who had been crippled
6 for thirty-eight years. When Jesus saw him lying there and was
   aware that he had been ill a long time, he asked him, 'Do you want
7 to recover?' 'Sir,' he replied, 'I have no one to put me in the pool
   when the water is disturbed, but while I am moving, someone else
8 is in the pool before me.' Jesus answered, 'Rise to your feet, take
9 up your bed and walk.' The man recovered instantly, took up his
   stretcher, and began to walk.
10   That day was a Sabbath. So the Jews said to the man who had
   been cured, 'It is the Sabbath. You are not allowed to carry your
11 bed on the Sabbath.' He answered, 'The man who cured me said,
12 "Take up your bed and walk."' They asked him, 'Who is the man
13 who told you to take up your bed and walk?' But the cripple who
   had been cured did not know; for the place was crowded and Jesus
14 had slipped away. A little later Jesus found him in the temple and
   said to him, 'Now that you are well again, leave your sinful ways,
15 or you may suffer something worse.' The man went away and told the
   Jews that it was Jesus who had cured him.
16   It was works of this kind done on the Sabbath that stirred the Jews
17 to persecute Jesus. He defended himself by saying, 'My Father has
18 never yet ceased his work, and I am working too.' This made the
   Jews still more determined to kill him, because he was not only
   breaking the Sabbath, but, by calling God his own Father, he
   claimed equality with God.
19   To this charge Jesus replied, 'In truth, in very truth I tell you,
   the Son can do nothing by himself; he does only what he sees the
20 Father doing: what the Father does, the Son does. For the Father
   loves the Son and shows him all his works, and will show greater yet,
21 to fill you with wonder. As the Father raises the dead and gives them
22 life, so the Son gives life to men, as he determines. And again, the
   Father does not judge anyone, but has given full jurisdiction to the

[*a*] *Some witnesses read* for the Jewish festival. [*b*] *Some witnesses add* waiting for the
disturbance of the water; *some further insert* (4) for from time to time an angel came
down into the pool and stirred up the water. The first to plunge in after this
disturbance recovered from whatever disease had afflicted him.

Son; it is his will that all should pay the same honour to the Son 23
as to the Father. To deny honour to the Son is to deny it to the
Father who sent him.

'In very truth, anyone who gives heed to what I say and puts his 24
trust in him who sent me has hold of eternal life, and does not come
up for judgement, but has already passed from death to life. In 25
truth, in very truth I tell you, a time is coming, indeed it is already
here, when the dead shall hear the voice of the Son of God, and all
who hear shall come to life. For as the Father has life-giving power 26
in himself, so has the Son, by the Father's gift.

'As Son of Man, he has also been given the right to pass judgement. 27
Do not wonder at this, because the time is coming when all who are 28
in the grave shall hear his voice and move forth: those who have 29
done right will rise to life; those who have done wrong will rise to
hear their doom. I cannot act by myself; I judge as I am bidden, 30
and my verdict is just, because my aim is not my own will, but the
will of him who sent me.

'If I testify on my own behalf, that testimony does not hold good. 31
There is another who bears witness for me, and I know that his 32
testimony holds. Your messengers have been to John; you have his 33
testimony to the truth. Not that I rely on human testimony, but 34
I remind you of it for your own salvation. John was a lamp, burning 35
brightly, and for a time you were ready to exult in his light. But I 36
rely on a testimony higher than John's. There is enough to testify
that the Father has sent me, in the works my Father gave me to do
and to finish—the very works I have in hand. This testimony to me 37
was given by the Father who sent me, although you never heard his
voice, or saw his form. But his word has found no home in you, 38
for you do not believe the one whom he sent. You study the scrip- 39
tures diligently, supposing that in having them you have eternal
life; yet, although their testimony points to me, you refuse to come 40
to me for that life.

'I do not look to men for honour. But with you it is different, 41, 42
as I know well, for you have no love for God in you. I have come 43
accredited by my Father, and you have no welcome for me; if
another comes self-accredited you will welcome him. How can you 44
have faith so long as you receive honour from one another, and care
nothing for the honour that comes from him who alone is God?
Do not imagine that I shall be your accuser at God's tribunal. 45

Your accuser is Moses, the very Moses on whom you have set your
46 hope. If you believed Moses you would believe what I tell you,
47 for it was about me that he wrote. But if you do not believe what
he wrote, how are you to believe what I say?'

6 SOME TIME later Jesus withdrew to the farther shore of the Sea of
2 Galilee (or Tiberias), and a large crowd of people followed who had
3 seen the signs he performed in healing the sick. Then Jesus went
4 up the hill-side and sat down with his disciples. It was near the
5 time of Passover, the great Jewish festival. Raising his eyes and
seeing a large crowd coming towards him, Jesus said to Philip,
6 'Where are we to buy bread to feed these people?' This he said to
7 test him; Jesus himself knew what he meant to do. Philip replied,
'Twenty pounds*a* would not buy enough bread for every one of them
8 to have a little.' One of his disciples, Andrew, the brother of Simon
9 Peter, said to him, 'There is a boy here who has five barley loaves
10 and two fishes; but what is that among so many?' Jesus said, 'Make
the people sit down.' There was plenty of grass there, so the men
11 sat down, about five thousand of them. Then Jesus took the loaves,
gave thanks, and distributed them to the people as they sat there.
He did the same with the fishes, and they had as much as they
12 wanted. When everyone had had enough, he said to his disciples,
13 'Collect the pieces left over, so that nothing may be lost.' This they
did, and filled twelve baskets with the pieces left uneaten of the five
barley loaves.
14   When the people saw the sign Jesus had performed, the word went
round, 'Surely this must be the prophet that was to come into the
15 world.' Jesus, aware that they meant to come and seize him to
proclaim him king, withdrew again to the hills by himself.
16, 17   At nightfall his disciples went down to the sea, got into their boat,
and pushed off to cross the water to Capernaum. Darkness had
18 already fallen, and Jesus had not yet joined them. By now a strong
19 wind was blowing and the sea grew rough. When they had
rowed about three or four miles they saw Jesus walking on the
20 sea and approaching the boat. They were terrified, but he called
21 out, 'It is I; do not be afraid.' Then they were ready to take
him aboard, and immediately the boat reached the land they were
making for.

[a] *Literally* 200 denarii.

NEXT MORNING the crowd was standing on the opposite shore. 22
They had seen only one boat there, and Jesus, they knew, had not
embarked with his disciples, who had gone away without him.
Boats from Tiberias, however, came ashore* near the place where 23
the people had eaten the bread over which the Lord gave thanks.*
When the people saw that neither Jesus nor his disciples were any 24
longer there, they themselves went aboard these boats and made for
Capernaum in search of Jesus. They found him on the other side. 25
'Rabbi,' they said, 'when did you come here?' Jesus replied, 'In 26
very truth I know that you have come looking for me because your
hunger was satisfied with the loaves you ate, not because you saw
signs. You must work, not for this perishable food, but for the food 27
that lasts, the food of eternal life.

'This food the Son of Man will give you, for he it is upon whom
the Father has set the seal of his authority.' 'Then what must we do', 28
they asked him, 'if we are to work as God would have us work?'
Jesus replied, 'This is the work that God requires: believe in the one 29
whom he has sent.'

They said, 'What sign can you give us to see, so that we may 30
believe you? What is the work you do? Our ancestors had manna 31
to eat in the desert; as Scripture says, "He gave them bread from
heaven to eat."' Jesus answered, 'I tell you this: the truth is, not 32
that Moses gave you the bread from heaven, but that my Father
gives you the real bread from heaven. The bread that God gives 33
comes down* from heaven and brings life to the world.' They said 34
to him, 'Sir, give us this bread now and always.' Jesus said to them, 35
'I am the bread of life. Whoever comes to me shall never be hungry,
and whoever believes in me shall never be thirsty. But you, as 36
I said, do not believe although you have seen.* All that the Father 37
gives me will come to me, and the man who comes to me I will never
turn away. I have come down from heaven, not to do my own will, 38
but the will of him who sent me. It is his will that I should not lose 39
even one of all that he has given me, but raise them all up on the last
day. For it is my Father's will that everyone who looks upon the 40
Son and puts his faith in him shall possess eternal life; and I will
raise him up on the last day.'

At this the Jews began to murmur disapprovingly because he said, 41

[a] *Some witnesses read* Other boats from Tiberias came ashore... [b] *Some witnesses
omit* over which...thanks. [c] *Or* is he who comes down... [d] *Some witnesses add* me.

42 'I am the bread which came down from heaven.' They said, 'Surely this is Jesus son of Joseph; we know his father and mother. How
43 can he now say, "I have come down from heaven"?' Jesus answered,
44 'Stop murmuring among yourselves. No man can come to me unless he is drawn by the Father who sent me; and I will raise him
45 up on the last day. It is written in the prophets: "And they shall all be taught by God." Everyone who has listened to the Father and learned from him comes to me.

46   'I do not mean that anyone has seen the Father. He who has
47 come from God has seen the Father, and he alone. In truth, in
48 very truth I tell you, the believer possesses eternal life. I am the
49 bread of life. Your forefathers ate the manna in the desert and they
50 are dead. I am speaking of the bread that comes down from heaven,
51 which a man may eat, and never die. I am that living bread which has come down from heaven: if anyone eats this bread he shall live for ever. Moreover, the bread which I will give is my own flesh; I give it for the life of the world.'

52   This led to a fierce dispute among the Jews. 'How can this man
53 give us his flesh to eat?' they said. Jesus replied, 'In truth, in very truth I tell you, unless you eat the flesh of the Son of Man and drink
54 his blood you can have no life in you. Whoever eats my flesh and drinks my blood possesses eternal life, and I will raise him up on the
55, 56 last day. My flesh is real food; my blood is real drink. Whoever eats my flesh and drinks my blood dwells continually in me and I dwell
57 in him. As the living Father sent me, and I live because of the Father,
58 so he who eats me shall live because of me. This is the bread which came down from heaven; and it is not like the bread which our fathers ate: they are dead, but whoever eats this bread shall live for ever.'

59 THIS WAS SPOKEN in synagogue when Jesus was teaching in
60 Capernaum. Many of his disciples on hearing it exclaimed, 'This is
61 more than we can stomach! Why listen to such words?' Jesus was aware that his disciples were murmuring about it and asked them,
62 'Does this shock you? What if you see the Son of Man ascending
63 to the place where he was before? The spirit alone gives life; the flesh is of no avail; the words which I have spoken to you are both
64 spirit and life. And yet there are some of you who have no faith.' For Jesus knew all along who were without faith and who was to

betray him. So he said, 'This is why I told you that no one can come 65
to me unless it has been granted to him by the Father.'

From that time on, many of his disciples withdrew and no longer 66
went about with him. So Jesus asked the Twelve, 'Do you also want 67
to leave me?' Simon Peter answered him, 'Lord, to whom shall 68
we go? Your words are words of eternal life. We have faith, and we 69
know that you are the Holy One of God.' Jesus answered, 'Have 70
I not chosen you, all twelve? Yet one of you is a devil.' He meant 71
Judas, son of Simon Iscariot. He it was who would betray him, and
he was one of the Twelve.

The Great Controversy

AFTERWARDS Jesus went about in Galilee. He wished to avoid 7
Judaea because the Jews were looking for a chance to kill him.
As the Jewish Feast of Tabernacles was close at hand, his brothers 2, 3
said to him, 'You should leave this district and go into Judaea, so
that your disciples there may see the great things you are doing.
Surely no one can hope to be in the public eye if he works in seclu- 4
sion. If you really are doing such things as these, show yourself to
the world.' For even his brothers were not believers in him. 5
Jesus said to them, 'The right time for me has not yet come, but 6
any time is right for you. The world cannot hate you; but it hates 7
me for exposing the wickedness of its ways. Go to the festival 8
yourselves. I am not*a* going up to this festival because the right
time for me has not yet come.' With this answer he stayed behind in 9
Galilee.

Later, when his brothers had gone to the festival, he went up 10
himself, not publicly, but almost in secret. The Jews were looking 11
for him at the festival and asking, 'Where is he?', and there was 12
much whispering about him in the crowds. 'He is a good man',
said some. 'No,' said others, 'he is leading the people astray.'
However, no one talked about him openly, for fear of the Jews. 13

WHEN THE FESTIVAL was already half over, Jesus went up to 14
the temple and began to teach. The Jews were astonished: 'How 15

[a] *Some witnesses read* not yet.

16 is it', they said, 'that this untrained man has such learning?' Jesus
replied, 'The teaching that I give is not my own; it is the teaching
17 of him who sent me. Whoever has the will to do the will of God shall
know whether my teaching comes from him or is merely my own.
18 Anyone whose teaching is merely his own, aims at honour for himself.
But if a man aims at the honour of him who sent him he is sincere,
and there is nothing false in him.
19   'Did not Moses give you the Law? Yet you all break it. Why are
20 you trying to kill me?' The crowd answered, 'You are possessed!
21 Who wants to kill you?' Jesus replied, 'Once only have I done
22 work on the Sabbath, and you are all taken aback. But consider:
Moses gave you the law of circumcision (not that it originated with
Moses but with the patriarchs) and you circumcise on the Sabbath.
23 Well then, if a child is circumcised on the Sabbath to avoid breaking the Law of Moses, why are you indignant with me for giving
24 health on the Sabbath to the whole of a man's body? Do not judge
superficially, but be just in your judgements.'
25   At this some of the people of Jerusalem began to say, 'Is not this
26 the man they want to put to death? And here he is, speaking openly,
and they have not a word to say to him. Can it be that our rulers
27 have actually decided that this is the Messiah? And yet we know
where this man comes from, but when the Messiah appears no one
28 is to know where he comes from.' Thereupon Jesus cried aloud
as he taught in the temple, 'No doubt you know me; no doubt you
know where I come from.*a* Yet I have not come of my own accord.
I was sent by the One who truly is, and him you do not know.
29 I know him because I come from him and he it is who sent me.'
30 At this they tried to seize him, but no one laid a hand on him because
31 his appointed hour had not yet come. Yet among the people many
believed in him. 'When the Messiah comes,' they said, 'is it likely
that he will perform more signs than this man?'
32   The Pharisees overheard these mutterings of the people about
him, so the chief priests and the Pharisees sent temple police to
33 arrest him. Then Jesus said, 'For a little longer I shall be with you;
34 then I am going away to him who sent me. You will look for me,
35 but you will not find me. Where I am, you cannot come.' So the
Jews said to one another, 'Where does he intend to go, that we should
not be able to find him? Will he go to the Dispersion among the

[a] Or Do you know me? And do you know where I come from?

Greeks, and teach the Greeks? What did he mean by saying, "You 36
will look for me, but you will not find me. Where I am, you cannot
come"?'*ᵃ*

ON THE LAST and greatest day of the festival Jesus stood and cried 37
aloud, 'If anyone is thirsty let him come to me; whoever believes 38
in me, let him drink.' As Scripture says, 'Streams of living water
shall flow out from within him.'*ᵇ* He was speaking of the Spirit 39
which believers in him would receive later; for the Spirit had not
yet been given, because Jesus had not yet been glorified.

On hearing this some of the people said, 'This must certainly be 40
the expected prophet.' Others said, 'This is the Messiah.' Others 41
again, 'Surely the Messiah is not to come from Galilee? Does not 42
Scripture say that the Messiah is to be of the family of David,
from David's village of Bethlehem?' Thus he caused a split among the 43
people. Some were for seizing him, but no one laid hands on him. 44

The temple police came back to the chief priests and Pharisees, 45
who asked, 'Why have you not brought him?' 'No man', they 46
answered, 'ever spoke as this man speaks.' The Pharisees retorted, 47
'Have you too been misled? Is there a single one of our rulers who 48
has believed in him, or of the Pharisees? As for this rabble, which 49
cares nothing for the Law, a curse is on them.' Then one of their 50
number, Nicodemus (the man who had once visited Jesus), intervened. 'Does our law', he asked them, 'permit us to pass judge- 51
ment on a man unless we have first given him a hearing and learned
the facts?' 'Are you a Galilean too?' they retorted. 'Study the 52
scriptures and you will find that prophets do not come from Galilee.'*ᶜ*

ONCE AGAIN Jesus addressed the people: 'I am the light of the 8 12
world. No follower of mine shall wander in the dark; he shall have
the light of life.' The Pharisees said to him, 'You are witness in your 13
own cause; your testimony is not valid.' Jesus replied, 'My testimony 14
is valid, even though I do bear witness about myself; because I
know where I come from, and where I am going. You do not know
either where I come from or where I am going. You judge by worldly 15

[a] *Some witnesses here insert the passage printed on p. 193.* [b] *Or* 'If any man is thirsty
let him come to me and drink. He who believes in me, as Scripture says, streams of
living water shall flow out from within him.' [c] *Some witnesses here insert the passage
7. 53 – 8. 11, which is printed on p. 193.*

16 standards. I pass judgement on no man, but if I do judge, my judgement is valid because it is not I alone who judge, but I and

17 he who sent me. In your own law it is written that the testimony of

18 two witnesses is valid. Here am I, a witness in my own cause, and

19 my other witness is the Father who sent me.' They asked, 'Where is your father?' Jesus replied, 'You know neither me nor my Father; if you knew me you would know my Father as well.'

20 These words were spoken by Jesus in the treasury as he taught in the temple. Yet no one arrested him, because his hour had not yet come.

21 Again he said to them, 'I am going away. You will look for me, but you will die in your sin; where I am going you cannot come.'

22 The Jews then said, 'Perhaps he will kill himself: is that what he

23 means when he says, "Where I am going you cannot come"?' So Jesus continued, 'You belong to this world below, I to the world

24 above. Your home is in this world, mine is not. That is why I told you that you would die in your sins. If you do not believe that I am

25 what I am, you will die in your sins.' They asked him, 'Who are you?'

26 Jesus answered, 'Why should I speak to you at all?*a* I have much to say about you—and in judgement. But he who sent me speaks the truth, and what I heard from him I report to the world.'

27 They did not understand that he was speaking to them about the

28 Father. So Jesus said to them, 'When you have lifted up the Son of Man you will know that I am what I am. I do nothing on my own authority, but in all that I say, I have been taught by my Father.

29 He who sent me is present with me, and has not left me alone; for

30 I always do what is acceptable to him.' As he said this, many put their faith in him.

31 Turning to the Jews who had believed him, Jesus said, 'If you dwell within the revelation I have brought, you are indeed my

32 disciples; you shall know the truth, and the truth will set you free.'

33 They replied, 'We are Abraham's descendants; we have never been in slavery to any man. What do you mean by saying, "You will

34 become free men"?' 'In very truth I tell you', said Jesus, 'that

35 everyone who commits sin is a slave. The slave has no permanent

36 standing in the household, but the son belongs to it for ever. If then the Son sets you free, you will indeed be free.

37 'I know that you are descended from Abraham, but you are bent

[a] Or What I have told you all along.

166

on killing me because my teaching makes no headway with you. I am 38
revealing in words what I saw in my Father's presence; and you
are revealing in action what you learned from your father.' They 39
retorted, 'Abraham is our father.' 'If you were Abraham's children',
Jesus replied, 'you would do as Abraham did.^{a} As it is, you are bent 40
on killing me, a man who told you the truth, as I heard it from God.
That is not how Abraham acted. You are doing your own father's 41
work.'

They said, 'We are not base-born; God is our father, and God
alone.' Jesus said, 'If God were your father, you would love me, 42
for God is the source of my being, and from him I come. I have
not come of my own accord; he sent me. Why do you not under- 43
stand my language? It is because my revelation is beyond your grasp.

'Your father is the devil and you choose to carry out your father's 44
desires. He was a murderer from the beginning, and is not rooted
in the truth; there is no truth in him. When he tells a lie he is
speaking his own language, for he is a liar and the father of lies.
But I speak the truth and therefore you do not believe me. Which of 45, 46
you can prove me in the wrong?^{b} If what I say is true, why do you
not believe me? He who has God for his father listens to the words 47
of God. You are not God's children; that is why you do not listen.'

The Jews answered, 'Are we not right in saying that you are a 48
Samaritan, and that you are possessed?' 'I am not possessed,' said 49
Jesus; 'the truth is that I am honouring my Father, but you dishonour me. I do not care about my own glory; there is one who 50
does care, and he is judge. In very truth I tell you, if anyone obeys 51
my teaching he shall never know what it is to die.'

The Jews said, 'Now we are certain that you are possessed. 52
Abraham is dead; the prophets are dead; and yet you say, "If anyone
obeys my teaching he shall not know what it is to die." Are you 53
greater than our father Abraham, who is dead? The prophets are dead
too. What do you claim to be?'

Jesus replied, 'If I glorify myself, that glory of mine is worthless. 54
It is the Father who glorifies me, he of whom you say, "He is our
God", though you do not know him. But I know him; if I said that 55
I did not know him I should be a liar like you. But in truth I know
him and obey his word.

[a] *Some witnesses read* 'If you are Abraham's children', Jesus replied, 'do as Abraham
did.' [b] *Or* Which of you convicts me of sin?

56 'Your father Abraham was overjoyed to see my day; he saw it
57 and was glad.' The Jews protested, 'You are not yet fifty years old.
58 How can you have seen Abraham?'[a] Jesus said, 'In very truth I tell
you, before Abraham was born, I am.'
59 They picked up stones to throw at him, but Jesus was not to be
seen; and he left the temple.[b]

9 As HE WENT on his way Jesus saw a man blind from his birth.
2 His disciples put the question, 'Rabbi, who sinned, this man
3 or his parents? Why was he born blind?' 'It is not that this man or
his parents sinned,' Jesus answered; 'he was born blind that God's
4 power might be displayed in curing him. While daylight lasts we[c]
must carry on the work of him who sent me; night comes, when no
5 one can work. While I am in the world I am the light of the world.'
6 With these words he spat on the ground and made a paste with
7 the spittle; he spread it on the man's eyes, and said to him, 'Go and
wash in the pool of Siloam.' (The name means 'sent'.) The man
went away and washed, and when he returned he could see.
8 His neighbours and those who were accustomed to see him beg-
9 ging said, 'Is not this the man who used to sit and beg?' Others
said, 'Yes, this is the man.' Others again said, 'No, but it is someone
10 like him.' The man himself said, 'I am the man.' They asked him,
11 'How were your eyes opened?' He replied, 'The man called Jesus
made a paste and smeared my eyes with it, and told me to go to
12 Siloam and wash. I went and washed, and gained my sight.' 'Where
is he?' they asked. He answered, 'I do not know.'

13 THE MAN who had been blind was brought before the Pharisees.
14 As it was a Sabbath day when Jesus made the paste and opened his
15 eyes, the Pharisees now asked him by what means he had gained
his sight. The man told them, 'He spread a paste on my eyes; then
16 I washed, and now I can see.' Some of the Pharisees said, 'This
fellow is no man of God; he does not keep the Sabbath.' Others
said, 'How could such signs come from a sinful man?' So they took
different sides.
17 Then they continued to question him: 'What have you to say

[a] *Some witnesses read* How can Abraham have seen you? [b] *Or the division may be
made after the words* was not to be seen; *the paragraph following would then begin* Then
Jesus left the temple, and as he went... [c] *Some witnesses read* I.

about him? It was your eyes he opened.' He answered, 'He is a prophet.' The Jews would not believe that the man had been blind 18 and had gained his sight, until they had summoned his parents and questioned them: 'Is this man your son? Do you say that he 19 was born blind? How is it that he can see now?' The parents replied, 20 'We know that he is our son, and that he was born blind. But how 21 it is that he can now see, or who opened his eyes, we do not know. Ask him; he is of age; he will speak for himself.' His parents gave 22 this answer because they were afraid of the Jews; for the Jewish authorities had already agreed that anyone who acknowledged Jesus as Messiah should be banned from the synagogue. That is why the 23 parents said, 'He is of age; ask him.'

So for the second time they summoned the man who had been 24 blind, and said, 'Speak the truth before God. We know that this fellow is a sinner.' 'Whether or not he is a sinner, I do not know', 25 the man replied. 'All I know is this: once I was blind, now I can see.' 'What did he do to you?' they asked. 'How did he open your eyes?' 26 'I have told you already,' he retorted, 'but you took no notice. Why 27 do you want to hear it again? Do you also want to become his disciples?' Then they became abusive. 'You are that man's disciple,' 28 they said, 'but we are disciples of Moses. We know that God spoke to 29 Moses, but as for this fellow, we do not know where he comes from.'

The man replied, 'What an extraordinary thing! Here is a man 30 who has opened my eyes, yet you do not know where he comes from! It is common knowledge that God does not listen to sinners; he 31 listens to anyone who is devout and obeys his will. To open the eyes 32 of a man born blind—it is unheard of since time began. If that man 33 had not come from God he could have done nothing.' 'Who are you 34 to give us lessons,' they retorted, 'born and bred in sin as you are?' Then they expelled him from the synagogue.

Jesus heard that they had expelled him. When he found him he 35 asked, 'Have you faith in the Son of Man[a]?' The man answered, 36 'Tell me who he is, sir, that I should put my faith in him.' 'You have 37 seen him,' said Jesus; 'indeed, it is he who is speaking to you.' 'Lord, I believe', he said, and bowed before him. 38

Jesus said, 'It is for judgement that I have come into this world— 39 to give sight to the sightless and to make blind those who see.' Some Pharisees in his company asked, 'Do you mean that we are 40

[a] *Some witnesses read* Son of God.

41 blind?' 'If you were blind,' said Jesus, 'you would not be guilty, but because you say "We see", your guilt remains.

10 'IN TRUTH I tell you, in very truth, the man who does not enter the sheepfold by the door, but climbs in some other way, is nothing
2 but a thief or a robber. The man who enters by the door is the shep-
3 herd in charge of the sheep. The door-keeper admits him, and the sheep hear his voice; he calls his own sheep by name, and leads them
4 out. When he has brought them all out, he goes ahead and the sheep
5 follow, because they know his voice. They will not follow a stranger; they will run away from him, because they do not recognize the voice of strangers.'
6 This was a parable that Jesus told them, but they did not understand what he meant by it.
7 So Jesus spoke again: 'In truth, in very truth I tell you, I am the
8 door of the sheepfold. The sheep paid no heed to any who came
9 before me, for these were all thieves and robbers. I am the door; anyone who comes into the fold through me shall be safe. He shall go in and out and shall find pasturage.
10 'The thief comes only to steal, to kill, to destroy; I have come that
11 men may have life, and may have it in all its fullness. I am the good shepherd; the good shepherd lays down his life for the sheep.
12 The hireling, when he sees the wolf coming, abandons the sheep and runs away, because he is no shepherd and the sheep are not his.
13 Then the wolf harries the flock and scatters the sheep. The man runs away because he is a hireling and cares nothing for the sheep.
14 'I am the good shepherd; I know my own sheep and my sheep
15 know me—as the Father knows me and I know the Father—and I
16 lay down my life for the sheep. But there are other sheep of mine, not belonging to this fold, whom I must bring in; and they too will listen to my voice. There will then be one flock, one shepherd.
17 The Father loves me because I lay down my life, to receive it back
18 again. No one has robbed me of it; I am laying it down of my own free will. I have the right to lay it down, and I have the right to receive it back again; this charge I have received from my Father.'
19, 20 These words once again caused a split among the Jews. Many of them said, 'He is possessed, he is raving. Why listen to him?'
21 Others said, 'No one possessed by an evil spirit could speak like this. Could an evil spirit open blind men's eyes?'

IT WAS winter, and the festival of the Dedication was being held in 22
Jerusalem. Jesus was walking in the temple precincts, in Solomon's 23
Cloister. The Jews gathered round him and asked: 'How long must 24
you keep us in suspense? If you are the Messiah say so plainly.'
'I have told you,' said Jesus, 'but you do not believe. My deeds 25
done in my Father's name are my credentials, but because you are 26
not sheep of my flock you do not believe. My own sheep listen to 27
my voice; I know them and they follow me. I give them eternal life 28
and they shall never perish; no one shall snatch them from my care.
My Father who has given them to me is greater than all, and no one 29
can snatch them*ᵃ* out of the Father's care. My Father and I are one.' 30
Once again the Jews picked up stones to stone him. At this Jesus 31, 32
said to them, 'I have set before you many good deeds, done by my
Father's power; for which of these would you stone me?' The Jews 33
replied, 'We are not going to stone you for any good deed, but for
your blasphemy. You, a mere man, claim to be a god.' Jesus 34
answered, 'Is it not written in your own Law, "I said: You are
gods"? Those are called gods to whom the word of God was deli- 35
vered—and Scripture cannot be set aside. Then why do you charge 36
me with blasphemy because I, consecrated and sent into the world
by the Father, said, "I am God's son"?
'If I am not acting as my Father would, do not believe me. 37
But if I am, accept the evidence of my deeds, even if you do not 38
believe me, so that you may recognize and know that the Father is in
me, and I in the Father.'
This provoked them to one more attempt to seize him. But he 39
escaped from their clutches.

Victory over Death

JESUS WITHDREW again across the Jordan, to the place where 40
John had been baptizing earlier. There he stayed, while crowds 41
came to him. They said, 'John gave us no miraculous sign, but all that
he said about this man was true.' Many came to believe in him there. 42

[a] *Some witnesses read* My Father is greater than all, and that which he has given me
no one can snatch...; *others read* That which my Father has given me is greater than
all, and no one can snatch it...

11 There was a man named Lazarus who had fallen ill. His home
2 was at Bethany, the village of Mary and her sister Martha. (This
Mary, whose brother Lazarus had fallen ill, was the woman who
anointed the Lord with ointment and wiped his feet with her hair.)
3 The sisters sent a message to him: 'Sir, you should know that your
4 friend lies ill.' When Jesus heard this he said, 'This sickness will not
end in death; it has come for the glory of God, to bring glory to the
5 Son of God.' And therefore, though he loved Martha and her sister
6 and Lazarus, after hearing of his illness Jesus waited for two days in
the place where he was.
7 After this, he said to his disciples, 'Let us go back to Judaea.'
8 'Rabbi,' his disciples said, 'it is not long since the Jews there were
9 wanting to stone you. Are you going there again?' Jesus replied,
'Are there not twelve hours of daylight? Anyone can walk in day-time
10 without stumbling, because he sees the light of this world. But if he
walks after nightfall he stumbles, because the light fails him.'
11 After saying this he added, 'Our friend Lazarus has fallen asleep,
12 but I shall go and wake him.' The disciples said, 'Master, if he has
13 fallen asleep he will recover.' Jesus, however, had been speaking of
14 his death, but they thought that he meant natural sleep. Then Jesus
15 spoke out plainly: 'Lazarus is dead. I am glad not to have been
there; it will be for your good and for the good of your faith. But
16 let us go to him.' Thomas, called 'the Twin', said to his fellow-
disciples, 'Let us also go, that we may die with him.'

17 ON HIS ARRIVAL Jesus found that Lazarus had already been four
18 days in the tomb. Bethany was just under two miles from Jerusalem,
19 and many of the people had come from the city to Martha and Mary
20 to condole with them on their brother's death. As soon as she heard
that Jesus was on his way, Martha went to meet him, while Mary
stayed at home.
21 Martha said to Jesus, 'If you had been here, sir, my brother would
22 not have died. Even now I know that whatever you ask of God, God
23, 24 will grant you.' Jesus said, 'Your brother will rise again.' 'I know
that he will rise again', said Martha, 'at the resurrection on the last
25 day.' Jesus said, 'I am the resurrection and I am life.ᵃ If a man has
26 faith in me, even though he die, he shall come to life; and no one
27 who is alive and has faith shall ever die. Do you believe this?' 'Lord,

[a] *Some witnesses omit* and I am life.

I do,' she answered; 'I now believe that you are the Messiah, the Son of God who was to come into the world.'

With these words she went to call her sister Mary, and taking 28 her aside, she said, 'The Master is here; he is asking for you.' When Mary heard this she rose up quickly and went to him. Jesus 29, 30 had not yet reached the village, but was still at the place where Martha left him. The Jews who were in the house condoling with 31 Mary, when they saw her start up and leave the house, went after her, for they supposed that she was going to the tomb to weep there.

So Mary came to the place where Jesus was. As soon as she caught 32 sight of him she fell at his feet and said, 'O sir, if you had only been here my brother would not have died.' When Jesus saw her weeping 33 and the Jews her companions weeping, he sighed heavily and was deeply moved. 'Where have you laid him?' he asked. They replied, 34 'Come and see, sir.' Jesus wept. The Jews said, 'How dearly he 35, 36 must have loved him!' But some of them said, 'Could not this man, 37 who opened the blind man's eyes, have done something to keep Lazarus from dying?'

Jesus again sighed deeply; then he went over to the tomb. It was 38 a cave, with a stone placed against it. Jesus said, 'Take away the 39 stone.' Martha, the dead man's sister, said to him, 'Sir, by now there will be a stench; he has been there four days.' Jesus said, 'Did 40 I not tell you that if you have faith you will see the glory of God?' So they removed the stone.   41

Then Jesus looked upwards and said, 'Father, I thank thee: thou hast heard me. I knew already that thou always hearest me, but 42 I spoke for the sake of the people standing round, that they might believe that thou didst send me.'

Then he raised his voice in a great cry: 'Lazarus, come forth.' 43 The dead man came out, his hands and feet swathed in linen bands, 44 his face wrapped in a cloth. Jesus said, 'Loose him; let him go.'

NOW MANY of the Jews who had come to visit Mary and had seen 45 what Jesus did, put their faith in him. But some of them went off to 46 the Pharisees and reported what he had done.

Thereupon the chief priests and the Pharisees convened a meeting 47 of the Council. 'What action are we taking?' they said. 'This man is performing many signs. If we leave him alone like this the whole 48

populace will believe in him. Then the Romans will come and sweep
49 away our temple and our nation.' But one of them, Caiaphas, who
50 was High Priest that year, said, 'You know nothing whatever; you
do not use your judgement; it is more to your interest that one man
should die for the people, than that the whole nation should be
51 destroyed.' He did not say this of his own accord, but as the
High Priest in office that year, he was prophesying that Jesus would
52 die for the nation—die not for the nation alone but to gather together
53 the scattered children of God. So from that day on they plotted
his death.

54   Accordingly Jesus no longer went about publicly in Judaea, but
left that region for the country bordering on the desert, and came
to a town called Ephraim, where he stayed with his disciples.

55 THE JEWISH Passover was now at hand, and many people went up
from the country to Jerusalem to purify themselves before the
56 festival. They looked out for Jesus, and as they stood in the temple
they asked one another, 'What do you think? Perhaps he is not
57 coming to the festival.' Now the chief priests and the Pharisees
had given orders that anyone who knew where he was should give
information, so that they might arrest him.

12 SIX DAYS BEFORE the Passover festival Jesus came to Bethany,
 2 where Lazarus lived whom he had raised from the dead. There a
supper was given in his honour, at which Martha served, and Lazarus
 3 sat among the guests with Jesus. Then Mary brought a pound of
very costly perfume, oil of pure nard, and anointed the feet of Jesus
and wiped them with her hair, till the house was filled with the
 4 fragrance. At this, Judas Iscariot, a disciple of his—the one who
 5 was to betray him—said, 'Why was this perfume not sold for thirty
 6 pounds*a* and given to the poor?' He said this, not out of any care for
the poor, but because he was a thief; he used to pilfer the money put
 7 into the common purse, which was in his charge. 'Leave her alone',
said Jesus. 'Let her keep it till the day when she prepares for
 8 my burial; for you have the poor among you always, but you will
not always have me.'*b*
 9   A great number of the Jews heard that he was there, and came not
only to see Jesus but also Lazarus whom he had raised from the dead.

[a] *Literally* for 300 denarii. [b] *Some witnesses omit* for you have...have me.

The chief priests then resolved to do away with Lazarus as well, 10
since on his account many Jews were going over to Jesus and putting 11
their faith in him.

THE NEXT DAY the great body of pilgrims who had come to the 12
festival, hearing that Jesus was on the way to Jerusalem, took palm 13
branches and went out to meet him, shouting, 'Hosanna! Blessings
on him who comes in the name of the Lord! God bless the king of
Israel!' Jesus found a donkey and mounted it, in accordance with 14
the text of Scripture: 'Fear no more, daughter of Zion; see, your 15
king is coming, mounted on an ass's colt.'

At the time his disciples did not understand this, but after Jesus 16
had been glorified they remembered that this had been written about
him, and that this had happened to him. The people who were 17
present when he called Lazarus out of the tomb and raised him
from the dead told what they had seen and heard. That is why the 18
crowd went to meet him; they had heard of this sign that he had
performed. The Pharisees said to one another, 'You see you are 19
doing no good at all; why, all the world has gone after him.'

AMONG THOSE who went up to worship at the festival were some 20
Greeks. They came to Philip, who was from Bethsaida in Galilee, 21
and said to him, 'Sir, we should like to see Jesus.' So Philip went 22
and told Andrew, and the two of them went to tell Jesus. Then Jesus 23
replied: 'The hour has come for the Son of Man to be glorified.
In truth, in very truth I tell you, a grain of wheat remains a solitary 24
grain unless it falls into the ground and dies; but if it dies, it bears
a rich harvest. The man who loves himself is lost, but he who hates 25
himself in this world will be kept safe for eternal life. If anyone 26
serves me, he must follow me; where I am, my servant will be.
Whoever serves me will be honoured by my Father.

'Now my soul is in turmoil, and what am I to say? Father, save 27
me from this hour.[a] No, it was for this that I came to this hour.
Father, glorify thy name.' A voice sounded from heaven: 'I have 28
glorified it, and I will glorify it again.' The crowd standing by said 29
it was thunder, while others said, 'An angel has spoken to him.' Jesus 30
replied, 'This voice spoke for your sake, not mine. Now is the hour 31
of judgement for this world; now shall the Prince of this world be

[a] *Or* ...turmoil. Shall I say, "Father, save me from this hour"?

32 driven out. And I shall draw all men to myself, when I am lifted
33 up from the earth.' This he said to indicate the kind of death he was
to die.

34   The people answered, 'Our Law teaches us that the Messiah
continues for ever. What do you mean by saying that the Son of Man
35 must be lifted up? What Son of Man is this?' Jesus answered them:
'The light is among you still, but not for long. Go on your way
while you have the light, so that darkness may not overtake you. He
36 who journeys in the dark does not know where he is going. While
you have the light, trust to the light, that you may become men of
light.' After these words Jesus went away from them into hiding.

37 I N S P I T E O F the many signs which Jesus had performed in their
38 presence they would not believe in him, for the prophet Isaiah's
utterance had to be fulfilled: 'Lord, who has believed what we
39 reported, and to whom has the Lord's power been revealed?' So it
was that they could not believe, for there is another saying of Isaiah's:
40 'He has blinded their eyes and dulled their minds, lest they should
see with their eyes, and perceive with their minds, and turn to me
41 to heal them.' Isaiah said this because[a] he saw his glory and spoke
about him.

42   For all that, even among those in authority a number believed in
him, but would not acknowledge him on account of the Pharisees,
43 for fear of being banned from the synagogue. For they valued their
reputation with men rather than the honour which comes from God.

44 S O J E S U S cried aloud: 'When a man believes in me, he believes in
45 him who sent me rather than in me; seeing me, he sees him who sent
46 me. I have come into the world as light, so that no one who has
47 faith in me should remain in darkness. But if anyone hears my
words and pays no regard to them, I am not his judge; I have not
48 come to judge the world, but to save the world. There is a judge for
the man who rejects me and does not accept my words; the word
49 that I spoke will be his judge on the last day. I do not speak on my
own authority, but the Father who sent me has himself commanded
50 me what to say and how to speak. I know that his commands are
eternal life. What the Father has said to me, therefore—that is what
I speak.'

[a] *Some witnesses read* when.

Farewell Discourses

IT WAS BEFORE the Passover festival. Jesus knew that his hour 13
had come and he must leave this world and go to the Father.
He had always loved his own who were in the world, and now he was
to show the full extent of his love.

The devil had already put it into the mind of Judas son of Simon 2
Iscariot to betray him. During supper, Jesus, well aware that the 3
Father had entrusted everything to him, and that he had come from
God and was going back to God, rose from table, laid aside his 4
garments, and taking a towel, tied it round him. Then he poured 5
water into a basin, and began to wash his disciples' feet and to wipe
them with the towel.

When it was Simon Peter's turn, Peter said to him, 'You, Lord, 6
washing my feet?' Jesus replied, 'You do not understand now what 7
I am doing, but one day you will.' Peter said, 'I will never let you 8
wash my feet.' 'If I do not wash you,' Jesus replied, 'you are not in
fellowship with me.' 'Then, Lord,' said Simon Peter, 'not my feet 9
only; wash my hands and head as well!'

Jesus said, 'A man who has bathed needs no further washing;[a] 10
he is altogether clean; and you are clean, though not every one of
you.' He added the words 'not every one of you' because he knew 11
who was going to betray him.

After washing their feet and taking his garments again, he sat 12
down. 'Do you understand', he asked, 'what I have done for you?
You call me "Master" and "Lord", and rightly so, for that is what 13
I am. Then if I, your Lord and Master, have washed your feet, you 14
also ought to wash one another's feet. I have set you an example: 15
you are to do as I have done for you. In very truth I tell you, a 16
servant is not greater than his master, nor a messenger than the one
who sent him. If you know this, happy are you if you act upon it. 17

'I am not speaking about all of you; I know whom I have chosen. 18
But there is a text of Scripture to be fulfilled: "He who eats bread
with me has turned against me."[b] I tell you this now, before the 19
event, that when it happens you may believe that I am what I am.

[a] *Some witnesses read* needs only to wash his feet. [b] *Literally* has lifted his heel
against me.

20 In very truth I tell you, he who receives any messenger of mine receives me; receiving me, he receives the One who sent me.'

21 After saying this, Jesus exclaimed in deep agitation of spirit, 'In truth, in very truth I tell you, one of you is going to betray me.'

22 The disciples looked at one another in bewilderment: whom could
23 he be speaking of? One of them, the disciple he loved, was reclining
24 close beside Jesus. So Simon Peter nodded to him and said, 'Ask
25 who it is he means.' That disciple, as he reclined, leaned back close
26 to Jesus and asked, 'Lord, who is it?' Jesus replied, 'It is the man to whom I give this piece of bread when I have dipped it in the dish.' Then, after dipping it in the dish, he took it out and gave it to Judas
27 son of Simon Iscariot. As soon as Judas had received it Satan entered
28 him. Jesus said to him, 'Do quickly what you have to do.' No one
29 at the table understood what he meant by this. Some supposed that, as Judas was in charge of the common purse, Jesus was telling him to buy what was needed for the festival, or to make some gift to
30 the poor. Judas, then, received the bread and went out. It was night.

31 WHEN HE HAD gone out Jesus said, 'Now the Son of Man is
32 glorified, and in him God is glorified. If God is glorified in him,[a] God will also glorify him in himself; and he will glorify him
33 now. My children, for a little longer I am with you; then you will look for me, and, as I told the Jews, I tell you now, where I am
34 going you cannot come. I give you a new commandment: love one
35 another; as I have loved you, so you are to love one another. If there is this love among you, then all will know that you are my disciples.'

36 Simon Peter said to him, 'Lord, where are you going?' Jesus replied, 'Where I am going you cannot follow me now, but one day
37 you will.' Peter said, 'Lord, why cannot I follow you now? I will
38 lay down my life for you.' Jesus answered, 'Will you indeed lay down your life for me? I tell you in very truth, before the cock crows you will have denied me three times.

14 'Set your troubled hearts at rest. Trust in God always; trust also
2 in me. There are many dwelling-places in my Father's house; if it were not so I should have told you; for I am going there on purpose
3 to prepare a place for you.[b] And if I go and prepare a place for you, I shall come again and receive you to myself, so that where I am

[a] *Some witnesses omit* If God...in him. [b] *Or* if it were not so, should I have told you that I am going to prepare a place for you?

you may be also; and my way there is known to you.'*a* Thomas said, 4, 5
'Lord, we do not know where you are going, so how can we know
the way?' Jesus replied, 'I am the way; I am the truth and I am life; 6
no one comes to the Father except by me.

'If you knew me you would know my Father too.*b* From now on 7
you do know him; you have seen him.' Philip said to him, 'Lord, 8
show us the Father and we ask no more.' Jesus answered, 'Have I 9
been all this time with you, Philip, and you still do not know me?
Anyone who has seen me has seen the Father. Then how can you
say, "Show us the Father"? Do you not believe that I am in the 10
Father, and the Father in me? I am not myself the source of the
words I speak to you: it is the Father who dwells in me doing his own
work. Believe me when I say that I am in the Father and the Father 11
in me; or else accept the evidence of the deeds themselves. In truth, 12
in very truth I tell you, he who has faith in me will do what I am
doing; and he will do greater things still because I am going to the
Father. Indeed anything you ask in my name I will do, so that the 13
Father may be glorified in the Son. If you ask*c* anything in my name 14
I will do it.

'If you love me you will obey my commands; and I will ask the 15, 16
Father, and he will give you another to be your Advocate, who will be
with you for ever—the Spirit of truth. The world cannot receive him, 17
because the world neither sees nor knows him; but you know him,
because he dwells with you and is*d* in you. I will not leave you 18
bereft; I am coming back to you. In a little while the world will 19
see me no longer, but you will see me; because I live, you too will
live; then you will know that I am in my Father, and you in me and 20
I in you. The man who has received my commands and obeys them 21
—he it is who loves me; and he who loves me will be loved by my
Father; and I will love him and disclose myself to him.'

Judas asked him—the other Judas, not Iscariot—'Lord, what can 22
have happened, that you mean to disclose yourself to us alone and
not to the world?' Jesus replied, 'Anyone who loves me will heed 23
what I say; then my Father will love him, and we will come to him
and make our dwelling with him; but he who does not love me does 24
not heed what I say. And the word you hear is not mine: it is the

[*a*] *Some witnesses read* also. You know where I am going and you know the way.
[*b*] *Some witnesses read* If you know me you will know my Father too. [*c*] *Some witnesses
insert* me. [*d*] *Some witnesses read* shall be.

25 word of the Father who sent me. I have told you all this while I am
26 still here with you; but your Advocate, the Holy Spirit whom the
Father will send in my name, will teach you everything, and will call
to mind all that I have told you.

27 'Peace is my parting gift to you, my own peace, such as the world
cannot give. Set your troubled hearts at rest, and banish your fears.
28 You heard me say, "I am going away, and coming back to you." If
you loved me you would have been glad to hear that I was going
29 to the Father; for the Father is greater than I. I have told you now,
beforehand, so that when it happens you may have faith.

30 'I shall not talk much longer with you, for the Prince of this world
31 approaches. He has no rights over me; but the world must be shown
that I love the Father, and do exactly as he commands; so up, let us
go forward!*a*

15 1,2 'I AM THE real vine, and my Father is the gardener. Every barren
branch of mine he cuts away; and every fruiting branch he cleans, to
3 make it more fruitful still. You have already been cleansed by the
4 word that I spoke to you. Dwell in me, as I in you. No branch can
bear fruit by itself, but only if it remains united with the vine; no
more can you bear fruit, unless you remain united with me.
5 'I am the vine, and you the branches. He who dwells in me, as
I dwell in him, bears much fruit; for apart from me you can do
6 nothing. He who does not dwell in me is thrown away like a
withered branch. The withered branches are heaped together,
thrown on the fire, and burnt.
7 'If you dwell in me, and my words dwell in you, ask what you
8 will, and you shall have it. This is my Father's glory, that you may
9 bear fruit in plenty and so be my disciples.*b* As the Father has loved
10 me, so I have loved you. Dwell in my love. If you heed my commands, you will dwell in my love, as I have heeded my Father's
commands and dwell in his love.
11 'I have spoken thus to you, so that my joy may be in you, and
12 your joy complete.*c* This is my commandment: love one another, as
13 I have loved you. There is no greater love than this, that a man should

[a] *Or* for the Prince of this world is coming, though he has nothing in common with me.
But he is coming so that the world may recognize that I love the Father, and do exactly
as he commands. Up, and let us go forward to meet him! [b] *Or* that you may bear
fruit in plenty. Thus you will be my disciples. [c] *Or* so that I may have joy in you and
your joy may be complete.

lay down his life for his friends. You are my friends, if you do what 14
I command you. I call you servants no longer; a servant does not 15
know what his master is about. I have called you friends, because
I have disclosed to you everything that I heard from my Father.
You did not choose me: I chose you. I appointed you to go on and 16
bear fruit, fruit that shall last; so that the Father may give you all
that you ask in my name. This is my commandment to you: love 17
one another.

'If the world hates you, it hated me first, as you know well.*a* 18
If you belonged to the world, the world would love its own; but 19
because you do not belong to the world, because I have chosen you
out of the world, for that reason the world hates you. Remember 20
what I said: "A servant is not greater than his master." As they
persecuted me, they will persecute you; they will follow your teaching
as little as they have followed mine. It is on my account that they 21
will treat you thus, because they do not know the One who sent me.

'If I had not come and spoken to them, they would not be guilty 22
of sin; but now they have no excuse for their sin: he who hates me, 23
hates my Father. If I had not worked among them and accomplished 24
what no other man has done, they would not be guilty of sin; but
now they have both seen and hated both me and my Father.*b* How- 25
ever, this text in their Law had to come true:*c* "They hated me
without reason."

'But when your Advocate has come, whom I will send you from 26
the Father—the Spirit of truth that issues from the Father—he will
bear witness to me. And you also are my witnesses, because you 27
have been with me from the first.

'I have told you all this to guard you against the breakdown of **16**
your faith. They will ban you from the synagogue; indeed, the time 2
is coming when anyone who kills you will suppose that he is performing a religious duty. They will do these things because they 3
do not know either the Father or me. I have told you all this so 4
that when the time comes for it to happen you may remember my
warning. I did not tell you this at first, because then I was with you;
but now I am going away to him who sent me. None of you asks 5
me "Where are you going?" Yet you are plunged into grief because 6
of what I have told you. Nevertheless I tell you the truth: it is for 7

[a] *Or* bear in mind that it hated me first. [b] *Or* but now they have indeed seen my work
and yet have hated both me and my Father. [c] *Or* let this text in their Law come true.

your good that I am leaving you. If I do not go, your Advocate will
8 not come, whereas if I go, I will send him to you. When he comes,
he will confute the world, and show where wrong and right and
9 judgement lie. He will convict them of wrong, by their refusal to
10 believe in me; he will convince them that right is on my side, by
11 showing that I go to the Father when I pass from your sight; and he
will convince them of divine judgement, by showing that the Prince
of this world stands condemned.

12 'There is still much that I could say to you, but the burden would
13 be too great for you now. However, when he comes who is the
Spirit of truth, he will guide you into all the truth; for he will
not speak on his own authority, but will tell only what he hears; and
14 he will make known to you the things that are coming. He will
glorify me, for everything that he makes known to you he will draw
15 from what is mine. All that the Father has is mine, and that is why
I said, "Everything that he makes known to you he will draw from
what is mine."

16 'A LITTLE while, and you see me no more; again a little while, and
17 you will see me.' Some of his disciples said to one another, 'What
does he mean by this: "A little while, and you will not see me, and
again a little while, and you will see me", and by this: "Because I am
18 going to my Father"?' So they asked, 'What is this "little while" that
he speaks of? We do not know what he means.'

19   Jesus knew that they were wanting to question him, and said,
'Are you discussing what I said: "A little while, and you will not see
20 me, and again a little while, and you will see me"? In very truth
I tell you, you will weep and mourn, but the world will be glad.
But though you will be plunged in grief, your grief will be turned to
21 joy. A woman in labour is in pain because her time has come; but
when the child is born she forgets the anguish in her joy that a man
22 has been born into the world. So it is with you: for the moment
you are sad at heart; but I shall see you again, and then you will
23 be joyful, and no one shall rob you of your joy. When that day comes
you will ask nothing of me. In very truth I tell you, if you ask the
24 Father for anything in my name, he will give it you.[a] So far you
have asked nothing in my name. Ask and you will receive, that your
joy may be complete.

[a] *Some witnesses read* if you ask the Father for anything, he will give it you in my name.

'Till now I have been using figures of speech; a time is coming 25
when I shall no longer use figures, but tell you of the Father in plain
words. When that day comes you will make your request in my 26
name, and I do not say that I shall pray to the Father for you, for 27
the Father loves you himself, because you have loved me and
believed that I came from God. I came from the Father and have 28
come into the world. Now I am leaving the world again and going
to the Father.' His disciples said, 'Why, this is plain speaking; this 29
is no figure of speech. We are certain now that you know every- 30
thing, and do not need to be questioned; because of this we believe
that you have come from God.'

Jesus answered, 'Do you now believe? Look,[a] the hour is coming, 31, 32
has indeed already come, when you are all to be scattered, each to
his home, leaving me alone. Yet I am not alone, because the Father
is with me. I have told you all this so that in me you may find peace. 33
In the world you will have trouble. But courage! The victory is
mine; I have conquered the world.'

AFTER THESE WORDS Jesus looked up to heaven and said: 17
'Father, the hour has come. Glorify thy Son, that the Son may
glorify thee. For thou hast made him sovereign over all mankind, 2
to give eternal life to all whom thou hast given him. This is eternal 3
life: to know thee who alone art truly God, and Jesus Christ whom
thou hast sent.

'I have glorified thee on earth by completing the work which thou 4
gavest me to do; and now, Father, glorify me in thine own presence 5
with the glory which I had with thee before the world began.

'I have made thy name known to the men whom thou didst give 6
me out of the world. They were thine, thou gavest them to me, and
they have obeyed thy command. Now they know that all thy gifts 7
have come to me from thee; for I have taught them all that I learned 8
from thee, and they have received it: they know with certainty that
I came from thee; they have had faith to believe that thou didst
send me.

'I pray for them; I am not praying for the world but for those 9
whom thou hast given me, because they belong to thee. All that is 10
mine is thine, and what is thine is mine; and through them has my
glory shone.

[a] *Or* At the moment you believe; but look...

11 'I am to stay no longer in the world, but they are still in the world, and I am on my way to thee. Holy Father, protect by the power of thy name those whom thou hast given me,*a* that they may be one,
12 as we are one. When I was with them, I protected by the power of thy name those whom thou hast given me,*b* and kept them safe. Not one of them is lost except the man who must be lost, for Scripture has to be fulfilled.
13 'And now I am coming to thee; but while I am still in the world I speak these words, so that they may have my joy within them in
14 full measure. I have delivered thy word to them, and the world
15 hates them because they are strangers in the world, as I am. I pray thee, not to take them out of the world, but to keep them from the
16, 17 evil one. They are strangers in the world, as I am. Consecrate them
18 by the truth;*c* thy word is truth. As thou hast sent me into the
19 world, I have sent them into the world, and for their sake I now consecrate myself, that they too may be consecrated by the truth.*c*
20 'But it is not for these alone that I pray, but for those also who
21 through their words put their faith in me; may they all be one: as thou, Father, art in me, and I in thee, so also may they be in us,
22 that the world may believe that thou didst send me. The glory which thou gavest me I have given to them, that they may be one, as we
23 are one; I in them and thou in me, may they be perfectly one. Then the world will learn that thou didst send me, that thou didst love them as thou didst me.
24 'Father, I desire that these men, who are thy gift to me, may be with me where I am, so that they may look upon my glory, which thou hast given me because thou didst love me before the world
25 began. O righteous Father, although the world does not know thee,
26 I know thee, and these men know that thou didst send me. I made thy name known to them, and will make it known, so that the love thou hadst for me may be in them, and I may be in them.'

[*a*] *Or* protect them by the power of thy name which thou hast given me, *or* keep in loyalty to thee those whom thou hast given me. [*b*] *Or* protected them by the power of thy name which thou hast given me, *or* kept in loyalty to thee those whom thou hast given me. [*c*] *Or* in truth.

The Final Conflict

AFTER THESE WORDS, Jesus went out with his disciples, and crossed 18
the Kedron ravine. There was a garden there, and he and his
disciples went into it. The place was known to Judas, his betrayer, 2
because Jesus had often met there with his disciples. So Judas took 3
a detachment of soldiers, and police provided by the chief priests
and the Pharisees, equipped with lanterns, torches, and weapons,
and made his way to the garden. Jesus, knowing all that was coming 4
upon him, went out to them and asked, 'Who is it you want?'
'Jesus of Nazareth', they answered. Jesus said, 'I am he.' And 5
there stood Judas the traitor with them. When he said, 'I am he', they 6
drew back and fell to the ground. Again Jesus asked, 'Who is it you 7
want?' 'Jesus of Nazareth', they answered. Then Jesus said, 'I have 8
told you that I am he. If I am the man you want, let these others
go.' (This was to make good his words, 'I have not lost one of those 9
whom thou gavest me.') Thereupon Simon Peter drew the sword he 10
was wearing and struck at the High Priest's servant, cutting off his
right ear. (The servant's name was Malchus.) Jesus said to Peter, 11
'Sheathe your sword. This is the cup my Father has given me; shall
I not drink it?'

THE TROOPS with their commander, and the Jewish police, now 12
arrested Jesus and secured him. They took him first to Annas.*a* 13
Annas was father-in-law of Caiaphas, the High Priest for that year*a*—
the same Caiaphas who had advised the Jews that it would be to their 14
interest if one man died for the whole people. Jesus was followed 15
by Simon Peter and another disciple. This disciple, who was
acquainted with the High Priest, went with Jesus into the High
Priest's courtyard, but Peter halted at the door outside. So the other 16
disciple, the High Priest's acquaintance, went out again and spoke
to the woman at the door, and brought Peter in. The maid on duty 17
at the door said to Peter, 'Are you another of this man's disciples?'
'I am not', he said. The servants and the police had made a charcoal 18
fire, because it was cold, and were standing round it warming themselves. And Peter too was standing with them, sharing the warmth.

[a] See note on verse 24.

19 The High Priest questioned Jesus about his disciples and about
20 what he taught. Jesus replied, 'I have spoken openly to all the
    world; I have always taught in synagogue and in the temple, where
21 all Jews congregate; I have said nothing in secret. Why question me?
22 Ask my hearers what I told them; they know what I said.' When he
    said this, one of the police struck him on the face, exclaiming, 'Is
23 that the way to answer the High Priest?' Jesus replied, 'If I spoke
    amiss, state it in evidence; if I spoke well, why strike me?'
24 So Annas sent him bound to Caiaphas the High Priest.*a*
25 Meanwhile Peter stood warming himself. The others asked, 'Are
    you another of his disciples?' But he denied it: 'I am not', he said.
26 One of the High Priest's servants, a relation of the man whose ear
    Peter had cut off, insisted, 'Did I not see you with him in the garden?'
27 Peter denied again; and just then a cock crew.

28 FROM CAIAPHAS Jesus was led into the Governor's headquarters.
    It was now early morning, and the Jews themselves stayed outside
    the headquarters to avoid defilement, so that they could eat the
29 Passover meal.*b* So Pilate went out to them and asked, 'What charge
30 do you bring against this man?' 'If he were not a criminal,' they
31 replied, 'we should not have brought him before you.' Pilate said,
    'Take him away and try him by your own law.' The Jews answered,
32 'We are not allowed to put any man to death.' Thus they ensured
    the fulfilment of the words by which Jesus had indicated the manner
    of his death.
33 Pilate then went back into his headquarters and summoned Jesus.
34 'Are you the king of the Jews?' he asked.*c* Jesus said, 'Is that your
35 own idea, or have others suggested it to you?' 'What! am I a Jew?'
    said Pilate. 'Your own nation and their chief priests have brought
36 you before me. What have you done?' Jesus replied, 'My kingdom
    does not belong to this world. If it did, my followers would be
    fighting to save me from arrest by the Jews. My kingly authority
37 comes from elsewhere.' 'You are a king, then?' said Pilate. Jesus
    answered, '"King" is your word. My task is to bear witness to the
    truth. For this was I born; for this I came into the world, and all
38 who are not deaf to truth listen to my voice.' Pilate said, 'What is

[*a*] *Some witnesses give this verse after* first to Annas *in verse 13; others at the end of verse 13.*
[*b*] *Or* could share in the offerings of the Passover season. [*c*] *Or* 'You are king of
the Jews, I take it', he said.

truth?', and with those words went out again to the Jews. 'For my part,' he said, 'I find no case against him. But you have a custom that 39 I release one prisoner for you at Passover. Would you like me to release the king of the Jews?' Again the clamour rose: 'Not him; we 40 want Barabbas!' (Barabbas was a bandit.)

Pilate now took Jesus and had him flogged; and the soldiers 19 1, 2 plaited a crown of thorns and placed it on his head, and robed him in a purple cloak. Then time after time they came up to him, crying, 3 'Hail, King of the Jews!', and struck him on the face.

Once more Pilate came out and said to the Jews, 'Here he is; 4 I am bringing him out to let you know that I find no case against him'; and Jesus came out, wearing the crown of thorns and the 5 purple cloak. 'Behold the Man!' said Pilate. The chief priests and 6 their henchmen saw him and shouted, 'Crucify! crucify!' 'Take him and crucify him yourselves,' said Pilate; 'for my part I find no case against him.' The Jews answered, 'We have a law; and by that 7 law he ought to die, because he has claimed to be Son of God.'

When Pilate heard that, he was more afraid than ever, and going 8, 9 back into his headquarters he asked Jesus, 'Where have you come from?' But Jesus gave him no answer. 'Do you refuse to speak to 10 me?' said Pilate. 'Surely you know that I have authority to release you, and I have authority to crucify you?' 'You would have no 11 authority at all over me', Jesus replied, 'if it had not been granted you from above; and therefore the deeper guilt lies with the man who handed me over to you.'

From that moment Pilate tried hard to release him; but the Jews 12 kept shouting, 'If you let this man go, you are no friend to Caesar; any man who claims to be a king is defying Caesar.' When Pilate 13 heard what they were saying, he brought Jesus out and took his seat on the tribunal at the place known as 'The Pavement' ('Gabbatha' in the language of the Jews). It was the eve of Passover,ᵃ about 14 noon. Pilate said to the Jews, 'Here is your king.' They shouted, 15 'Away with him! Away with him! Crucify him!' 'Crucify your king?' said Pilate. 'We have no king but Caesar', the Jews replied. Then at last, to satisfy them, he handed Jesus over to be crucified. 16

JESUS WAS now taken in charge and, carrying his own cross, went 17 out to the Place of the Skull, as it is called (or, in the Jews'

[a] *Or* It was Friday in Passover.

18 language, 'Golgotha'), where they crucified him, and with him two others, one on the right, one on the left, and Jesus between them.
19 And Pilate wrote an inscription to be fastened to the cross; it
20 read, 'Jesus of Nazareth King of the Jews.' This inscription was read by many Jews, because the place where Jesus was crucified was not far from the city, and the inscription was in Hebrew, Latin, and
21 Greek. Then the Jewish chief priests said to Pilate, 'You should not write "King of the Jews"; write, "He claimed to be king of the
22 Jews."' Pilate replied, 'What I have written, I have written.'
23 The soldiers, having crucified Jesus, took possession of his clothes, and divided them into four parts, one for each soldier, leaving out the tunic. The tunic was seamless, woven in one piece throughout;
24 so they said to one another, 'We must not tear this; let us toss for it'; and thus the text of Scripture came true: 'They shared my garments among them, and cast lots for my clothing.'
25 That is what the soldiers did. But meanwhile near the cross where Jesus hung stood his mother, with her sister, Mary wife of
26 Clopas, and Mary of Magdala. Jesus saw his mother, with the disciple whom he loved standing beside her. He said to her,
27 'Mother, there is your son'; and to the disciple, 'There is your mother'; and from that moment the disciple took her into his home.
28 After that, Jesus, aware that all had now come to its appointed
29 end, said in fulfilment of Scripture, 'I thirst.' A jar stood there full of sour wine; so they soaked a sponge with the wine, fixed it on a
30 javelin,[a] and held it up to his lips. Having received the wine, he said, 'It is accomplished!' He bowed his head and gave up his spirit.[b]
31 Because it was the eve of Passover,[c] the Jews were anxious that the bodies should not remain on the cross for the coming Sabbath, since that Sabbath was a day of great solemnity; so they requested
32 Pilate to have the legs broken and the bodies taken down. The soldiers accordingly came to the first of his fellow-victims and to
33 the second, and broke their legs; but when they came to Jesus, they
34 found that he was already dead, so they did not break his legs. But one of the soldiers stabbed his side with a lance, and at once there
35 was a flow of blood and water. This is vouched for by an eyewitness, whose evidence is to be trusted. He knows that he speaks the truth,
36 so that you too may believe; for this happened in fulfilment of the

[a] *So one witness; the others read* on marjoram. [b] *Or* breathed out his life. [c] *Or* Because it was Friday in Passover...

text of Scripture: 'No bone of his shall be broken.' And another 37
text says, 'They shall look on him whom they pierced.'

AFTER THAT, Pilate was approached by Joseph of Arimathaea, 38
a disciple of Jesus, but a secret disciple for fear of the Jews, who[a]
asked to be allowed to remove the body of Jesus. Pilate gave the
permission; so Joseph came and took the body away. He was joined 39
by Nicodemus (the man who had first visited Jesus by night), who
brought with him a mixture of myrrh and aloes, more than half a
hundredweight. They took the body of Jesus and wrapped it, with 40
the spices, in strips of linen cloth according to Jewish burial-customs.
Now at the place where he had been crucified there was a garden, 41
and in the garden a new tomb, not yet used for burial. There, 42
because the tomb was near at hand and it was the eve of the Jewish
Sabbath, they laid Jesus.

EARLY ON THE Sunday morning, while it was still dark, Mary of 20
Magdala came to the tomb. She saw that the stone had been moved
away from the entrance, and ran to Simon Peter and the other dis- 2
ciple, the one whom Jesus loved. 'They have taken the Lord out of
his tomb,' she cried, 'and we do not know where they have laid him.'
So Peter and the other set out and made their way to the tomb. 3
They were running side by side, but the other disciple outran Peter 4
and reached the tomb first. He peered in and saw the linen wrap- 5
pings lying there, but did not enter. Then Simon Peter came up, 6
following him, and he went into the tomb. He saw the linen
wrappings lying, and the napkin which had been over his head, not 7
lying with the wrappings but rolled together in a place by itself. Then 8
the disciple who had reached the tomb first went in too, and he
saw and believed; until then they had not understood the scriptures, 9
which showed that he must rise from the dead.
    So the disciples went home again; but Mary stood at the tomb 10, 11
outside, weeping. As she wept, she peered into the tomb; and she 12
saw two angels in white sitting there, one at the head, and one at
the feet, where the body of Jesus had lain. They said to her, 'Why 13
are you weeping?' She answered, 'They have taken my Lord away,
and I do not know where they have laid him.' With these words she 14

[a] *Or* of Arimathaea. He was a disciple of Jesus, but had gone into hiding for fear
of the Jews. He now...

turned round and saw Jesus standing there, but did not recognize

15 him. Jesus said to her, 'Why are you weeping? Who is it you are looking for?' Thinking it was the gardener, she said, 'If it is you, sir, who removed him, tell me where you have laid him, and I will

16 take him away.' Jesus said, 'Mary!' She turned to him and said,

17 'Rabbuni!' (which is Hebrew for 'My Master'). Jesus said, 'Do not cling to me,^{a} for I have not yet ascended to the Father. But go to my brothers, and tell them that I am now ascending^b to my Father

18 and your Father, my God and your God.' Mary of Magdala went to the disciples with her news: 'I have seen the Lord!' she said, and gave them his message.

19 Late that Sunday evening, when the disciples were together behind locked doors, for fear of the Jews, Jesus came and stood among

20 them. 'Peace be with you!' he said, and then showed them his hands and his side. So when the disciples saw the Lord, they were filled

21 with joy. Jesus repeated, 'Peace be with you!', and then said, 'As the

22 Father sent me, so I send you.' He then breathed on them, saying,

23 'Receive the Holy Spirit! If you forgive any man's sins, they stand forgiven; if you pronounce them unforgiven, unforgiven they remain.'

24 One of the Twelve, Thomas, that is 'the Twin', was not with the

25 rest when Jesus came. So the disciples told him, 'We have seen the Lord.' He said, 'Unless I see the mark of the nails on his hands, unless I put my finger into the place where the nails were, and my hand into his side, I will not believe it.'

26 A week later his disciples were again in the room, and Thomas was with them. Although the doors were locked, Jesus came and

27 stood among them, saying, 'Peace be with you!' Then he said to Thomas, 'Reach your finger here: see my hands; reach your hand here and put it into my side; be unbelieving no longer, but believe.'

28, 29 Thomas said, 'My Lord and my God!' Jesus said, 'Because you have seen me you have found faith. Happy are they who never saw me and yet have found faith.'

30 There were indeed many other signs that Jesus performed in the presence of his disciples, which are not recorded in this book.

31 Those here written have been recorded in order that you may hold the faith^c that Jesus is the Christ, the Son of God, and that through this faith you may possess eternal life by his name.

[a] Or Touch me no more. [b] Or I am going to ascend... [c] Some witnesses read that you may come to believe...

SOME TIME LATER, Jesus showed himself to his disciples once 21
again, by the Sea of Tiberias; and in this way. Simon Peter 2
and Thomas 'the Twin' were together with Nathanael of Cana-in-
Galilee. The sons of Zebedee and two other disciples were also there.
Simon Peter said, 'I am going out fishing.' 'We will go with you', 3
said the others. So they started and got into the boat. But that night
they caught nothing.

Morning came, and there stood Jesus on the beach, but the 4
disciples did not know that it was Jesus. He called out to them, 5
'Friends, have you caught anything?' They answered 'No.' He 6
said, 'Shoot the net to starboard, and you will make a catch.' They
did so, and found they could not haul the net aboard, there were so
many fish in it. Then the disciple whom Jesus loved said to Peter, 7
'It is the Lord!' When Simon Peter heard that, he wrapped his
coat about him (for he had stripped) and plunged into the sea. The 8
rest of them came on in the boat, towing the net full of fish; for
they were not far from land, only about a hundred yards.

When they came ashore, they saw a charcoal fire there, with fish 9
laid on it, and some bread. Jesus said, 'Bring some of your catch.' 10
Simon Peter went aboard and dragged the net to land, full of big 11
fish, a hundred and fifty-three of them; and yet, many as they were,
the net was not torn. Jesus said, 'Come and have breakfast.' None 12
of the disciples dared to ask 'Who are you?' They knew it was the
Lord. Jesus now came up, took the bread, and gave it to them, and 13
the fish in the same way.

This makes the third time that Jesus appeared to his disciples 14
after his resurrection from the dead.

After breakfast, Jesus said to Simon Peter, 'Simon son of John, 15
do you love me more than all else[a]?' 'Yes, Lord,' he answered, 'you
know that I love you.'[b] 'Then feed my lambs', he said. A second 16
time he asked, 'Simon son of John, do you love me?' 'Yes, Lord,
you know I love you.'[b] 'Then tend my sheep.' A third time he said, 17
'Simon son of John, do you love me[c]?' Peter was hurt that he asked
him a third time, 'Do you love me?'[d] 'Lord,' he said, 'you know
everything; you know I love you.'[b] Jesus said, 'Feed my sheep.

'And further, I tell you this in very truth: when you were young 18
you fastened your belt about you and walked where you chose; but

[*a*] *Or* more than they do. [*b*] *Or* that I am your friend. [*c*] *Or* are you my friend.
[*d*] *Or* that at the third asking he should have said, 'Are you my friend?'

when you are old you will stretch out your arms, and a stranger
19 will bind you fast, and carry you where you have no wish to go.' He
said this to indicate the manner of death by which Peter was to
glorify God. Then he added, 'Follow me.'

20   Peter looked round, and saw the disciple whom Jesus loved
following—the one who at supper had leaned back close to him to
21 ask the question, 'Lord, who is it that will betray you?' When he
caught sight of him, Peter asked, 'Lord, what will happen to him?'
22 Jesus said, 'If it should be my will that he wait until I come, what is
it to you? Follow me.'

23   That saying of Jesus became current in the brotherhood, and
was taken to mean that that disciple would not die. But in fact Jesus
did not say that he would not die; he only said, 'If it should be my
will that he wait until I come, what is it to you?'

24   It is this same disciple who attests what has here been written.
It is in fact he who wrote it, and we know that his testimony is true.

25   There is much else that Jesus did. If it were all to be recorded
in detail, I suppose the whole world would not hold the books that
would be written.

An Incident in the Temple*

AND THEY WENT each to his home, and Jesus to the Mount of 53, 1*
Olives. At daybreak he appeared again in the temple, and all the 2
people gathered round him. He had taken his seat and was engaged
in teaching them when the doctors of the law and the Pharisees 3
brought in a woman detected in adultery. Making her stand out
in the middle they said to him, 'Master, this woman was caught in 4
the very act of adultery. In the Law Moses has laid down that such 5
women are to be stoned. What do you say about it?' They put the 6
question as a test, hoping to frame a charge against him. Jesus bent
down and wrote with his finger on the ground. When they continued 7
to press their question he sat up straight and said, 'That one of you
who is faultless shall throw the first stone.' Then once again he bent 8
down and wrote on the ground. When they heard what he said, one 9
by one they went away,ᵃ the eldest first; and Jesus was left alone,
with the woman still standing there. Jesus again sat up andᵇ said 10
to the woman, 'Where are they? Has no one condemned you?' 'No 11
one, sir', she said. Jesus replied, 'No more do I. You may go; do not
sin again.'

* *This passage, which in the most widely received editions of the New Testament is printed*
in the text of John, 7. 53 – 8. 11, has no fixed place in our ancient witnesses. Some of them
do not contain it at all. Some place it after Luke 21. 38, others after John 7. 36, or 7. 52,
or 21. 24.
[a] *Some witnesses insert* convicted by their conscience. [b] *Some witnesses insert* seeing
no one but the woman.

ACTS OF THE
APOSTLES

ACTS OF THE
APOSTLES

The Beginnings of the Church

IN THE FIRST PART of my work, Theophilus, I wrote of 1
all that Jesus did and taught from the beginning until the day 2
when, after giving instructions through the Holy Spirit to the
apostles whom he had chosen, he was taken up to heaven. He 3
showed himself to these men after his death, and gave ample proof
that he was alive: over a period of forty days he appeared to them
and taught them about the kingdom of God. While he was in their 4
company he told them not to leave Jerusalem. 'You must wait', he
said, 'for the promise made by my Father, about which you have
heard me speak: John, as you know, baptized with water, but you 5
will be baptized with the Holy Spirit, and within the next few days.'

So, when they were all together, they asked him, 'Lord, is this 6
the time when you are to establish once again the sovereignty of
Israel?' He answered, 'It is not for you to know about dates or 7
times, which the Father has set within his own control. But you 8
will receive power when the Holy Spirit comes upon you; and you
will bear witness for me in Jerusalem, and all over Judaea and
Samaria, and away to the ends of the earth.'

When he had said this, as they watched, he was lifted up, and 9
a cloud removed him from their sight. As he was going, and as they 10
were gazing intently into the sky, all at once there stood beside
them two men in white who said, 'Men of Galilee, why stand there 11
looking up into the sky? This Jesus, who has been taken away from
you up to heaven, will come in the same way as you have seen him go.'

Then they returned to Jerusalem from the hill called Olivet, which 12
is near Jerusalem, no farther than a Sabbath day's journey. Entering 13
the city they went to the room upstairs where they were lodging:
Peter and John and James and Andrew, Philip and Thomas,
Bartholomew and Matthew, James son of Alphaeus and Simon the
Zealot, and Judas son of James. All these were constantly at prayer 14

together, and with them a group of women, including Mary the mother of Jesus, and his brothers.

15 It was during this time that Peter stood up before the assembled
16 brotherhood, about one hundred and twenty in all, and said: 'My friends, the prophecy in Scripture was bound to come true, which the Holy Spirit, through the mouth of David, uttered about Judas who
17 acted as guide to those who arrested Jesus. For he was one of our
18 number and had his place in this ministry.' (This Judas, be it noted, after buying a plot of land with the price of his villainy, fell forward
19 on the ground, and burst open, so that his entrails poured out. This became known to everyone in Jerusalem, and they named the property in their own language Akeldama, which means 'Blood Acre'.)
20 'The text I have in mind', Peter continued, 'is in the Book of Psalms: "Let his homestead fall desolate; let there be none to inhabit it";
21 and again, "Let another take over his charge." Therefore one of those who bore us company all the while we had the Lord Jesus
22 with us, coming and going, from John's ministry of baptism until the day when he was taken up from us—one of those must now join us as a witness to his resurrection.'
23 Two names were put forward: Joseph, who was known as Barsabbas, and bore the added name of Justus; and Matthias.
24 Then they prayed and said, 'Thou, Lord, who knowest the hearts of
25 all men, declare which of these two thou hast chosen to receive this office of ministry and apostleship which Judas abandoned to go
26 where he belonged.' They drew lots and the lot fell on Matthias, who was then assigned a place among the twelve apostles.[a]

2 WHILE THE DAY of Pentecost was running its course they were
2 all together in one place, when suddenly there came from the sky a noise like that of a strong driving wind, which filled the whole
3 house where they were sitting. And there appeared to them tongues like flames of fire, dispersed among them and resting on each one.
4 And they were all filled with the Holy Spirit and began to talk in other tongues, as the Spirit gave them power of utterance.
5 Now there were living in Jerusalem devout Jews[b] drawn from every
6 nation under heaven; and at this sound the crowd gathered, all bewildered because each one heard the apostles talking in his own

[a] *Some witnesses read* was then appointed a colleague of the eleven apostles. [b] *Some witnesses read* devout men.

language. They were amazed and in their astonishment exclaimed, 7
'Why, they are all Galileans, are they not, these men who are
speaking? How is it then that we hear them, each of us in his own 8
native language? Parthians, Medes, Elamites; inhabitants of Meso- 9
potamia, of Judaea and Cappadocia, of Pontus and Asia, of Phrygia 10
and Pamphylia, of Egypt and the districts of Libya around Cyrene;
visitors from Rome, both Jews and proselytes, Cretans and Arabs, 11
we hear them telling in our own tongues the great things God has
done.' And they were all amazed and perplexed, saying to one 12
another, 'What can this mean?' Others said contemptuously, 'They 13
have been drinking!'

But Peter stood up with the Eleven, raised his voice, and addressed 14
them: 'Fellow Jews, and all you who live in Jerusalem, mark this
and give me a hearing. These men are not drunk, as you imagine; 15
for it is only nine in the morning. No, this is what the prophet 16
spoke of: "God says, 'This will happen in the last days: I will pour 17
out upon everyone a portion of my spirit; and your sons and daughters shall prophesy; your young men shall see visions, and your old
men shall dream dreams. Yes, I will endue even my slaves, both 18
men and women, with a portion of my spirit, and they shall prophesy.
And I will show portents in the sky above, and signs on the earth 19
below—blood and fire and drifting smoke. The sun shall be turned 20
to darkness, and the moon to blood, before that great, resplendent
day, the day of the Lord, shall come. And then, everyone who 21
invokes the name of the Lord shall be saved.'"

'Men of Israel, listen to me: I speak of Jesus of Nazareth, a man 22
singled out by God and made known to you through miracles,
portents, and signs, which God worked among you through him, as
you well know. When he had been given up to you, by the deliberate 23
will and plan of God, you used heathen men to crucify and kill
him. But God raised him to life again, setting him free from 24
the pangs of death,[a] because it could not be that death should keep
him in its grip.

'For David says of him: 25

"I foresaw that the presence of the Lord would be with me always,
For he is at my right hand so that I may not be shaken;
Therefore my heart was glad and my tongue spoke my joy;   26

[a] *Some witnesses read* of Hades.

Moreover, my flesh shall dwell in hope,
27   For thou wilt not abandon my soul to Hades,
Nor let thy loyal servant suffer corruption.
28   Thou hast shown me the ways of life,
Thou wilt fill me with gladness by thy presence."

29   'Let me tell you plainly, my friends, that the patriarch David
30 died and was buried, and his tomb is here to this very day. It is
clear therefore that he spoke as a prophet who knew that God had
sworn to him that one of his own direct descendants should sit on
31 his throne; and when he said he was not abandoned to Hades, and
his flesh never suffered corruption, he spoke with foreknowledge
32 of the resurrection of the Messiah. The Jesus we speak of has been
33 raised by God, as we can all bear witness. Exalted thus with*a* God's
right hand, he received the Holy Spirit from the Father, as was
34 promised, and all that you now see and hear flows from him. For it
was not David who went up to heaven; his own words are: "The
35 Lord said to my Lord, 'Sit at my right hand until I make your
36 enemies your footstool.'" Let all Israel then accept as certain that
God has made this Jesus, whom you crucified, both Lord and
Messiah.'

37   When they heard this they were cut to the heart, and said to Peter
38 and the apostles,*b* 'Friends, what are we to do?' 'Repent,' said
Peter, 'repent and be baptized, every one of you, in the name of
Jesus the Messiah for the forgiveness of your sins; and you will
39 receive the gift of the Holy Spirit. For the promise is to you, and to
your children, and to all who are far away, everyone whom the
Lord our God may call.'

40   In these and many other words he pressed his case and pleaded
with them: 'Save yourselves', he said, 'from this crooked age.'
41 Then those who accepted his word were baptized, and some three
thousand were added to their number that day.

42   They met constantly to hear the apostles teach, and to share the
43 common life, to break bread, and to pray. A sense of awe was
everywhere, and many marvels and signs were brought about
44 through the apostles. All whose faith had drawn them together held
45 everything in common:*c* they would sell their property and posses-

[a] *Or* at. [b] *Some witnesses read* the rest of the apostles. [c] *Or* All who had become believers held everything together in common.

sions and make a general distribution as the need of each required. With one mind they kept up their daily attendance at the temple, 46 and, breaking bread in private houses, shared their meals with unaffected joy, as they praised God and enjoyed the favour of the 47 whole people. And day by day the Lord added to their number those whom he was saving.

ONE DAY at three in the afternoon, the hour of prayer, Peter and 3 John were on their way up to the temple. Now a man who had been 2 a cripple from birth used to be carried there and laid every day by the gate of the temple called 'Beautiful Gate', to beg from people as they went in. When he saw Peter and John on their way into the 3 temple he asked for charity. But Peter fixed his eyes on him, as 4 John did also, and said, 'Look at us.' Expecting a gift from them, 5 the man was all attention. And Peter said, 'I have no silver or gold; 6 but what I have I give you: in the name of Jesus Christ of Nazareth, walk.' Then he grasped him by the right hand and pulled him up; 7 and at once his feet and ankles grew strong; he sprang up, stood on 8 his feet, and started to walk. He entered the temple with them, leaping and praising God as he went. Everyone saw him walking 9 and praising God, and when they recognized him as the man who 10 used to sit begging at Beautiful Gate, they were filled with wonder and amazement at what had happened to him.

And as he was clutching Peter and John all the people came run- 11 ning in astonishment towards them in Solomon's Cloister, as it is called. Peter saw them coming and met them with these words: 12 'Men of Israel, why be surprised at this? Why stare at us as if we had made this man walk by some power or godliness of our own? The God of Abraham, Isaac, and Jacob, the God of our fathers, 13 has given the highest honour to his servant Jesus, whom you com- mitted for trial and repudiated in Pilate's court—repudiated the one 14 who was holy and righteous when Pilate had decided to release him. You begged as a favour the release of a murderer, and killed him 15 who has led the way to life. But God raised him from the dead; of that we are witnesses. And the name of Jesus, by awakening faith, 16 has strengthened this man, whom you see and know, and this faith has made him completely well, as you can all see for yourselves.

'And now, my friends, I know quite well that you acted in ignor- 17 ance, and so did your rulers; but this is how God fulfilled what he 18

had foretold in the utterances of all the prophets: that his Messiah
19 should suffer. Repent then and turn to God, so that your sins may
be wiped out. Then the Lord may grant you a time of recovery
20 and send you the Messiah he has already appointed, that is, Jesus.
21 He must be received into heaven until the time of universal restora-
22 tion comes, of which God spoke by his holy prophets.*a* Moses said,
"The Lord God will raise up a prophet for you from among yourselves as he raised me;*b* you shall listen to everything he says to you,
23 and anyone who refuses to listen to that prophet must be extirpated
24 from Israel." And so said all the prophets, from Samuel onwards;
with one voice they all predicted this present time.

25 'You are the heirs of the prophets; you are within the covenant
which God made with your fathers, when he said to Abraham,
"And in your offspring all the families on earth shall find blessing."
26 When God raised up his Servant, he sent him to you first, to bring
you blessing by turning every one of you from your wicked ways.'

4 They were still addressing the people when the chief*c* priests
came upon them, together with the Controller of the Temple and
2 the Sadducees, exasperated at their teaching the people and proclaiming the resurrection from the dead—the resurrection of Jesus.
3 They were arrested and put in prison for the night, as it was already
4 evening. But many of those who had heard the message became
believers. The number of men now reached about five thousand.

5 Next day the Jewish rulers, elders, and doctors of the law met
6 in Jerusalem. There were present Annas the High Priest, Caiaphas,
Jonathan,*d* Alexander, and all who were of the high-priestly family.
7 They brought the apostles before the court and began the examination. 'By what power', they asked, 'or by what name have such
8 men as you done this?' Then Peter, filled with the Holy Spirit,
9 answered, 'Rulers of the people and elders, if the question put to us
today is about help given to a sick man, and we are asked by what
10 means he was cured, here is the answer, for all of you and for all the
people of Israel: it was by the name of Jesus Christ of Nazareth,
whom you crucified, whom God raised from the dead; it is by his
11 name*e* that this man stands here before you fit and well. This Jesus
is the stone rejected by the builders which has become the keystone
12 —and you are the builders. There is no salvation in anyone else

[a] *Some witnesses add* from the beginning of the world. [b] *Or* like me. [c] *Some witnesses omit* chief. [d] *Some witnesses read* John. [e] *Some witnesses insert* and no other.

at all,*ª* for there is no other name under heaven granted to men, by
which we may receive salvation.'

Now as they observed the boldness of Peter and John, and noted 13
that they were untrained laymen, they began to wonder, then recognized them as former companions of Jesus. And when they saw 14
the man who had been cured standing with them, they had nothing
to say in reply. So they ordered them to leave the court, and then 15
discussed the matter among themselves. 'What are we to do with 16
these men?' they said; 'for it is common knowledge in Jerusalem
that a notable miracle has come about through them; and we cannot
deny it. But to stop this from spreading further among the people, 17
we had better caution them never again to speak to anyone in this
name.' They then called them in and ordered them to refrain from 18
all public speaking and teaching in the name of Jesus.

But Peter and John said to them in reply: 'Is it right in God's 19
eyes for us to obey you rather than God? Judge for yourselves. We 20
cannot possibly give up speaking of things we have seen and heard.'

The court repeated the caution and discharged them. They could 21
not see how they were to punish them, because the people were all
giving glory to God for what had happened. The man upon whom 22
this miracle of healing had been performed was over forty years old.

As soon as they were discharged they went back to their friends 23
and told them everything that the chief priests and elders had said.
When they heard it, they raised their voices as one man and called 24
upon God:

'Sovereign Lord, maker of heaven and earth and sea and of everything in them, who by the Holy Spirit,*ᵇ* through the mouth of David 25
thy servant, didst say,

"Why did the Gentiles rage and the peoples lay their plots in vain?
The kings of the earth took their stand and the rulers made common 26
      cause
Against the Lord and against his Messiah."

They did indeed make common cause in this very city against thy 27
holy servant Jesus whom thou didst anoint as Messiah. Herod and
Pontius Pilate conspired with the Gentiles and peoples of Israel to 28
do all the things which, under thy hand and by thy decree, were

[a] *Some witnesses omit* There is no ... at all. [b] *Some witnesses omit* by the Holy
Spirit.

29 foreordained. And now, O Lord, mark their threats, and enable thy
30 servants to speak thy word with all boldness. Stretch out thy hand
to heal and cause signs and wonders to be done through the name
of thy holy servant Jesus.'
31   When they had ended their prayer, the building where they were
assembled rocked, and all were filled with the Holy Spirit and spoke
the word of God with boldness.

32 THE WHOLE body of believers was united in heart and soul. Not
a man of them claimed any of his possessions as his own, but every-
33 thing was held in common, while the apostles bore witness with
great power to the resurrection of the Lord Jesus. They were all
34 held in high esteem; for they had never a needy person among them,
because all who had property in land or houses sold it, brought the
35 proceeds of the sale, and laid the money at the feet of the apostles;
it was then distributed to any who stood in need.
36   For instance, Joseph, surnamed by the apostles Barnabas (which
37 means 'Son of Exhortation'), a Levite, by birth a Cypriot, owned an
estate, which he sold; he brought the money, and laid it at the
apostles' feet.
5   But there was another man, called Ananias, with his wife Sapphira,
2 who sold a property. With the full knowledge of his wife he kept
back part of the purchase-money, and part he brought and laid at
3 the apostles' feet. But Peter said, 'Ananias, how was it that Satan
so possessed your mind that you lied to the Holy Spirit, and kept
4 back part of the price of the land? While it remained, did it not
remain yours? When it was turned into money, was it not still at
your own disposal? What made you think of doing this thing? You
5 have lied not to men but to God.' When Ananias heard these words
6 he dropped dead; and all the others who heard were awestruck. The
younger men rose and covered his body, then carried him out and
buried him.
7   About three hours passed, and then his wife came in, unaware of
8 what had happened. Peter turned to her and said, 'Tell me, were
you paid such and such a price for the land?' 'Yes,' she said, 'that
9 was the price.' Then Peter said, 'Why did you both conspire to put
the Spirit of the Lord to the test? Hark! there at the door are the
footsteps of those who buried your husband; and they will carry
10 you away.' And suddenly she dropped dead at his feet. When the

young men came in, they found her dead; and they carried her out and buried her beside her husband. And a great awe fell upon the 11 whole church, and upon all who heard of these events; and many 12 remarkable and wonderful things took place among the people at the hands of the apostles.

THEY USED to meet by common consent in Solomon's Cloister, no one from outside their number venturing to join with them. 13 But people in general spoke highly of them,^a and more than that, 14 numbers of men and women were added to their ranks as believers in the Lord.^b In the end the sick were actually carried out into the 15 streets and laid there on beds and stretchers, so that even the shadow of Peter might fall on one or another as he passed by; and the people 16 from the towns round Jerusalem flocked in, bringing those who were ill or harassed by unclean spirits, and all of them were cured.

Then the High Priest and his colleagues, the Sadducean party 17 as it then was, were goaded into action by jealousy. They proceeded 18 to arrest the apostles, and put them in official custody. But an angel 19 of the Lord opened the prison doors during the night, brought them out, and said, 'Go, take your place in the temple and speak to the 20 people, and tell them about this new life and all it means.' Accor- 21 dingly they entered the temple at daybreak and went on with their teaching.

When the High Priest arrived with his colleagues they summoned the 'Sanhedrin', that is, the full senate of the Israelite nation, and sent to the jail to fetch the prisoners. But the police who went to 22 the prison failed to find them there, so they returned and reported, 'We found the jail securely locked at every point, with the warders 23 at their posts by the doors, but when we opened them we found no one inside.' When they heard this, the Controller of the Temple 24 and the chief priests were wondering what could have become of them,^c and then a man arrived with the report, 'Look! the men you 25 put in prison are there in the temple teaching the people.' At that 26 the Controller went off with the police and fetched them, but without using force for fear of being stoned by the people.

[*a*] *Or* ...Cloister. Although others did not venture to join them, the common people spoke highly of them. [*b*] *Or* and an ever-increasing number of believers, both men and women, were added to the Lord. [*c*] *Or* wondering about them, what this could possibly mean.

27 So they brought them and stood them before the Council; and
28 the High Priest began his examination. 'We expressly ordered you',
he said, 'to desist from teaching in that name; and what has happened? You have filled Jerusalem with your teaching, and you are
29 trying to make us responsible for that man's death.' Peter replied for
30 himself and the apostles: 'We must obey God rather than men. The
God of our fathers raised up Jesus whom you had done to death*a* by
31 hanging him on a gibbet. He it is whom God has exalted with his
own right hand*b* as leader and saviour, to grant Israel repentance
32 and forgiveness of sins. And we are witnesses to all this, and so is
the Holy Spirit given by God to those who are obedient to him.'
33 This touched them on the raw, and they wanted to put them to
34 death. But a member of the Council rose to his feet, a Pharisee
called Gamaliel, a teacher of the law held in high regard by all the
35 people. He moved that the men be put outside for a while. Then he
said, 'Men of Israel, be cautious in deciding what to do with these
36 men. Some time ago Theudas came forward, claiming to be somebody, and a number of men, about four hundred, joined him. But
he was killed and his whole following was broken up and disappeared.
37 After him came Judas the Galilean at the time of the census; he
induced some people to revolt under his leadership, but he too
38 perished and his whole following was scattered. And so now: keep
clear of these men, I tell you; leave them alone. For if this idea of
39 theirs or its execution is of human origin, it will collapse; but if it
is from God, you will never be able to put them down, and you risk
finding yourselves at war with God.'
40 They took his advice. They sent for the apostles and had them
flogged; then they ordered them to give up speaking in the name
41 of Jesus, and discharged them. So the apostles went out from the
Council rejoicing that they had been found worthy to suffer indignity
42 for the sake of the Name. And every day they went steadily on with
their teaching in the temple and in private houses, telling the good
news of Jesus the Messiah.*c*

[a] Or ... Jesus, and you did him to death... [b] Or at his right hand. [c] Or the
good news that the Messiah was Jesus.

206

The Church Moves Outwards

DURING THIS PERIOD, when disciples were growing in number, 6
there was disagreement between those of them who spoke Greek[a]
and those who spoke the language of the Jews.[b] The former party
complained that their widows were being overlooked in the daily
distribution. So the Twelve called the whole body of disciples 2
together and said, 'It would be a grave mistake for us to neglect the
word of God in order to wait at table. Therefore, friends, look out 3
seven men of good reputation from your number, men full of the
Spirit and of wisdom, and we will appoint them to deal with these
matters, while we devote ourselves to prayer and to the ministry of 4
the Word.' This proposal proved acceptable to the whole body. They 5
elected Stephen, a man full of faith and of the Holy Spirit, Philip,
Prochorus, Nicanor, Timon, Parmenas, and Nicolas of Antioch,
a former convert to Judaism. These they presented to the apostles, 6
who prayed and laid their hands on them.

The word of God now spread more and more widely; the number 7
of disciples in Jerusalem went on increasing rapidly, and very many
of the priests adhered to the Faith.

Stephen, who was full of grace and power, began to work great 8
miracles and signs among the people. But some members of the 9
synagogue called the Synagogue of Freedmen, comprising Cyrenians
and Alexandrians and people from Cilicia and Asia, came forward
and argued with Stephen, but could not hold their own against the 10
inspired wisdom with which he spoke. They then put up men who 11
alleged that they had heard him make blasphemous statements against
Moses and against God. They stirred up the people and the elders 12
and doctors of the law, set upon him and seized him, and brought
him before the Council. They produced false witnesses who said, 13
'This man is for ever saying things against this holy place and
against the Law. For we have heard him say that Jesus of Nazareth 14
will destroy this place and alter the customs handed down to us by
Moses.' And all who were sitting in the Council fixed their eyes on 15
him, and his face appeared to them like the face of an angel.

Then the High Priest asked, 'Is this so?' And he said, 'My brothers, 7 1, 2

[a] Literally the Hellenists. [b] Literally the Hebrews.

207

fathers of this nation, listen to me. The God of glory appeared to Abraham our ancestor while he was in Mesopotamia, before he had
3 settled in Harran, and said: "Leave your country and your kinsfolk
4 and come away to a land that I will show you." Thereupon he left the land of the Chaldaeans and settled in Harran. From there, after his father's death, God led him to migrate to this land where you now
5 live. He gave him nothing in it to call his own, not one yard; but promised to give it in possession to him and his descendants after
6 him, though he was then childless. God spoke in these terms: "Abraham's descendants shall live as aliens in a foreign land, held
7 in slavery and oppression for four hundred years. And I will pass judgement", said God, "on the nation whose slaves they are; and after that they shall come out free, and worship me in this place."
8 He then gave him the covenant of circumcision, and so, after Isaac was born, he circumcised him on the eighth day; and Isaac begot Jacob, and Jacob the twelve patriarchs.
9   'The patriarchs out of jealousy sold Joseph into slavery in Egypt,
10 but God was with him and rescued him from all his troubles. He also gave him a presence and powers of mind which so commended him to Pharaoh king of Egypt, that he appointed him chief administrator for Egypt and the whole of the royal household.
11   'But famine struck the whole of Egypt and Canaan, and caused
12 great hardship; and our ancestors could find nothing to eat. But Jacob heard that there was food in Egypt and sent our fathers there.
13 This was their first visit. On the second visit Joseph was recognized by his brothers, and his family connexions were disclosed to Pharaoh.
14 So Joseph sent an invitation to his father Jacob and all his relatives,
15 seventy-five persons altogether; and Jacob went down into Egypt.
16 There he ended his days, as also our forefathers did. Their remains were later removed to Shechem and buried in the tomb which Abraham had bought and paid for from the clan of Emmor at Shechem.
17   'Now as the time approached for God to fulfil the promise he had made to Abraham, our nation in Egypt grew and increased
18 in numbers. At length another king, who knew nothing of Joseph,
19 ascended the throne of Egypt. He made a crafty attack on our race, and cruelly forced our ancestors to expose their children so that they
20 should not survive. At this time Moses was born. He was a fine child, and pleasing to God. For three months he was nursed in his

father's house, and when he was exposed, Pharaoh's daughter herself 21
adopted him and brought him up as her own son. So Moses was 22
trained in all the wisdom of the Egyptians, a powerful speaker and a
man of action.

'He was approaching the age of forty, when it occurred to him 23
to look into the conditions of his fellow-countrymen the Israelites.
He saw one of them being ill-treated, so he went to his aid, and 24
avenged the victim by striking down the Egyptian. He thought his 25
fellow-countrymen would understand that God was offering them
deliverance through him, but they did not understand. The next 26
day he came upon two of them fighting, and tried to bring them to
make up their quarrel. "My men," he said, "you are brothers; why
are you ill-treating one another?" But the man who was at fault 27
pushed him away. "Who set you up as a ruler and judge over us?"
he said. "Are you going to kill me like the Egyptian you killed 28
yesterday?" At this Moses fled the country and settled in Midianite 29
territory. There two sons were born to him.

'After forty years had passed, an angel appeared to him in the 30
flame of a burning bush in the desert near Mount Sinai. Moses was 31
amazed at the sight. But as he approached to look closely, the voice
of the Lord was heard: "I am the God of your fathers, the God of 32
Abraham, Isaac, and Jacob." Moses was terrified and dared not
look. Then the Lord said to him, "Take off your shoes; the place 33
where you are standing is holy ground. I have indeed seen how my 34
people are oppressed in Egypt and have heard their groans; and I
have come down to rescue them. Up, then; let me send you to
Egypt."

'This Moses, whom they had rejected with the words, "Who made 35
you ruler and judge?"—this very man was commissioned as ruler
and liberator by God himself, speaking through the angel who
appeared to him in the bush. It was Moses who led them out, 36
working miracles and signs in Egypt, at the Red Sea, and for forty
years in the desert. It was he again who said to the Israelites, "God 37
will raise up a prophet for you from among yourselves as he
raised me."[a] He it was who, when they were assembled there in 38
the desert, conversed with the angel who spoke to him on Mount
Sinai, and with our forefathers; he received the living utterances of
God, to pass on to us.

[a] Or like me.

39 'But our forefathers would not accept his leadership. They thrust
40 him aside. They wished themselves back in Egypt, and said to Aaron,
"Make us gods to go before us. As for that Moses, who brought
41 us out of Egypt, we do not know what has become of him." That was
when they made the bull-calf, and offered sacrifice to the idol, and
42 held a feast in honour of the thing their hands had made. But God
turned away from them and gave them over to the worship of the
hosts of heaven, as it stands written in the book of the prophets:
"Did you bring me victims and offerings those forty years in the
43 desert, you house of Israel? No, you carried aloft the shrine of
Moloch and the star of the god Rephan, the images which you had
made for your adoration. I will banish you beyond Babylon."

44   'Our forefathers had the Tent of the Testimony in the desert, as
God commanded when he told Moses to make it after the pattern
45 which he had seen. Our fathers of the next generation, with Joshua,
brought it with them when they dispossessed the nations whom God
drove out before them, and there it was until the time of David.
46 David found favour with God and asked to be allowed to provide
47 a dwelling-place for the God of Jacob;[a] but it was Solomon who
48 built him a house. However, the Most High does not live in houses
49 made by men: as the prophet says, "Heaven is my throne and earth
my footstool. What kind of house will you build for me, says the
50 Lord; where is my resting-place? Are not all these things of my own
making?"

51   'How stubborn you are, heathen still at heart and deaf to the
truth! You always fight against the Holy Spirit. Like fathers, like
52 sons. Was there ever a prophet whom your fathers did not persecute?
They killed those who foretold the coming of the Righteous One;
53 and now you have betrayed him and murdered him, you who
received the Law as God's angels gave it to you, and yet have not
kept it.'

54   This touched them on the raw and they ground their teeth with
55 fury. But Stephen, filled with the Holy Spirit, and gazing intently
up to heaven, saw the glory of God, and Jesus standing at God's
56 right hand. 'Look,' he said, 'there is a rift in the sky; I can see the
57 Son of Man standing at God's right hand!' At this they gave a great
58 shout and stopped their ears. Then they made one rush at him and,
flinging him out of the city, set about stoning him. The witnesses

[a] *Some witnesses read* for the house of Jacob.

laid their coats at the feet of a young man named Saul. So they stoned 59
Stephen, and as they did so, he called out, 'Lord Jesus, receive my
spirit.' Then he fell on his knees and cried aloud, 'Lord, do not 60
hold this sin against them', and with that he died. And Saul was 8
among those who approved of his murder.

THIS WAS the beginning of a time of violent persecution for the
church in Jerusalem; and all except the apostles were scattered
over the country districts of Judaea and Samaria. Stephen was 2
given burial by certain devout men, who made a great lamentation
for him. Saul, meanwhile, was harrying the church; he entered 3
house after house, seizing men and women, and sending them to
prison.

As for those who had been scattered, they went through the 4
country preaching the Word. Philip came down to a city in Samaria 5
and began proclaiming the Messiah to them. The crowds, to a man, 6
listened eagerly to what Philip said, when they heard him and saw
the miracles that he performed. For in many cases of possession the 7
unclean spirits came out with a great outcry; and many paralysed
and crippled folk were cured; and there was great joy in that city. 8
A man named Simon had been in the city for some time, and had 9
swept the Samaritans off their feet with his magical arts, claiming
to be someone great. All of them, high and low, listened eagerly 10
to him. 'This man', they said, 'is that power of God which is called
"The Great Power".' They listened because they had for so long 11
been carried away by his magic. But when they came to believe 12
Philip with his good news about the kingdom of God and the name
of Jesus Christ, they were baptized, men and women alike. Even 13
Simon himself believed, and was baptized, and thereupon was constantly in Philip's company. He was carried away when he saw the
powerful signs and miracles that were taking place.

The apostles in Jerusalem now heard that Samaria had accepted 14
the word of God. They sent off Peter and John, who went down there 15
and prayed for the converts, asking that they might receive the
Holy Spirit. For until then the Spirit had not come upon any of 16
them. They had been baptized into the name of the Lord Jesus,
that and nothing more. So Peter and John laid their hands on them 17
and they received the Holy Spirit.

When Simon saw that the Spirit was bestowed through the 18

19 laying on of the apostles' hands, he offered them money and said, 'Give me the same power too, so that when I lay my hands on any-
20 one, he will receive the Holy Spirit.' 'You and your money,' said Peter sternly, 'may you come to a bad end, for thinking God's gift is for
21 sale! You have no part nor lot in this, for you are dishonest with
22 God. Repent of this wickedness and pray the Lord to forgive you
23 for imagining such a thing. I can see that you are doomed to taste
24 the bitter fruit and wear the fetters of sin.'*a* Simon answered, 'Pray to the Lord for me yourselves and ask that none of the things you have spoken of may fall upon me.'
25   And so, after giving their testimony and speaking the word of the Lord, they took the road back to Jerusalem, bringing the good news to many Samaritan villages on the way.
26   Then the angel of the Lord said to Philip, 'Start out and go south to the road that leads down from Jerusalem to Gaza.' (This is the
27 desert road.) So he set out and was on his way when he caught sight of an Ethiopian. This man was a eunuch, a high official of the Kandake, or Queen, of Ethiopia, in charge of all her treasure. He
28 had been to Jerusalem on a pilgrimage and was now on his way home,
29 sitting in his carriage and reading aloud the prophet Isaiah. The Spirit
30 said to Philip, 'Go and join the carriage.' When Philip ran up he heard him reading the prophet Isaiah and said, 'Do you understand
31 what you are reading?' He said, 'How can I understand unless someone will give me the clue?' So he asked Philip to get in and sit beside him.
32   The passage he was reading was this: 'He was led like a sheep to be slaughtered; and like a lamb that is dumb before the shearer,
33 he does not open his mouth. He has been humiliated and has no redress. Who will be able to speak of his posterity? For his life is cut off and he is gone from the earth.'
34   'Now', said the eunuch to Philip, 'tell me, please, who it is that the prophet is speaking about here: himself or someone else?'
35 Then Philip began. Starting from this passage, he told him the
36 good news of Jesus. As they were going along the road, they came to some water. 'Look,' said the eunuch, 'here is water: what is
38 there to prevent my being baptized?';*b* and he ordered the carriage

[a] *Literally* you are for gall of bitterness and a fetter of unrighteousness. [b] *Some witnesses insert* (37) Philip said, 'If you whole-heartedly believe, it is permitted.' He replied, 'I believe that Jesus Christ is the Son of God.'

to stop. Then they both went down into the water, Philip and the eunuch; and he baptized him. When they came up out of the water 39 the Spirit snatched Philip away, and the eunuch saw no more of him, but went on his way well content. Philip appeared at Azotus, 40 and toured the country, preaching in all the towns till he reached Caesarea.

MEANWHILE SAUL was still breathing murderous threats against 9 the disciples of the Lord. He went to the High Priest and applied 2 for letters to the synagogues at Damascus authorizing him to arrest anyone he found, men or women, who followed the new way, and bring them to Jerusalem. While he was still on the road and nearing 3 Damascus, suddenly a light flashed from the sky all around him. He 4 fell to the ground and heard a voice saying, 'Saul, Saul, why do you persecute me?' 'Tell me, Lord,' he said, 'who you are.' The voice 5 answered, 'I am Jesus, whom you are persecuting. But get up and 6 go into the city, and you will be told what you have to do.' Mean- 7 while the men who were travelling with him stood speechless; they heard the voice but could see no one. Saul got up from the ground, 8 but when he opened his eyes he could not see; so they led him by the hand and brought him into Damascus. He was blind for three days, 9 and took no food or drink.

There was a disciple in Damascus named Ananias. He had a vision 10 in which he heard the voice of the Lord: 'Ananias!' 'Here I am, Lord', he answered. The Lord said to him, 'Go at once to Straight 11 Street, to the house of Judas, and ask for a man from Tarsus named Saul. You will find him at prayer; he has had a vision of a man 12 named Ananias coming in and laying his hands on him to restore his sight.' Ananias answered, 'Lord, I have often heard about this 13 man and all the harm he has done to thy people in Jerusalem. And 14 here he is with authority from the chief priests to arrest all who invoke thy name.' But the Lord said to him, 'You must go, for this 15 man is my chosen instrument to bring my name before the nations and their kings, and before the people of Israel. I myself will show 16 him all that he must go through for my name's sake.'

So Ananias went. He entered the house, laid his hands on him 17 and said, 'Saul, my brother, the Lord Jesus, who appeared to you on your way here, has sent me to you so that you may recover your sight, and be filled with the Holy Spirit.' And immediately it 18

seemed that scales fell from his eyes, and he regained his sight.
19 Thereupon he was baptized, and afterwards he took food and his strength returned.

20 He stayed some time with the disciples in Damascus. Soon he was proclaiming Jesus publicly in the synagogues: 'This', he said,
21 'is the Son of God.' All who heard were astounded. 'Is not this the man', they said, 'who was in Jerusalem trying to destroy those who invoke this name? Did he not come here for the sole purpose
22 of arresting them and taking them to the chief priests?' But Saul grew more and more forceful, and silenced the Jews of Damascus with his cogent proofs that Jesus was the Messiah.

23 As the days mounted up, the Jews hatched a plot against his life;
24 but their plans became known to Saul. They kept watch on the city
25 gates day and night so that they might murder him; but his converts took him one night and let him down by the wall, lowering him in a basket.

26 When he reached Jerusalem he tried to join the body of disciples there; but they were all afraid of him, because they did not believe
27 that he was really a convert. Barnabas, however, took him by the hand and introduced him to the apostles. He described to them how Saul had seen the Lord on his journey, and heard his voice, and how
28 he had spoken out boldly in the name of Jesus at Damascus. Saul
29 now stayed with them, moving about freely in Jerusalem. He spoke out boldly and openly in the name of the Lord, talking and debating with the Greek-speaking Jews.[a] But they planned to murder him,
30 and when the brethren learned of this they escorted him to Caesarea and saw him off to Tarsus.

31 MEANWHILE the church, throughout Judaea, Galilee, and Samaria, was left in peace to build up its strength. In the fear of the Lord, upheld by the Holy Spirit, it held on its way and grew in numbers.
32 Peter was making a general tour, in the course of which he went
33 down to visit God's people at Lydda. There he found a man named Aeneas who had been bed-ridden with paralysis for eight years.
34 Peter said to him, 'Aeneas, Jesus Christ cures you; get up and make
35 your bed', and immediately he stood up. All who lived in Lydda and Sharon saw him; and they turned to the Lord.

[a] *Literally* the Hellenists.

In Joppa there was a disciple named Tabitha (in Greek, Dorcas, 36 meaning a gazelle), who filled her days with acts of kindness and charity. At that time she fell ill and died; and they washed her body 37 and laid it in a room upstairs. As Lydda was near Joppa, the dis- 38 ciples, who had heard that Peter was there, sent two men to him with the urgent request, 'Please come over to us without delay.' Peter thereupon went off with them. When he arrived they took him 39 upstairs to the room, where all the widows came and stood round him in tears, showing him the shirts and coats that Dorcas used to make while she was with them. Peter sent them all outside, and 40 knelt down and prayed. Then, turning towards the body, he said, 'Tabitha, arise.' She opened her eyes, saw Peter, and sat up. He 41 gave her his hand and helped her to her feet. Then he called the members of the congregation and the widows and showed her to them alive. The news spread all over Joppa, and many came to 42 believe in the Lord. Peter stayed on in Joppa for some time with 43 one Simon, a tanner.

At Caesarea there was a man named Cornelius, a centurion in the 10 Italian Cohort, as it was called. He was a religious man, and he and 2 his whole family joined in the worship of God. He gave generously to help the Jewish people, and was regular in his prayers to God. One day about three in the afternoon he had a vision in which he 3 clearly saw an angel of God, who came into his room and said, 'Cornelius!' He stared at him in terror. 'What is it, my lord?' he 4 asked. The angel said, 'Your prayers and acts of charity have gone up to heaven to speak for you before God. And now send to Joppa 5 for a man named Simon, also called Peter: he is lodging with another 6 Simon, a tanner, whose house is by the sea.' So when the angel who 7 was speaking to him had gone, he summoned two of his servants and a military orderly who was a religious man, told them the whole 8 story, and sent them to Joppa.

Next day, while they were still on their way and approaching the 9 city, about noon Peter went up on the roof to pray. He grew hungry 10 and wanted something to eat. While they were getting it ready, he fell into a trance. He saw a rift in the sky, and a thing coming down 11 that looked like a great sheet of sail-cloth. It was slung by the four corners, and was being lowered to the ground. In it he saw creatures 12 of every kind, whatever walks or crawls or flies. Then there was a 13 voice which said to him, 'Up, Peter, kill and eat.' But Peter said, 14

15 'No, Lord, no: I have never eaten anything profane or unclean.' The voice came again a second time: 'It is not for you to call profane what
16 God counts clean.' This happened three times; and then the thing was taken up again into the sky.

17   While Peter was still puzzling over the meaning of the vision he had seen, the messengers of Cornelius had been asking the way to
18 Simon's house, and now arrived at the entrance. They called out and
19 asked if Simon Peter was lodging there. But Peter was thinking over the vision, when the Spirit said to him, 'Some*a* men are here
20 looking for you; make haste and go downstairs. You may go with
21 them without any misgiving, for it was I who sent them.' Peter came down to the men and said, 'You are looking for me? Here I
22 am. What brings you here?' 'We are from the centurion Cornelius,' they replied, 'a good and religious man, acknowledged as such by the whole Jewish nation. He was directed by a holy angel to send for
23 you to his house and to listen to what you have to say.' So Peter asked them in and gave them a night's lodging. Next day he set out with them, accompanied by some members of the congregation at Joppa.

24   The day after that, he arrived at Caesarea. Cornelius was expect-
25 ing them and had called together his relatives and close friends. When Peter arrived, Cornelius came to meet him, and bowed to the ground
26 in deep reverence. But Peter raised him to his feet and said, 'Stand
27 up; I am a man like anyone else.' Still talking with him he went in
28 and found a large gathering. He said to them, 'I need not tell you that a Jew is forbidden by his religion to visit or associate with a man of another race; yet God has shown me clearly that I must not call
29 any man profane or unclean. That is why I came here without demur when you sent for me. May I ask what was your reason for sending?'

30   Cornelius said, 'Four days ago, just about this time, I was in the house here saying the afternoon prayers, when suddenly a man in
31 shining robes stood before me. He said: "Cornelius, your prayer has been heard and your acts of charity remembered before God.
32 Send to Joppa, then, to Simon Peter, and ask him to come. He is
33 lodging in the house of Simon the tanner, by the sea." So I sent to you there and then; it was kind of you to come. And now we are all met here before God, to hear all that the Lord has ordered you to say.'

[a] *One witness reads* Two; *others read* Three.

Peter began: 'I now see how true it is that God has no favourites, 34
but that in every nation the man who is godfearing and does what 35
is right is acceptable to him. He sent his word to the Israelites and 36
gave the good news of peace through Jesus Christ, who is Lord of all.
I need not tell you what happened lately all over the land of the 37
Jews, starting from Galilee after the baptism proclaimed by John.
You know about Jesus of Nazareth, how God anointed him with the 38
Holy Spirit and with power. He went about doing good and healing
all who were oppressed by the devil, for God was with him. And 39
we can bear witness to all that he did in the Jewish country-side and
in Jerusalem. He was put to death by hanging on a gibbet; but God 40
raised him to life on the third day, and allowed him to appear, not 41
to the whole people, but to witnesses whom God had chosen in
advance—to us, who ate and drank with him after he rose from the
dead. He commanded us to proclaim him to the people, and affirm 42
that he is the one who has been designated by God as judge of
the living and the dead. It is to him that all the prophets testify, 43
declaring that everyone who trusts in him receives forgiveness of
sins through his name.'

Peter was still speaking when the Holy Spirit came upon all who 44
were listening to the message. The believers who had come with 45
Peter, men of Jewish birth, were astonished that the gift of the Holy
Spirit should have been poured out even on Gentiles. For they 46
could hear them speaking in tongues of ecstasy and acclaiming the
greatness of God. Then Peter spoke: 'Is anyone prepared to with- 47
hold the water for baptism from these persons, who have received
the Holy Spirit just as we did ourselves?' Then he ordered them to 48
be baptized in the name of Jesus Christ. After that they asked him
to stay on with them for a time.

News came to the apostles and the members of the church in 11
Judaea that Gentiles too had accepted the word of God; and when 2
Peter came up to Jerusalem those who were of Jewish birth raised
the question with him. 'You have been visiting men who are un- 3
circumcised,' they said, 'and sitting at table with them!' Peter 4
began by laying before them the facts as they had happened.

'I was in the city of Joppa', he said, 'at prayer; and while in a 5
trance I had a vision: a thing was coming down that looked like a
great sheet of sail-cloth, slung by the four corners and lowered from
the sky till it reached me. I looked intently to make out what was in 6

it and I saw four-footed creatures of the earth, wild beasts, and things
7 that crawl or fly. Then I heard a voice saying to me, "Up, Peter,
8 kill and eat." But I said, "No, Lord, no: nothing profane or unclean
9 has ever entered my mouth." A voice from heaven answered a
second time, "It is not for you to call profane what God counts
10 clean." This happened three times, and then they were all drawn
11 up again into the sky. At that moment three men, who had been
sent to me from Caesarea, arrived at the house where I was*a* staying;
12 and the Spirit told me to go with them.*b* My six companions here
13 came with me and we went into the man's house. He told us how
he had seen an angel standing in his house who said, "Send to Joppa
14 for Simon also called Peter. He will speak words that will bring
15 salvation to you and all your household." Hardly had I begun
speaking, when the Holy Spirit came upon them, just as upon us
16 at the beginning. Then I recalled what the Lord had said: "John
baptized with water, but you will be baptized with the Holy Spirit."
17 God gave them no less a gift than he gave us when we put our trust
in the Lord Jesus Christ; then how could I possibly stand in God's
way?'
18   When they heard this their doubts were silenced. They gave
praise to God and said, 'This means that God has granted life-
giving repentance to the Gentiles also.'

19 MEANWHILE those who had been scattered after the persecution
that arose over Stephen made their way to Phoenicia, Cyprus, and
Antioch, bringing the message to Jews only and to no others.
20 But there were some natives of Cyprus and Cyrene among them,
and these, when they arrived at Antioch, began to speak to pagans
21 as well, telling them the good news of the Lord Jesus. The power of
the Lord was with them, and a great many became believers, and
turned to the Lord.
22   The news reached the ears of the church in Jerusalem; and they
23 sent Barnabas to Antioch. When he arrived and saw the divine
grace at work, he rejoiced, and encouraged them all to hold fast to
24 the Lord with resolute hearts; for he was a good man, full of the
Holy Spirit and of faith. And large numbers were won over to the
Lord.

[a] *Some witnesses read* we were. [b] *Some witnesses add* making no distinctions; *others
add* without any misgiving, *as in 10. 20.*

He then went off to Tarsus to look for Saul; and when he had 25, 26
found him, he brought him to Antioch. For a whole year the two of
them lived in fellowship with the congregation there, and gave instruction to large numbers. It was in Antioch that the disciples first got
the name of Christians.

During this period some prophets came down from Jerusalem to 27
Antioch. One of them, Agabus by name, was inspired to stand up 28
and predict a severe and world-wide famine, which in fact occurred
in the reign of Claudius. So the disciples agreed to make a contribu- 29
tion, each according to his means, for the relief of their fellow-
Christians in Judaea. This they did, and sent it off in the charge of 30
Barnabas and Saul to the elders.

I t w a s about this time that King Herod attacked certain members 12
of the church. He beheaded James, the brother of John, and then, 2, 3
when he saw that the Jews approved, proceeded to arrest Peter also.
This happened during the festival of Unleavened Bread. Having 4
secured him, he put him in prison under a military guard, four
squads of four men each, meaning to produce him in public after
Passover. So Peter was kept in prison under constant watch, while 5
the church kept praying fervently for him to God.

On the very night before Herod had planned to bring him for- 6
ward, Peter was asleep between two soldiers, secured by two chains,
while outside the doors sentries kept guard over the prison. All at 7
once an angel of the Lord stood there, and the cell was ablaze with
light. He tapped Peter on the shoulder and woke him. 'Quick!
Get up', he said, and the chains fell away from his wrists. The angel 8
then said to him, 'Do up your belt and put your shoes on.' He
did so. 'Now wrap your cloak round you and follow me.' He 9
followed him out, with no idea that the angel's intervention was real:
he thought it was just a vision. But they passed the first guard-post, 10
then the second, and reached the iron gate leading out into the city,
which opened for them of its own accord. And so they came out
and walked the length of one street; and the angel left him.

Then Peter came to himself. 'Now I know it is true,' he said; 11
'the Lord has sent his angel and rescued me from Herod's clutches
and from all that the Jewish people were expecting.' When he 12
realized how things stood, he made for the house of Mary, the mother
of John Mark, where a large company was at prayer. He knocked at 13

14 the outer door and a maid called Rhoda came to answer it. She recognized Peter's voice and was so overjoyed that instead of opening the door she ran in and announced that Peter was standing outside.
15 'You are crazy', they told her; but she insisted that it was so. Then they said, 'It must be his guardian angel.'
16 Meanwhile Peter went on knocking, and when they opened the
17 door and saw him, they were astounded. With a movement of the hand he signed to them to keep quiet, and told them how the Lord had brought him out of prison. 'Report this to James and the members of the church', he said. Then he left the house and went off elsewhere.
18 When morning came, there was consternation among the soldiers:
19 what could have become of Peter? Herod made close search, but failed to find him, so he interrogated the guards and ordered their execution.
20 Afterwards he left Judaea to reside for a time at Caesarea. He had for some time been furiously angry with the people of Tyre and Sidon, who now by common agreement presented themselves at his court. There they won over Blastus the royal chamberlain, and sued for peace, because their country drew its supplies from
21 the king's territory. So, on an appointed day, attired in his royal
22 robes and seated on the rostrum, Herod harangued them; and the
23 populace shouted back, 'It is a god speaking, not a man!' Instantly an angel of the Lord struck him down, because he had usurped the honour due to God; he was eaten up with worms and died.
24 Meanwhile the word of God continued to grow and spread.
25 Barnabas and Saul, their task fulfilled, returned from Jerusalem,*ᵃ* taking John Mark with them.

The Church Breaks Barriers

13 THERE WERE at Antioch, in the congregation there, certain prophets and teachers: Barnabas, Simeon called Niger, Lucius of Cyrene, Manaen, who had been at the court of Prince Herod,
2 and Saul. While they were keeping a fast and offering worship to

[a] *Some witnesses read* their task fulfilled, returned to Jerusalem; *or, as it might be rendered,* their task at Jerusalem fulfilled, returned.

the Lord, the Holy Spirit said, 'Set Barnabas and Saul apart for me, to do the work to which I have called them.' Then, after further 3 fasting and prayer, they laid their hands on them and let them go.

So these two, sent out on their mission by the Holy Spirit, came 4 down to Seleucia, and from there sailed to Cyprus. Arriving at 5 Salamis, they declared the word of God in the Jewish synagogues. They had John with them as their assistant. They went through 6 the whole island as far as Paphos, and there they came upon a sorcerer, a Jew who posed as a prophet, Bar-Jesus by name. He was 7 in the retinue of the Governor, Sergius Paulus, an intelligent man, who had sent for Barnabas and Saul and wanted to hear the word of God. This Elymas the sorcerer (so his name may be translated) 8 opposed them, trying to turn the Governor away from the Faith. But Saul, also known as Paul, filled with the Holy Spirit, looked 9 him in the face and said, 'You utter impostor and charlatan! You 10 son of the devil and enemy of all goodness, will you never stop falsifying the straight ways of the Lord? Look now, the hand of the 11 Lord strikes: you shall be blind, and for a time you shall not see the sunlight.' Instantly mist and darkness came over him and he groped about for someone to lead him by the hand. When the Governor saw 12 what had happened he became a believer, deeply impressed by what he learned about the Lord.

Leaving Paphos, Paul and his companions went by sea to Perga 13 in Pamphylia; John, however, left them and returned to Jerusalem. From Perga they continued their journey as far as Pisidian Antioch. 14 On the Sabbath they went to synagogue and took their seats; and 15 after the readings from the Law and the prophets, the officials of the synagogue sent this message to them: 'Friends, if you have anything to say to the people by way of exhortation, let us hear it.' Paul rose, made a gesture with his hand, and began: 16

'Men of Israel and you who worship our God, listen to me! The God of this people of Israel chose our fathers. When they were 17 still living as aliens in Egypt he made them into a nation and brought them out of that country with arm outstretched. For some forty 18 years he bore with their conduct[a] in the desert. Then in the Canaan- 19 ite country he overthrew seven nations, whose lands he gave them to be their heritage for some four hundred and fifty years, and afterwards 20 appointed judges for them until the time of the prophet Samuel.

[a] *Some witnesses read* he sustained them.

21 'Then they asked for a king and God gave them Saul the son of Kish, a man of the tribe of Benjamin, who reigned for forty years.
22 Then he removed him and set up David as their king, giving him his approval in these words: "I have found David son of Jesse to be a man after my own heart, who will carry out all my purposes."
23 This is the man from whose posterity God, as he promised, has
24 brought Israel a saviour, Jesus. John made ready for his coming by proclaiming baptism as a token of repentance to the whole people of
25 Israel. And when John was nearing the end of his course, he said, "I am not what you think I am. No, after me comes one whose shoes I am not fit to unfasten."

26 'My brothers, you who come of the stock of Abraham, and others among you who revere our God, we are the people to whom the
27 message of this salvation has been sent. The people of Jerusalem and their rulers did not recognize him, or understand the words of the prophets which are read Sabbath by Sabbath; indeed they
28 fulfilled them by condemning him. Though they failed to find grounds for the sentence of death, they asked Pilate to have him
29 executed. And when they had carried out all that the scriptures said about him, they took him down from the gibbet and laid him in
30, 31 a tomb. But God raised him from the dead; and there was a period of many days during which he appeared to those who had come up with him from Galilee to Jerusalem.

32 'They are now his witnesses before our nation; and we are here to give you the good news that God, who made the promise to the
33 fathers, has fulfilled it for the children[a] by raising Jesus from the dead, as indeed it stands written, in the second[b] Psalm: "You are
34 my son; this day have I begotten you." Again, that he raised him from the dead, never again to revert to corruption, he declares in these words: "I will give you the blessings promised to David, holy
35 and sure." This is borne out by another passage: "Thou wilt not
36 let thy loyal servant suffer corruption." As for David, when he had served the purpose of God in his own generation, he died, and was
37 gathered to his fathers, and suffered corruption; but the one whom
38 God raised up did not suffer corruption; and you must understand, my brothers, that it is through him that forgiveness of sins is now
39 being proclaimed to you. It is through him that everyone who has

[a] *Some witnesses read* our children; *others read* us their children. [b] *Some witnesses read* first.

faith is acquitted of everything for which there was no acquittal under the Law of Moses. Beware, then, lest you bring down upon 40 yourselves the doom proclaimed by the prophets: "See this, you 41 scoffers, wonder, and begone; for I am doing a deed in your days, a deed which you will never believe when you are told of it."'

As they were leaving the synagogue they were asked to come again 42 and speak on these subjects next Sabbath; and after the congregation 43 had dispersed, many Jews and gentile worshippers went along with Paul and Barnabas, who spoke to them and urged them to hold fast to the grace of God.

On the following Sabbath almost the whole city gathered to hear 44 the word of God. When the Jews saw the crowds, they were filled 45 with jealous resentment, and contradicted what Paul and Barnabas said, with violent abuse. But Paul and Barnabas were outspoken in 46 their reply. 'It was necessary', they said, 'that the word of God should be declared to you first. But since you reject it and thus condemn yourselves as unworthy of eternal life, we now turn to the Gentiles. For these are our instructions from the Lord: "I have 47 appointed you to be a light for the Gentiles, and a means of salvation to earth's farthest bounds."' When the Gentiles heard this, they 48 were overjoyed and thankfully acclaimed the word of the Lord, and those who were marked out for eternal life became believers. So the word of the Lord spread far and wide through the region. 49 But the Jews stirred up feeling among the women of standing who 50 were worshippers, and among the leading men of the city; a persecution was started against Paul and Barnabas, and they were expelled from the district. So they shook the dust off their feet in protest 51 against them and went to Iconium. And the converts were filled with 52 joy and with the Holy Spirit.

At Iconium similarly they went*ᵃ* into the Jewish synagogue and 14 spoke to such purpose that a large body both of Jews and Greeks became believers. But the unconverted Jews stirred up the Gentiles 2 and poisoned their minds against the Christians. For some time 3 Paul and Barnabas stayed on and spoke boldly and openly in reliance on the Lord; and he confirmed the message of his grace by causing signs and miracles to be worked at their hands. The mass of the 4 townspeople were divided, some siding with the Jews, others with the apostles. But when a move was made by Gentiles and Jews together, 5

[a] *Or* At Iconium they went together...

with the connivance of the city authorities, to maltreat them and
6 stone them, they got wind of it and made their escape to the Lycao-
7 nian cities of Lystra and Derbe and the surrounding country, where
they continued to spread the good news.

8 At Lystra sat a crippled man, lame from birth, who had never
9 walked in his life. This man listened while Paul was speaking. Paul
10 looked him in the face and saw that he had the faith to be cured, so
he said to him in a loud voice, 'Stand up straight on your feet'; and
11 he sprang up and started to walk. When the crowds saw what Paul
had done, they shouted, in their native Lycaonian, 'The gods have
12 come down to us in human form.' And they called Barnabas Jupiter,
13 and Paul they called Mercury, because he was the spokesman. And
the priest of Jupiter, whose temple was just outside the city, brought
oxen and garlands to the gates, and he and all the people were about
to offer sacrifice.

14 But when the apostles Barnabas and Paul heard of it, they tore
15 their clothes and rushed into the crowd shouting, 'Men, what is this
that you are doing? We are only human beings, no less mortal than
you. The good news we bring tells you to turn from these follies to
the living God, who made heaven and earth and sea and everything
16 in them. In past ages he allowed all nations to go their own way;
17 and yet he has not left you without some clue to his nature, in the
kindness he shows: he sends you rain from heaven and crops in
their seasons, and gives you food and good cheer in plenty.'
18 With these words they barely managed to prevent the crowd from
offering sacrifice to them.

19 Then Jews from Antioch and Iconium came on the scene and
won over the crowds. They stoned Paul, and dragged him out of the
20 city, thinking him dead. The converts formed a ring round him,
and he got to his feet and went into the city. Next day he left with
Barnabas for Derbe.

21 After bringing the good news to that town, where they gained
many converts, they returned to Lystra, then to Iconium, and then
22 to Antioch, heartening the converts and encouraging them to be
true to their religion. They warned them that to enter the kingdom
23 of God we must pass through many hardships. They also appointed
elders for them in each congregation, and with prayer and fasting
committed them to the Lord in whom they had put their faith.
24 Then they passed through Pisidia and came into Pamphylia.

When they had given the message at Perga, they went down to 25
Attalia, and from there set sail for Antioch, where they had origi- 26
nally been commended to the grace of God for the task which they
had now completed. When they arrived and had called the congrega- 27
tion together, they reported all that God had helped them to do,
and how he had thrown open the gates of faith to the Gentiles.
And they stayed for some time with the disciples there.   28

NOW CERTAIN persons who had come down from Judaea began 15
to teach the brotherhood that those who were not circumcised in
accordance with Mosaic practice could not be saved. That brought 2
them into fierce dissension and controversy with Paul and Barnabas.
And so it was arranged that these two and some others from Antioch
should go up to Jerusalem to see the apostles and elders about this
question.

They were sent on their way by the congregation, and travelled 3
through Phoenicia and Samaria, telling the full story of the conversion of the Gentiles. The news caused great rejoicing among all the
Christians there.

When they reached Jerusalem they were welcomed by the church 4
and the apostles and elders, and reported all that God had helped
them to do. Then some of the Pharisaic party who had become 5
believers came forward and said, 'They must be circumcised and
told to keep the Law of Moses.'

The apostles and elders held a meeting to look into this matter; 6
and, after a long debate, Peter rose and addressed them. 'My friends,' 7
he said, 'in the early days, as you yourselves know, God made his
choice among you and ordained that from my lips the Gentiles
should hear and believe the message of the Gospel. And God, who 8
can read men's minds, showed his approval of them by giving the
Holy Spirit to them, as he did to us. He made no difference between 9
them and us; for he purified their hearts by faith. Then why do you 10
now provoke God by laying on the shoulders of these converts a yoke
which neither we nor our fathers were able to bear? No, we believe 11
that it is by the grace of the Lord Jesus that we are saved, and so are
they.'

At that the whole company fell silent and listened to Barnabas and 12
Paul as they told of all the signs and miracles that God had worked
among the Gentiles through them.

13 When they had finished speaking, James summed up: 'My
14 friends,' he said, 'listen to me. Simeon has told how it first happened that God took notice of the Gentiles, to choose from among
15 them a people to bear his name; and this agrees with the words of
the prophets, as Scripture has it:

16   "Thereafter I will return and rebuild the fallen house of David;
    Even from its ruins I will rebuild it, and set it up again,
17   That they may seek the Lord—all the rest of mankind,
    And the Gentiles, whom I have claimed for my own.
    Thus says the Lord, whose work it is,
18   Made known long ago."

19 'My judgement therefore is that we should impose no irksome
20 restrictions on those of the Gentiles who are turning to God, but
instruct them by letter to abstain from things polluted by contact
with idols, from fornication, from anything that has been strangled,
21 and from blood.*a* Moses, after all, has never lacked spokesmen in
every town for generations past; he is read in the synagogues
Sabbath by Sabbath.'
22 Then the apostles and elders, with the agreement of the whole
church, resolved to choose representatives and send them to Antioch
with Paul and Barnabas. They chose two leading men in the com-
23 munity, Judas Barsabbas and Silas, and gave them this letter to
deliver:
   'We, the apostles and elders, send greetings as brothers to our
24 brothers of gentile origin in Antioch, Syria, and Cilicia. Foras-
much as we have heard that some of our number, without any
instructions from us, have*b* disturbed you with their talk and
25 unsettled your minds, we have resolved unanimously to send to you
our chosen representatives with our well-beloved Barnabas and
26 Paul, who have devoted themselves to the cause of our Lord Jesus
27 Christ. We are therefore sending Judas and Silas, who will them-
28 selves confirm this by word of mouth. It is the decision of the Holy
Spirit, and our decision, to lay no further burden upon you beyond
29 these essentials: you are to abstain from meat that has been offered
to idols, from blood, from anything that has been strangled,*c* and

[a] *Some witnesses omit* from fornication; *others omit* from anything that has been
strangled; *some add (after* blood) and to refrain from doing to others what they
would not like done to themselves. [b] *Some witnesses read* have gone out and...
[c] *Some witnesses omit* from anything that has been strangled.

from fornication.*ᵃ* If you keep yourselves free from these things you will be doing right. Farewell.'

So they were sent off on their journey and travelled down to 30 Antioch, where they called the congregation together, and delivered the letter. When it was read, they all rejoiced at the encouragement 31 it brought. Judas and Silas, who were prophets themselves, said 32 much to encourage and strengthen the members, and, after spend- 33 ing some time there, were dismissed with the good wishes of the brethren, to return to those who had sent them.*ᵇ* But Paul and 35 Barnabas stayed on at Antioch, and there, along with many others, they taught and preached the word of the Lord.

Paul Leads the Advance

AFTER A WHILE Paul said to Barnabas, 'Ought we not to go 36 back now to see how our brothers are faring in the various towns where we proclaimed the word of the Lord?' Barnabas 37 wanted to take John Mark with them; but Paul judged that the man 38 who had deserted them in Pamphylia and had not gone on to share in their work was not the man to take with them now. The dispute was 39 so sharp that they parted company. Barnabas took Mark with him and sailed for Cyprus, while Paul chose Silas. He started on his journey, 40 commended by the brothers to the grace of the Lord, and travelled 41 through Syria and Cilicia bringing new strength to the congregations.

He went on to Derbe and to Lystra, and there he found a disciple 16 named Timothy, the son of a Jewish Christian mother and a Greek father. He was well spoken of by the Christians at Lystra and 2 Iconium, and Paul wanted to have him in his company when he 3 left the place. So he took him and circumcised him, out of considera- tion for the Jews who lived in those parts; for they all knew that his father was a Greek. As they made their way from town to town they 4 handed on the decisions taken by the apostles and elders in Jerusalem and enjoined their observance. And so, day by day, the congrega- 5 tions grew stronger in faith and increased in numbers.

[*a*] *Some witnesses omit* and from fornication; *and some add* and refrain from doing to others what you would not like done to yourselves. [*b*] *Some witnesses add* (34) But Silas decided to remain there.

6   They travelled through the Phrygian and Galatian region,*ᵃ* because they were prevented by the Holy Spirit from delivering the
7 message in the province of Asia; and when they approached the Mysian border they tried to enter Bithynia; but the Spirit of Jesus
8 would not allow them, so they skirted*ᵇ* Mysia and reached the coast
9 at Troas. During the night a vision came to Paul: a Macedonian stood there appealing to him and saying, 'Come across to Macedonia and
10 help us.' After he had seen this vision we at once set about getting a passage to Macedonia, concluding that God had called us to bring them the good news.

11   So we sailed from Troas and made a straight run to Samothrace,
12 the next day to Neapolis, and from there to Philippi, a city of the first rank in that district of Macedonia, and a Roman colony. Here
13 we stayed for some days, and on the Sabbath day we went outside the city gate by the river-side, where we thought there would be a place of prayer,*ᶜ* and sat down and talked to the women who had
14 gathered there. One of them named Lydia, a dealer in purple fabric from the city of Thyatira, who was a worshipper of God, was listening, and the Lord opened her heart to respond to what Paul
15 said. She was baptized, and her household with her, and then she said to us, 'If you have judged me to be a believer in the Lord, I beg you to come and stay in my house.' And she insisted on our going.

16   Once, when we were on our way to the place of prayer, we met a slave-girl who was possessed by an oracular spirit and brought
17 large profits to her owners by telling fortunes. She followed Paul and the rest of us, shouting, 'These men are servants of the Supreme
18 God, and are declaring to you a way of salvation.' She did this day after day, until Paul could bear it no longer. Rounding on the spirit he said, 'I command you in the name of Jesus Christ to come out of her', and it went out there and then.

19   When the girl's owners saw that their hope of gain had gone, they seized Paul and Silas and dragged them to the city authorities in
20 the main square; and bringing them before the magistrates, they said, 'These men are causing a disturbance in our city; they are
21 Jews; they are advocating customs which it is illegal for us Romans
22 to adopt and follow.' The mob joined in the attack; and the magistrates

[a] *Or* through Phrygia and the Galatian region.   [b] *Possibly* traversed.   [c] *Some witnesses read* where there was a recognized place of prayer.

tore off the prisoners' clothes and ordered them to be flogged. After 23
giving them a severe beating they flung them into prison and ordered
the jailer to keep them under close guard. In view of these orders, 24
he put them in the inner prison and secured their feet in the stocks.

About midnight Paul and Silas, at their prayers, were singing 25
praises to God, and the other prisoners were listening, when sud- 26
denly there was such a violent earthquake that the foundations of
the jail were shaken; all the doors burst open and all the prisoners
found their fetters unfastened. The jailer woke up to see the prison 27
doors wide open, and assuming that the prisoners had escaped, drew
his sword intending to kill himself. But Paul shouted, 'Do yourself 28
no harm; we are all here.' The jailer called for lights, rushed in and 29
threw himself down before Paul and Silas, trembling with fear. He 30
then escorted them out and said, 'Masters, what must I do to be
saved?' They said, 'Put your trust in the Lord Jesus, and you will 31
be saved, you and your household.' Then they spoke the word of 32
the Lord^a to him and to everyone in his house. At that late hour of 33
the night he took them and washed their wounds; and immediately
afterwards he and his whole family were baptized. He brought them 34
into his house, set out a meal, and rejoiced with his whole household
in his new-found faith in God.

When daylight came the magistrates sent their officers with instruc- 35
tions to release the men. The jailer reported the message to Paul: 36
'The magistrates have sent word that you are to be released. So
now you may go free, and blessings on your journey.'^b But Paul 37
said to the officers: 'They gave us a public flogging, though we are
Roman citizens and have not been found guilty; they threw us into
prison, and are they now to smuggle us out privately? No indeed!
Let them come in person and escort us out.' The officers reported 38
his words. The magistrates were alarmed to hear that they were
Roman citizens, and came and apologized to them. Then they escorted 39
them out and requested them to go away from the city. On leaving 40
the prison, they went to Lydia's house, where they met their fellow-
Christians, and spoke words of encouragement to them; then they
departed.

THEY NOW travelled by way of Amphipolis and Apollonia 17
and came to Thessalonica, where there was a Jewish synagogue.

[a] *Some witnesses read* of God.   [b] *Some witnesses read* . . . free and take your journey.

2 Following his usual practice Paul went to their meetings; and for the next three Sabbaths he argued with them, quoting texts of Scripture
3 which he expounded and applied to show that the Messiah had to suffer and rise from the dead. 'And this Jesus,' he said, 'whom I am
4 proclaiming to you, is the Messiah.' Some of them were convinced and joined Paul and Silas; so did a great number of godfearing Greeks and a good many influential women.*a*
5 But the Jews in their jealousy recruited some low fellows from the dregs of the populace, roused the rabble, and had the city in an uproar. They mobbed Jason's house, with the intention of bringing
6 Paul and Silas before the town assembly. Failing to find them, they dragged Jason himself and some members of the congregation before the magistrates, shouting, 'The men who have made trouble all over
7 the world have now come here; and Jason has harboured them. They all flout the Emperor's laws, and assert that there is a rival king,
8 Jesus.' These words caused a great commotion in the mob, which
9 affected the magistrates also. They bound over Jason and the others, and let them go.
10 As soon as darkness fell, the members of the congregation sent Paul and Silas off to Beroea. On arrival, they made their way to
11 the synagogue. The Jews here were more liberal-minded than those at Thessalonica: they received the message with great eagerness, studying the scriptures every day to see whether it was as they said.
12 Many of them therefore became believers, and so did a fair number
13 of Greeks, women of standing as well as men. But when the Thessalonian Jews learned that the word of God had now been proclaimed by Paul in Beroea, they came on there to stir up trouble and rouse
14 the rabble. Thereupon the members of the congregation sent Paul off at once to go down to the coast, while Silas and Timothy both
15 stayed behind. Paul's escort brought him as far as Athens, and came away with instructions for Silas and Timothy to rejoin him with all speed.
16 Now while Paul was waiting for them at Athens he was exasperated
17 to see how the city was full of idols. So he argued in the synagogue with the Jews and gentile worshippers, and also in the city square
18 every day with casual passers-by. And some of the Epicurean and Stoic philosophers joined issue with him. Some said, 'What can this charlatan be trying to say?'; others, 'He would appear to be a propa-

[a] *Some witnesses read* a good many wives of leading men.

gandist for foreign deities'—this because he was preaching about
Jesus and Resurrection. So they took him and brought him before 19
the Court of Areopagus*a* and said, 'May we know what this new
doctrine is that you propound? You are introducing ideas that sound 20
strange to us, and we should like to know what they mean.' (Now 21
the Athenians in general and the foreigners there had no time for
anything but talking or hearing about the latest novelty.)

Then Paul stood up before the Court of Areopagus*b* and said: 22
'Men of Athens, I see that in everything that concerns religion you
are uncommonly scrupulous. For as I was going round looking 23
at the objects of your worship, I noticed among other things an altar
bearing the inscription "To an Unknown God". What you worship
but do not know—this is what I now proclaim.

'The God who created the world and everything in it, and who 24
is Lord of heaven and earth, does not live in shrines made by men.
It is not because he lacks anything that he accepts service at men's 25
hands, for he is himself the universal giver of life and breath and all
else. He created every race of men of one stock, to inhabit the whole 26
earth's surface. He fixed the epochs of their history*c* and the limits
of their territory. They were to seek God, and, it might be, touch 27
and find him; though indeed he is not far from each one of us,
for in him we live and move, in him we exist; as some of your own 28
poets*d* have said, "We are also his offspring." As God's offspring, 29
then, we ought not to suppose that the deity is like an image in gold
or silver or stone, shaped by human craftsmanship and design. As 30
for the times of ignorance, God has overlooked them; but now he
commands mankind, all men everywhere, to repent, because he has 31
fixed the day on which he will have the world judged, and justly
judged, by a man of his choosing; of this he has given assurance to
all by raising him from the dead.'

When they heard about the raising of the dead, some scoffed; and 32
others said, 'We will hear you on this subject some other time.'
And so Paul left the assembly. However, some men joined him and 33, 34
became believers, including Dionysius, a member of the Court of
Areopagus; also a woman named Damaris, and others besides.

After this he left Athens and went to Corinth. There he fell in 18 1, 2
with a Jew named Aquila, a native of Pontus, and his wife Priscilla;

[a] *Or* brought him to Mars' Hill. [b] *Or* in the middle of Mars' Hill. [c] *Or* fixed the
ordered seasons... [d] *Some witnesses read* some among you.

he had recently arrived from Italy because Claudius had issued an
3 edict that all Jews should leave Rome. Paul approached them and,
because he was of the same trade, he made his home with them, and
4 they carried on business together; they were tent-makers. He also
held discussions in the synagogue Sabbath by Sabbath, trying to
convince both Jews and pagans.

5 Then Silas and Timothy came down from Macedonia, and Paul
devoted himself entirely to preaching, affirming before the Jews
6 that the Messiah was Jesus. But when they opposed him and re-
sorted to abuse, he shook out the skirts of his cloak and said to them,
'Your blood be on your own heads! My conscience is clear; now
7 I shall go to the Gentiles.' With that he left, and went to the house
of a worshipper of God named Titius Justus, who lived next door
8 to the synagogue. Crispus, who held office in the synagogue, now
became a believer in the Lord, with all his household; and a number
9 of Corinthians listened and believed, and were baptized. One night
in a vision the Lord said to Paul, 'Have no fear: go on with your
10 preaching and do not be silenced, for I am with you and no one
shall attempt to do you harm;*a* and there are many in this city who
11 are my people.' So he settled down for eighteen months, teaching
the word of God among them.

12 But when Gallio was proconsul of Achaia, the Jews set upon Paul
13 in a body and brought him into court. 'This man', they said, 'is
inducing people to worship God in ways that are against the law.'
14 Paul was just about to speak when Gallio said to them, 'If it had been
a question of crime or grave misdemeanour, I should, of course, have
15 given you Jews a patient hearing, but if it is some bickering about
words and names and your Jewish law, you may see to it yourselves;
16 I have no mind to be a judge of these matters.' And he had them
17 ejected from the court. Then there was a general attack on Sosthenes,
who held office in the synagogue, and they gave him a beating in
full view of the bench. But all this left Gallio quite unconcerned.

18 Paul stayed on for some time, and then took leave of the brotherhood and set sail for Syria, accompanied by Priscilla and Aquila.
At Cenchreae he had his hair cut off, because he was under a vow.
19 When they reached Ephesus he parted from them and went himself
20 into the synagogue, where he held a discussion with the Jews. He
21 was asked to stay longer, but declined and set out from Ephesus,

[a] Or and you will not be harmed by anyone's attacks.

saying, as he took leave of them, 'I shall come back to you if it is God's will.' On landing at Caesarea, he went up and paid his 22 respects to the church, and then went down to Antioch. After 23 spending some time there, he set out again and made a journey through the Galatian country and on through Phrygia, bringing new strength to all the converts.

NOW THERE arrived at Ephesus a Jew named Apollos, an Alexan- 24 drian by birth, an eloquent man,*a* powerful in his use of the scriptures. He had been instructed in the way of the Lord and was full 25 of spiritual fervour; and in his discourses he taught accurately the facts about Jesus,*b* though he knew only John's baptism. He now 26 began to speak boldly in the synagogue, where Priscilla and Aquila heard him; they took him in hand and expounded the new way*c* to him in greater detail. Finding that he wished to go across to 27 Achaia, the brotherhood gave him their support, and wrote to the congregation there to make him welcome. From the time of his arrival, he was very helpful to those who had by God's grace become believers; for he was indefatigable in confuting the Jews, 28 demonstrating publicly from the scriptures that the Messiah is Jesus.

While Apollos was at Corinth, Paul travelled through the inland **19** regions till he came to Ephesus. There he found a number of converts, to whom he said, 'Did you receive the Holy Spirit when you became 2 believers?' 'No,' they replied, 'we have not even heard that there is a Holy Spirit.' He said, 'Then what baptism were you given?' 3 'John's baptism', they answered. Paul then said, 'The baptism that 4 John gave was a baptism in token of repentance, and he told the people to put their trust in one who was to come after him, that is, in Jesus.' On hearing this they were baptized into the name of the 5 Lord Jesus; and when Paul had laid his hands on them, the Holy 6 Spirit came upon them and they spoke in tongues of ecstasy and prophesied. Altogether they were about a dozen men. 7

During the next three months he attended the synagogue and, 8 using argument and persuasion, spoke boldly and freely about the kingdom of God. But when some proved obdurate and would not 9 believe, speaking evil of the new way before the whole congregation, he left them, withdrew his converts, and continued to hold

[*a*] *Or* a learned man.   [*b*] *Some witnesses read* about the Lord.   [*c*] *Some witnesses read* the way of God.

10 discussions daily in the lecture-hall of Tyrannus. This went on for two years, with the result that the whole population of the province
11 of Asia, both Jews and pagans, heard the word of the Lord. And
12 through Paul God worked miracles of an unusual kind: when handkerchiefs and scarves which had been in contact with his skin were carried to the sick, they were rid of their diseases and the evil spirits came out of them.
13 But some strolling Jewish exorcists tried their hand at using the name of the Lord Jesus on those possessed by evil spirits; they would
14 say, 'I adjure you by Jesus whom Paul proclaims.' There were seven sons of Sceva, a Jewish chief priest, who were using this method,
15 when the evil spirit answered back and said, 'Jesus I acknowledge,
16 and I know about Paul, but who are you?' And the man with the evil spirit flew at them, overpowered them all, and handled them with such violence that they ran out of the house stripped and
17 battered. This became known to everybody in Ephesus, whether Jew or pagan; they were all awestruck, and the name of the Lord
18 Jesus gained in honour. Moreover many of those who had become believers came and openly confessed that they had been using
19 magical spells. And a good many of those who formerly practised magic collected their books and burnt them publicly. The total value
20 was reckoned up and it came to fifty thousand pieces of silver. In such ways the word of the Lord showed its power, spreading more and more widely and effectively.
21 When things had reached this stage, Paul made up his mind[a] to visit Macedonia and Achaia and then go on to Jerusalem; and he said,
22 'After I have been there, I must see Rome also.' So he sent two of his assistants, Timothy and Erastus, to Macedonia, while he himself stayed some time longer in the province of Asia.
23 Now about that time, the Christian movement gave rise to a
24 serious disturbance. There was a man named Demetrius, a silver-smith who made silver shrines of Diana and provided a great deal
25 of employment for the craftsmen. He called a meeting of these men and the workers in allied trades, and addressed them. 'Men,' he said, 'you know that our high standard of living depends on this industry.
26 And you see and hear how this fellow Paul with his propaganda has perverted crowds of people, not only at Ephesus but also in practically the whole of the province of Asia. He is telling them that

[a] *Or* Paul, led by the Spirit, resolved...

gods made by human hands are not gods at all. There is danger for 27
us here; it is not only that our line of business will be discredited,
but also that the sanctuary of the great goddess Diana will cease to
command respect; and then it will not be long before she who is
worshipped by all Asia and the civilized world is brought down from
her divine pre-eminence.'

When they heard this they were roused to fury and shouted, 'Great 28
is Diana of the Ephesians!' The whole city was in confusion; they 29
seized Paul's travelling-companions, the Macedonians Gaius and
Aristarchus, and made a concerted rush with them into the theatre.
Paul wanted to appear before the assembly but the other Christians 30
would not let him. Even some of the dignitaries of the province, who 31
were friendly towards him, went and urged him not to venture into
the theatre. Meanwhile some were shouting one thing, some another; 32
for the assembly was in confusion and most of them did not know
what they had all come for. But some of the crowd explained the 33
trouble to Alexander, whom the Jews had pushed to the front, and
he, motioning for silence, attempted to make a defence before the
assembly. But when they recognized that he was a Jew, a single 34
cry arose from them all: for about two hours they kept on shouting,
'Great is Diana of the Ephesians!'

The town clerk, however, quieted the crowd. 'Men of Ephesus,' 35
he said, 'all the world knows that our city of Ephesus is temple-
warden of the great Diana and of that symbol of her which fell
from heaven. Since these facts are beyond dispute, your proper 36
course is to keep quiet and do nothing rash. These men whom you 37
have brought here as culprits have committed no sacrilege and uttered
no blasphemy against our goddess. If therefore Demetrius and his 38
craftsmen have a case against anyone, assizes are held and there are
such people as proconsuls; let the parties bring their charges and
countercharges. If, on the other hand, you have some further ques- 39
tion to raise, it will be dealt with in the statutory assembly. We 40
certainly run the risk of being charged with riot for this day's work.
There is no justification for it, and if the issue is raised we shall be
unable to give any explanation of this uproar.' With that he dismissed 41
the assembly.

WHEN THE disturbance had ceased, Paul sent for the disciples and, 20
after encouraging them, said good-bye and set out on his journey

2 to Macedonia. He travelled through those parts of the country, often speaking words of encouragement to the Christians there, and
3 so came into Greece. When he had spent three months there and was on the point of embarking for Syria, a plot was laid against him
4 by the Jews, so he decided to return by way of Macedonia. He was accompanied by Sopater son of Pyrrhus, from Beroea, the Thessalonians Aristarchus and Secundus, Gaius the Doberian[a] and
5 Timothy, and the Asians Tychicus and Trophimus. These went
6 ahead and waited for us at Troas; we ourselves set sail from Philippi after the Passover season,[b] and in five days reached them at Troas, where we spent a week.

7   On the Saturday night, in our assembly for the breaking of bread, Paul, who was to leave next day, addressed them, and went on speak-
8 ing until midnight. Now there were many lamps in the upper room
9 where we were assembled; and a youth named Eutychus, who was sitting on the window-ledge, grew more and more sleepy as Paul went on talking. At last he was completely overcome by sleep, fell from the third floor to the ground, and was picked up for dead.
10 Paul went down, threw himself upon him, seizing him in his arms, and said to them, 'Stop this commotion: there is still life in him.'
11 He then went upstairs, broke bread and ate, and after much conver-
12 sation, which lasted until dawn, he departed. And they took the boy away alive and were immensely comforted.

13   We went ahead to the ship and sailed for Assos, where we were to take Paul aboard. He had made this arrangement, as he was going
14 to travel by road. When he met us at Assos, we took him aboard and
15 went on to Mitylene. Next day we sailed from there and arrived opposite Chios, and on the second day we made Samos. On the
16 following day[c] we reached Miletus. For Paul had decided to pass by Ephesus and so avoid having to spend time in the province of Asia; he was eager to be in Jerusalem, if he possibly could, on the day of
17 Pentecost. He did, however, send from Miletus to Ephesus and
18 summon the elders of the congregation; and when they joined him, he spoke as follows:

    'You know how, from the day that I first set foot in the province
19 of Asia, for the whole time that I was with you, I served the Lord

---

[a] *Some witnesses read* the Derbaean.   [b] *Literally* after the days of Unleavened Bread.
[c] *Some witnesses read* . . . Samos, and, after stopping at Trogyllium, on the following day . . .

in all humility amid the sorrows and trials that came upon me through
the machinations of the Jews. You know that I kept back nothing 20
that was for your good: I delivered the message to you; I taught you,
in public and in your homes; with Jews and pagans alike I insisted 21
on repentance before God and trust in our Lord Jesus. And now, as 22
you see, I am on my way to Jerusalem, under the constraint of the
Spirit.*a* Of what will befall me there I know nothing, except that 23
in city after city the Holy Spirit assures me that imprisonment and
hardships await me. For myself, I set no store by life; I only want 24
to finish the race, and complete the task which the Lord Jesus
assigned to me, of bearing my testimony to the gospel of God's grace.

'One word more: I have gone about among you proclaiming the 25
Kingdom, but now I know that none of you will see my face again.
That being so, I here and now declare that no man's fate can be 26
laid at my door; for I have kept back nothing; I have disclosed to 27
you the whole purpose of God. Keep watch over yourselves and 28
over all the flock of which the Holy Spirit has given you charge, as
shepherds of the church of the Lord,*b* which he won for himself by
his own blood.*c* I know that when I am gone, savage wolves will 29
come in among you and will not spare the flock. Even from your 30
own body there will be men coming forward who will distort the
truth to induce the disciples to break away and follow them. So be 31
on the alert; remember how for three years, night and day, I never
ceased to counsel each of you, and how I wept over you.

'And now I commend you to God and to his gracious word, which 32
has power to build you up and give you your heritage among all
who are dedicated to him. I have not wanted anyone's money or 33
clothes for myself; you all know that these hands of mine earned 34
enough for the needs of me and my companions. I showed you that 35
it is our duty to help the weak in this way, by hard work, and that
we should keep in mind the words of the Lord Jesus, who himself
said, "Happiness lies more in giving than in receiving."'

As he finished speaking, he knelt down with them all and prayed. 36
Then there were loud cries of sorrow from them all, as they folded 37
Paul in their arms and kissed him. What distressed them most was 38
his saying that they would never see his face again. So they escorted
him to his ship.

[a] Or under an inner compulsion. [b] *Some witnesses read* of God. [c] Or by the blood
of his Own.

237

21   When we had parted from them and set sail, we made a straight run
2   and came to Cos; next day to Rhodes, and thence to Patara.[a] There
     we found a ship bound for Phoenicia, so we went aboard and sailed in
3   her. We came in sight of Cyprus, and leaving it on our port beam, we
     continued our voyage to Syria, and put in at Tyre, for there the ship
4   was to unload her cargo. We went and found the disciples and stayed
     there a week; and they, warned by the Spirit, urged Paul to abandon
5   his visit to Jerusalem. But when our time ashore was ended, we
     left and continued our journey; and they and their wives and children
     all escorted us out of the city. We knelt down on the beach and prayed,
6   then bade each other good-bye; we went aboard, and they returned
     home.
7   We made the passage from Tyre and reached Ptolemais, where
8   we greeted the brotherhood and spent one day with them. Next day
     we left and came to Caesarea. We went to the home of Philip the
9   evangelist, who was one of the Seven, and stayed with him. He had
     four unmarried daughters, who possessed the gift of prophecy.
10   When we had been there several days, a prophet named Agabus
11   arrived from Judaea. He came to us, took Paul's belt, bound his
     own feet and hands with it, and said, 'These are the words of the
     Holy Spirit: Thus will the Jews in Jerusalem bind the man to
     whom this belt belongs, and hand him over to the Gentiles.'
12   When we heard this, we and the local people begged and implored
13   Paul to abandon his visit to Jerusalem. Then Paul gave his answer:
     'Why all these tears? Why are you trying to weaken my resolution?
     For my part I am ready not merely to be bound but even to die
14   for the name of the Lord Jesus.' So, as he would not be persuaded,
     we gave up and said, 'The Lord's will be done.'
15   At the end of our stay we packed our baggage and took the road
16   up to Jerusalem. Some of the disciples from Caesarea came along
     with us, bringing a certain Mnason of Cyprus, a Christian from the
17   early days, with whom we were to lodge. So we reached Jerusalem,
     where the brotherhood welcomed us gladly.
18   Next day Paul paid a visit to James; we were with him, and all the
19   elders attended. He greeted them, and then described in detail all
20   that God had done among the Gentiles through his ministry. When
     they heard this, they gave praise to God. Then they said to Paul:
     'You see, brother, how many thousands of converts we have among

[a] *Some witnesses add* and Myra.

the Jews, all of them staunch upholders of the Law. Now they 21
have been given certain information about you: it is said that you
teach all the Jews in the gentile world to turn their backs on Moses,
telling them to give up circumcising their children and following
our way of life. What is the position, then? They are sure to hear 22
that you have arrived. You must therefore do as we tell you. We have 23
four men here who are under a vow; take them with you and go 24
through the ritual of purification with them, paying their expenses,
after which they may shave their heads. Then everyone will know
that there is nothing in the stories they were told about you, but that
you are a practising Jew and keep the Law yourself. As for the 25
gentile converts, we sent them our decision that they must abstain
from meat that has been offered to idols, from blood, from anything
that has been strangled,[a] and from fornication.' So Paul took the 26
four men, and next day, after going through the ritual of purification
with them, he went into the temple to give notice of the date when
the period of purification would end and the offering be made for
each one of them.

From Jerusalem to Rome

B UT JUST BEFORE the period of seven days was up, the Jews from 27
the province of Asia saw him in the temple. They stirred up the
whole crowd, and seized him, shouting, 'Men of Israel, help, help! 28
This is the fellow who spreads his doctrine all over the world,
attacking our people, our law, and this sanctuary. On top of all this
he has brought Greeks into the temple and profaned this holy place.'
For they had previously seen Trophimus the Ephesian with him in 29
the city, and assumed that Paul had brought him into the temple.

The whole city was in a turmoil, and people came running from 30
all directions. They seized Paul and dragged him out of the temple;
and at once the doors were shut. While they were clamouring for his 31
death, a report reached the officer commanding the cohort, that all
Jerusalem was in an uproar. He immediately took a force of soldiers 32
with their centurions and came down on the rioters at the double.
As soon as they saw the commandant and his troops, they stopped
beating Paul. The commandant stepped forward, arrested him, and 33

[a] *Some witnesses omit* from anything that has been strangled.

239

ordered him to be shackled with two chains; he then asked who
34 the man was and what he had been doing. Some in the crowd
shouted one thing, some another. As he could not get at the truth
because of the hubbub, he ordered him to be taken into barracks.
35 When Paul reached the steps, he had to be carried by the soldiers
36 because of the violence of the mob. For the whole crowd were at
their heels yelling, 'Kill him!'
37 Just before Paul was taken into the barracks he said to the commandant, 'May I say something to you?' The commandant said,
38 'So you speak Greek, do you? Then you are not the Egyptian who
started a revolt some time ago and led a force of four thousand
39 terrorists out into the wilds?' Paul replied, 'I am a Jew, a Tarsian
from Cilicia, a citizen of no mean city. I ask your permission to speak
40 to the people.' When permission had been given, Paul stood on the
steps and with a gesture called for the attention of the people. As
soon as quiet was restored, he addressed them in the Jewish language:
22 'Brothers and fathers, give me a hearing while I make my defence
2 before you.' When they heard him speaking to them in their own
3 language, they listened the more quietly. 'I am a true-born Jew,'
he said, 'a native of Tarsus in Cilicia. I was brought up in this city,
and as a pupil of Gamaliel I was thoroughly trained in every point
of our ancestral law. I have always been ardent in God's service,
4 as you all are today. And so I began to persecute this movement to
the death, arresting its followers, men and women alike, and putting
5 them in chains. For this I have as witnesses the High Priest and
the whole Council of Elders. I was given letters from them to our
fellow-Jews at Damascus, and had started out to bring the Christians
6 there to Jerusalem as prisoners for punishment; and this is what
happened. I was on the road and nearing Damascus, when suddenly
about midday a great light flashed from the sky all around me,
7 and I fell to the ground. Then I heard a voice saying to me, "Saul,
8 Saul, why do you persecute me?" I answered, "Tell me, Lord,
who you are." "I am Jesus of Nazareth," he said, "whom you are
9 persecuting." My companions saw the light, but did not hear the
10 voice that spoke to me. "What shall I do, Lord?" I said, and the
Lord replied, "Get up and continue your journey to Damascus;
there you will be told of all the tasks that are laid upon you."
11 As I had been blinded by the brilliance of that light, my companions
led me by the hand, and so I came to Damascus.

'There, a man called Ananias, a devout observer of the Law and 12
well spoken of by all the Jews of that place, came and stood beside 13
me and said, "Saul, my brother, recover your sight." Instantly I
recovered my sight and saw him. He went on: "The God of our 14
fathers appointed you to know his will and to see the Righteous One
and to hear his very voice, because you are to be his witness before 15
the world, and testify to what you have seen and heard. And now why 16
delay? Be baptized at once, with invocation of his name, and wash
away your sins."

'After my return to Jerusalem, I was praying in the temple when 17
I fell into a trance and saw him there, speaking to me. "Make haste", 18
he said, "and leave Jerusalem without delay, for they will not accept
your testimony about me." "Lord," I said, "they know that I 19
imprisoned those who believe in thee, and flogged them in every
synagogue; and when the blood of Stephen thy witness was shed 20
I stood by, approving, and I looked after the clothes of those who
killed him." But he said to me, "Go, for I am sending you far away 21
to the Gentiles."'

Up to this point they had given him a hearing; but now they began 22
shouting, 'Down with him! A scoundrel like that is better dead!'
And as they were yelling and waving their cloaks and flinging dust 23
in the air, the commandant ordered him to be brought into the 24
barracks and gave instructions to examine him by flogging, and
find out what reason there was for such an outcry against him.
But when they tied him up for the lash,*a* Paul said to the centurion 25
who was standing there, 'Can you legally flog a man who is a Roman
citizen, and moreover has not been found guilty?' When the centurion 26
heard this, he went and reported it to the commandant. 'What
do you mean to do?' he said. 'This man is a Roman citizen.'
The commandant came to Paul. 'Tell me, are you a Roman citizen?' 27
he asked. 'Yes', said he. The commandant rejoined, 'It cost me a 28
large sum to acquire this citizenship.' Paul said, 'But it was mine
by birth.' Then those who were about to examine him withdrew 29
hastily, and the commandant himself was alarmed when he realized
that Paul was a Roman citizen and that he had put him in irons.

THE FOLLOWING day, wishing to be quite sure what charge the 30
Jews were bringing against Paul, he released him and ordered the

[a] *Or* tied him up with thongs.

chief priests and the entire Council to assemble. He then took Paul down and stood him before them.

23   Paul fixed his eyes on the Council and said, 'My brothers, I have lived all my life, and still live today, with a perfectly clear conscience
2 before God.' At this the High Priest Ananias ordered his attendants
3 to strike him on the mouth. Paul retorted, 'God will strike you, you whitewashed wall! You sit there to judge me in accordance with the Law; and then in defiance of the Law you order me to be struck!'
4, 5 The attendants said, 'Would you insult God's High Priest?' 'My brothers,' said Paul, 'I had no idea that he was High Priest; Scripture, I know, says: "You must not abuse the ruler of your people."'
6   Now Paul was well aware that one section of them were Sadducees and the other Pharisees, so he called out in the Council, 'My brothers, I am a Pharisee, a Pharisee born and bred; and the true
7 issue in this trial is our hope of the resurrection of the dead.' At these words the Pharisees and Sadducees fell out among themselves,
8 and the assembly was divided. (The Sadducees deny that there is any resurrection, or angel, or spirit, but the Pharisees accept them.)
9 So a great uproar broke out; and some of the doctors of the law belonging to the Pharisaic party openly took sides and declared, 'We can find no fault with this man; perhaps an angel or spirit has
10 spoken to him.' The dissension was mounting, and the commandant was afraid that Paul would be torn in pieces, so he ordered the troops to go down, pull him out of the crowd, and bring him into the barracks.
11   The following night the Lord appeared to him and said, 'Keep up your courage; you have affirmed the truth about me in Jerusalem, and you must do the same in Rome.'
12   When day broke, the Jews banded together and took an oath not
13 to eat or drink until they had killed Paul. There were more than forty
14 in this conspiracy. They came to the chief priests and elders and said, 'We have bound ourselves by a solemn oath not to taste food
15 until we have killed Paul. It is now for you, acting with the Council, to apply to the commandant to bring him down to you, on the pretext of a closer investigation of his case; and we have arranged to do away with him before he arrives.'
16 But the son of Paul's sister heard of the ambush; he went to the
17 barracks, obtained entry, and reported it to Paul. Paul called one of the centurions and said, 'Take this young man to the commandant;
18 he has something to report.' The centurion took him and brought

him to the commandant. 'The prisoner Paul', he said, 'sent for me and asked me to bring this young man to you; he has something to tell you.' The commandant took him by the arm, drew him aside, and asked him, 'What is it you have to report?' He said, 'The Jews have made a plan among themselves and will request you to bring Paul down to the Council tomorrow, on the pretext of obtaining more precise information about him. Do not listen to them; for a party more than forty strong are lying in wait for him. They have sworn not to eat or drink until they have done away with him; they are now ready, and wait only for your consent.' So the commandant dismissed the young man, with orders not to let anyone know that he had given him this information.

Then he called a couple of his centurions and issued these orders: 'Get ready two hundred infantry to proceed to Caesarea, together with seventy cavalrymen and two hundred light-armed troops;*ᵃ* parade three hours after sunset. Provide also mounts for Paul so that he may ride through under safe escort to Felix the Governor.' And he wrote a letter to this effect:

'Claudius Lysias to His Excellency the Governor Felix. Your Excellency: This man was seized by the Jews and was on the point of being murdered when I intervened with the troops and removed him, because I discovered that he was a Roman citizen. As I wished to ascertain the charge on which they were accusing him, I took him down to their Council. I found that the accusation had to do with controversial matters in their law, but there was no charge against him meriting death or imprisonment. However, I have now been informed of an attempt to be made on the man's life, so I am sending him to you at once, and have also instructed his accusers to state their case against him before you.'ᵇ

Acting on their orders, the infantry took Paul and brought him by night to Antipatris. Next day they returned to their barracks, leaving the cavalry to escort him the rest of the way. The cavalry entered Caesarea, delivered the letter to the Governor, and handed Paul over to him. He read the letter, asked him what province he was from, and learned that he was from Cilicia. 'I will hear your case', he said, 'when your accusers arrive.' He then ordered him to be held in custody at his headquarters in Herod's palace.

[a] Or two hundred spearmen (*the meaning of the Greek word is uncertain*). [b] *Some witnesses read* '. . . before you. Farewell.'

24 FIVE DAYS later the High Priest Ananias came down, accompanied
by some of the elders and an advocate named Tertullus, and they
2 laid an information against Paul before the Governor. When the
prisoner was called, Tertullus opened the case.

'Your Excellency,' he said, 'we owe it to you that we enjoy unbroken
peace. It is due to your provident care that, in all kinds of ways and
in all sorts of places, improvements are being made for the good of
3, 4 this province. We welcome this, sir, most gratefully. And now, not
to take up too much of your time, I crave your indulgence for a brief
5 statement of our case. We have found this man to be a perfect pest,
a fomenter of discord among the Jews all over the world, a ring-
6 leader of the sect of the Nazarenes. He even made an attempt to
8 profane the temple; and then we arrested him.*a* If you will examine
him yourself you can ascertain from him the truth of all the charges
9 we bring.' The Jews supported the attack, alleging that the facts
were as he stated.

10   Then the Governor motioned to Paul to speak, and he began his
reply: 'Knowing as I do that for many years you have administered
11 justice in this province, I make my defence with confidence. You
can ascertain the facts for yourself. It is not more than twelve days
12 since I went up to Jerusalem on a pilgrimage. They did not find
me arguing with anyone, or collecting a crowd, either in the temple
13 or in the synagogues or up and down the city; and they cannot make
14 good the charges they bring against me. But this much I will admit:
I am a follower of the new way (the "sect" they speak of), and it
is in that manner that I worship the God of our fathers; for I believe
15 all that is written in the Law and the prophets, and in reliance on
God I hold the hope, which my accusers too accept, that there is to
16 be a resurrection of good and wicked alike. Accordingly I, no less
than they, train myself to keep at all times a clear conscience before
God and man.

17   'After an absence of several years I came to bring charitable gifts
18 to my nation and to offer sacrifices. They found me in the temple
ritually purified and engaged in this service. I had no crowd with
me, and there was no disturbance. But some Jews from the province
19 of Asia were there, and if they had any charge against me it is they

[a] *Some witnesses insert* (7) It was our intention to try him under our law; but Lysias
the commandant intervened and took him by force out of our hands, ordering his
accusers to come before you.

who ought to have been in court to state it. Failing that, it is for 20
these persons here present to say what crime they discovered when
I was brought before the Council, apart from this one open assertion 21
which I made as I stood there: "The true issue in my trial before
you today is the resurrection of the dead."'

Then Felix, who happened to be well informed about the Christian 22
movement, adjourned the hearing. 'When Lysias the commanding
officer comes down', he said, 'I will go into your case.' He gave orders 23
to the centurion to keep Paul under open arrest and not to prevent
any of his friends from making themselves useful to him.

Some days later Felix came with his wife Drusilla, who was a 24
Jewess, and sending for Paul he let him talk to him about faith in
Christ Jesus. But when the discourse turned to questions of morals, 25
self-control, and the coming judgement, Felix became alarmed and
exclaimed, 'That will do for the present; when I find it convenient
I will send for you again.' At the same time he had hopes of a bribe 26
from Paul; and for this reason he sent for him very often and talked
with him. When two years had passed, Felix was succeeded by 27
Porcius Festus. Wishing to curry favour with the Jews, Felix left
Paul in custody.

THREE DAYS after taking up his appointment Festus went up from **25**
Caesarea to Jerusalem, where the chief priests and the Jewish 2
leaders brought before him the case against Paul. They asked Festus 3
to favour them against him, and pressed for him to be brought up
to Jerusalem, for they were planning an ambush to kill him on the
way. Festus, however, replied, 'Paul is in safe custody at Caesarea, 4
and I shall be leaving Jerusalem shortly myself; so let your leading 5
men come down with me, and if there is anything wrong, let them
prosecute him.'

After spending eight or ten days at most in Jerusalem, he went 6
down to Caesarea, and next day he took his seat in court and ordered
Paul to be brought up. When he appeared, the Jews who had come 7
down from Jerusalem stood round bringing many grave charges,
which they were unable to prove. Paul's plea was: 'I have committed 8
no offence, either against the Jewish law, or against the temple, or
against the Emperor.' Festus, anxious to ingratiate himself with the 9
Jews, turned to Paul and asked, 'Are you willing to go up to Jerusalem and stand trial on these charges before me there?' But Paul 10

said, 'I am now standing before the Emperor's tribunal, and that is where I must be tried. Against the Jews I have committed no
11 offence, as you very well know. If I am guilty of any capital crime, I do not ask to escape the death penalty; but if there is no substance in the charges which these men bring against me, it is not open to anyone to hand me over as a sop to them. I appeal to Caesar!'
12 Then Festus, after conferring with his advisers, replied, 'You have appealed to Caesar: to Caesar you shall go.'
13 After an interval of some days King Agrippa and Bernice arrived
14 at Caesarea on a courtesy visit to Festus. They spent several days there, and during this time Festus laid Paul's case before the king.
15 'We have a man', he said, 'left in custody by Felix; and when I was in Jerusalem the chief priests and elders of the Jews laid an informa-
16 tion against him, demanding his condemnation. I answered them, "It is not Roman practice to hand over any accused man before he is confronted with his accusers and given an opportunity of answer-
17 ing the charge." So when they had come here with me I lost no time; the very next day I took my seat in court and ordered the
18 man to be brought up. But when his accusers rose to speak, they
19 brought none of the charges I was expecting; they merely had certain points of disagreement with him about their peculiar religion, and about someone called Jesus, a dead man whom Paul alleged to
20 be alive. Finding myself out of my depth in such discussions, I asked if he was willing to go to Jerusalem and stand his trial there on these
21 issues. But Paul appealed to be remanded in custody for His Imperial Majesty's decision, and I ordered him to be detained until
22 I could send him to the Emperor.' Agrippa said to Festus, 'I should rather like to hear the man myself.' 'Tomorrow', he answered, 'you shall hear him.'
23 So next day Agrippa and Bernice came in full state and entered the audience-chamber accompanied by high-ranking officers and prominent citizens; and on the orders of Festus Paul was brought
24 up. Then Festus said, 'King Agrippa, and all you gentlemen here present with us, you see this man: the whole body of the Jews approached me both in Jerusalem and here, loudly insisting that he
25 had no right to remain alive. But it was clear to me that he had committed no capital crime, and when he himself appealed to His
26 Imperial Majesty, I decided to send him. But I have nothing definite about him to put in writing for our Sovereign. Accordingly

I have brought him up before you all and particularly before you,
King Agrippa, so that as a result of this preliminary inquiry I may
have something to report. There is no sense, it seems to me, in 27
sending on a prisoner without indicating the charges against him.'

Agrippa said to Paul, 'You have our permission to speak for 26
yourself.' Then Paul stretched out his hand and began his defence:

'I consider myself fortunate, King Agrippa, that it is before you 2
that I am to make my defence today upon all the charges brought
against me by the Jews, particularly as you are expert in all Jewish 3
matters, both our customs and our disputes. And therefore I beg
you to give me a patient hearing.

'My life from my youth up, the life I led from the beginning 4
among my people and in Jerusalem, is familiar to all Jews. Indeed 5
they have known me long enough and could testify, if they only
would, that I belonged to the strictest group in our religion: I lived
as a Pharisee. And it is for a hope kindled by God's promise to our 6
forefathers that I stand in the dock today. Our twelve tribes hope 7
to see the fulfilment of that promise, worshipping with intense
devotion day and night; and for this very hope I am impeached, and
impeached by Jews, Your Majesty. Why is it considered incredible 8
among you that God should raise dead men to life?

'I myself once thought it my duty to work actively against the 9
name of Jesus of Nazareth; and I did so in Jerusalem. It was I who 10
imprisoned many of God's people by authority obtained from the
chief priests; and when they were condemned to death, my vote was
cast against them. In all the synagogues I tried by repeated punish- 11
ment to make them renounce their faith; indeed my fury rose to such
a pitch that I extended my persecution to foreign cities.

'On one such occasion I was travelling to Damascus with authority 12
and commission from the chief priests; and as I was on my way, 13
Your Majesty, in the middle of the day I saw a light from the sky,
more brilliant than the sun, shining all around me and my travelling-
companions. We all fell to the ground, and then I heard a voice saying 14
to me in the Jewish language, "Saul, Saul, why do you persecute me?
It is hard for you, this kicking against the goad." I said, "Tell me, 15
Lord, who you are"; and the Lord replied, "I am Jesus, whom you
are persecuting. But now, rise to your feet and stand upright. I have 16
appeared to you for a purpose: to appoint you my servant and witness, to testify both to what you have seen and to what you shall yet

17 see of me. I will rescue you from this people and from the Gentiles
18 to whom I am sending you. I send you to open their eyes and turn
them from darkness to light, from the dominion of Satan to God,
so that, by trust in me, they may obtain forgiveness of sins, and a
place with those whom God has made his own."
19   'And so, King Agrippa, I did not disobey the heavenly vision.
20 I turned first to the inhabitants of Damascus, and then to Jerusalem
and all the country of Judaea, and to the Gentiles, and sounded the
call to repent and turn to God, and to prove their repentance by deeds.
21 That is why the Jews seized me in the temple and tried to do away
22 with me. But I had God's help, and so to this very day I stand and
testify to great and small alike. I assert nothing beyond what was
23 foretold by the prophets and by Moses: that the Messiah must
suffer, and that he, the first to rise from the dead, would announce the
dawn to Israel and to the Gentiles.'
24   While Paul was thus making his defence, Festus shouted at the
top of his voice, 'Paul, you are raving; too much study is driving
25 you mad.' 'I am not mad, Your Excellency,' said Paul; 'what I am
26 saying is sober truth. The king is well versed in these matters, and
to him I can speak freely. I do not believe that he can be unaware
of any of these facts, for this has been no hole-and-corner business.
27 King Agrippa, do you believe the prophets? I know you do.'
28 Agrippa said to Paul, 'You think it will not take much to win me
29 over and make a Christian of me.' 'Much or little,' said Paul, 'I wish
to God that not only you, but all those also who are listening to me
today, might become what I am, apart from these chains.'
30   With that the king rose, and with him the Governor, Bernice, and
31 the rest of the company, and after they had withdrawn they talked it
over. 'This man', they said, 'is doing nothing that deserves death or
32 imprisonment.' Agrippa said to Festus, 'The fellow could have been
discharged, if he had not appealed to the Emperor.'

27 WHEN IT WAS decided that we should sail for Italy, Paul and some
other prisoners were handed over to a centurion named Julius, of the
2 Augustan Cohort. We embarked in a ship of Adramyttium, bound
for ports in the province of Asia, and put out to sea. In our party
3 was Aristarchus, a Macedonian from Thessalonica. Next day we
landed at Sidon; and Julius very considerately allowed Paul to go
4 to his friends to be cared for. Leaving Sidon we sailed under the

lee of Cyprus because of the head-winds, then across the open sea 5
off the coast of Cilicia and Pamphylia, and so reached Myra in
Lycia.

There the centurion found an Alexandrian vessel bound for Italy 6
and put us aboard. For a good many days we made little headway, 7
and we were hard put to it to reach Cnidus. Then, as the wind
continued against us, off Salmone we began to sail under the lee of
Crete, and, hugging the coast, struggled on to a place called Fair 8
Havens, not far from the town of Lasea.

By now much time had been lost, the Fast was already over, and 9
it was risky to go on with the voyage. Paul therefore gave them this
advice: 'I can see, gentlemen,' he said, 'that this voyage will be 10
disastrous: it will mean grave loss, loss not only of ship and cargo
but also of life.' But the centurion paid more attention to the captain 11
and to the owner of the ship than to what Paul said; and as the 12
harbour was unsuitable for wintering, the majority were in favour
of putting out to sea, hoping, if they could get so far, to winter at
Phoenix, a Cretan harbour exposed south-west and north-west.
So when a southerly breeze sprang up, they thought that their pur- 13
pose was as good as achieved, and, weighing anchor, they sailed
along the coast of Crete hugging the land. But before very long a 14
fierce wind, the 'North-easter' as they call it, tore down from the
landward side. It caught the ship and, as it was impossible to keep 15
head to wind, we had to give way and run before it. We ran under the 16
lee of a small island called Cauda, and with a struggle managed to get
the ship's boat under control. When they had hoisted it aboard, 17
they made use of tackle and undergirded the ship. Then, because they
were afraid of running on to the shallows of Syrtis, they lowered
the mainsail and let her drive. Next day, as we were making very 18
heavy weather, they began to lighten the ship; and on the third day 19
they jettisoned the ship's gear with their own hands. For days on end 20
there was no sign of either sun or stars, a great storm was raging,
and our last hopes of coming through alive began to fade.

When they had gone for a long time without food, Paul stood up 21
among them and said, 'You should have taken my advice, gentlemen, not to sail from Crete; then you would have avoided this
damage and loss. But now I urge you not to lose heart; not a single 22
life will be lost, only the ship. For last night there stood by me an 23
angel of the God whose I am and whom I worship. "Do not be 24

afraid, Paul," he said; "it is ordained that you shall appear before the Emperor; and, be assured, God has granted you the lives of all who
25 are sailing with you." So keep up your courage: I trust in God that
26 it will turn out as I have been told; though we have to be cast ashore on some island.'
27 The fourteenth night came and we were still drifting in the Sea of Adria. In the middle of the night the sailors felt that land was
28 getting nearer. They sounded and found twenty fathoms. Sounding
29 again after a short interval they found fifteen fathoms; and fearing that we might be cast ashore on a rugged coast they dropped four
30 anchors from the stern and prayed for daylight to come. The sailors tried to abandon ship; they had already lowered the ship's boat, pretending they were going to lay out anchors from the bows,
31 when Paul said to the centurion and the soldiers, 'Unless these men
32 stay on board you can none of you come off safely.' So the soldiers cut the ropes of the boat and let her drop away.
33 Shortly before daybreak Paul urged them all to take some food. 'For the last fourteen days', he said, 'you have lived in suspense and
34 gone hungry; you have eaten nothing whatever. So I beg you to have something to eat; your lives depend on it. Remember, not a
35 hair of your heads will be lost.' With these words, he took bread, gave thanks to God in front of them all, broke it, and began eating.
36 Then they all plucked up courage, and took food themselves.
37 There were on board two hundred and seventy-six of us in all.
38 When they had eaten as much as they wanted they lightened the ship by dumping the corn in the sea.
39 When day broke they could not recognize the land, but they noticed a bay with a sandy beach, on which they planned, if possible,
40 to run the ship ashore. So they slipped the anchors and let them go; at the same time they loosened the lashings of the steering-paddles,
41 set the foresail to the wind, and let her drive to the beach. But they found themselves caught between cross-currents and ran the ship aground, so that the bow stuck fast and remained immovable, while
42 the stern was being pounded to pieces by the breakers. The soldiers thought they had better kill the prisoners for fear that any should
43 swim away and escape; but the centurion wanted to bring Paul safely through and prevented them from carrying out their plan. He gave orders that those who could swim should jump overboard
44 first and get to land; the rest were to follow, some on planks,

some on parts of the ship. And thus it was that all came safely to land.

Once we had made our way to safety we identified the island as 28 Malta. The rough islanders treated us with uncommon kindness: 2 because it was cold and had started to rain, they lit a bonfire and made us all welcome. Paul had got together an armful of sticks 3 and put them on the fire, when a viper, driven out by the heat, fastened on his hand. The islanders, seeing the snake hanging on 4 to his hand, said to one another, 'The man must be a murderer; he may have escaped from the sea, but divine justice has not let him live.' Paul, however, shook off the snake into the fire and was 5 none the worse. They still expected that any moment he would 6 swell up or drop down dead, but after waiting a long time without seeing anything extraordinary happen to him, they changed their minds and now said, 'He is a god.'

In the neighbourhood of that place there were lands belonging 7 to the chief magistrate of the island, whose name was Publius. He took us in and entertained us hospitably for three days. It so happened that 8 this man's father was in bed suffering from recurrent bouts of fever and dysentery. Paul visited him and, after prayer, laid his hands upon him and healed him; whereupon the other sick people on the 9 island came also and were cured. They honoured us with many 10 marks of respect, and when we were leaving they put on board provision for our needs.

Three months had passed when we set sail in a ship which had 11 wintered in the island; she was the *Castor and Pollux* of Alexandria. We put in at Syracuse and spent three days there; then we sailed 12, 13 round and arrived at Rhegium. After one day a south wind sprang up and we reached Puteoli in two days. There we found fellow- 14 Christians and were invited to stay a week with them. And so to Rome. The Christians there had had news of us and came out to 15 meet us as far as Appii Forum and Tres Tabernae, and when Paul saw them, he gave thanks to God and took courage.

WHEN WE ENTERED Rome Paul was allowed to lodge by himself 16 with a soldier in charge of him. Three days later he called together 17 the local Jewish leaders; and when they were assembled, he said to them: 'My brothers, I, who never did anything against our people or the customs of our forefathers, am here as a prisoner; I was

18 handed over to the Romans at Jerusalem. They examined me and would have liked to release me because there was no capital charge
19 against me; but the Jews objected, and I had no option but to appeal to the Emperor; not that I had any accusation to bring against my
20 own people. That is why I have asked to see you and talk to you, because it is for the sake of the hope of Israel that I am in chains,
21 as you see.' They replied, 'We have had no communication from Judaea, nor has any countryman of ours arrived with any report
22 or gossip to your discredit. We should like to hear from you what your views are; all we know about this sect is that no one has a good word to say for it.'
23   So they fixed a day, and came in large numbers as his guests. He dealt at length with the whole matter; he spoke urgently of the kingdom of God and sought to convince them about Jesus by appealing to the Law of Moses and the prophets. This went on from dawn
24 to dusk. Some were won over by his arguments; others remained
25 sceptical. Without reaching any agreement among themselves they began to disperse, but not before Paul had said one thing more: 'How well the Holy Spirit spoke to your fathers through the prophet
26 Isaiah when he said, "Go to this people and say: You will hear and hear, but never understand; you will look and look, but never see.
27 For this people has grown gross at heart; their ears are dull, and their eyes are closed. Otherwise, their eyes might see, their ears hear, and their heart understand, and then they might turn again, and I
28 would heal them." Therefore take notice that this salvation of God has been sent to the Gentiles: the Gentiles will listen.'ᵃ
30   He stayed there two full years at his own expense, with a welcome
31 for all who came to him, proclaiming the kingdom of God and teaching the facts about the Lord Jesus Christ quite openly and without hindrance.

[a] *Some witnesses add* (29) After he had spoken, the Jews went away, arguing vigorously among themselves.

LETTERS

THE
LETTER OF PAUL TO THE
ROMANS

The Gospel according to Paul

FROM PAUL, servant of Christ Jesus, apostle by God's call, 1
set apart for the service of the Gospel.
   This gospel God announced beforehand in sacred scrip- 2
tures through his prophets. It is about his Son: on the human level 3
he was born of David's stock, but on the level of the spirit—the 4
Holy Spirit—he was declared Son of God by a mighty act in that
he rose from the dead:[a] it is about Jesus Christ our Lord. Through 5
him I received the privilege of a commission in his name to lead
to faith and obedience men in all nations, yourselves among them, 6
you who have heard the call and belong to Jesus Christ.

   I send greetings to all of you in Rome whom God loves and has 7
called to be his dedicated people. Grace and peace to you from God
our Father and the Lord Jesus Christ.

   Let me begin by thanking my God, through Jesus Christ, for you 8
all, because all over the world they are telling the story of your faith.
God is my witness, the God to whom I offer the humble service 9
of my spirit by preaching the gospel of his Son: God knows how
continually I make mention of you in my prayers, and am always 10
asking that by his will I may, somehow or other, succeed at long
last in coming to visit you. For I long to see you; I want to bring 11
you some spiritual gift to make you strong; or rather, I want to be 12
among you to receive encouragement myself through the influence
of your faith on me as of mine on you.

   But I should like you to know,[b] my brothers, that I have often 13
planned to come, though so far without success, in the hope of
achieving something among you, as I have in other parts of the world.
I am under obligation to Greek and non-Greek, to learned and 14
simple; hence my eagerness to declare the Gospel to you in Rome 15

[a] Or declared Son of God with full powers from the time when he rose from the dead.
[b] Some witnesses read I believe you know.

255

16 as well as to others. For I am not ashamed of the Gospel. It is the saving power of God for everyone who has faith—the Jew first,

17 but the Greek also—because here is revealed God's way of righting wrong, a way that starts from faith and ends in faith;[a] as Scripture says, 'he shall gain life who is justified through faith'.

18 FOR WE SEE divine retribution revealed from heaven and falling upon all the godless wickedness of men. In their wickedness they are

19 stifling the truth. For all that may be known of God by men lies plain before their eyes; indeed God himself has disclosed it to them.

20 His invisible attributes, that is to say his everlasting power and deity, have been visible, ever since the world began, to the eye of reason, in the things he has made. There is therefore no possible defence for

21 their conduct; knowing God, they have refused to honour him as God, or to render him thanks. Hence all their thinking has ended in

22 futility, and their misguided minds are plunged in darkness. They boast of their wisdom, but they have made fools of themselves,

23 exchanging the splendour of immortal God for an image shaped like mortal man, even for images like birds, beasts, and creeping things.

24 For this reason God has given them up to the vileness of their

25 own desires, and the consequent degradation of their bodies, because they have bartered away the true God for a false one,[b] and have offered reverence and worship to created things instead of to the Creator, who is blessed for ever; amen.

26 In consequence, I say, God has given them up to shameful passions. Their women have exchanged natural intercourse for un-

27 natural, and their men in turn, giving up natural relations with women, burn with lust for one another; males behave indecently with males, and are paid in their own persons the fitting wage of such perversion.

28 Thus, because they have not seen fit to acknowledge God, he has given them up to their own depraved reason. This leads them to

29 break all rules of conduct. They are filled with every kind of injustice, mischief, rapacity, and malice; they are one mass of envy, murder,

30 rivalry, treachery, and malevolence; whisperers and scandal-mongers, hateful to God, insolent, arrogant, and boastful; they invent new

31 kinds of mischief, they show no loyalty to parents, no conscience,

[a] Or . . . wrong. It is based on faith and addressed to faith. [b] Or the truth of God for the lie.

no fidelity to their plighted word; they are without natural affection and without pity. They know well enough the just decree of God, 32 that those who behave like this deserve to die, and yet they do it; not only so, they actually applaud such practices.

You therefore have no defence—you who sit in judgement, who- 2 ever you may be—for in judging your fellow-man you condemn yourself, since you, the judge, are equally guilty. It is admitted 2 that God's judgement is rightly passed upon all who commit such crimes as these; and do you imagine—you who pass judgement on 3 the guilty while committing the same crimes yourself—do you imagine that you, any more than they, will escape the judgement of God? Or do you think lightly of his wealth of kindness, of tolerance, 4 and of patience, without recognizing that God's kindness is meant to lead you to a change of heart? In the rigid obstinacy of your heart 5 you are laying up for yourself a store of retribution for the day of retribution, when God's just judgement will be revealed, and he 6 will pay every man for what he has done. To those who pursue glory, 7 honour, and immortality by steady persistence in well-doing, he will give eternal life; but for those who are governed by selfish 8 ambition, who refuse obedience to the truth and take the wrong for their guide, there will be the fury of retribution. There will be 9 grinding misery for every human being who is an evil-doer, for the Jew first and for the Greek also; and for every well-doer there will 10 be glory, honour, and peace, for the Jew first and also for the Greek.

For God has no favourites: those who have sinned outside the pale 11, 12 of the Law of Moses will perish outside its pale, and all who have sinned under that law will be judged by the law. It is not by hearing 13 the law, but by doing it, that men will be justified before God. When Gentiles who do not possess the law carry out its precepts 14 by the light of nature, then, although they have no law, they are their own law, for they display the effect of the law inscribed on their 15 hearts. Their conscience is called as witness, and their own thoughts argue the case on either side, against them or even for them, on the 16 day when God judges the secrets of human hearts through Christ Jesus. So my gospel declares.

But as for you—you may bear the name of Jew; you rely upon the 17 law and are proud of your God; you know his will; you are aware of 18 moral distinctions because you receive instruction from the law; you are confident that you are the one to guide the blind, to enlighten 19

20 the benighted, to train the stupid, and to teach the immature, because
21 in the law you see the very shape of knowledge and truth. You, then,
who teach your fellow-man, do you fail to teach yourself? You
22 proclaim, 'Do not steal'; but are you yourself a thief? You say,
'Do not commit adultery'; but are you an adulterer? You abominate
23 false gods; but do you rob their shrines? While you take pride in
24 the law, you dishonour God by breaking it. For, as Scripture says,
'Because of you the name of God is dishonoured among the Gentiles.'
25 Circumcision has value, provided you keep the law; but if you
break the law, then your circumcision is as if it had never been.
26 Equally, if an uncircumcised man keeps the precepts of the law,
27 will he not count as circumcised? He may be uncircumcised in his
natural state, but by fulfilling the law he will pass judgement on you
28 who break it, for all your written code and your circumcision. The
true Jew is not he who is such in externals, neither is the true circum-
29 cision the external mark in the flesh. The true Jew is he who is such
inwardly, and the true circumcision is of the heart, directed not
by written precepts but by the Spirit; such a man receives his
commendation not from men but from God.

3 Then what advantage has the Jew? What is the value of circum-
2 cision? Great, in every way. In the first place, the Jews were en-
3 trusted with the oracles of God. What if some of them were unfaithful?
4 Will their faithlessness cancel the faithfulness of God? Certainly not!
God must be true though every man living were a liar; for we read
in Scripture, 'When thou speakest thou shalt be vindicated, and win
the verdict when thou art on trial.'

5 Another question: if our injustice serves to bring out God's
justice, what are we to say? Is it unjust of God (I speak of him in
6 human terms) to bring retribution upon us? Certainly not! If God
were unjust, how could he judge the world?

7 Again, if the truth of God brings him all the greater honour because of my falsehood, why should I any longer be condemned as
8 a sinner? Why not indeed 'do evil that good may come', as some
libellously report me as saying? To condemn such men as these is
surely no injustice.

9 What then? Are we Jews any better off?*a* No, not at all!*b* For
we have already formulated the charge that Jews and Greeks alike
10 are all under the power of sin. This has scriptural warrant:

[*a*] Or Are we Jews any worse off? [*b*] Or Not in all respects.

'There is no just man, not one;
No one who understands, no one who seeks God.   11
All have swerved aside, all alike have become debased;   12
There is no one to show kindness; no, not one.

Their throat is an open grave,   13
They use their tongues for treachery,
Adders' venom is on their lips,
And their mouth is full of bitter curses.   14

Their feet hasten to shed blood,   15
Ruin and misery lie along their paths,   16
They are strangers to the high-road of peace,   17
And reverence for God does not enter their thoughts.'   18

Now all the words of the law are addressed, as we know, to those 19
who are within the pale of the law, so that no one may have anything
to say in self-defence, but the whole world may be exposed to the
judgement of God. For (again from Scripture) 'no human being can 20
be justified in the sight of God' for having kept the law: law brings
only the consciousness of sin.

BUT NOW, quite independently of law, God's justice has been 21
brought to light. The Law and the prophets both bear witness to it:
it is God's way of righting wrong, effective through faith in Christ 22
for all who have such faith—all, without distinction. For all alike 23
have sinned, and are deprived of the divine splendour, and all are 24
justified by God's free grace alone, through his act of liberation in
the person of Christ Jesus. For God designed him to be the means 25
of expiating sin by his sacrificial death, effective through faith. God
meant by this to demonstrate his justice, because in his forbearance
he had overlooked the sins of the past—to demonstrate his justice 26
now in the present, showing that he is both himself just and justifies
any man who puts his faith in Jesus.

What room then is left for human pride? It is excluded. And on 27
what principle? The keeping of the law would not exclude it, but
faith does. For our argument is that a man is justified by faith quite 28
apart from success in keeping the law.

Do you suppose God is the God of the Jews alone? Is he not the 29
God of Gentiles also? Certainly, of Gentiles also, if it be true that 30

God is one. And he will therefore justify both the circumcised in virtue of their faith, and the uncircumcised through their faith.

31 Does this mean that we are using faith to undermine law? By no means: we are placing law itself on a firmer footing.

4 WHAT, THEN, are we to say about Abraham, our ancestor in the
2 natural line? If Abraham was justified by anything he had done, then he has a ground for pride. But he has no such ground before God;
3 for what does Scripture say? 'Abraham put his faith in God, and
4 that faith was counted to him as righteousness.' Now if a man does a piece of work, his wages are not 'counted' as a favour; they are
5 paid as debt. But if without any work to his credit he simply puts his faith in him who acquits the guilty, then his faith is indeed
6 'counted as righteousness'. In the same sense David speaks of the happiness of the man whom God 'counts' as just, apart from any
7 specific acts of justice: 'Happy are they', he says, 'whose lawless
8 deeds are forgiven, whose sins are buried away; happy is the man
9 whose sins the Lord does not count against him.' Is this happiness confined to the circumcised, or is it for the uncircumcised also? Consider: we say, 'Abraham's faith was counted as righteousness';
10 in what circumstances was it so counted? Was he circumcised at the time, or not? He was not yet circumcised, but uncircumcised;
11 and he later received the symbolic rite of circumcision as the hallmark of the righteousness which faith had given him when he was still uncircumcised. Consequently, he is the father of all who have faith when uncircumcised, so that righteousness is 'counted' to
12 them; and at the same time he is the father of such of the circumcised as do not rely upon their circumcision alone, but also walk in the footprints of the faith which our father Abraham had while he was yet uncircumcised.
13 For it was not through law that Abraham, or his posterity, was given the promise that the world should be his inheritance, but
14 through the righteousness that came from faith. For if those who hold by the law, and they alone, are heirs, then faith is empty and
15 the promise goes for nothing, because law can bring only retribution;
16 but where there is no law there can be no breach of law. The promise was made on the ground of faith, in order that it might be a matter of sheer grace, and that it might be valid for all Abraham's posterity, not only for those who hold by the law, but for those also who have

the faith of Abraham. For he is the father of us all, as Scripture 17 says: 'I have appointed you to be father of many nations.' This promise, then, was valid before God, the God in whom he put his faith, the God who makes the dead live and summons things that are not yet in existence as if they already were. When hope seemed hope- 18 less, his faith was such that he became 'father of many nations', in agreement with the words which had been spoken to him: 'Thus shall your posterity be.' Without any weakening of faith he contem- 19 plated his own body, as good as dead (for he was about a hundred years old), and the deadness of Sarah's womb, and never doubted 20 God's promise, but, strong in faith, gave honour to God, in the 21 firm conviction of his power to do what he had promised. And that 22 is why Abraham's faith was 'counted to him as righteousness'.

Those words were written, not for Abraham's sake alone, but 23, 24 for our sake too: it is to be 'counted' in the same way to us who have faith in the God who raised Jesus our Lord from the dead; for he was delivered to death for our misdeeds, and raised to life to 25 justify us.[a]

THEREFORE, NOW THAT we have been justified through faith, 5 let us continue at peace[b] with God through our Lord Jesus Christ, through whom we have been allowed to enter the sphere of God's 2 grace, where we now stand. Let us exult[c] in the hope of the divine splendour that is to be ours. More than this: let us even exult[d] in 3 our present sufferings, because we know that suffering trains us to endure, and endurance brings proof that we have stood the test, 4 and this proof is the ground of hope. Such a hope is no mockery, 5 because God's love has flooded our inmost heart through the Holy Spirit he has given us.

For at the very time when we were still powerless, then Christ 6 died for the wicked. Even for a just man one of us would hardly die, 7 though perhaps for a good man one might actually brave death; but Christ died for us while we were yet sinners, and that is God's 8 own proof of his love towards us. And so, since we have now been 9 justified by Christ's sacrificial death, we shall all the more certainly be saved through him from final retribution. For if, when we were 10 God's enemies, we were reconciled to him through the death of his

[a] *Or* raised to life because we were now justified. [b] *Some witnesses read* we are at peace. [c] *Or* We exult. [d] *Or* we even exult.

Son, much more, now that we are reconciled, shall we be saved by
11 his life. But that is not all: we also exult in God through our Lord
Jesus, through whom we have now been granted reconciliation.

12   Mark what follows. It was through one man that sin entered the
world, and through sin death, and thus death pervaded the whole
13 human race, inasmuch as all men have sinned. For sin was already
in the world before there was law, though in the absence of law no
14 reckoning is kept of sin. But death held sway from Adam to Moses,
even over those who had not sinned as Adam did, by disobeying a
direct command—and Adam foreshadows the Man who was to come.

15   But God's act of grace is out of all proportion to Adam's wrongdoing. For if the wrongdoing of that one man brought death upon
so many, its effect is vastly exceeded by the grace of God and the gift
that came to so many by the grace of the one man, Jesus Christ.
16 And again, the gift of God is not to be compared in its effect with
that one man's sin; for the judicial action, following upon the one
offence, issued in a verdict of condemnation, but the act of grace,
following upon so many misdeeds, issued in a verdict of acquittal.
17 For if by the wrongdoing of that one man death established its reign,
through a single sinner, much more shall those who receive in far
greater measure God's grace, and his gift of righteousness, live and
reign through the one man, Jesus Christ.

18   It follows, then, that as the issue of one misdeed was condemnation
for all men, so the issue of one just act is acquittal and life for all men.
19 For as through the disobedience of the one man the many were made
sinners, so through the obedience of the one man the many will be
made righteous.

20   Law intruded into this process to multiply law-breaking. But
where sin was thus multiplied, grace immeasurably exceeded it,
21 in order that, as sin established its reign by way of death, so God's
grace might establish its reign in righteousness, and issue in eternal
life through Jesus Christ our Lord.

6   What are we to say, then? Shall we persist in sin, so that there
2 may be all the more grace? No, no! We died to sin: how can we
3 live in it any longer? Have you forgotten that when we were baptized into union with Christ Jesus we were baptized into his death?
4 By baptism we were buried with him, and lay dead, in order that,
as Christ was raised from the dead in the splendour of the Father,
so also we might set our feet upon the new path of life.

For if we have become incorporate with him in a death like his, 5
we shall also be one with him in a resurrection like his. We know 6
that the man we once were has been crucified with Christ, for the
destruction of the sinful self, so that we may no longer be the slaves
of sin, since a dead man is no longer answerable for his sin. But if 7, 8
we thus died with Christ, we believe that we shall also come to life
with him. We know that Christ, once raised from the dead, is never 9
to die again: he is no longer under the dominion of death. For in 10
dying as he died, he died to sin, once for all, and in living as he lives,
he lives to God. In the same way you must regard yourselves as dead 11
to sin and alive to God, in union with Christ Jesus.

So sin must no longer reign in your mortal body, exacting obedi- 12
ence to the body's desires. You must no longer put its several parts 13
at sin's disposal, as implements for doing wrong. No: put yourselves
at the disposal of God, as dead men raised to life; yield your bodies
to him as implements for doing right; for sin shall no longer be your 14
master, because you are no longer under law, but under the grace
of God.

What then? Are we to sin, because we are not under law but 15
under grace? Of course not. You know well enough that if you 16
put yourselves at the disposal of a master, to obey him, you are
slaves of the master whom you obey; and this is true whether you
serve sin, with death as its result; or obedience, with righteousness
as its result. But God be thanked, you, who once were slaves of sin, 17
have yielded whole-hearted obedience to the pattern of teaching
to which you were made subject,[a] and, emancipated from sin, have 18
become slaves of righteousness (to use words that suit your human 19
weakness)—I mean, as you once yielded your bodies to the service
of impurity and lawlessness, making for moral anarchy, so now you
must yield them to the service of righteousness, making for a holy
life.

When you were slaves of sin, you were free from the control of 20
righteousness; and what was the gain? Nothing but what now 21
makes you ashamed, for the end of that is death. But now, freed 22
from the commands of sin, and bound to the service of God, your
gains are such as make for holiness, and the end is eternal life.
For sin pays a wage, and the wage is death, but God gives freely, 23
and his gift is eternal life, in union with Christ Jesus our Lord.

[a] *Or* which was handed on to you.

7 You cannot be unaware, my friends—I am speaking to those who have some knowledge of law—that a person is subject to the law so
2 long as he is alive, and no longer. For example, a married woman is by law bound to her husband while he lives; but if her husband dies,
3 she is discharged from the obligations of the marriage-law. If, therefore, in her husband's lifetime she consorts with another man, she will incur the charge of adultery; but if her husband dies she is free of the law, and she does not commit adultery by consorting with
4 another man. So you, my friends, have died to the law by becoming identified with the body of Christ, and accordingly you have found another husband in him who rose from the dead, so that we may
5 bear fruit for God. While we lived on the level of our lower nature, the sinful passions evoked by the law worked in our bodies, to bear
6 fruit for death. But now, having died to that which held us bound, we are discharged from the law, to serve God in a new way, the way of the spirit, in contrast to the old way, the way of a written code.
7 What follows? Is the law identical with sin? Of course not. But except through law I should never have become acquainted with sin. For example, I should never have known what it was to covet,
8 if the law had not said, 'Thou shalt not covet.' Through that commandment sin found its opportunity, and produced in me all kinds
9 of wrong desires. In the absence of law, sin is a dead thing. There was a time when, in the absence of law, I was fully alive; but when
10 the commandment came, sin sprang to life and I died. The commandment which should have led to life proved in my experience to lead
11 to death, because sin found its opportunity in the commandment, seduced me, and through the commandment killed me.
12 Therefore the law is in itself holy, and the commandment is
13 holy and just and good. Are we to say then that this good thing was the death of me? By no means. It was sin that killed me, and thereby sin exposed its true character: it used a good thing to bring about my death, and so, through the commandment, sin became more sinful than ever.
14 We know that the law is spiritual; but I am not: I am unspiritual,
15 the purchased slave of sin. I do not even acknowledge my own actions as mine, for what I do is not what I want to do, but what I
16 detest. But if what I do is against my will, it means that I agree with
17 the law and hold it to be admirable. But as things are, it is no longer
18 I who perform the action, but sin that lodges in me. For I know

that nothing good lodges in me—in my unspiritual nature, I mean— for though the will to do good is there, the deed is not. The good 19 which I want to do, I fail to do; but what I do is the wrong which is against my will; and if what I do is against my will, clearly it is 20 no longer I who am the agent, but sin that has its lodging in me.

I discover this principle, then: that when I want to do the right, 21 only the wrong is within my reach. In my inmost self I delight in 22 the law of God, but I perceive that there is in my bodily members 23 a different law, fighting against the law that my reason approves and making me a prisoner under the law*a* that is in my members, the law of sin. Miserable creature that I am, who is there to rescue 24 me out of this body doomed to death*b*? God alone, through Jesus 25 Christ our Lord! Thanks be to God! In a word then, I myself, subject to God's law as a rational being, am yet,*c* in my unspiritual nature, a slave to the law of sin.

The conclusion of the matter is this: there is no condemnation for 8 those who are united with Christ Jesus, because in Christ Jesus 2 the life-giving law of the Spirit has set you free from the law of sin and death. What the law could never do, because our lower nature 3 robbed it of all potency, God has done: by sending his own Son in a form like that of our own sinful nature, and as a sacrifice for sin,*d* he has passed judgement against sin within that very nature, so that the 4 commandment of the law may find fulfilment in us, whose conduct, no longer under the control of our lower nature, is directed by the Spirit.

Those who live on the level of our lower nature have their outlook 5 formed by it, and that spells death; but those who live on the level 6 of the spirit have the spiritual outlook, and that is life and peace. For the outlook of the lower nature is enmity with God; it is not 7 subject to the law of God; indeed it cannot be: those who live on 8 such a level cannot possibly please God.

But that is not how you live. You are on the spiritual level, if 9 only God's Spirit dwells within you; and if a man does not possess the Spirit of Christ, he is no Christian. But if Christ is dwelling 10 within you, then although the body is a dead thing because you sinned, yet the spirit is life itself because you have been justified.*e*

[a] *Or* by means of the law. [b] *Or* out of the body doomed to this death. [c] *Or* Thus, left to myself, while subject...rational being, I am yet... [d] *Or* and to deal with sin. [e] *Or* so that you may live rightly.

11   Moreover, if the Spirit of him who raised Jesus from the dead dwells within you, then the God who raised Christ Jesus from the dead will also give new life to your mortal bodies through his indwelling Spirit.

12   It follows, my friends, that our lower nature has no claim upon us;
13   we are not obliged to live on that level. If you do so, you must die. But if by the Spirit you put to death all the base pursuits of the body, then you will live.

14, 15   For all who are moved by the Spirit of God are sons of God. The Spirit you have received is not a spirit of slavery leading you back into a life of fear, but a Spirit that makes us sons, enabling us to cry
16   'Abba! Father!' In that cry the Spirit of God joins with our spirit
17   in testifying that we are God's children; and if children, then heirs. We are God's heirs and Christ's fellow-heirs, if we share his sufferings now in order to share his splendour hereafter.

18   For I reckon that the sufferings we now endure bear no comparison
19   with the splendour, as yet unrevealed, which is in store for us. For the created universe waits with eager expectation for God's sons
20   to be revealed. It was made the victim of frustration, not by its own choice, but because of him who made it so;^a yet always there was
21   hope, because^b the universe itself is to be freed from the shackles of mortality and enter upon the liberty and splendour of the children
22   of God. Up to the present, we know, the whole created universe
23   groans in all its parts as if in the pangs of childbirth. Not only so, but even we, to whom the Spirit is given as firstfruits of the harvest to come, are groaning inwardly while we wait for God to make us
24   his sons and^c set our whole body free. For we have been saved, though only in hope. Now to see is no longer to hope: why should
25   a man endure and wait^d for what he already sees? But if we hope for something we do not yet see, then, in waiting for it, we show our endurance.

26   In the same way the Spirit comes to the aid of our weakness. We do not even know how we ought to pray,^e but through our
27   inarticulate groans the Spirit himself is pleading for us, and God who searches our inmost being knows what the Spirit means, because
28   he pleads for God's own people in God's own way; and in every-

[a] *Or* because God subjected it.   [b] *Or* with the hope that...   [c] *Some witnesses omit* make us his sons and.   [d] *Some witnesses read* why should a man hope...   [e] *Or* what it is right to pray for.

thing, as we know, he co-operates for good with those who love
God*a* and are called according to his purpose. For God knew his   29
own before ever they were, and also ordained that they should be
shaped to the likeness of his Son, that he might be the eldest among
a large family of brothers; and it is these, so fore-ordained, whom   30
he has also called. And those whom he called he has justified, and to
those whom he justified he has also given his splendour.

With all this in mind, what are we to say? If God is on our side,   31
who is against us? He did not spare his own Son, but surrendered   32
him for us all; and with this gift how can he fail to lavish upon us all
he has to give? Who will be the accuser of God's chosen ones?   33
It is God who pronounces acquittal: then who can condemn? It is   34
Christ—Christ who died, and, more than that, was raised from the
dead—who is at God's right hand, and indeed pleads our cause.*b*
Then what can separate us from the love of Christ? Can affliction or   35
hardship? Can persecution, hunger, nakedness, peril, or the sword?
'We are being done to death for thy sake all day long,' as Scripture   36
says; 'we have been treated like sheep for slaughter'—and yet, in   37
spite of all, overwhelming victory is ours through him who loved us.
For I am convinced that there is nothing in death or life, in the realm   38
of spirits or superhuman powers, in the world as it is or the world
as it shall be, in the forces of the universe, in heights or depths—   39
nothing in all creation that can separate us from the love of God
in Christ Jesus our Lord.

The Purpose of God in History

I AM SPEAKING the truth as a Christian, and my own conscience,   9
enlightened by the Holy Spirit, assures me it is no lie: in my heart   2
there is great grief and unceasing sorrow. For I could even pray to   3
be outcast from Christ myself for the sake of my brothers, my
natural kinsfolk. They are Israelites: they were made God's sons;   4
theirs is the splendour of the divine presence, theirs the covenants,

[a] *Or* and, as we know, all things work together for good for those who love God; *some*
witnesses read and we know God himself co-operates for good with those who love God.
[b] *Or* Who will be the accuser of God's chosen ones? Will it be God himself? No,
he it is who pronounces acquittal. Who will be the judge to condemn? Will it be Christ
—he who died, and, more than that, . . . right hand? No, he it is who pleads our cause.

5 the law, the temple worship, and the promises. Theirs are the patriarchs, and from them, in natural descent, sprang the Messiah.*ᵃ* May God, supreme above all, be blessed for ever!*ᵇ* Amen.

6 It is impossible that the word of God should have proved false.
7 For not all descendants of Israel are truly Israel, nor, because they are Abraham's offspring, are they all his true children;*ᶜ* but, in the words of Scripture, 'Through the line of Isaac your posterity
8 shall be traced.'*ᵈ* That is to say, it is not those born in the course of nature who are children of God; it is the children born through
9 God's promise who are reckoned as Abraham's descendants. For the promise runs: 'At the time fixed I will come, and Sarah shall have a son.'

10 But that is not all, for Rebekah's children had one and the same
11 father, our ancestor Isaac; and yet, in order that God's selective purpose might stand, based not upon men's deeds but upon the call
12 of God, she was told, even before they were born, when they had as yet done nothing, good or ill, 'The elder shall be servant to the
13 younger'; and that accords with the text of Scripture, 'Jacob I loved and Esau I hated.'

14 What shall we say to that? Is God to be charged with injustice?
15 By no means. For he says to Moses, 'Where I show mercy, I will
16 show mercy, and where I pity, I will pity.' Thus it does not depend
17 on man's will or effort, but on God's mercy. For Scripture says to Pharaoh, 'I have raised you up for this very purpose, to exhibit my power in my dealings with you, and to spread my fame over all
18 the world.' Thus he not only shows mercy as he chooses, but also makes men stubborn as he chooses.

19 You will say, 'Then why does God blame a man? For who can
20 resist his will?' Who are you, sir, to answer God back? Can the pot
21 speak to the potter and say, 'Why did you make me like this?'? Surely the potter can do what he likes with the clay. Is he not free to make out of the same lump two vessels, one to be treasured, the other for common use?

22 But what if God, desiring to exhibit*ᵉ* his retribution at work and to make his power known, tolerated very patiently those vessels

---

[a] *Greek* Christ. [b] *Or* sprang the Messiah, supreme above all, God blessed for ever; *or* sprang the Messiah, who is supreme above all. Blessed be God for ever! [c] *Or* all children of God. [d] *Or* God's call shall be for your descendants in the line of Isaac. [e] *Or* although he had the will to exhibit...

which were objects of retribution due for destruction, and did so 23
in order to make known the full wealth of his splendour upon
vessels which were objects of mercy, and which from the first had
been prepared for this splendour?

Such vessels are we, whom he has called from among Gentiles 24
as well as Jews, as it says in the Book of Hosea: 'Those who were not 25
my people I will call My People, and the unloved nation I will call
My Beloved. For in the very place where they were told "you are 26
no people of mine", they shall be called Sons of the living God.'
But Isaiah makes this proclamation about Israel: 'Though the 27
Israelites be countless as the sands of the sea, it is but a remnant
that shall be saved; for the Lord's sentence on the land will be 28
summary and final'; as also he said previously, 'If the Lord of 29
Hosts had not left us the mere germ of a nation, we should have
become like Sodom, and no better than Gomorrah.'

Then what are we to say? That Gentiles, who made no effort after 30
righteousness, nevertheless achieved it, a righteousness based on
faith; whereas Israel made great efforts after a law of righteousness, 31
but never attained to it. Why was this? Because their efforts were not 32
based on faith, but (as they supposed) on deeds. They stumbled over
the 'stumbling-stone' mentioned in Scripture: 'Here I lay in Zion 33
a stumbling-stone and a rock to trip them up; but he who has faith
in him will not be put to shame.'

BROTHERS, my deepest desire and my prayer to God is for their 10
salvation. To their zeal for God I can testify; but it is an ill-informed 2
zeal. For they ignore God's way of righteousness, and try to set 3
up their own, and therefore they have not submitted themselves to
God's righteousness. For Christ ends the law and brings righteous- 4
ness for everyone who has faith.[a]

Of legal righteousness Moses writes, 'The man who does this 5
shall gain life by it.' But the righteousness that comes by faith says, 6
'Do not say to yourself, "Who can go up to heaven?"' (that is to
bring Christ down), 'or, "Who can go down to the abyss?"' (to bring 7
Christ up from the dead). But what does it say? 'The word is near 8
you: it is upon your lips and in your heart.' This means the word
of faith which we proclaim. If on your lips is the confession, 'Jesus 9

[a] *Or* Christ is the end of the law as a way to righteousness for everyone who has
faith.

is Lord', and in your heart the faith that God raised him from the
10 dead, then you will find salvation. For the faith that leads to
righteousness is in the heart, and the confession that leads to salvation
is upon the lips.

11   Scripture says, 'Everyone who has faith in him will be saved
12 from shame'—everyone: there is no distinction between Jew and
Greek, because the same Lord is Lord of all, and is rich enough for
13 the need of all who invoke him. For everyone, as it says again—
14 'everyone who invokes the name of the Lord will be saved'. How
could they invoke one in whom they had no faith? And how could
they have faith in one they had never heard of? And how hear
15 without someone to spread the news? And how could anyone spread
the news without a commission to do so? And that is what Scripture
affirms: 'How welcome are the feet of the messengers of good
news!'

16   But not all have responded to the good news. For Isaiah says,
17 'Lord, who has believed our message?' We conclude that faith is
awakened by the message, and the message that awakens it comes
through the word of Christ.

18   But, I ask, can it be that they never heard it? Of course they did:
'Their voice has sounded all over the earth, and their words to the
19 bounds of the inhabited world.' But, I ask again, can it be that
Israel failed to recognize the message? In reply, I first cite Moses,
who says, 'I will use a nation that is no nation to stir your envy, and
20 a foolish nation to rouse your anger.' But Isaiah is still more daring:
'I was found', he says, 'by those who were not looking for me; I was
21 clearly shown to those who never asked about me'; while to Israel
he says, 'All day long I have stretched out my hands to an unruly
and recalcitrant people.'

11 I ASK THEN, has God rejected his people? I cannot believe it!
I am an Israelite myself, of the stock of Abraham, of the tribe of
2 Benjamin. No! God has not rejected the people which he acknowledged of old as his own. You know (do you not?) what Scripture
says in the story of Elijah—how Elijah pleads with God against
3 Israel: 'Lord, they have killed thy prophets, they have overthrown
thine altars, and I alone am left, and they are seeking my life.'
4 But what does the oracle say to him? 'I have left myself seven
5 thousand men who have not done homage to Baal.' In just the same

way at the present time a 'remnant' has come into being, selected by
the grace of God. But if it is by grace, then it does not rest on deeds 6
done, or grace would cease to be grace.

What follows? What Israel sought, Israel has not achieved, but 7
the selected few have achieved it. The rest were made blind to the
truth, exactly as it stands written: 'God brought upon them a numb- 8
ness of spirit; he gave them blind eyes and deaf ears, and so it is still.'
Similarly David says: 9

> 'May their table be a snare and a trap,
> Both stumbling-block and retribution!
> May their eyes be darkened so that they do not see!   10
> Bow down their back for ever!'

I now ask, did their failure mean complete downfall? Far from it! 11
Because they offended, salvation has come to the Gentiles, to stir
Israel to emulation. But if their offence means the enrichment of 12
the world, and if their falling-off means the enrichment of the
Gentiles, how much more their coming to full strength!

But I have something to say to you Gentiles. I am a missionary 13
to the Gentiles, and as such I give all honour to that ministry
when I try to stir emulation in the men of my own race, and so to 14
save some of them. For if their rejection has meant the reconciliation 15
of the world, what will their acceptance mean? Nothing less than
life from the dead! If the first portion of dough is consecrated, so 16
is the whole lump. If the root is consecrated, so are the branches.
But if some of the branches have been lopped off, and you, a wild 17
olive, have been grafted in among them, and have come to share the
same root and sap as the olive, do not make yourself superior to the 18
branches. If you do so, remember that it is not you who sustain the
root: the root sustains you.

You will say, 'Branches were lopped off so that I might be grafted 19
in.' Very well: they were lopped off for lack of faith, and by faith 20
you hold your place. Put away your pride, and be on your guard;
for if God did not spare the native branches, no more will he spare 21
you. Observe the kindness and the severity of God—severity to 22
those who fell away, divine kindness to you, if only you remain
within its scope; otherwise you too will be cut off, whereas they, if 23
they do not continue faithless, will be grafted in; for it is in God's
power to graft them in again. For if you were cut from your native 24

wild olive and against all nature grafted into the cultivated olive, how much more readily will they, the natural olive-branches, be grafted into their native stock!

25 For there is a deep truth here, my brothers, of which I want you to take account, so that you may not be complacent about your own discernment: this partial blindness has come upon Israel only until 26 the Gentiles have been admitted in full strength; when that has happened, the whole of Israel will be saved, in agreement with the text of Scripture:

> 'From Zion shall come the Deliverer;
> He shall remove wickedness from Jacob.
27 And this is the covenant I will grant them,
> When I take away their sins.'

28 In the spreading of the Gospel they are treated as God's enemies for your sake; but God's choice stands, and they are his friends for 29 the sake of the patriarchs. For the gracious gifts of God and his 30 calling are irrevocable. Just as formerly you were disobedient to God, 31 but now have received mercy in the time of their disobedience, so now, when you receive mercy, they have proved disobedient, but 32 only in order that they too may receive mercy. For in making all mankind prisoners to disobedience, God's purpose was to show mercy to all mankind.

33 O depth of wealth, wisdom, and knowledge in God! How un- 34 searchable his judgements, how untraceable his ways! Who knows 35 the mind of the Lord? Who has been his counsellor? Who has ever 36 made a gift to him, to receive a gift in return? Source, Guide, and Goal of all that is—to him be glory for ever! Amen.

Christian Behaviour

12 THEREFORE, MY BROTHERS, I implore you by God's mercy to offer your very selves to him: a living sacrifice, dedicated and fit for his acceptance, the worship offered by mind and heart.[a] 2 Adapt yourselves no longer to the pattern of this present world, but let your minds be remade and your whole nature thus trans-

[a] *Or* ... acceptance, for such is the worship which you, as rational creatures, should offer.

formed. Then you will be able to discern the will of God, and to know what is good, acceptable, and perfect.

In virtue of the gift that God in his grace has given me I say to ₃ everyone among you: do not be conceited or think too highly of yourself; but think your way to a sober estimate based on the measure of faith that God has dealt to each of you. For just as in ₄ a single human body there are many limbs and organs, all with different functions, so all of us, united with Christ, form one body, ₅ serving individually as limbs and organs to one another.

The gifts we possess differ as they are allotted to us by God's grace, ₆ and must be exercised accordingly: the gift of inspired utterance, for example, in proportion to a man's faith; or the gift of administra- ₇ tion, in administration. A teacher should employ his gift in teaching, and one who has the gift of stirring speech should use it to stir his ₈ hearers. If you give to charity, give with all your heart; if you are a leader, exert yourself to lead; if you are helping others in distress, do it cheerfully.

Love in all sincerity, loathing evil and clinging to the good. Let ₉, ₁₀ love for our brotherhood breed warmth of mutual affection. Give pride of place to one another in esteem.

With unflagging energy, in ardour of spirit, serve the Lord.ᵃ   ₁₁

Let hope keep you joyful; in trouble stand firm; persist in ₁₂ prayer.

Contribute to the needs of God's people, and practise hospitality. ₁₃

Call down blessings on your persecutors—blessings, not curses. ₁₄

With the joyful be joyful, and mourn with the mourners. ₁₅

Have equal regard for one another. Do not be haughty, but go ₁₆ about with humble folk. Do not keep thinking how wise you are.

Never pay back evil for evil. Let your aims be such as all men count ₁₇ honourable. If possible, so far as it lies with you, live at peace with ₁₈ all men. My dear friends, do not seek revenge, but leave a place ₁₉ for divine retribution; for there is a text which reads, 'Justice is mine, says the Lord, I will repay.' But there is another text: 'If your ₂₀ enemy is hungry, feed him; if he is thirsty, give him a drink; by doing this you will heap live coals on his head.' Do not let evil ₂₁ conquer you, but use good to defeat evil.

Every person must submit to the supreme authorities. There is **13** no authority but by act of God, and the existing authorities are

[a] *Some witnesses read* meet the demands of the hour.

2 instituted by him; consequently anyone who rebels against authority is resisting a divine institution, and those who so resist have them-
3 selves to thank for the punishment they will receive. For government, a terror to crime, has no terrors for good behaviour. You wish to have no fear of the authorities? Then continue to do right and you
4 will have their approval, for they are God's agents working for your good. But if you are doing wrong, then you will have cause to fear them; it is not for nothing that they hold the power of the sword, for they are God's agents of punishment, for retribution on the
5 offender. That is why you are obliged to submit. It is an obligation
6 imposed not merely by fear of retribution but by conscience. That is also why you pay taxes. The authorities are in God's service and to these duties they devote their energies.
7 Discharge your obligations to all men; pay tax and toll, reverence
8 and respect, to those to whom they are due. Leave no claim outstanding against you, except that of mutual love. He who loves his
9 neighbour has satisfied every claim of the law. For the commandments, 'Thou shalt not commit adultery, thou shalt not kill, thou shalt not steal, thou shalt not covet', and any other commandment there may be, are all summed up in the one rule, 'Love your neigh-
10 bour as yourself.' Love cannot wrong a neighbour; therefore the whole law is summed up in love.[a]
11 In all this, remember how critical the moment is. It is time for you to wake out of sleep, for deliverance is nearer to us now than
12 it was when first we believed. It is far on in the night; day is near. Let us therefore throw off the deeds of darkness and put on our
13 armour as soldiers of the light. Let us behave with decency as befits the day: no revelling or drunkenness, no debauchery or vice, no
14 quarrels or jealousies! Let Christ Jesus himself be the armour that you wear; give no more thought to satisfying the bodily appetites.

14 IF A MAN is weak in his faith you must accept him without attempt-
2 ing to settle doubtful points. For instance, one man will have faith enough to eat all kinds of food, while a weaker man eats only
3 vegetables. The man who eats must not hold in contempt the man who does not, and he who does not eat must not pass judgement on
4 the one who does; for God has accepted him. Who are you to pass judgement on someone else's servant? Whether he stands or falls

[a] *Or* the whole law is fulfilled by love.

is his own Master's business; and stand he will, because his Master has power to enable him to stand.

Again, this man regards one day more highly than another, while 5 that man regards all days alike. On such a point everyone should have reached conviction in his own mind. He who respects the day 6 has the Lord in mind in doing so, and he who eats meat has the Lord in mind when he eats, since he gives thanks to God; and he who abstains has the Lord in mind no less, since he too gives thanks to God.

For no one of us lives, and equally no one of us dies, for himself 7 alone. If we live, we live for the Lord; and if we die, we die for the 8 Lord. Whether therefore we live or die, we belong to the Lord. This is why Christ died and came to life again, to establish his lord- 9 ship over dead and living. You, sir, why do you pass judgement 10 on your brother? And you, sir, why do you hold your brother in contempt? We shall all stand before God's tribunal. For Scripture 11 says, 'As I live, says the Lord, to me every knee shall bow and every tongue acknowledge God.' So, you see, each of us will have to 12 answer for himself.

Let us therefore cease judging one another, but rather make this 13 simple judgement: that no obstacle or stumbling-block be placed in a brother's way. I am absolutely convinced, as a Christian, that noth- 14 ing is impure in itself; only, if a man considers a particular thing impure, then to him it is impure. If your brother is outraged by what 15 you eat, then your conduct is no longer guided by love. Do not by your eating bring disaster to a man for whom Christ died! What for 16 you is a good thing must not become an occasion for slanderous talk; for the kingdom of God is not eating and drinking, but justice, peace, 17 and joy, inspired by the Holy Spirit. He who thus shows himself 18 a servant of Christ is acceptable to God and approved by men.

Let us then pursue the things that make for peace and build up 19 the common life. Do not ruin the work of God for the sake of food. 20 Everything is pure in itself, but anything is bad for the man who by his eating causes another to fall. It is a fine thing to abstain 21 from eating meat or drinking wine, or doing anything which causes your brother's downfall. If you have a clear conviction, apply it to 22 yourself in the sight of God. Happy is the man who can make his decision with a clear conscience![a] But a man who has doubts is 23 guilty if he eats, because his action does not arise from his conviction,

[a] *Or* who does not bring judgement upon himself by what he approves!

15 and anything which does not arise from conviction is sin.^a Those of us who have a robust conscience must accept as our own burden the
2 tender scruples of weaker men, and not consider ourselves. Each of us must consider his neighbour and think what is for his good
3 and will build up the common life. For Christ too did not consider himself, but might have said, in the words of Scripture, 'The
4 reproaches of those who reproached thee fell upon me.' For all the ancient scriptures were written for our own instruction, in order that through the encouragement they give us we may maintain our hope
5 with fortitude. And may God, the source of all fortitude and all encouragement, grant that you may agree with one another after the
6 manner of Christ Jesus, so that with one mind and one voice you may praise the God and Father of our Lord Jesus Christ.
7 In a word, accept one another as Christ accepted us, to the glory
8 of God. I mean that Christ became a servant of the Jewish people to maintain the truth of God by making good his promises to the
9 patriarchs, and at the same time to give the Gentiles cause to glorify God for his mercy. As Scripture says, 'Therefore I will praise thee
10 among the Gentiles and sing hymns to thy name'; and again,
11 'Gentiles, make merry together with his own people'; and yet again,
12 'All Gentiles, praise the Lord; let all peoples praise him.' Once again, Isaiah says, 'There shall be the Root of Jesse, the one raised up
13 to govern the Gentiles; on him the Gentiles shall set their hope.' And may the God of hope fill you with all joy and peace by your faith in him, until, by the power of the Holy Spirit, you overflow with hope.

14 MY FRIENDS, I have no doubt in my own mind that you yourselves are quite full of goodness and equipped with knowledge of every
15 kind, well able to give advice to one another; nevertheless I have written to refresh your memory, and written somewhat boldly at
16 times, in virtue of the gift I have from God. His grace has made me a minister of Christ Jesus to the Gentiles; my priestly service is the preaching of the gospel of God, and it falls to me to offer the Gentiles to him as^b an acceptable sacrifice, consecrated by the Holy Spirit.
17 Thus in the fellowship of Christ Jesus I have ground for pride
18 in the service of God. I will venture to speak of those things alone in which I have been Christ's instrument to bring the Gentiles into

[a] *See p. 279, note c.*   [b] *Or* ...of God, so that the worship which the Gentiles offer may be...

his allegiance, by word and deed, by the force of miraculous signs 19
and by the power of the Holy Spirit. As a result I have completed
the preaching of the gospel of Christ from Jerusalem as far round as
Illyricum. It is my ambition to bring the gospel to places where the 20
very name of Christ has not been heard, for I do not want to build
on another man's foundation; but, as Scripture says, 21

> 'They who had no news of him shall see,
> And they who never heard of him shall understand.'

That is why I have been prevented all this time from coming to 22
you. But now I have no further scope in these parts, and I have 23
been longing for many years to visit you on my way to Spain; for 24
I hope to see you as I travel through, and to be sent there with your
support after having enjoyed your company for a while. But at the 25
moment I am on my way to Jerusalem, on an errand to God's people
there. For Macedonia and Achaia have resolved to raise a common 26
fund for the benefit of the poor among God's people at Jerusalem.
They have resolved to do so, and indeed they are under an obligation 27
to them. For if the Jewish Christians shared their spiritual treasures
with the Gentiles, the Gentiles have a clear duty to contribute to their
material needs. So when I have finished this business and delivered 28
the proceeds under my own seal, I shall set out for Spain by way of
your city, and I am sure that when I arrive I shall come to you with 29
a full measure of the blessing of Christ.

I implore you by our Lord Jesus Christ and by the love that the 30
Spirit inspires, be my allies in the fight; pray to God for me that 31
I may be saved from unbelievers in Judaea and that my errand to
Jerusalem may find acceptance with God's people, so that by his 32
will I may come to you in a happy frame of mind and enjoy a time
of rest with you. The God of peace be with you all. Amen.[a] 33

I COMMEND to you Phoebe, a fellow-Christian who holds office **16**
in the congregation at Cenchreae. Give her, in the fellowship of 2
Christ, a welcome worthy of God's people, and stand by her in any
business in which she may need your help, for she has herself been
a good friend to many, including myself.

Give my greetings to Prisca and Aquila, my fellow-workers in 3
Christ. They risked their necks to save my life, and not I alone 4

[a] *See p. 279, note c.*

ROMANS 16 *Christian Behaviour*

5 but all the gentile congregations are grateful to them. Greet also the congregation at their house.

Give my greetings to my dear friend Epaenetus, the first convert
6,7 to Christ in Asia, and to Mary, who toiled hard for you. Greet Andronicus and Junias*a* my fellow-countrymen and comrades in captivity. They are eminent among the apostles, and they were Christians before I was.

8 Greetings to Ampliatus, my dear friend in the fellowship of the
9 Lord, to Urban my comrade in Christ, and to my dear Stachys.
10 My greetings to Apelles, well proved in Christ's service, to the house-
11 hold of Aristobulus, and my countryman Herodion, and to those of
12 the household of Narcissus who are in the Lord's fellowship. Greet Tryphaena and Tryphosa, who toil in the Lord's service, and dear
13 Persis who has toiled in his service so long. Give my greetings to Rufus, an outstanding follower of the Lord, and to his mother,
14 whom I call mother too. Greet Asyncritus, Phlegon, Hermes,
15 Patrobas, Hermas, and all friends in their company. Greet Philologus and Julia,*b* Nereus and his sister, and Olympas, and all God's people associated with them.

16 Greet one another with the kiss of peace. All Christ's congregations send you their greetings.

17 I implore you, my friends, keep your eye on those who stir up quarrels and lead others astray, contrary to the teaching you received.
18 Avoid them, for such people are servants not of Christ our Lord but of their own appetites, and they seduce the minds of innocent people
19 with smooth and specious words. The fame of your obedience has spread everywhere. This makes me happy about you; yet I should
20 wish you to be experts in goodness but simpletons in evil; and the God of peace will soon crush Satan beneath your feet. The grace of our Lord Jesus be with you!*c*

21 Greetings to you from my colleague Timothy, and from Lucius,
22 Jason, and Sosipater my fellow-countrymen. (I Tertius, who took
23 this letter down, add my Christian greetings.) Greetings also from Gaius, my host and host of the whole congregation, and from Erastus, treasurer of this city, and our brother Quartus.*d*

[a] *Or* Junia; *some ancient witnesses read* Julia, *or* Julias. [b] *Or* Julias; *some witnesses read* Junia, *or* Junias. [c] *The words* The grace...with you *are omitted at this point in some witnesses; in some, these or similar words are given as verse 24, and in some others after verse 27 (see note on verse 23).* [d] *Some witnesses add* (24) The grace of our Lord Jesus Christ be with you all!

278

To HIM who has power to make your standing sure, according to 25 the Gospel I brought you and the proclamation of Jesus Christ, according to the revelation of that divine secret kept in silence for long ages but now disclosed, and through prophetic scriptures by 26 eternal God's command made known to all nations, to bring them to faith and obedience—to God who alone is wise, through Jesus 27 Christ,[a] be glory for endless ages! Amen.[b][c]

[a] *Some witnesses insert* to whom. [b] *Here some witnesses add* The grace of our Lord Jesus Christ be with you! [c] *Some witnesses place verses 25–27 at the end of chapter 14, one other places them at the end of chapter 15, and others omit them altogether.*

THE
FIRST LETTER OF PAUL TO THE
CORINTHIANS

Unity and Order in the Church

1 FROM PAUL, apostle of Jesus Christ at God's call and
2 by God's will, together with our colleague Sosthenes, to the
congregation of God's people at Corinth, dedicated to him in
Christ Jesus, claimed by him as his own, along with all men everywhere who invoke the name of our Lord Jesus Christ—their Lord
as well as ours.

3 Grace and peace to you from God our Father and the Lord Jesus
Christ.

4 I am always thanking God for you. I thank him for his grace
5 given to you in Christ Jesus. I thank him for all the enrichment that
has come to you in Christ. You possess full knowledge and you can
6 give full expression to it, because in you the evidence for the truth
7 of Christ has found confirmation. There is indeed no single gift you
lack, while you wait expectantly for our Lord Jesus Christ to reveal
8 himself. He will keep you firm to the end, without reproach on
9 the Day of our Lord Jesus. It is God himself who called you
to share in the life of his Son Jesus Christ our Lord; and God
keeps faith.

10 I appeal to you, my brothers, in the name of our Lord Jesus Christ:
agree among yourselves, and avoid divisions; be firmly joined in
11 unity of mind and thought. I have been told, my brothers, by
12 Chloe's people that there are quarrels among you. What I mean is
this: each of you is saying, 'I am Paul's man', or 'I am for Apollos';
13 'I follow Cephas', or 'I am Christ's.' Surely Christ has not been
divided among you! Was it Paul who was crucified for you? Was
14 it in the name of Paul that you were baptized? Thank God, I never
15 baptized one of you—except Crispus and Gaius. So no one can say
16 you were baptized in my name.—Yes, I did baptize the household of
17 Stephanas; I cannot think of anyone else. Christ did not send me
to baptize, but to proclaim the Gospel; and to do it without relying

on the language of worldly wisdom, so that the fact of Christ on his cross might have its full weight.

This doctrine of the cross is sheer folly to those on their way to 18 ruin, but to us who are on the way to salvation it is the power of God. Scripture says, 'I will destroy the wisdom of the wise, and bring to 19 nothing the cleverness of the clever.' Where is your wise man now, 20 your man of learning, or your subtle debater—limited, all of them, to this passing age? God has made the wisdom of this world look foolish. As God in his wisdom ordained, the world failed to find him 21 by its wisdom, and he chose to save those who have faith by the folly of the Gospel. Jews call for miracles, Greeks look for wisdom; 22 but we proclaim Christ—yes, Christ nailed to the cross; and though 23 this is a stumbling-block to Jews and folly to Greeks, yet to those 24 who have heard his call, Jews and Greeks alike, he is the power of God and the wisdom of God.

Divine folly is wiser than the wisdom of man, and divine weakness 25 stronger than man's strength. My brothers, think what sort of 26 people you are, whom God has called. Few of you are men of wisdom, by any human standard; few are powerful or highly born. Yet, 27 to shame the wise, God has chosen what the world counts folly, and to shame what is strong, God has chosen what the world counts weakness. He has chosen things low and contemptible, mere 28 nothings, to overthrow the existing order. And so there is no place 29 for human pride in the presence of God. You are in Christ Jesus by 30 God's act, for God has made him our wisdom; he is our righteousness; in him we are consecrated and set free. And so (in the words of 31 Scripture), 'If a man is proud, let him be proud of the Lord.'

As for me, brothers, when I came to you, I declared the 2 attested truth of God[a] without display of fine words or wisdom. I resolved that while I was with you I would think of nothing but 2 Jesus Christ—Christ nailed to the cross. I came before you weak, 3 as I was then, nervous and shaking with fear. The word I spoke, the 4 gospel I proclaimed, did not sway you with subtle arguments; it carried conviction by spiritual power, so that your faith might be 5 built not upon human wisdom but upon the power of God.

And yet I do speak words of wisdom to those who are ripe for it, 6 not a wisdom belonging to this passing age, nor to any of its governing powers, which are declining to their end; I speak God's hidden 7

[a] *Some witnesses read* I declared God's secret purpose. . .

wisdom, his secret purpose framed from the very beginning to bring
8 us to our full glory. The powers that rule the world have never known
it; if they had, they would not have crucified the Lord of glory.
9 But, in the words of Scripture, 'Things beyond our seeing, things
beyond our hearing, things beyond our imagining, all prepared by
10 God for those who love him', these it is that God has revealed to us
through the Spirit.

For the Spirit explores everything, even the depths of God's own
11 nature. Among men, who knows what a man is but the man's own
spirit within him? In the same way, only the Spirit of God knows
12 what God is. This is the Spirit that we have received from God, and
not the spirit of the world, so that we may know all that God of his
13 own grace gives us; and, because we are interpreting spiritual truths
to those who have the Spirit, we speak of these gifts of God in words
14 found for us not by our human wisdom but by the Spirit. A man who
is unspiritual refuses what belongs to the Spirit of God; it is folly to
him; he cannot grasp it, because it needs to be judged in the light of
15 the Spirit. A man gifted with the Spirit can judge the worth of everything, but is not himself subject to judgement by his fellow-
16 men. For (in the words of Scripture) 'who knows the mind of the
Lord? Who can advise him?' We, however, possess the mind of
Christ.

3 FOR MY PART, my brothers, I could not speak to you as I should
speak to people who have the Spirit. I had to deal with you on the
2 merely natural plane, as infants in Christ. And so I gave you milk
to drink, instead of solid food, for which you were not yet ready.
3 Indeed, you are still not ready for it, for you are still on the merely
natural plane. Can you not see that while there is jealousy and
strife among you, you are living on the purely human level of your
4 lower nature? When one says, 'I am Paul's man', and another, 'I am
for Apollos', are you not all too human?

5 After all, what is Apollos? What is Paul? We are simply God's
agents in bringing you to the faith. Each of us performed the task
6 which the Lord allotted to him: I planted the seed, and Apollos
7 watered it; but God made it grow. Thus it is not the gardeners with
their planting and watering who count, but God, who makes it grow.
8 Whether they plant or water, they work as a team,[a] though each will

[a] *Or* Whether they plant or water, it is all the same.

get his own pay for his own labour. We are God's fellow-workers;[a] 9 and you are God's garden.

Or again, you are God's building. I am like a skilled master- 10 builder who by God's grace laid the foundation, and someone else is putting up the building. Let each take care how he builds. There 11 can be no other foundation beyond that which is already laid; I mean Jesus Christ himself. If anyone builds on that foundation with 12 gold, silver, and fine stone, or with wood, hay, and straw, the work 13 that each man does will at last be brought to light; the day of judgement will expose it. For that day dawns in fire, and the fire will test the worth of each man's work. If a man's building stands, he will be 14 rewarded; if it burns, he will have to bear the loss; and yet he will 15 escape with his life, as one might from a fire. Surely you know that 16 you are God's temple, where the Spirit of God dwells. Anyone who 17 destroys God's temple will himself be destroyed[b] by God, because the temple of God is holy; and that temple you are.

Make no mistake about this: if there is anyone among you who 18 fancies himself wise—wise, I mean, by the standards of this passing age—he must become a fool to gain true wisdom. For the wisdom of 19 this world is folly in God's sight. Scripture says, 'He traps the wise in their own cunning', and again, 'The Lord knows that the argu- 20 ments of the wise are futile.' So never make mere men a cause for 21 pride. For though everything belongs to you—Paul, Apollos, and 22 Cephas, the world, life, and death, the present and the future, all of them belong to you—yet you belong to Christ, and Christ to God. 23

We must be regarded as Christ's underlings and as stewards of the 4 secrets of God. Well then, stewards are expected to show themselves 2 trustworthy. For my part, if I am called to account by you or by 3 any human court of judgement, it does not matter to me in the least. Why, I do not even pass judgement on myself, for I have nothing on my conscience; but that does not mean I stand acquitted. My judge 4 is the Lord. So pass no premature judgement; wait until the Lord 5 comes. For he will bring to light what darkness hides, and disclose men's inward motives; then will be the time for each to receive from God such praise as he deserves.

Into this general picture, my friends, I have brought Apollos and 6 myself on your account, so that you may take our case as an example,

[a] *Or* We are fellow-workers in God's service. [b] *Some witnesses read* is himself destroyed.

and learn to 'keep within the rules', as they say, and may not be

7 inflated with pride as you patronize one and flout the other. Who makes you, my friend, so important? What do you possess that was not given you? If then you really received it all as a gift, why take the credit to yourself?

8 All of you, no doubt, have everything you could desire. You have come into your fortune already. You have come into your kingdom— and left us out. How I wish you had indeed won your kingdom; then

9 you might share it with us! For it seems to me God has made us apostles the most abject of mankind. We are like men condemned to death in the arena, a spectacle to the whole universe—angels as well

10 as men. We are fools for Christ's sake, while you are such sensible Christians. We are weak; you are so powerful. We are in disgrace;

11 you are honoured. To this day we go hungry and thirsty and in rags;

12 we are roughly handled; we wander from place to place; we wear ourselves out working with our own hands. They curse us, and we

13 bless; they persecute us, and we submit to it; they slander us, and we humbly make our appeal. We are treated as the scum of the earth, the dregs of humanity, to this very day.

14 I am not writing thus to shame you, but to bring you to reason;

15 for you are my dear children. You may have ten thousand tutors in Christ, but you have only one father. For in Christ Jesus you are my offspring, and mine alone, through the preaching of the Gospel.

16, 17 I appeal to you therefore to follow my example. That is the very reason why I have sent Timothy, who is a dear son to me and a most trustworthy Christian; he will remind you of the way of life in Christ which I follow, and which I teach everywhere in all our con-

18 gregations. There are certain persons who are filled with self-

19 importance because they think I am not coming to Corinth. I shall come very soon, if the Lord will; and then I shall take the measure of these self-important people, not by what they say, but by what

20 power is in them. The kingdom of God is not a matter of talk, but

21 of power. Choose, then: am I to come to you with a rod in my hand, or in love and a gentle spirit?

5 I ACTUALLY HEAR reports of sexual immorality among you, im-morality such as even pagans do not tolerate: the union of a man

2 with his father's wife. And you can still be proud of yourselves! You ought to have gone into mourning; a man who has done such a deed

should have been rooted out of your company. For my part, though 3 I am absent in body, I am present in spirit, and my judgement upon the man who did this thing is already given, as if I were indeed present: you all being assembled in the name of our Lord Jesus, and 4 I with you in spirit, with the power of our Lord Jesus over us, this 5 man is to be consigned to Satan for the destruction of the body, so that his spirit may be saved on the Day of the Lord.

Your self-satisfaction ill becomes you. Have you never heard the 6 saying, 'A little leaven leavens all the dough'? The old leaven of 7 corruption is working among you. Purge it out, and then you will be bread of a new baking, as it were unleavened Passover bread. For indeed our Passover has begun; the sacrifice is offered—Christ himself. So we who observe the festival must not use the old leaven, the 8 leaven of corruption and wickedness, but only the unleavened bread which is sincerity and truth.

In my letter I wrote that you must have nothing to do with loose 9 livers. I was not, of course, referring to pagans who lead loose 10 lives or are grabbers and swindlers or idolaters. To avoid them you would have to get right out of the world. I now write that you must 11 have nothing to do with any so-called Christian who leads a loose life, or is grasping, or idolatrous, a slanderer, a drunkard, or a swindler. You should not even eat with any such person. What 12 business of mine is it to judge outsiders? God is their judge. You 13 are judges within the fellowship. Root out the evil-doer from your community.

IF ONE of your number has a dispute with another, has he the face 6 to take it to pagan law-courts instead of to the community of God's people? It is God's people who are to judge the world; surely you 2 know that. And if the world is to come before you for judgement, are you incompetent to deal with these trifling cases? Are you not 3 aware that we are to judge angels? How much more, mere matters of business! If therefore you have such business disputes, how can you 4 entrust jurisdiction to outsiders, men who count for nothing in our community? I write this to shame you. Can it be that there is not 5 a single wise man among you able to give a decision in a brother-Christian's cause? Must brother go to law with brother—and before 6 unbelievers? Indeed, you already fall below your standard in going 7 to law with one another at all. Why not rather suffer injury? Why not

8 rather let yourself be robbed? So far from this, you actually injure
9 and rob—injure and rob your brothers! Surely you know that the
unjust will never come into possession of the kingdom of God.
Make no mistake: no fornicator or idolater, none who are guilty either
10 of adultery or of homosexual perversion, no thieves or grabbers or
drunkards or slanderers or swindlers, will possess the kingdom of
11 God. Such were some of you. But you have been through the
purifying waters; you have been dedicated to God and justified
through the name of the Lord Jesus and the Spirit of our God.
12 'I am free to do anything', you say. Yes, but not everything is for
my good. No doubt I am free to do anything, but I for one will
13 not let anything make free with me. 'Food is for the belly and the
belly for food', you say. True; and one day God will put an end to
both. But it is not true that the body is for lust; it is for the Lord—
14 and the Lord for the body. God not only raised our Lord from
15 the dead; he will also raise us by his power. Do you not know that
your bodies are limbs and organs of Christ? Shall I then take from
Christ his bodily parts and make them over to a harlot? Never!
16 You surely know that anyone who links himself with a harlot
becomes physically one with her (for Scripture says, 'The pair shall
17 become one flesh'); but he who links himself with Christ is one with
18 him, spiritually. Shun fornication. Every other sin that a man can
commit is outside the body; but the fornicator sins against his own
19 body. Do you not know that your body is a shrine of the indwelling
Holy Spirit, and the Spirit is God's gift to you? You do not belong
20 to yourselves; you were bought at a price. Then honour God in your
body.

The Christian in a Pagan Society

7 AND NOW FOR the matters you wrote about.
It is a good thing for a man to have nothing to do with women;[a]
2 but because there is so much immorality, let each man have his own
3 wife and each woman her own husband. The husband must give the
wife what is due to her, and the wife equally must give the husband
4 his due. The wife cannot claim her body as her own; it is her
husband's. Equally, the husband cannot claim his body as his own;

[a] *Or* You say, 'It is a good thing...women';...

it is his wife's. Do not deny yourselves to one another, except when 5
you agree upon a temporary abstinence in order to devote yourselves
to prayer; afterwards you may come together again; otherwise, for
lack of self-control, you may be tempted by Satan.

All this I say by way of concession, not command. I should like 6, 7
you all to be as I am myself; but everyone has the gift God has
granted him, one this gift and another that.

To the unmarried and to widows I say this: it is a good thing if 8
they stay as I am myself; but if they cannot control themselves, they 9
should marry. Better be married than burn with vain desire.

To the married I give this ruling, which is not mine but the 10
Lord's: a wife must not separate herself from her husband; if she 11
does, she must either remain unmarried or be reconciled to her
husband; and the husband must not divorce his wife.

To the rest I say this, as my own word, not as the Lord's: if a 12
Christian has a heathen wife, and she is willing to live with him, he
must not divorce her; and a woman who has a heathen husband 13
willing to live with her must not divorce her husband. For the hea- 14
then husband now belongs to God through his Christian wife, and
the heathen wife through her Christian husband. Otherwise your
children would not belong to God, whereas in fact they do. If on the 15
other hand the heathen partner wishes for a separation, let him have
it. In such cases the Christian husband or wife is under no compulsion; but God's call is a call to live in peace. Think of it: as a wife 16
you may be your husband's salvation; as a husband you may be your
wife's salvation.

However that may be, each one must order his life according to 17
the gift the Lord has granted him and his condition when God called
him. That is what I teach in all our congregations. Was a man 18
called with the marks of circumcision on him? Let him not remove
them. Was he uncircumcised when he was called? Let him not be
circumcised. Circumcision or uncircumcision is neither here nor 19
there; what matters is to keep God's commands. Every man should 20
remain in the condition in which he was called. Were you a slave 21
when you were called? Do not let that trouble you; but if a chance of
liberty should come, take it.[a] For the man who as a slave received the 22
call to be a Christian is the Lord's freedman, and, equally, the free

[a] *Or* but even if a chance of liberty should come, choose rather to make good use of
your servitude.

23 man who received the call is a slave in the service of Christ. You were
24 bought at a price; do not become slaves of men. Thus each one, my
friends, is to remain before God in the condition in which he received
his call.

25   On the question of celibacy, I have no instructions from the Lord,
but I give my judgement as one who by God's mercy is fit to be
trusted.

26   It is my opinion, then, that in a time of stress like the present
this is the best way for a man to live—it is best for a man to be as
27 he is. Are you bound in marriage? Do not seek a dissolution. Has
28 your marriage been dissolved? Do not seek a wife. If, however, you
do marry, there is nothing wrong in it; and if a virgin marries, she
has done no wrong. But those who marry will have pain and grief in
this bodily life, and my aim is to spare you.

29   What I mean, my friends, is this. The time we live in will not
last long. While it lasts, married men should be as if they had no
30 wives; mourners should be as if they had nothing to grieve them, the
joyful as if they did not rejoice; buyers must not count on keeping
31 what they buy, nor those who use the world's wealth on using it to
the full. For the whole frame of this world is passing away.

32   I want you to be free from anxious care. The unmarried man
33 cares for the Lord's business; his aim is to please the Lord. But
the married man cares for worldly things; his aim is to please his
34 wife; and he has a divided mind. The unmarried or celibate woman
cares[a] for the Lord's business; her aim is to be dedicated to him in
body as in spirit; but the married woman cares for worldly things;
her aim is to please her husband.

35   In saying this I have no wish to keep you on a tight rein. I am
thinking simply of your own good, of what is seemly, and of your
freedom to wait upon the Lord without distraction.

36   But if a man has a partner in celibacy[b] and feels that he is not
behaving properly towards her, if, that is, his instincts are too
strong for him,[c] and something must be done, he may do as he
37 pleases; there is nothing wrong in it; let them marry.[d] But if a man is
steadfast in his purpose, being under no compulsion, and has complete control of his own choice; and if he has decided in his own mind

[a] *Some witnesses read* . . . his wife. And there is a difference between the wife and the
virgin. The unmarried woman cares. . .   [b] *Or* a virgin daughter (*or* ward).   [c] *Or* if she
is ripe for marriage.   [d] *Or* let the girl and her lover marry.

to preserve his partner*^a* in her virginity, he will do well. Thus, he 38
who marries his partner*^b* does well, and he who does not will do
better.

A wife is bound to her husband as long as he lives. But if the 39
husband die, she is free to marry whom she will, provided the
marriage is within the Lord's fellowship. But she is better off as 40
she is; that is my opinion, and I believe that I too have the Spirit
of God.

NOW ABOUT FOOD consecrated to heathen deities.   8

Of course we all 'have knowledge', as you say. This 'knowledge'
breeds conceit; it is love that builds. If anyone fancies that he knows, 2
he knows nothing yet, in the true sense of knowing. But if a man 3
loves,*^c* he is acknowledged by God.*^d*

Well then, about eating this consecrated food: of course, as you 4
say, 'a false god has no existence in the real world. There is no god
but one.' For indeed, if there be so-called gods, whether in heaven 5
or on earth—as indeed there are many 'gods' and many 'lords'—
yet for us there is one God, the Father, from whom all being comes, 6
towards whom we move; and there is one Lord, Jesus Christ,
through whom all things came to be, and we through him.

But not everyone knows this. There are some who have been so 7
accustomed to idolatry*^e* that even now they eat this food with a sense
of its heathen consecration, and their conscience, being weak, is
polluted by the eating. Certainly food will not bring us into God's 8
presence: if we do not eat, we are none the worse, and if we eat, we
are none the better. But be careful that this liberty of yours does 9
not become a pitfall for the weak. If a weak character sees you 10
sitting down to a meal in a heathen temple—you, who 'have knowledge'—will not his conscience be emboldened to eat food consecrated to the heathen deity? This 'knowledge' of yours is utter 11
disaster to the weak, the brother for whom Christ died. In thus 12
sinning against your brothers and wounding their conscience,*^f* you
sin against Christ. And therefore, if food be the downfall of my 13
brother, I will never eat meat any more, for I will not be the cause
of my brother's downfall.

[a] *Or* his daughter. [b] *Or* gives his daughter in marriage. [c] *Some witnesses read*
loves God. [d] *Or* he is recognized. [e] *Some witnesses read* in whom the consciousness
of the false god is so persistent… [f] *Some witnesses insert* weak as it is.

9 AM I NOT a free man? Am I not an apostle? Did I not see
2 Jesus our Lord? Are not you my own handiwork, in the Lord? If
   others do not accept me as an apostle, you at least are bound to
   do so, for you are yourselves the very seal of my apostolate, in the
   Lord.
3,4   To those who put me in the dock this is my answer: Have I no
5 right to eat and drink? Have I no right to take a Christian wife about
   with me, like the rest of the apostles and the Lord's brothers, and
6 Cephas? Or are Barnabas and I alone bound to work for our living?
7 Did you ever hear of a man serving in the army at his own expense?
   or planting a vineyard without eating the fruit of it? or tending a
8 flock without using its milk? Do not suppose I rely on these human
9 analogies; in the Law of Moses we read, 'A threshing ox shall not be
10 muzzled.' Do you suppose God's concern is with oxen? Or is the
   reference clearly to ourselves? Of course it refers to us, in the sense
   that the ploughman should plough and the thresher thresh in the
11 hope of getting some of the produce. If we have sown a spiritual
12 crop for you, is it too much to expect from you a material harvest? If
   you allow others these rights, have not we a stronger claim?
      But I have availed myself of no such right. On the contrary, I
   put up with all that comes my way rather than offer any hindrance to
13 the gospel of Christ. You know (do you not?) that those who perform
   the temple service eat the temple offerings, and those who wait upon
14 the altar claim their share of the sacrifice. In the same way the
   Lord gave instructions that those who preach the Gospel should
15 earn their living by the Gospel. But I have never taken advantage of
   any such right, nor do I intend to claim it in this letter. I had rather
16 die! No one shall make my boast an empty boast. Even if I preach
   the Gospel, I can claim no credit for it; I cannot help myself; it
17 would be misery to me not to preach. If I did it of my own choice,
   I should be earning my pay; but since I do it apart from my own
18 choice, I am simply discharging a trust.[a] Then what is my pay?
   The satisfaction of preaching the Gospel without expense to anyone; in other words, of waiving the rights which my preaching
   gives me.
19   I am a free man and own no master; but I have made myself every
20 man's servant, to win over as many as possible. To Jews I became like

[a] *Or* If I do it willingly I am earning my pay; if I did it unwillingly I should still have
a trust laid upon me.

a Jew, to win Jews; as they are subject to the Law of Moses, I put myself under that law to win them although I am not myself subject to it. To win Gentiles, who are outside the Law, I made myself like one of them, although I am not in truth outside God's law, being under the law of Christ. To the weak I became weak, to win the weak. Indeed, I have become everything in turn to men of every sort, so that in one way or another I may save some. All this I do for the sake of the Gospel, to bear my part in proclaiming it.

You know (do you not?) that at the sports all the runners run the race, though only one wins the prize. Like them, run to win! But every athlete goes into strict training. They do it to win a fading wreath; we, a wreath that never fades. For my part, I run with a clear goal before me; I am like a boxer who does not beat the air; I bruise my own body and make it know its master, for fear that after preaching to others I should find myself rejected.

You should understand, my brothers, that our ancestors were all under the pillar of cloud, and all of them passed through the Red Sea; and so they all received baptism into the fellowship of Moses in cloud and sea. They all ate the same supernatural food, and all drank the same supernatural drink; I mean, they all drank from the super-natural rock that accompanied their travels—and that rock was Christ. And yet, most of them were not accepted by God, for the desert was strewn with their corpses.

These events happened as symbols to warn us not to set our de-sires on evil things, as they did. Do not be idolaters, like some of them; as Scripture has it, 'the people sat down to feast and stood up to play'. Let us not commit fornication, as some of them did—and twenty-three thousand died in one day. Let us not put the power of the Lord[a] to the test, as some of them did—and were destroyed by serpents. Do not grumble against God, as some of them did—and were destroyed by the Destroyer.

All these things that happened to them were symbolic, and were recorded for our benefit as a warning. For upon us the fulfilment of the ages has come. If you feel sure that you are standing firm, beware! You may fall. So far you have faced no trial beyond what man can bear. God keeps faith, and he will not allow you to be tested above your powers, but when the test comes he will at the same time provide a way out, by enabling you to sustain it.

[a] *Some witnesses read* of Christ.

14, 15 SO THEN, dear friends, shun idolatry. I speak to you as men of
16 sense. Form your own judgement on what I say. When we bless 'the
cup of blessing', is it not a means of sharing in the blood of Christ?
When we break the bread, is it not a means of sharing in the body of
17 Christ? Because there is one loaf, we, many as we are, are one
body;*a* for it is one loaf of which we all partake.

18   Look at the Jewish people. Are not those who partake in the
19 sacrificial meal sharers in the altar? What do I imply by this? that
an idol is anything but an idol? or food offered to it anything more
20 than food? No: but the sacrifices the heathen offer are offered (in
the words of Scripture) 'to demons and to that which is not God';
21 and I will not have you become partners with demons. You cannot
drink the cup of the Lord and the cup of demons. You cannot
22 partake of the Lord's table and the table of demons. Can we defy the
Lord? Are we stronger than he?

23   'We are free to do anything', you say. Yes, but is everything good
for us? 'We are free to do anything', but does everything help the
24 building of the community? Each of you must regard, not his own
interests, but the other man's.

25   You may eat anything sold in the meat-market without raising
26 questions of conscience; for the earth is the Lord's and everything
in it.

27   If an unbeliever invites you to a meal and you care to go, eat
whatever is put before you, without raising questions of conscience.
28 But if somebody says to you, 'This food has been offered in sacrifice',
then, out of consideration for him, and for conscience' sake, do not
29 eat it—not your conscience, I mean, but the other man's.

'What?' you say, 'is my freedom to be called in question by
30 another man's conscience? If I partake with thankfulness, why am I
31 blamed for eating food over which I have said grace?' Well, whether
you eat or drink, or whatever you are doing, do all for the honour
32 of God: give no offence to Jews, or Greeks, or to the church of God.
33 For my part I always try to meet everyone half-way, regarding not
my own good but the good of the many, so that they may be saved.
11 Follow my example as I follow Christ's.

2 I COMMEND YOU for always keeping me in mind, and maintaining
3 the tradition I handed on to you. But I wish you to understand that,

[*a*] *Or* For we, many as we are, are one loaf, one body.

while every man has Christ for his Head, woman's head is man,[a] as
Christ's Head is God. A man who keeps his head covered when he 4
prays or prophesies brings shame on his head; a woman, on the con- 5
trary, brings shame on her head if she prays or prophesies bare-
headed: it is as bad as if her head were shaved. If a woman is not 6
to wear a veil she might as well have her hair cut off; but if it is a
disgrace for her to be cropped and shaved, then she should wear a
veil. A man has no need to cover his head, because man is the image 7
of God, and the mirror of his glory, whereas woman reflects the
glory of man.[b] For man did not originally spring from woman, but 8
woman was made out of man; and man was not created for woman's 9
sake, but woman for the sake of man; and therefore it is woman's 10
duty to have a sign of authority[c] on her head, out of regard for the
angels.[d] And yet, in Christ's fellowship woman is as essential to man 11
as man to woman. If woman was made out of man, it is through 12
woman that man now comes to be; and God is the source of all.

Judge for yourselves: is it fitting for a woman to pray to God 13
bare-headed? Does not Nature herself teach you that while flowing 14
locks disgrace a man, they are a woman's glory? For her locks were 15
given for covering.

However, if you insist on arguing, let me tell you, there is no such 16
custom among us, or in any of the congregations of God's people.

In giving you these injunctions I must mention a practice which 17
I cannot commend: your meetings tend to do more harm than good.
To begin with, I am told that when you meet as a congregation 18
you fall into sharply divided groups; and I believe there is some truth
in it (for dissensions are necessary if only to show which of your 19
members are sound). The result is that when you meet as a congrega- 20
tion, it is impossible for you to eat the Lord's Supper, because each 21
of you is in such a hurry to eat his own, and while one goes hungry
another has too much to drink. Have you no homes of your own 22
to eat and drink in? Or are you so contemptuous of the church of
God that you shame its poorer members? What am I to say? Can
I commend you? On this point, certainly not!

For the tradition which I handed on to you came to me from the 23
Lord himself: that the Lord Jesus, on the night of his arrest, took

[a] *Or* a woman's head is her husband. [b] *Or* a woman reflects her husband's glory.
[c] *Some witnesses read* to have a veil. [d] *Or* and therefore a woman should keep her
dignity on her head, for fear of the angels.

24 bread and, after giving thanks to God, broke it and said: 'This is
25 my body, which is for you; do this as a memorial of me.' In the
same way, he took the cup after supper, and said: 'This cup is the
new covenant sealed by my blood. Whenever you drink it, do this as
26 a memorial of me.' For every time you eat this bread and drink the
cup, you proclaim the death of the Lord, until he comes.

27   It follows that anyone who eats the bread or drinks the cup of the
Lord unworthily will be guilty of desecrating the body and blood of
28 the Lord. A man must test himself before eating his share of the bread
29 and drinking from the cup. For he who eats and drinks eats and drinks
30 judgement on himself if he does not discern the Body. That is why
31 many of you are feeble and sick, and a number have died. But if we
32 examined ourselves, we should not thus fall under judgement. When,
however, we do fall under the Lord's judgement, he is disciplining
us, to save us from being condemned with the rest of the world.

33   Therefore, my brothers, when you meet for a meal, wait for one
34 another. If you are hungry, eat at home, so that in meeting together
you may not fall under judgement. The other matters I will arrange
when I come.

Spiritual Gifts

12   ABOUT GIFTS of the Spirit, there are some things of which I do
    not wish you to remain ignorant.
2   You know how, in the days when you were still pagan, you were
swept off to those dumb heathen gods, however you happened to
3 be led.*a* For this reason I must impress upon you that no one
who says 'A curse on Jesus!' can be speaking under the influence
of the Spirit of God. And no one can say 'Jesus is Lord!' except
under the influence of the Holy Spirit.
4, 5   There are varieties of gifts, but the same Spirit. There are varieties
6 of service, but the same Lord. There are many forms of work, but
7 all of them, in all men, are the work of the same God. In each of us
the Spirit is manifested in one particular way, for some useful pur-
8 pose. One man, through the Spirit, has the gift of wise speech, while
another, by the power of the same Spirit, can put the deepest know-
9 ledge into words. Another, by the same Spirit, is granted faith;

[a] Or . . . pagan, you would be seized by some power which drove you to those dumb
heathen gods.

another, by the one Spirit, gifts of healing, and another miraculous 10
powers; another has the gift of prophecy, and another ability to
distinguish true spirits from false; yet another has the gift of ecstatic
utterance of different kinds, and another the ability to interpret
it. But all these gifts are the work of one and the same Spirit, 11
distributing them separately to each individual at will.

For Christ is like a single body with its many limbs and organs, 12
which, many as they are, together make up one body. For indeed 13
we were all brought into one body by baptism, in the one Spirit,
whether we are Jews or Greeks, whether slaves or free men, and
that one Holy Spirit was poured out for all of us to drink.

A body is not one single organ, but many. Suppose the foot 14, 15
should say, 'Because I am not a hand, I do not belong to the body',
it does belong to the body none the less. Suppose the ear were to 16
say, 'Because I am not an eye, I do not belong to the body', it does
still belong to the body. If the body were all eye, how could it 17
hear? If the body were all ear, how could it smell? But, in fact, 18
God appointed each limb and organ to its own place in the body,
as he chose. If the whole were one single organ, there would not 19
be a body at all; in fact, however, there are many different organs, 20
but one body. The eye cannot say to the hand, 'I do not need you'; 21
nor the head to the feet, 'I do not need you.' Quite the contrary: 22
those organs of the body which seem to be more frail than others are
indispensable, and those parts of the body which we regard as less 23
honourable are treated with special honour. To our unseemly parts
is given a more than ordinary seemliness, whereas our seemly parts 24
need no adorning. But God has combined the various parts of the
body, giving special honour to the humbler parts, so that there 25
might be no sense of division in the body, but that all its organs might
feel the same concern for one another. If one organ suffers, they all 26
suffer together. If one flourishes, they all rejoice together.

Now you are Christ's body, and each of you a limb or organ of it. 27
Within our community God has appointed, in the first place apostles, 28
in the second place prophets, thirdly teachers; then miracle-workers,
then those who have gifts of healing, or ability to help others or
power to guide them, or the gift of ecstatic utterance of various kinds.
Are all apostles? all prophets? all teachers? Do all work miracles? 29
Have all gifts of healing? Do all speak in tongues of ecstasy? Can 30
all interpret them? The higher gifts are those you should aim at. 31

And now I will show you the best way of all.

╳ 13 I may speak in tongues of men or of angels, but if I am without
2 love, I am a sounding gong or a clanging cymbal. I may have the
gift of prophecy, and know every hidden truth; I may have faith
strong enough to move mountains; but if I have no love, I am nothing.
3 I may dole out all I possess, or even give my body to be burnt,[a] but
if I have no love, I am none the better.

4 Love is patient; love is kind and envies no one. Love is never
5 boastful, nor conceited, nor rude; never selfish, not quick to take
6 offence. Love keeps no score of wrongs; does not gloat over other
7 men's sins, but delights in the truth. There is nothing love cannot
face; there is no limit to its faith, its hope, and its endurance.

8 Love will never come to an end. Are there prophets? their work
will be over. Are there tongues of ecstasy? they will cease. Is there
9 knowledge? it will vanish away; for our knowledge and our prophecy
10 alike are partial, and the partial vanishes when wholeness comes.
11 When I was a child, my speech, my outlook, and my thoughts were
all childish. When I grew up, I had finished with childish things.
12 Now we see only puzzling reflections in a mirror, but then we shall
see face to face. My knowledge now is partial; then it will be
13 whole, like God's knowledge of me. In a word, there are three
things that last for ever: faith, hope, and love; but the greatest of
them all is love.

14 Put love first; but there are other gifts of the Spirit at which you
2 should aim also, and above all prophecy. When a man is using the
language of ecstasy he is talking with God, not with men, for no man
understands him; he is no doubt inspired, but he speaks mysteries.
3 On the other hand, when a man prophesies, he is talking to men,
and his words have power to build; they stimulate and they en-
4 courage. The language of ecstasy is good for the speaker himself,
5 but it is prophecy that builds up a Christian community. I should
be pleased for you all to use the tongues of ecstasy, but better pleased
for you to prophesy. The prophet is worth more than the man of
ecstatic speech—unless indeed he can explain its meaning, and so
6 help to build up the community. Suppose, my friends, that when
I come to you I use ecstatic language: what good shall I do you,
unless what I say contains something by way of revelation, or
enlightenment, or prophecy, or instruction?

[a] *Some witnesses read* even seek glory by self-sacrifice.

Even with inanimate things that produce sounds—a flute, say, 7
or a lyre—unless their notes mark definite intervals, how can you
tell what tune is being played? Or again, if the trumpet-call is 8
not clear, who will prepare for battle? In the same way if your 9
ecstatic utterance yields no precise meaning, how can anyone tell
what you are saying? You will be talking into the air. How many 10
different kinds of sound there are, or may be, in the world! Nothing
is altogether soundless. Well then, if I do not know the meaning of 11
the sound the speaker makes, his words will be gibberish to me,
and mine to him. You are, I know, eager for gifts of the Spirit; then 12
aspire above all to excel in those which build up the church.

I say, then, that the man who falls into ecstatic utterance should 13
pray for the ability to interpret. If I use such language in my prayer, 14
the Spirit in me prays, but my intellect lies fallow. What then? 15
I will pray as I am inspired to pray, but I will also pray intelligently.
I will sing hymns as I am inspired to sing, but I will sing intelligently
too. Suppose you are praising God in the language of inspiration: 16
how will the plain man who is present be able to say 'Amen' to your
thanksgiving, when he does not know what you are saying? Your 17
prayer of thanksgiving may be all that could be desired, but it is no
help to the other man. Thank God, I am more gifted in ecstatic 18
utterance than any of you,[a] but in the congregation I would rather 19
speak five intelligible words, for the benefit of others as well as
myself, than thousands of words in the language of ecstasy.

Do not be childish, my friends. Be as innocent of evil as babes, 20
but at least be grown-up in your thinking. We read in the Law: 21
'I will speak to this nation through men of strange tongues, and by
the lips of foreigners; and even so they will not heed me, says the
Lord.' Clearly then these 'strange tongues' are not intended as a 22
sign for believers, but for unbelievers, whereas prophecy is designed
not for unbelievers but for those who hold the faith. So if the whole 23
congregation is assembled and all are using the 'strange tongues'
of ecstasy, and some uninstructed persons or unbelievers should
enter, will they not think you are mad? But if all are uttering 24
prophecies, the visitor, when he enters, hears from everyone something that searches his conscience and brings conviction, and the
secrets of his heart are laid bare. So he will fall down and worship 25
God, crying, 'God is certainly among you!'

[a] *Or* ...man. I say the thanksgiving; I use ecstatic speech more than any of you.

26 To sum up, my friends: when you meet for worship, each of you contributes a hymn, some instruction, a revelation, an ecstatic utterance, or the interpretation of such an utterance. All of these
27 must aim at one thing: to build up the church. If it is a matter of ecstatic utterance, only two should speak, or at most three, one
28 at a time, and someone must interpret. If there is no interpreter, the speaker had better not address the meeting at all, but speak to
29 himself and to God. Of the prophets, two or three may speak, while
30 the rest exercise their judgement upon what is said. If someone else,
31 sitting in his place, receives a revelation, let the first speaker stop. You can all prophesy, one at a time, so that the whole congregation may
32 receive instruction and encouragement. It is for prophets to control
33 prophetic inspiration, for the God who inspires them is not a God of disorder but of peace.

34 As in all congregations of God's people, women[a] should not address the meeting. They have no licence to speak, but should
35 keep their place as the law directs. If there is something they want to know, they can ask their own husbands at home. It is a shocking thing that a woman should address the congregation.

36 Did the word of God originate with you? Or are you the only
37 people to whom it came? If anyone claims to be inspired or a pro-
38 phet, let him recognize that what I write has the Lord's authority. If he does not recognize this, he himself should not be recognized.[b]

39 In short, my friends, be eager to prophesy; do not forbid ecstatic
40 utterance; but let all be done decently and in order.

Life After Death

15 AND NOW, MY BROTHERS, I must remind you of the gospel that I preached to you; the gospel which you received, on which you
2 have taken your stand, and which is now bringing you salvation. Do you still hold fast the Gospel as I preached it to you? If not, your conversion was in vain.[c]

[a] *Or* of peace, as in all communities of God's people. Women... [b] *Some witnesses read* If he does not acknowledge this, he is not acknowledged (by God). [c] *Or* Do you remember the terms in which I preached the Gospel to you?—for I assume you did not accept it thoughtlessly.

First and foremost, I handed on to you the facts which had been 3
imparted to me: that Christ died for our sins, in accordance with the
scriptures; that he was buried; that he was raised to life on the third 4
day, according to the scriptures; and that he appeared to Cephas, and 5
afterwards to the Twelve. Then he appeared to over five hundred of 6
our brothers at once, most of whom are still alive, though some have
died. Then he appeared to James, and afterwards to all the apostles. 7

In the end he appeared even to me; though this birth of mine 8
was monstrous, for I had persecuted the church and am therefore 9
inferior to all other apostles—indeed not fit to be called an apostle.
However, by God's grace I am what I am, nor has his grace been 10
given to me in vain; on the contrary, in my labours I have outdone
them all—not I, indeed, but the grace of God working with me. But 11
what matter, I or they? This is what we all proclaim, and this is what
you believed.

Now if this is what we proclaim, that Christ was raised from the 12
dead, how can some of you say there is no resurrection of the dead?
If there be no resurrection, then Christ was not raised; and if Christ 13, 14
was not raised, then our gospel is null and void, and so is your faith;
and we turn out to be lying witnesses for God, because we bore 15
witness that he raised Christ to life, whereas, if the dead are not
raised, he did not raise him. For if the dead are not raised, it follows 16
that Christ was not raised; and if Christ was not raised, your faith has 17
nothing in it and you are still in your old state of sin. It follows also 18
that those who have died within Christ's fellowship are utterly lost.
If it is for this life only that Christ has given us hope,*a* we of all men 19
are most to be pitied.

But the truth is, Christ was raised to life—the firstfruits of the 20
harvest of the dead. For since it was a man who brought death into 21
the world, a man also brought resurrection of the dead. As in Adam 22
all men die, so in Christ all will be brought to life; but each in his 23
own proper place: Christ the firstfruits, and afterwards, at his
coming, those who belong to Christ. Then comes the end, when he 24
delivers up the kingdom to God the Father, after abolishing every
kind of domination, authority, and power. For he is destined to 25
reign until God has put all enemies under his feet; and the last 26
enemy to be abolished is death.*b* Scripture says, 'He has put all 27

[*a*] *Or* If it is only an uncertain hope that our life in Christ has given us... [*b*] *Or* Then
at the end, when...power (for he...feet), the last enemy, death, will be abolished.

things in subjection under his feet.' But in saying 'all things', it
²⁸ clearly means to exclude God who subordinates them; and when all
things are thus subject to him, then the Son himself will also be
made subordinate to God who made all things subject to him, and
thus God will be all in all.

²⁹ Again, there are those who receive baptism on behalf of the dead.
Why should they do this? If the dead are not raised to life at all, what
do they mean by being baptized on their behalf?

³⁰ And we ourselves—why do we face these dangers hour by hour?
³¹ Every day I die: I swear it by my pride in you, my brothers—for in
³² Christ Jesus our Lord I am proud of you. If, as the saying is, I
'fought wild beasts' at Ephesus, what have I gained by it?ᵃ If the
dead are never raised to life, 'let us eat and drink, for tomorrow we
die'.

³³ Make no mistake: 'Bad company is the ruin of a good character.'
³⁴ Come back to a sober and upright life and leave your sinful ways.
There are some who know nothing of God; to your shame I say it.

³⁵ But, you may ask, how are the dead raised? In what kind of body?
³⁶ A senseless question! The seed you sow does not come to life unless
³⁷ it has first died; and what you sow is not the body that shall be, but
³⁸ a naked grain, perhaps of wheat, or of some other kind; and God
clothes it with the body of his choice, each seed with its own particu-
³⁹ lar body. All flesh is not the same flesh: there is flesh of men, flesh of
⁴⁰ beasts, of birds, and of fishes—all different. There are heavenly bodies
and earthly bodies; and the splendour of the heavenly bodies is one
⁴¹ thing, the splendour of the earthly, another. The sun has a splendour
of its own, the moon another splendour, and the stars another, for
⁴² star differs from star in brightness. So it is with the resurrection of
the dead. What is sown in the earth as a perishable thing is raised
⁴³ imperishable. Sown in humiliation, it is raised in glory; sown in
⁴⁴ weakness, it is raised in power; sown as an animal body, it is raised as
a spiritual body.

If there is such a thing as an animal body, there is also a spiritual
⁴⁵ body. It is in this sense that Scripture says, 'The first man,
Adam, became an animate being', whereas the last Adam has become
⁴⁶ a life-giving spirit. Observe, the spiritual does not come first; the

[a] *Or* If, as men do, I had fought wild beasts at Ephesus, what good would it be to me?
or If I had been in no better case than one fighting beasts in the arena at Ephesus, what
good would it be to me?

animal body comes first, and then the spiritual. The first man was 47
made 'of the dust of the earth': the second man is from heaven. The 48
man made of dust is the pattern of all men of dust, and the heavenly
man is the pattern of all the heavenly. As we have worn the likeness 49
of the man made of dust, so we shall wear the likeness of the heavenly
man.

What I mean, my brothers, is this: flesh and blood can never 50
possess the kingdom of God, and the perishable cannot possess
immortality. Listen! I will unfold a mystery: we shall not all die, 51
but we shall all be changed in a flash, in the twinkling of an eye, at 52
the last trumpet-call. For the trumpet will sound, and the dead will
rise immortal, and we shall be changed. This perishable being must 53
be clothed with the imperishable, and what is mortal must be clothed
with immortality. And when[a] our mortality has been clothed with 54
immortality, then the saying of Scripture will come true: 'Death
is swallowed up; victory is won!' 'O Death, where is your victory? 55
O Death, where is your sting?' The sting of death is sin, and sin 56
gains its power from the law; but, God be praised, he gives us the 57
victory through our Lord Jesus Christ.

Therefore, my beloved brothers, stand firm and immovable, and 58
work for the Lord always, work without limit, since you know that
in the Lord your labour cannot be lost.

Christian Giving

AND NOW ABOUT the collection in aid of God's people: you 16
should follow my directions to our congregations in Galatia.
Every Sunday each of you is to put aside and keep by him a sum in 2
proportion to his gains, so that there may be no collecting when I
come. When I arrive, I will give letters of introduction to persons 3
approved by you, and send them to carry your gift to Jerusalem.
If it should seem worth while for me to go as well, they shall go 4
with me.

I shall come to Corinth after passing through Macedonia—for I 5
am travelling by way of Macedonia—and I may stay with you, 6

[a] *Some witnesses insert* our perishable nature has been clothed with the imperishable, and...

perhaps even for the whole winter, and then you can help me on my

7 way wherever I go next. I do not want this to be a flying visit;

8 I hope to spend some time with you, if the Lord permits. But I shall

9 remain at Ephesus until Whitsuntide, for a great opportunity has opened for effective work, and there is much opposition.

10 If Timothy comes, see that you put him at his ease; for it is the Lord's work that he is engaged upon, as I am myself; so no one must

11 slight him. Send him happily on his way to join me, since I am

12 waiting for him with our friends. As for our friend Apollos, I urged him strongly to go to Corinth with the others, but he was quite determined not to go*a* at present; he will go when opportunity offers.

13, 14 Be alert; stand firm in the faith; be valiant and strong. Let all you do be done in love.

15 I have a request to make of you, my brothers. You know that the Stephanas family were the first converts in Achaia, and have laid

16 themselves out to serve God's people. I wish you to give their due position to such persons, and indeed to everyone who labours hard

17 at our common task. It is a great pleasure to me that Stephanas, Fortunatus, and Achaicus have arrived, because they have done what

18 you had no chance to do; they have relieved my mind—and no doubt yours too. Such men deserve recognition.

19 Greetings from the congregations in Asia. Many greetings in the Lord from Aquila and Prisca and the congregation at their house.

20 Greetings from all the brothers. Greet one another with the kiss of peace.

21 This greeting is in my own hand—PAUL.

22 If anyone does not love the Lord, let him be outcast. *Marana tha*—Come, O Lord!

23 The grace of the Lord Jesus Christ be with you.

24 My love to you all in Christ Jesus. Amen.

[a] *Or* but it was by no means the will of God that he should go . . .

THE
SECOND LETTER OF PAUL TO THE
CORINTHIANS

Personal Religion and the Ministry

FROM PAUL, apostle of Christ Jesus by God's will, and 1
our colleague Timothy, to the congregation of God's people at
Corinth, together with all who are dedicated to him throughout
the whole of Achaia.

Grace and peace to you from God our Father and the Lord Jesus 2
Christ.

Praise be to the God and Father of our Lord Jesus Christ, the 3
all-merciful Father, the God whose consolation never fails us! He 4
comforts us in all our troubles, so that we in turn may be able to
comfort others in any trouble of theirs and to share with them the
consolation we ourselves receive from God. As Christ's cup of 5
suffering overflows, and we suffer with him, so also through Christ
our consolation overflows. If distress be our lot, it is the price we 6
pay for your consolation, for your salvation; if our lot be consolation, it is to help us to bring you comfort, and strength to face with
fortitude the same sufferings we now endure. And our hope for 7
you is firmly grounded;[a] for we know that if you have part in the
suffering, you have part also in the divine consolation.

In saying this, we should like you to know, dear friends, how 8
serious was the trouble that came upon us in the province of Asia.
The burden of it was far too heavy for us to bear, so heavy that
we even despaired of life. Indeed, we felt in our hearts that 9
we had received a death-sentence. This was meant to teach us not
to place reliance on ourselves, but on God who raises the dead.
From such mortal peril God delivered us; and he will deliver us 10
again,[b] he on whom our hope is fixed. Yes, he will continue to 11
deliver us, if you will co-operate by praying for us. Then, with so
many people praying for our deliverance, there will be many to

[a] *Some witnesses give these clauses* If distress... firmly grounded *in different sequence.*
[b] *Some witnesses read* and he still delivers us.

give thanks on our behalf for the gracious favour God has shown towards us.

12 There is one thing we are proud of: our conscience assures us that in our dealings with our fellow-men, and above all in our dealings with you, our conduct has been governed by a devout and godly

13 sincerity,[a] by the grace of God and not by worldly wisdom. There is nothing in our letters to you but what you can read for yourselves,

14 and understand too. Partial as your present knowledge of us is, you will I hope come to understand fully that you have as much reason to be proud of us, as we of you, on the Day of our Lord Jesus.

15 It was because I felt so confident about all this that I had intended to come first of all to you[b] and give you the benefit of a double visit:

16 I meant to visit you on my way to Macedonia, and after leaving Macedonia, to return to you, and you would then send me on my

17 way to Judaea. That was my intention; did I lightly change my mind?[c] Or do I, when I frame my plans, frame them as a worldly man might, so that it should rest with me to say 'yes' and 'yes',

18 or 'no' and 'no'? As God is true, the language in which we address

19 you is not an ambiguous blend of Yes and No. The Son of God, Christ Jesus, proclaimed among you by us (by Silvanus and Timothy, I mean, as well as myself), was never a blend of Yes and No. With

20 him it was, and is, Yes. He is the Yes pronounced upon God's promises, every one of them. That is why, when we give glory to God,

21 it is through Christ Jesus that we say 'Amen'. And if you and we belong to Christ, guaranteed as his and anointed, it is all God's

22 doing; it is God also who has set his seal upon us, and as a pledge of what is to come has given the Spirit to dwell in our hearts.

23 I appeal to God to witness what I am going to say; I stake my life upon it: it was out of consideration for you that I did not after all

24 come to Corinth. Do not think we are dictating the terms of your faith; your hold on the faith is secure enough. We are working with

2 you for your own happiness. So I made up my mind that my next

2 visit to you must not be another painful one. If I cause pain to you, who is left to cheer me up, except you, whom I have offended?

3 This is precisely the point I made in my letter: I did not want, I said, to come and be made miserable by the very people who ought to have made me happy; and I had sufficient confidence in you all

[a] *Some witnesses read* by sincere and godly singleness of mind. [b] *Or* had originally intended to come to you... [c] *Or* In forming this intention, did I act irresponsibly?

to know that for me to be happy is for all of you to be happy. That letter I sent you came out of great distress and anxiety; how 4 many tears I shed as I wrote it! But I never meant to cause you pain; I wanted you rather to know the love, the more than ordinary love, that I have for you.

Any injury that has been done, has not been done to me; to some 5 extent, not to labour the point, it has been done to you all. The 6 penalty on which the general meeting has agreed has met the offence well enough. Something very different is called for now: you must 7 forgive the offender and put heart into him; the man's sorrow must not be made so severe as to overwhelm him. I urge you therefore 8 to assure him of your love for him by a formal act. I wrote, I may 9 say, to see how you stood the test, whether you fully accepted my authority. But anyone who has your forgiveness has mine too; and 10 when I speak of forgiving (so far as there is anything for me to forgive), I mean that as the representative of Christ I have forgiven him for your sake.*ª* For Satan must not be allowed to get the better 11 of us; we know his wiles all too well.

Then when I came to Troas, where I was to preach the gospel 12 of Christ, and where an opening awaited me for the Lord's work, I still found no relief of mind, for my colleague Titus was not there 13 to meet me; so I took leave of the people there and went off to Macedonia. But thanks be to God, who continually leads us about, 14 captives in Christ's triumphal procession, and everywhere uses us to reveal and spread abroad the fragrance of the knowledge of himself! We are indeed the incense offered by Christ to God, both for those 15 who are on the way to salvation, and for those who are on the way to perdition: to the latter it is a deadly fume that kills, to the former 16 a vital fragrance that brings life. Who is equal to such a calling? At least we do not go hawking the word of God about, as so many do; 17 when we declare the word we do it in sincerity, as from God and in God's sight, as members of Christ.

ARE WE BEGINNING all over again to produce our credentials? Do 3 we, like some people, need letters of introduction to you, or from you? No, you are all the letter we need, a letter written on our heart; 2 any man can see it for what it is and read it for himself. And as for 3 you, it is plain that you are a letter that has come from Christ, given

[a] *Or* that I have forgiven him for your sake, in the presence of Christ.

to us to deliver: a letter written not with ink but with the Spirit
of the living God, written not on stone tablets but on the pages of
the human heart.

4 It is in full reliance upon God, through Christ, that we make such
5 claims. There is no question of our being qualified in ourselves: we
cannot claim anything as our own. Such qualification as we have
6 comes from God; it is he who has qualified us to dispense his new
covenant—a covenant expressed not in a written document, but in
a spiritual bond; for the written law condemns to death, but the
Spirit gives life.

7 The law, then, engraved letter by letter upon stone, dispensed
death, and yet it was inaugurated with divine splendour. That splendour, though it was soon to fade, made the face of Moses so bright
8 that the Israelites could not gaze steadily at him. But if so, must
not even greater splendour rest upon the divine dispensation of the
9 Spirit? If splendour accompanied the dispensation under which we
are condemned, how much richer in splendour must that one be
10 under which we are acquitted! Indeed, the splendour that once
was is now no splendour at all; it is outshone by a splendour greater
11 still. For if that which was soon to fade had its moment of splendour,
how much greater is the splendour of that which endures!

12, 13 With such a hope as this we speak out boldly; it is not for us to
do as Moses did: he put a veil over his face to keep the Israelites
14 from gazing on that fading splendour until it was gone. But in any
case their minds had been made insensitive, for that same veil is
there to this very day when the lesson is read from the old covenant;
and it is never lifted, because only in Christ is the old covenant
15 abrogated. But to this very day, every time the Law of Moses is read,
16 a veil lies over the minds of the hearers. However, as Scripture says
of Moses, 'whenever he turns to the Lord the veil is removed'.[a]
17 Now the Lord of whom this passage speaks is the Spirit; and where
18 the Spirit of the Lord is, there is liberty. And because for us there
is no veil over the face, we all reflect as in a mirror the splendour of
the Lord; thus we are transfigured into his likeness, from splendour
to splendour; such is the influence of the Lord who is Spirit.

4 SEEING THEN that we have been entrusted with this commission,
2 which we owe entirely to God's mercy, we never lose heart. We

[a] *Or* as Scripture says, when one turns to the Lord the veil is removed.

have renounced the deeds that men hide for very shame; we neither practise cunning nor distort the word of God; only by declaring the truth openly do we recommend ourselves, and then it is to the common conscience of our fellow-men and in the sight of God. And if indeed our gospel be found veiled, the only people who find 3 it so are those on the way to perdition. Their unbelieving minds are 4 so blinded by the god of this passing age, that the gospel of the glory of Christ, who is the very image of God, cannot dawn upon them and bring them light. It is not ourselves that we proclaim; we proclaim 5 Christ Jesus as Lord, and ourselves as your servants, for Jesus' sake. For the same God who said, 'Out of darkness let light shine', has 6 caused his light to shine within us, to give the light of revelation— the revelation of the glory of God in the face of Jesus Christ.

We are no better than pots of earthenware to contain this treasure, 7 and this proves that such transcendent power does not come from us, but is God's alone. Hard-pressed on every side, we are never 8 hemmed in; bewildered, we are never at our wits' end; hunted, we 9 are never abandoned to our fate; struck down, we are not left to die. Wherever we go we carry death with us in our body, the death that 10 Jesus died, that in this body also life may reveal itself, the life that Jesus lives. For continually, while still alive, we are being surren- 11 dered into the hands of death, for Jesus' sake, so that the life of Jesus also may be revealed in this mortal body of ours. Thus death 12 is at work in us, and life in you.

But Scripture says, 'I believed, and therefore I spoke out', and 13 we too, in the same spirit of faith, believe and therefore speak out; for we know that he who raised the Lord Jesus to life will with Jesus 14 raise us too, and bring us to his presence, and you with us. Indeed, 15 it is for your sake that all things are ordered, so that, as the abounding grace of God is shared by more and more, the greater may be the chorus of thanksgiving that ascends to the glory of God.

No wonder we do not lose heart! Though our outward humanity 16 is in decay, yet day by day we are inwardly renewed. Our troubles 17 are slight and short-lived; and their outcome an eternal glory which outweighs them far. Meanwhile our eyes are fixed, not on the things 18 that are seen, but on the things that are unseen: for what is seen passes away; what is unseen is eternal. For we know that if the 5 earthly frame that houses us today should be demolished, we possess a building which God has provided—a house not made by human

2 hands, eternal, and in heaven. In this present body we do indeed groan; we yearn to have our heavenly habitation put on over this one
3 —in the hope that, being thus clothed, we shall not find ourselves
4 naked. We groan indeed, we who are enclosed within this earthly frame; we are oppressed because we do not want to have the old body stripped off. Rather our desire is to have the new body put on over it, so that our mortal part may be absorbed into life immortal.
5 God himself has shaped us for this very end; and as a pledge of it he has given us the Spirit.
6   Therefore we never cease to be confident. We know that so long
7 as we are at home in the body we are exiles from the Lord; faith is
8 our guide, we do not see him.*ᵃ* We are confident, I repeat, and would
9 rather leave our home in the body and go to live with the Lord. We therefore make it our ambition, wherever we are, here or there, to be
10 acceptable to him. For we must all have our lives laid open before the tribunal of Christ, where each must receive what is due to him for his conduct in the body, good or bad.

11 WITH THIS FEAR of the Lord before our eyes we address our appeal to men. To God our lives lie open, as I hope they also lie open to you
12 in your heart of hearts. This is not another attempt to recommend ourselves to you: we are rather giving you a chance to show yourselves proud of us; then you will have something to say to those whose
13 pride is all in outward show and not in inward worth. It may be we are beside ourselves, but it is for God; if we are in our right mind,
14 it is for you. For the love of Christ leaves us no choice, when once we have reached the conclusion that one man died for all and there-
15 fore all mankind has died. His purpose in dying for all was that men, while still in life, should cease to live for themselves, and should live
16 for him who for their sake died and was raised to life. With us therefore worldly standards have ceased to count in our estimate of any man; even if once they counted in our understanding of Christ,
17 they do so now no longer. When anyone is united to Christ, there is a new world;*ᵇ* the old order has gone, and a new order has already begun.*ᶜ*
18   From first to last this has been the work of God. He has reconciled

[a] Or faith is our guide and not the things we see.   [b] Or a new act of creation.   [c] Or When anyone is united to Christ he is a new creature: his old life is over; a new life has already begun.

us men to himself through Christ, and he has enlisted us in this service of reconciliation. What I mean is, that God was in Christ 19 reconciling the world to himself,*ᵃ* no longer holding men's misdeeds against them, and that he has entrusted us with the message of reconciliation. We come therefore as Christ's ambassadors. It is 20 as if God were appealing to you through us: in Christ's name, we implore you, be reconciled to God! Christ was innocent of sin, 21 and yet for our sake God made him one with the sinfulness of men,*ᵇ* so that in him we might be made one with the goodness of God himself. Sharing in God's work, we urge this appeal upon you: 6 you have received the grace of God; do not let it go for nothing. God's own words are: 2

> 'In the hour of my favour I gave heed to you;
> On the day of deliverance I came to your aid.'

The hour of favour has now come; now, I say, has the day of deliverance dawned.

In order that our service may not be brought into discredit, we 3 avoid giving offence in anything. As God's servants, we try to 4 recommend ourselves in all circumstances by our steadfast endurance: in hardships and dire straits; flogged, imprisoned, mobbed; 5 overworked, sleepless, starving. We recommend ourselves by the 6 innocence of our behaviour, our grasp of truth, our patience and kindliness; by gifts of the Holy Spirit, by sincere love, by declaring 7 the truth, by the power of God. We wield the weapons of righteousness in right hand and left. Honour and dishonour, praise and 8 blame, are alike our lot: we are the impostors who speak the truth, the unknown men whom all men know; dying we still live on; 9 disciplined by suffering, we are not done to death; in our sorrows 10 we have always cause for joy; poor ourselves, we bring wealth to many; penniless, we own the world.

Men of Corinth, we have spoken very frankly to you; we have 11 opened our heart wide to you all. On our part there is no constraint; 12 any constraint there may be is in yourselves. In fair exchange then 13 (may a father speak so to his children?) open wide your hearts to us.

[*a*] *Or* God was reconciling the world to himself by Christ. [*b*] *Or* and yet God made him a sin-offering for us.

Problems of Church Life and Discipline

14 DO NOT UNITE yourselves with unbelievers; they are no fit mates for you. What has righteousness to do with wickedness?
15 Can light consort with darkness? Can Christ agree with Belial, or a
16 believer join hands with an unbeliever? Can there be a compact between the temple of God and the idols of the heathen? And the temple of the living God is what we are. God's own words are: 'I will live and move about among them; I will be their God, and
17 they shall be my people.' And therefore, 'come away and leave them, separate yourselves, says the Lord; do not touch what is unclean.
18 Then I will accept you, says the Lord, the Ruler of all being; I will
7 be a father to you, and you shall be my sons and daughters.' Such are the promises that have been made to us, dear friends. Let us therefore cleanse ourselves from all that can defile flesh or spirit, and in the fear of God complete our consecration.

2 DO MAKE A PLACE for us in your hearts! We have wronged no one,
3 ruined no one, taken advantage of no one. I do not want to blame you. Why, as I have told you before, the place you have in our heart
4 is such that, come death, come life, we meet it together. I am perfectly frank with you. I have great pride in you. In all our many troubles my cup is full of consolation, and overflows with joy.
5 Even when we reached Macedonia there was still no relief for this poor body of ours: instead, there was trouble at every turn, quarrels
6 all round us, forebodings in our heart. But God, who brings com-
7 fort to the downcast, has comforted us by the arrival of Titus, and not merely by his arrival, but by his being so greatly comforted about you. He has told us how you long for me, how sorry you are, and how eager to take my side; and that has made me happier still.
8 Even if I did wound you by the letter I sent, I do not now regret it. I may have been sorry for it when I saw that the letter had caused
9 you pain, even if only for a time; but now I am happy, not that your feelings were wounded but that the wound led to a change of heart. You bore the smart as God would have you bear it, and so you are
10 no losers by what we did. For the wound which is borne in God's way brings a change of heart too salutary to regret; but the hurt

which is borne in the world's way brings death. You bore your hurt 11
in God's way, and see what its results have been! It made you take
the matter seriously and vindicate yourselves. How angered you
were, how apprehensive! How your longing for me awoke, yes, and
your devotion and your eagerness to see justice done! At every
point you have cleared yourselves of blame in this trouble. And so, 12
although I did send you that letter, it was not the offender or his
victim that most concerned me. My aim in writing was to help to
make plain to you, in the sight of God, how truly you are devoted to
us. That is why we have been so encouraged. 13

But besides being encouraged ourselves we have also been delighted beyond everything by seeing how happy Titus is: you have
all helped to set his mind completely at rest. Anything I may have 14
said to him to show my pride in you has been justified. Every word
we ever addressed to you bore the mark of truth; and the same holds
of the proud boast we made in the presence of Titus: that also has
proved true. His heart warms all the more to you as he recalls 15
how ready you all were to do what he asked, meeting him as you
did in fear and trembling. How happy I am now to have complete 16
confidence in you!

WE MUST TELL YOU, friends, about the grace of generosity which 8
God has imparted to*a* our congregations in Macedonia. The troubles 2
they have been through have tried them hard, yet in all this they have
been so exuberantly happy that from the depths of their poverty they
have shown themselves lavishly open-handed. Going to the limit 3
of their resources, as I can testify, and even beyond that limit,
they begged us most insistently, and on their own initiative, to be 4
allowed to share in this generous service to their fellow-Christians.
And their giving surpassed our expectations; for they gave their very 5
selves, offering them in the first instance to the Lord, but also, under
God, to us. The upshot is that we have asked Titus, who began it 6
all, to visit you and bring this work of generosity also to completion.
You are so rich in everything—in faith, speech, knowledge, and zeal 7
of every kind, as well as in the loving regard you have for us*b*—
surely you should show yourselves equally lavish in this generous
service! This is not meant as an order; by telling you how keen 8

[a] *Or* how gracious God has been to... [b] *Some witnesses read* the love we have for
you, *or* the love which we have kindled in your hearts.

9 others are I am putting your love to the test. For you know how generous our Lord Jesus Christ has been: he was rich, yet for your sake he became poor, so that through his poverty you might become rich.

10 Here is my considered opinion on the matter. What I ask you to do is in your own interests. You made a good beginning last year both in the work you did and in your willingness to undertake it.

11 Now I want you to go on and finish it: be as eager to complete the scheme as you were to adopt it, and give according to your means.

12 Provided there is an eager desire to give, God accepts what a man has;

13 he does not ask for what he has not. There is no question of relieving

14 others at the cost of hardship to yourselves; it is a question of equality. At the moment your surplus meets their need, but one day your need may be met from their surplus. The aim is equality;

15 as Scripture has it, 'The man who got much had no more than enough, and the man who got little did not go short.'

16 I thank God that he has made Titus as keen on your behalf as we

17 are! For Titus not only welcomed our request; he is so eager that

18 by his own desire he is now leaving to come to you. With him we are sending one of our company whose reputation is high among our

19 congregations everywhere for his services to the Gospel. Moreover they have duly appointed him to travel with us and help in this beneficent work, by which we do honour to the Lord himself and

20 show our own eagerness to serve. We want to guard against any

21 criticism of our handling of this generous gift; for our aims are entirely honourable, not only in the Lord's eyes, but also in the eyes of men.

22 With these men we are sending another of our company whose enthusiasm we have had many opportunities of testing, and who is now all the more earnest because of the great confidence he has in

23 you. If there is any question about Titus, he is my partner and my associate in dealings with you; as for the others, they are delegates

24 of our congregations, an honour to Christ.[a] Then give them clear expression of your love and justify our pride in you; justify it to them, and through them to the congregations.

9 About the provision of aid for God's people, it is superfluous for

2 me to write to you. I know how eager you are to help; I speak of it with pride to the Macedonians: I tell them that Achaia had everything ready last year; and most of them have been fired by your zeal.

[a] *Or* they are...congregations; they reflect Christ.

My purpose in sending these friends is to ensure that what we have 3
said about you in this matter should not prove to be an empty boast.
By that I mean, I want you to be prepared, as I told them you
were; for if I bring with me men from Macedonia and they find you 4
are not prepared, what a disgrace it will be to us, let alone to you,
after all the confidence we have shown! I have accordingly thought 5
it necessary to ask these friends to go on ahead to Corinth, to see
that your promised bounty is in order before I come; it will then be
awaiting me as a bounty indeed, and not as an extortion.

Remember: sparse sowing, sparse reaping; sow bountifully, and 6
you will reap bountifully. Each person should give as he has decided 7
for himself; there should be no reluctance, no sense of compulsion;
God loves a cheerful giver. And it is in God's power to provide you 8
richly with every good gift; thus you will have ample means in yourselves to meet each and every situation, with enough and to spare
for every good cause. Scripture says of such a man: 'He has lavished 9
his gifts on the needy, his benevolence stands fast for ever.' Now 10
he who provides seed for sowing and bread for food will provide
the seed for you to sow; he will multiply it and swell the harvest of
your benevolence, and you will always be rich enough to be generous. 11
Through our action such generosity will issue in thanksgiving to
God, for as a piece of willing service this is not only a contribution 12
towards the needs of God's people; more than that, it overflows
in a flood of thanksgiving to God. For through the proof which this 13
affords, many will give honour to God when they see how humbly
you obey him and how faithfully you confess the gospel of Christ;
and will thank him for your liberal contribution to their need and
to the general good. And as they join in prayer on your behalf, their 14
hearts will go out to you because of the richness of the grace which
God has imparted to you. Thanks be to God for his gift beyond 15
words!

Trials of a Christian Missionary

BUT I, PAUL, appeal to you by the gentleness and magnanimity 10
of Christ—I, so feeble (you say) when I am face to face with you,
so brave when I am away. Spare me, I beg you, the necessity of 2
such bravery when I come, for I reckon I could put on as bold a face

as you please against those who charge us with moral weakness.
3 Weak men we may be, but it is not as such that we fight our battles.
4 The weapons we wield are not merely human,*a* but divinely potent to
5 demolish strongholds; we demolish sophistries and all that rears its
proud head against the knowledge of God; we compel every human
6 thought to surrender in obedience to Christ; and we are prepared to
punish all rebellion when once you have put yourselves in our hands.
7   Look facts in the face.*b* Someone is convinced, is he, that he
belongs to Christ? Let him think again, and reflect that we belong
8 to Christ as much as he does. Indeed, if I am somewhat over-
boastful about our authority—an authority given by the Lord to
build you up, not pull you down—I shall make my boast good.
9 So you must not think of me as one who scares you by the letters
10 he writes. 'His letters', so it is said, 'are weighty and powerful;
but when he appears he has no presence, and as a speaker he is
11 beneath contempt.' People who talk in that way should reckon with
this: when I come, my actions will show the same man as my letters
showed in my absence.
12   We should not dare to class ourselves or compare ourselves with
any of those who put forward their own claims. What fools they are
to measure themselves by themselves, to find in themselves their own
13 standard of comparison!*c* With us there will be no attempt to boast
beyond our proper sphere; and our sphere is determined by the limit
God laid down for us, which permitted us to come as far as Corinth.
14 We are not overstretching our commission, as we should be if it
did not extend to you, for we were the first to reach Corinth in
15 preaching the gospel of Christ. And we do not boast of work done
where others have laboured, work beyond our proper sphere. Our
hope is rather that, as your faith grows, we may attain a position
among you greater than ever before, but still within the limits of
16 our sphere. Then we can carry the Gospel to lands that lie beyond you, never priding ourselves on work already done in another
17, 18 man's sphere. If a man must boast, let him boast of the Lord. Not
the man who recommends himself, but the man whom the Lord
recommends—he and he alone is to be accepted.

[a] Or charge us with worldly standards. We live, no doubt, in the world; but it is not
on that level that we fight our battles. The weapons we wield are not those of the world...
[b] Or You are looking only at what catches the eye. [c] Some witnesses read On the
contrary we measure ourselves by ourselves, by our own standard of comparison.

I wish you would bear with me in a little of my folly; please do 11
bear with me. I am jealous for you, with a divine jealousy; for I 2
betrothed you to Christ, thinking to present you as a chaste virgin
to her true and only husband. But as the serpent in his cunning 3
seduced Eve, I am afraid that your thoughts may be corrupted and
you may lose your*a* single-hearted devotion to Christ. For if some- 4
one comes who proclaims another Jesus, not the Jesus whom we
proclaimed, or if you then receive a spirit different from the Spirit
already given to you, or a gospel different from the gospel you have
already accepted, you manage to put up with that well enough. Have 5
I in any way come short of those superlative apostles? I think not.
I may be no speaker, but knowledge I have; at all times we have 6
made known to you the full truth.

Or was this my offence, that I made no charge for preaching the 7
gospel of God, lowering myself to help in raising you? It is true 8
that I took toll of other congregations, accepting*b* support from them
to serve you. Then, while I was with you, if I ran short I sponged 9
on no one; anything I needed was fully met by our friends who
came from Macedonia; I made it a rule, as I always shall, never to
be a burden to you. As surely as the truth of Christ is in me, I will 10
preserve my pride in this matter throughout Achaia, and nothing
shall stop me. Why? Is it that I do not love you? God knows 11
I do.

And I shall go on doing as I am doing now, to cut the ground 12
from under those who would seize any chance to put their vaunted
apostleship on the same level as ours. Such men are sham-apostles, 13
crooked in all their practices, masquerading as apostles of Christ.
There is nothing surprising about that; Satan himself masquerades 14
as an angel of light. It is therefore a simple thing for his agents to 15
masquerade as agents of good. But they will meet the end their
deeds deserve.

I repeat: let no one take me for a fool; but if you must, then give 16
me the privilege of a fool, and let me have my little boast like others.
I am not speaking here as a Christian, but like a fool, if it comes to 17
bragging. So many people brag of their earthly distinctions that 18
I shall do so too. How gladly you bear with fools, being yourselves 19
so wise! If a man tyrannizes over you, exploits you, gets you in his 20

[a] *Some witnesses insert* purity and...   [b] *Or* Did I take toll of other congregations
by accepting...?

clutches, puts on airs, and hits you in the face, you put up with it.
21 And we, you say, have been weak! I admit the reproach.

But if there is to be bravado (and here I speak as a fool), I can
22 indulge in it too. Are they Hebrews? So am I. Israelites? So am I.
23 Abraham's descendants? So am I. Are they servants of Christ?
I am mad to speak like this, but I can outdo them. More overworked
than they, scourged more severely, more often imprisoned, many
24 a time face to face with death. Five times the Jews have given me the
25 thirty-nine strokes; three times I have been beaten with rods; once I
was stoned; three times I have been shipwrecked, and for twenty-four
26 hours I was adrift on the open sea. I have been constantly on the
road; I have met dangers from rivers, dangers from robbers, dangers
from my fellow-countrymen, dangers from foreigners, dangers in
towns, dangers in the country, dangers at sea, dangers from false
27 friends. I have toiled and drudged, I have often gone without sleep;
hungry and thirsty, I have often gone fasting; and I have suffered
from cold and exposure.
28 Apart from these external things,[a] there is the responsibility that
weighs on me every day, my anxious concern for all our congrega-
29 tions. If anyone is weak, do I not share his weakness? If anyone
is made to stumble, does my heart not blaze with indignation?
30 If boasting there must be, I will boast of the things that show up
31 my weakness. The God and Father of the Lord Jesus (blessed be
32 his name for ever!) knows that what I say is true. When I was in
Damascus, the commissioner of King Aretas kept the city under
33 observation so as to have me arrested; and I was let down in a
basket, through a window in the wall, and so escaped his clutches.

12 I AM OBLIGED to boast. It does no good; but I shall go on to tell
2 of visions and revelations granted by the Lord. I know a Christian
man who fourteen years ago (whether in the body or out of it,
I do not know—God knows) was caught up as far as the third
3 heaven. And I know that this same man (whether in the body or out
4 of it, I do not know—God knows) was caught up into paradise, and
5 heard words so secret that human lips may not repeat them. About
such a man as that I am ready to boast; but I will not boast on my
6 own account, except of my weaknesses. If I should choose to boast,
it would not be the boast of a fool, for I should be speaking the truth.

[a] *Or* Apart from things which I omit.

But I refrain, because I should not like anyone to form an estimate of me which goes beyond the evidence of his own eyes and ears. And so, to keep me from being unduly elated by the magnificence of such revelations, I was given[a] a sharp pain in my body[b] which came as Satan's messenger to bruise me; this was to save me from being unduly elated. Three times I begged the Lord to rid me of it, but his answer was: 'My grace is all you need; power comes to its full strength in weakness.' I shall therefore prefer to find my joy and pride in the very things that are my weakness; and then the power of Christ will come and rest upon me. Hence I am well content, for Christ's sake, with weakness, contempt, persecution, hardship, and frustration; for when I am weak, then I am strong.

I AM BEING very foolish, but it was you who drove me to it; my credentials should have come from you. In no respect did I fall short of these superlative apostles, even if I am a nobody. The marks of a true apostle were there, in the work I did among you, which called for such constant fortitude, and was attended by signs, marvels, and miracles. Is there anything in which you were treated worse than the other congregations—except this, that I never sponged upon you? How unfair of me! I crave forgiveness.

Here am I preparing to pay you a third visit; and I am not going to sponge upon you. It is you I want, not your money; parents should make provision for their children, not children for their parents. As for me, I will gladly spend what I have for you—yes, and spend myself to the limit. If I love you overmuch, am I to be loved the less? But, granted that I did not prove a burden to you, still I was unscrupulous enough, you say, to use a trick to catch you. Who, of the men I have sent to you, was used by me to defraud you? I begged Titus to visit you, and I sent our friend with him. Did Titus defraud you? Have we not both been guided by the same Spirit, and followed the same course?

Perhaps you think that all this time we have been addressing our defence to you. No; we are speaking in God's sight, and as Christian men. Our whole aim, my own dear people, is to build you up. I fear that when I come I may perhaps find you different from what

[a] *Some witnesses read*...ears, and because of the magnificence of the revelations themselves. Therefore to keep me from being unduly elated I was given...   [b] *Or* a painful wound to my pride (*literally* a stake, *or* thorn, for the flesh).

I wish you to be, and that you may find me also different from what you wish. I fear I may find quarrelling and jealousy, angry tempers and personal rivalries, backbiting and gossip, arrogance and general

21 disorder. I am afraid that, when I come again, my God may humiliate me in your presence, that I may have tears to shed over many of those who have sinned in the past and have not repented of their unclean lives, their fornication and sensuality.

13 This will be my third visit to you; and all facts must be established

2 by the evidence of two or three witnesses. To those who have sinned in the past, and to everyone else, I repeat the warning I gave before; I gave it in person on my second visit, and I give it now in absence.

3 It is that when I come this time, I will show no leniency. Then you will have the proof you seek of the Christ who speaks through me, the Christ who, far from being weak with you, makes his power

4 felt among you. True, he died on the cross in weakness, but he lives by the power of God; and we who share his weakness shall by the power of God live with him in your service.

5 Examine yourselves: are you living the life of faith? Put yourselves to the test. Surely you recognize that Jesus Christ is among

6 you?—unless of course you prove unequal to the test. I hope you

7 will come to see that we are not unequal to it. Our prayer to God is that we may not have to hurt you; we are not concerned to be vindicated ourselves; we want you to do what is right, even if we

8 should seem to be discredited. For we have no power to act against

9 the truth, but only for it. We are well content to be weak at any time if only you are strong. Indeed, my whole prayer is that all may be

10 put right with you. My purpose in writing this letter before I come, is to spare myself, when I come, any sharp exercise of authority— authority which the Lord gave me for building up and not for pulling down.

11 And now, my friends, farewell. Mend your ways; take our appeal to heart; agree with one another; live in peace; and the God of love

12 and peace will be with you. Greet one another with the kiss of

13 peace. All God's people send you greetings.

14 The grace of the Lord Jesus Christ, and the love of God, and fellowship in the Holy Spirit, be with you all.

THE
LETTER OF PAUL TO THE
GALATIANS

Faith and Freedom

FROM PAUL, an apostle, not by human appointment or 1
human commission, but by commission from Jesus Christ
and from God the Father who raised him from the dead.
I and the group of friends now with me send greetings to the 2
Christian congregations of Galatia.

Grace and peace to you from God the Father and our Lord Jesus 3
Christ,*a* who sacrificed himself for our sins, to rescue us out of this 4
present age of wickedness, as our God and Father willed: to whom 5
be glory for ever and ever. Amen.

I am astonished to find you turning so quickly away from him 6
who called you by grace,*b* and following a different gospel. Not that 7
it is in fact another gospel; only there are persons who unsettle your
minds by trying to distort the gospel of Christ. But if anyone, if we 8
ourselves or an angel from heaven, should preach a gospel at variance
with the gospel we preached to you, he shall be held outcast. I now 9
repeat what I have said before: if anyone preaches a gospel at
variance with the gospel which you received, let him be outcast!

Does my language now sound as if I were canvassing for men's 10
support? Whose support do I want but God's alone? Do you
think I am currying favour with men? If I still sought men's
favour, I should be no servant of Christ.

I must make it clear to you, my friends, that the gospel you heard 11
me preach is no human invention. I did not take it over from any 12
man; no man taught it me; I received it through a revelation of
Jesus Christ.

You have heard what my manner of life was when I was still a 13
practising Jew: how savagely I persecuted the church of God, and

[a] *Some witnesses read* God our Father and the Lord Jesus Christ. [b] *Some witnesses
read* from Christ who called you by grace, *or* from him who called you by grace of
Christ.

14 tried to destroy it; and how in the practice of our national religion I was outstripping many of my Jewish contemporaries in my bound-
15 less devotion to the traditions of my ancestors. But then in his good pleasure God, who had set me apart from birth and called me
16 through his grace, chose to reveal his Son to me and through me, in order that I might proclaim him among the Gentiles. When that
17 happened, without consulting any human being, without going up to Jerusalem to see those who were apostles before me, I went off at once to Arabia, and afterwards returned to Damascus.
18 Three years later I did go up to Jerusalem to get to know Cephas.
19 I stayed with him for a fortnight, without seeing any other of the
20 apostles, except*a* James the Lord's brother. What I write is plain truth; before God I am not lying.
21, 22 Next I went to the regions of Syria and Cilicia, and remained
23 unknown by sight*b* to Christ's congregations in Judaea. They only heard it said, 'Our former persecutor is preaching the good news of
24 the faith which once he tried to destroy'; and they praised God for me.
2 Next, fourteen years later, I went again*c* to Jerusalem with
2 Barnabas, taking Titus with us. I went up because it had been revealed by God that I should do so. I laid before them—but at a private interview with the men of repute—the gospel which I am accustomed to preach to the Gentiles, to make sure that the race I
3 had run, and was running, should not be run in vain. Yet even my companion Titus, Greek though he is, was not compelled to be
4 circumcised. That course was urged only as a concession to certain*d* sham-Christians, interlopers who had stolen in to spy upon the liberty we enjoy in the fellowship of Christ Jesus. These men wanted
5 to bring us into bondage, but not for one moment did I yield to their dictation; I was determined that the full truth of the Gospel should be maintained for you.*e*
6 But as for the men of high reputation (not that their importance matters to me: God does not recognize these personal distinc-tions)—these men of repute, I say, did not prolong the consultation,*f*

[a] Or but only. [b] Or unknown personally. [c] Some witnesses omit again. [d] Or The question was later raised because of certain... [e] Or, following the reading of some witnesses, Yet even...is, was under no absolute compulsion to be circumcised, but for the sake of certain...of Christ Jesus, with the intention of bringing us into bondage, I yielded to their demand for the moment, to ensure that gospel truth should not be prevented from reaching you. [f] Or gave me no further instructions.

but on the contrary acknowledged that I had been entrusted with 7
the Gospel for Gentiles as surely as Peter had been entrusted with
the Gospel for Jews. For God whose action made Peter an apostle 8
to the Jews, also made me an apostle to the Gentiles.

Recognizing, then, the favour thus bestowed upon me, those 9
reputed pillars of our society, James, Cephas, and John, accepted
Barnabas and myself as partners, and shook hands upon it, agreeing
that we should go to the Gentiles while they went to the Jews. All 10
they asked was that we should keep their poor in mind, which was
the very thing I made*a* it my business to do.

But when Cephas came to Antioch, I opposed him to his face, 11
because he was clearly in the wrong. For until certain persons*b* 12
came from James he was taking his meals with gentile Christians;
but when they*c* came he drew back and began to hold aloof, because
he was afraid of the advocates of circumcision. The other Jewish 13
Christians showed the same lack of principle; even Barnabas was
carried away and played false like the rest. But when I saw that 14
their conduct did not square with*d* the truth of the Gospel, I said to
Cephas, before the whole congregation, 'If you, a Jew born and
bred, live like a Gentile, and not like a Jew, how can you insist that
Gentiles must live like Jews?'

We ourselves are Jews by birth, not Gentiles and sinners. But we 15, 16
know that no man is ever justified by doing what the law demands,
but only through faith in Christ Jesus; so we too have put our faith
in Jesus Christ, in order that we might be justified through this faith,
and not through deeds dictated by law; for by such deeds, Scripture
says, no mortal man shall be justified.

If now, in seeking to be justified in Christ, we ourselves no less 17
than the Gentiles turn out to be sinners against the law,*e* does that
mean that Christ is an abettor of sin? No, never! No, if I start 18
building up again a system which I have pulled down, then it is
that I show myself up as a transgressor of the law. For through the 19
law I died to law—to live for God. I have been crucified with 20
Christ: the life I now live is not my life, but the life which Christ
lives in me; and my present bodily life is lived by faith in the Son
of God, who loved me and sacrificed himself for me. I will not 21

[a] *Or* had made, *or* have made. [b] *Some witnesses read* a certain person. [c] *Some
witnesses read* he. [d] *Or* I saw that they were not making progress towards... [e] *Or* no
less than the Gentiles have accepted the position of sinners against the law.

nullify the grace of God; if righteousness comes by law, then Christ died for nothing.

3 YOU STUPID GALATIANS! You must have been bewitched—you before whose eyes Jesus Christ was openly displayed upon his cross!
2 Answer me one question: did you receive the Spirit by keeping the
3 law or by believing the gospel message[a]? Can it be that you are so stupid? You started with the spiritual; do you now look to the
4 material to make you perfect? Have all your great experiences been
5 in vain—if vain indeed they should be? I ask then: when God gives you the Spirit and works miracles among you, why is this? Is it because you keep the law, or is it because you have faith in the
6 gospel message? Look at Abraham: he put his faith in God, and that faith was counted to him as righteousness.
7   You may take it, then, that it is the men of faith who are Abraham's
8 sons. And Scripture, foreseeing that God would justify the Gentiles through faith, declared the Gospel to Abraham beforehand: 'In you
9 all nations shall find blessing.' Thus it is the men of faith who share the blessing with faithful Abraham.
10   On the other hand those who rely on obedience to the law are under a curse; for Scripture says, 'Cursed are all who do not persevere in doing everything that is written in the Book of the Law.'
11 It is evident that no one is ever justified before God in terms of law; because we read, 'he shall gain life who is justified through faith'.
12 Now law is not at all a matter of having faith: we read, 'he who does this shall gain life by what he does'.
13   Christ bought us freedom from the curse of the law by becoming for our sake an accursed thing; for Scripture says,'Cursed is everyone
14 who is hanged on a tree.' And the purpose of it all was that the blessing of Abraham should in Jesus Christ be extended to the Gentiles, so that we might receive the promised Spirit through faith.
15   My brothers, let me give you an illustration. Even in ordinary life, when a man's will and testament has been duly executed, no one
16 else can set it aside or add a codicil. Now the promises were pronounced to Abraham and to his 'issue'. It does not say 'issues' in the plural, but in the singular, 'and to your issue'; and the 'issue'
17 intended is Christ. What I am saying is this: a testament, or covenant, had already been validated by God; it cannot be invalidated, and its

[a] Or or by the message of faith, *or* or by hearing and believing.

promises rendered ineffective, by a law made four hundred and thirty years later. If the inheritance is by legal right, then it is not 18 by promise; but it was by promise that God bestowed it as a free gift on Abraham.

Then what of the law? It was added to make wrongdoing a legal 19 offence.*ᵃ* It was a temporary measure pending the arrival of the 'issue' to whom the promise was made. It was promulgated through angels, and there was an intermediary; but an intermediary is not 20 needed for one party acting alone, and God is one.

Does the law, then, contradict the promises? No, never! If a law 21 had been given which had power to bestow life, then indeed righteousness would have come from keeping the law. But Scripture has 22 declared the whole world to be prisoners in subjection to sin, so that faith in Jesus Christ may be the ground on which the promised blessing is given, and given to those who have such faith.

Before this faith came, we were close prisoners in the custody of 23 law, pending the revelation of faith. Thus the law was a kind of tutor 24 in charge of us until Christ should come,*ᵇ* when we should be justified through faith; and now that faith has come, the tutor's charge 25 is at an end.

For through faith you are all sons of God in union with Christ 26 Jesus. Baptized into union with him, you have all put on Christ as 27 a garment. There is no such thing as Jew and Greek, slave and free- 28 man, male and female; for you are all one person in Christ Jesus. But if you thus belong to Christ, you are the 'issue' of Abraham, and 29 so heirs by promise.

This is what I mean: so long as the heir is a minor, he is no better 4 off than a slave, even though the whole estate is his; he is under 2 guardians and trustees until the date fixed by his father. And so 3 it was with us. During our minority we were slaves to the elemental spirits of the universe,*ᶜ* but when the term was completed, God sent 4 his own Son, born of a woman, born under the law, to purchase 5 freedom for the subjects of the law, in order that we might attain the status of sons.

To prove that you are sons, God has sent into our hearts the Spirit 6 of his Son, crying 'Abba! Father!' You are therefore no longer a 7 slave but a son, and if a son, then also by God's own act an heir.

[*a*] *Or* added because of offences.   [*b*] *Or* a kind of tutor to conduct us to Christ.
[*c*] *Or* the elements of the natural world, *or* elementary ideas belonging to this world.

8 Formerly, when you did not acknowledge God, you were the
9 slaves of beings which in their nature are no gods.*ᵃ* But now that
you do acknowledge God—or rather, now that he has acknowledged
you—how can you turn back to the mean and beggarly spirits of
the elements?*ᵇ* Why do you propose to enter their service all over
10 again? You keep special days and months and seasons and years.
11 You make me fear that all the pains I spent on you may prove to be
labour lost.

12 PUT YOURSELVES in my place, my brothers, I beg you, for I have
13 put myself in yours. It is not that you did me any wrong. As you
know, it was bodily illness that originally*ᶜ* led to my bringing you the
14 Gospel, and you resisted any temptation to show scorn or disgust at
the state of my poor body;*ᵈ* you welcomed me as if I were an angel
15 of God, as you might have welcomed Christ Jesus himself. Have
you forgotten how happy you thought yourselves in having me with
you? I can say this for you: you would have torn out your very eyes,
16 and given them to me, had that been possible! And have I now made
myself your enemy by being honest with you?
17 The persons I have referred to are envious of you, but not with
an honest envy:*ᵉ* what they really want is to bar the door to you so
18 that you may come to envy*ᶠ* them. It is always a fine thing to deserve
an honest envy*ᵍ*—always, and not only when I am present with you,
19 dear children. For my children you are, and I am in travail with
20 you over again until you take the shape of Christ. I wish I could
be with you now; then I could modify my tone;*ʰ* as it is, I am at my
wits' end about you.

21 TELL ME NOW, you who are so anxious to be under law, will you
22 not listen to what the Law says? It is written there that Abraham
had two sons, one by his slave and the other by his free-born wife.
23 The slave-woman's son was born in the course of nature, the free
24 woman's through God's promise. This is an allegory. The two women
stand for two covenants. The one bearing children into slavery is
25 the covenant that comes from Mount Sinai: that is Hagar. Sinai is

[a] Or were slaves to 'gods' which in reality do not exist. [b] *See note on 4.3.* [c] Or
formerly, or on the first of my two visits. [d] Or you showed neither scorn nor disgust
at the trial my poor body was enduring. [e] Or paying court to you, but not with honest
intentions. [f] Or pay court to. [g] Or to be honourably wooed. [h] Or now, and
could exchange words with you.

a mountain in Arabia and it represents the Jerusalem of today, for
she and her children are in slavery. But the heavenly Jerusalem is 26
the free woman; she is our mother. For Scripture says, 'Rejoice, 27
O barren woman who never bore child; break into a shout of joy, you
who never knew a mother's pangs; for the deserted wife shall have
more children than she who lives with the husband.'

And you, my brothers, like Isaac, are children of God's promise. 28
But just as in those days the natural-born son persecuted the spiritual 29
son, so it is today. But what does Scripture say? 'Drive out the 30
slave-woman and her son, for the son of the slave shall not share the
inheritance with the free woman's sons.' You see, then, my brothers, 31
we are no slave-woman's children; our mother is the free woman.
Christ set us free, to be free men.*ª* Stand firm, then, and refuse 5
to be tied to the yoke of slavery again.

Mark my words: I, Paul, say to you that if you receive circumci- 2
sion Christ will do you no good at all. Once again, you can take it 3
from me that every man who receives circumcision is under obligation to keep the entire law. When you seek to be justified by way of 4
law, your relation with Christ is completely severed: you have fallen
out of the domain of God's grace. For to us, our hope of attaining 5
that righteousness which we eagerly await is the work of the Spirit
through faith. If we are in union with Christ Jesus circumcision 6
makes no difference at all, nor does the want of it; the only thing
that counts is faith active in love.*ᵇ*

You were running well; who was it hindered you from following 7
the truth? Whatever persuasion he used, it did not come from God 8
who is calling you; 'a little leaven', remember, 'leavens all the 9
dough'. United with you in the Lord, I am confident that you will 10
not take the wrong view; but the man who is unsettling your minds,
whoever he may be, must bear God's judgement. And I, my friends, 11
if I am still advocating circumcision, why is it I am still persecuted?
In that case, my preaching of the cross is a stumbling-block no more.
As for these agitators, they had better go the whole way and make 12
eunuchs of themselves!

You, my friends, were called to be free men; only do not turn 13
your freedom into licence for your lower nature, but be servants
to one another in love. For the whole law can be summed up in 14

[a] *Or* What Christ has done is to set us free. [b] *Or* inspired by love.

15 a single commandment: 'Love your neighbour as yourself.' But if
you go on fighting one another, tooth and nail, all you can expect is
mutual destruction.

16 I mean this: if you are guided by the Spirit you will not fulfil the
17 desires of your lower nature. That nature sets its desires against the
Spirit, while the Spirit fights against it. They are in conflict with one
18 another so that what you will to do you cannot do. But if you are led
by the Spirit, you are not under law.

19 Anyone can see the kind of behaviour that belongs to the lower
20 nature: fornication, impurity, and indecency; idolatry and sorcery;
quarrels, a contentious temper, envy, fits of rage, selfish ambitions,
21 dissensions, party intrigues, and jealousies; drinking bouts, orgies,
and the like. I warn you, as I warned you before, that those who
behave in such ways will never inherit the kingdom of God.

22 But the harvest of the Spirit is love, joy, peace, patience, kindness,
23 goodness, fidelity, gentleness, and self-control. There is no law
24 dealing with such things as these. And those who belong to Christ
Jesus have crucified the lower nature with its passions and desires.
25 If the Spirit is the source of our life, let the Spirit also direct our
course.

26 We must not be conceited, challenging one another to rivalry,
6 jealous of one another. If a man should do something wrong, my
brothers, on a sudden impulse,*a* you who are endowed with the
Spirit must set him right again very gently. Look to yourself, each
2 one of you: you may be tempted too. Help one another to carry these
heavy loads, and in this way you will fulfil the law of Christ.

3 For if a man imagines himself to be somebody, when he is nothing,
4 he is deluding himself. Each man should examine his own conduct
for himself; then he can measure his achievement by comparing
5 himself with himself and not with anyone else. For everyone has his
own proper burden to bear.

6 When anyone is under instruction in the faith, he should give his
teacher a share of all good things he has.

7 Make no mistake about this: God is not to be fooled; a man reaps
8 what he sows. If he sows seed in the field of his lower nature, he
will reap from it a harvest of corruption, but if he sows in the field
of the Spirit, the Spirit will bring him a harvest of eternal life.
9 So let us never tire of doing good, for if we do not slacken our efforts

[a] *Or* If a man is caught doing something wrong, my brothers,...

we shall in due time reap our harvest. Therefore, as opportunity 10
offers, let us work for the good of all, especially members of the
household of the faith.

YOU SEE these big letters? I am now writing to you in my own hand. 11
It is all those who want to make a fair outward and bodily show who 12
are trying to force circumcision upon you; their sole object is to
escape persecution for the cross of Christ. For even those who do 13
receive circumcision are not thoroughgoing observers of the law:
they only want you to be circumcised in order to boast of your
having submitted to that outward rite. But God forbid that I should 14
boast of anything but the cross of our Lord Jesus Christ, through
which*a* the world is crucified to me and I to the world! Circumcision 15
is nothing; uncircumcision is nothing; the only thing that counts is
new creation! Whoever they are who take this principle for their 16
guide, peace and mercy be upon them, and upon the whole Israel of
God!
    In future let no one make trouble for me, for I bear the marks of 17
Jesus branded on my body.
    The grace of our Lord Jesus Christ be with your spirit, my 18
brothers. Amen.

[a] *Or* whom.

THE
LETTER OF PAUL TO THE
EPHESIANS

The Glory of Christ in the Church

1 FROM PAUL, apostle of Christ Jesus, commissioned by the
will of God, to God's people at Ephesus,[a] believers incorporate
in Christ Jesus.

2   Grace to you and peace from God our Father and the Lord Jesus
Christ.

3   Praise be to the God and Father of our Lord Jesus Christ, who
has bestowed on us in Christ every spiritual blessing in the heavenly

4 realms. In Christ he chose us before the world was founded, to be
5 dedicated, to be without blemish in his sight, to be full of love; and
he[b] destined us—such was his will and pleasure—to be accepted as

6 his sons through Jesus Christ, that the glory of his gracious gift,
so graciously bestowed on us in his Beloved, might redound to his

7 praise. For in Christ our release is secured and our sins are forgiven
through the shedding of his blood. Therein lies the richness of God's

8 free grace lavished upon us, imparting full wisdom and insight.
9 He has made known to us his hidden purpose—such was his will

10 and pleasure determined beforehand in Christ—to be put into effect
when the time was ripe: namely, that the universe, all in heaven and
on earth, might be brought into a unity in Christ.

11   In Christ indeed we have been given our share in the heritage,
as was decreed in his design whose purpose is everywhere at work.

12 For it was his will that we, who were the first to set our hope on
13 Christ,[c] should cause his glory to be praised. And you too, when
you had heard the message of the truth, the good news of your salvation, and had believed it, became incorporate in Christ and received

14 the seal of the promised Holy Spirit; and that Spirit is the pledge that
we shall enter upon our heritage, when God has redeemed what is his
own, to his praise and glory.

[a] *Some witnesses omit* at Ephesus. [b] *Or* ...sight. In his love he... [c] *Or* who
already enjoyed the hope of Christ, *or* whose expectation and hope are in Christ.

Because of all this, now that I have heard of the faith you have in 15
the Lord Jesus and of the love you bear towards all God's people, I 16
never cease to give thanks for you when I mention you in my prayers.
I pray that the God of our Lord Jesus Christ, the all-glorious Father, 17
may give you the spiritual powers of wisdom and vision, by which
there comes the knowledge of him. I pray that your inward eyes 18
may be illumined, so that you may know what is the hope to which
he calls you, what the wealth and glory of the share he offers you
among his people in their heritage, and how vast the resources of 19
his power open to us who trust in him. They are measured by his
strength and the might which he exerted in Christ when he raised 20
him from the dead, when he enthroned him at his right hand in the
heavenly realms, far above all government and authority, all power 21
and dominion, and any title of sovereignty that can be named, not
only in this age but in the age to come. He put everything in subjec- 22
tion beneath his feet, and appointed him as supreme head to the
church, which is his body and as such holds within it the fullness 23
of him who himself receives the entire fullness of God.[a]

TIME WAS when you were dead in your sins and wickedness, 2
when you followed the evil ways of this present age, when you 2
obeyed the commander of the spiritual powers of the air, the spirit
now at work among God's rebel subjects. We too were of their 3
number: we all lived our lives in sensuality, and obeyed the prompt-
ings of our own instincts and notions. In our natural condition we,
like the rest, lay under the dreadful judgement of God. But God, 4
rich in mercy, for the great love he bore us, brought us to life with 5
Christ even when we were dead in our sins; it is by his grace you
are saved. And in union with Christ Jesus he raised us up and 6
enthroned us with him in the heavenly realms, so that he might 7
display in the ages to come how immense are the resources of his
grace, and how great his kindness to us in Christ Jesus. For it is 8
by his grace you are saved, through trusting him; it is not your own
doing. It is God's gift, not a reward for work done. There is nothing 9
for anyone to boast of. For we are God's handiwork, created in 10

[a] *Or* as supreme head to the church, which is his body and as such holds within it
the fullness of him who fills the universe in all its parts; *or* as supreme head to the
church which is his body, and to be all that he himself is who fills the universe in all
its parts.

Christ Jesus to devote ourselves to the good deeds for which God has designed us.

11   Remember then your former condition: you, Gentiles as you are outwardly,*ᵃ* you, 'the uncircumcised' so called by those who are called 'the circumcised' (but only with reference to an outward

12 rite)—you were at that time separate from Christ, strangers to the community of Israel, outside God's covenants and the promise that goes with them. Your world was a world without hope and without

13 God. But now in union with Christ Jesus you who once were far off have been brought near through the shedding of Christ's blood.

14 For he is himself our peace. Gentiles and Jews, he has made the two one, and in his own body of flesh and blood has broken down

15 the enmity which stood like a dividing wall between them; for he annulled the law with its rules and regulations, so as to create out of the two a single new humanity in himself, thereby making peace.

16 This was his purpose, to reconcile the two in a single body to God through the cross, on which he killed the enmity.*ᵇ*

17   So he came and proclaimed the good news: peace to you who were

18 far off, and peace to those who were near by; for through him we

19 both alike have access to the Father in the one Spirit. Thus you are no longer aliens in a foreign land, but fellow-citizens with God's

20 people, members of God's household. You are built upon the foundation laid by the apostles and prophets, and Christ Jesus himself is the

21 foundation-stone.*ᶜ* In him the whole building*ᵈ* is bonded together

22 and grows into a holy temple in the Lord. In him you too are being built with all the rest into a spiritual dwelling for God.

3 WITH THIS in mind I make my prayer, I, Paul, who in the cause

2 of you Gentiles am now the prisoner of Christ Jesus—for surely you have heard how God has assigned the gift of his grace to me for your

3 benefit. It was by a revelation that his secret was made known to me.

4 I have already written a brief account of this, and by reading it

5 you may perceive that I understand the secret of Christ. In former generations this was not disclosed to the human race; but now it has been revealed by inspiration to his dedicated apostles and prophets,

6 that through the Gospel the Gentiles are joint heirs with the

---

[a] *Or* by birth. [b] *Or* . . . cross. Thus in his own person he put the enmity to death.
[c] *Or* built upon the foundation of the apostles and prophets, and Christ Jesus himself is the keystone. [d] *Or* every structure.

Jews, part of the same body, sharers together in the promise made in Christ Jesus. Such is the gospel of which I was made 7 a minister, by God's gift, bestowed unmerited on me in the working of his power. To me, who am less than the least of all God's 8 people, he has granted of his grace the privilege of proclaiming to the Gentiles the good news of the unfathomable riches of Christ, and of 9 bringing to light how this hidden purpose was to be put into effect. It was hidden for long ages in God the creator of the universe, in 10 order that now, through the church, the wisdom of God in all its varied forms might be made known to the rulers and authorities in the realms of heaven. This is in accord with his age-long purpose, 11 which he achieved in Christ Jesus our Lord. In him we have access 12 to God with freedom, in the confidence born of trust in him. I beg 13 you, then, not to lose heart over my sufferings for you: indeed, they are your glory.

With this in mind, then, I kneel in prayer to the Father, from 14, 15 whom every family*a* in heaven and on earth takes its name, that out 16 of the treasures of his glory he may grant you strength and power through his Spirit in your inner being, that through faith Christ 17 may dwell in your hearts in love. With deep roots and firm foundations, may you be strong to grasp, with all God's people, what is the 18 breadth and length and height and depth of the love of Christ, and 19 to know it, though it is beyond knowledge. So may you attain to fullness of being, the fullness of God himself.*b*

Now to him who is able to do immeasurably more than all we 20 can ask or conceive, by the power which is at work among us, to 21 him be glory in the church and in Christ Jesus from generation to generation evermore! Amen.

I ENTREAT YOU, then—I, a prisoner for the Lord's sake: as God 4 has called you, live up to your calling. Be humble always and gentle, 2 and patient too. Be forbearing with one another and charitable. Spare no effort to make fast with bonds of peace the unity which the 3 Spirit gives. There is one body and one Spirit, as there is also one hope 4 held out in God's call to you; one Lord, one faith, one baptism; one 5, 6 God and Father of all, who is over all and through all and in all.

But each of us has been given his gift, his due portion of Christ's 7 bounty. Therefore Scripture says: 8

[a] *Or* his whole family. [b] *Or* the fullness which God requires.

331

'He ascended into the heights
With captives in his train;
He gave gifts to men.'

9 Now, the word 'ascended' implies that he also descended to the
10 lowest level, down to the very earth.[a] He who descended is no other
than he who ascended far above all heavens, so that he might fill the
11 universe. And these were his gifts: some to be apostles, some pro-
12 phets, some evangelists, some pastors and teachers, to equip God's
people for work in his service, to the building up of the body of
13 Christ. So shall we all at last attain to the unity inherent in our faith
and our knowledge of the Son of God—to mature manhood, mea-
14 sured by nothing less than the full stature of Christ. We are no
longer to be children, tossed by the waves and whirled about by
every fresh gust of teaching, dupes of crafty rogues and their deceit-
15 ful schemes. No, let us speak the truth in love; so shall we fully
16 grow up into Christ. He is the head, and on him the whole body
depends. Bonded and knit together by every constituent joint, the
whole frame grows through the due activity of each part, and builds
itself up in love.

17 This then is my word to you, and I urge it upon you in the Lord's
name. Give up living like pagans with their good-for-nothing
18 notions. Their wits are beclouded, they are strangers to the life
that is in God, because ignorance prevails among them and their
19 minds have grown hard as stone. Dead to all feeling, they have
abandoned themselves to vice, and stop at nothing to satisfy their
20, 21 foul desires. But that is not how you learned Christ. For were you
not told of him, were you not as Christians taught the truth as it is
22 in Jesus?—that, leaving your former way of life, you must lay aside
that old human nature which, deluded by its lusts, is sinking towards
23, 24 death. You must be made new in mind and spirit, and put on the
new nature of God's creating, which shows itself in the just and
devout life called for by the truth.

25 Then throw off falsehood; speak the truth to each other, for all of
us are the parts of one body.

26 If you are angry, do not let anger lead you into sin; do not let
27 sunset find you still nursing it; leave no loop-hole for the devil.

28 The thief must give up stealing, and instead work hard and honestly

[a] *Or* descended to the regions beneath the earth.

with his own hands, so that he may have something to share with the needy.

No bad language must pass your lips, but only what is good and 29 helpful to the occasion, so that it brings a blessing to those who hear it. And do not grieve the Holy Spirit of God, for that Spirit is the 30 seal with which you were marked for the day of our final liberation. Have done with spite and passion, all angry shouting and cursing, 31 and bad feeling of every kind.

Be generous to one another, tender-hearted, forgiving one another 32 as God in Christ forgave you.

In a word, as God's dear children, try to be like him, and live in 5 1, 2 love as Christ loved you, and gave himself up on your behalf as an offering and sacrifice whose fragrance is pleasing to God.

Fornication and indecency of any kind, or ruthless greed, must not 3 be so much as mentioned among you, as befits the people of God. No 4 coarse, stupid, or flippant talk; these things are out of place; you should rather be thanking God. For be very sure of this: no one 5 given to fornication or indecency, or the greed which makes an idol of gain, has any share in the kingdom of Christ and of God.

Let no one deceive you with shallow arguments; it is for all these 6 things that God's dreadful judgement is coming upon his rebel subjects. Have no part or lot with them. For though you were once 7, 8 all darkness, now as Christians you are light. Live like men who are at home in daylight, for where light is, there all goodness springs up, 9 all justice and truth. Make sure what would have the Lord's appro- 10 val; take no part in the barren deeds of darkness, but show them up 11 for what they are. The things they do in secret it would be shameful 12 even to mention. But everything, when once the light has shown it 13 up, is illumined, and everything thus illumined is all light. And so 14 the hymn says:

> 'Awake, sleeper,
> Rise from the dead,
> And Christ will shine upon you.'

Be most careful then how you conduct yourselves: like sensible 15 men, not like simpletons. Use the present opportunity to the full, 16 for these are evil days. So do not be fools, but try to understand 17 what the will of the Lord is. Do not give way to drunkenness and 18 the dissipation that goes with it, but let the Holy Spirit fill you:

19 speak to one another in psalms, hymns, and[a] songs; sing and make
20 music in your hearts to the Lord; and in the name of our Lord Jesus
Christ give thanks every day for everything to our God and Father.
21 Be subject to one another out of reverence for Christ.
22, 23 Wives, be subject to your husbands as to the Lord; for the man
is the head of the woman, just as Christ also is the head of the church.
24 Christ is, indeed, the Saviour of the body; but just as the church
is subject to Christ, so must women be to their husbands in
everything.
25 Husbands, love your wives, as Christ also loved the church and
26 gave himself up for it, to consecrate it, cleansing it by water and
27 word, so that he might present the church to himself all glorious,
with no stain or wrinkle or anything of the sort, but holy and without
28 blemish. In the same way men also are bound to love their wives,
as they love their own bodies. In loving his wife a man loves himself.
29 For no one ever hated his own body: on the contrary, he provides and
30 cares for it; and that is how Christ treats the church, because it is his
31 body, of which we are living parts. Thus it is that (in the words of
Scripture) 'a man shall leave his father and mother and shall be
32 joined to his wife, and the two shall become a single body'. It is a
great truth that is hidden here. I for my part refer it to Christ and
33 to the church, but it applies also individually: each of you must love
his wife as his very self; and the woman must see to it that she pays
her husband all respect.
6 Children, obey your parents, for it is right that you should.
2 'Honour your father and mother' is the first commandment with
3 a promise attached, in the words: 'that it may be well with you and
that you may live long in the land'.
4 You fathers, again, must not goad your children to resentment,
but give them the instruction, and the correction, which belong to
a Christian upbringing.
5 Slaves, obey your earthly masters with fear and trembling, single-
6 mindedly, as serving Christ. Do not offer merely the outward show
of service, to curry favour with men, but, as slaves of Christ, do
7 whole-heartedly the will of God. Give the cheerful service of those
8 who serve the Lord, not men. For you know that whatever good
each man may do, slave or free, will be repaid him by the Lord.
9 You masters, also, must do the same by them. Give up using

[a] *Some witnesses insert* spiritual, *as in Colossians 3.16.*

threats; remember you both have the same Master in heaven, and
he has no favourites.

    Finally then, find your strength in the Lord, in his mighty power. 10
Put on all the armour which God provides, so that you may be able 11
to stand firm against the devices of the devil. For our fight is not 12
against human foes, but against cosmic powers, against the authorities and potentates of this dark world, against the superhuman forces
of evil in the heavens. Therefore, take up God's armour; then you 13
will be able to stand your ground when things are at their worst,
to complete every task and still to stand. Stand firm, I say. Buckle 14
on the belt of truth; for coat of mail put on integrity; let the shoes 15
on your feet be the gospel of peace, to give you firm footing; and, 16
with all these, take up the great shield of faith, with which you will
be able to quench all the flaming arrows of the evil one. Take salva- 17
tion for helmet; for sword, take that which the Spirit gives you—the
words that come from God. Give yourselves wholly to prayer and 18
entreaty; pray on every occasion in the power of the Spirit. To this
end keep watch and persevere, always interceding for all God's
people; and pray for me, that I may be granted the right words when 19
I open my mouth, and may boldly and freely make known his hidden
purpose, for which I am an ambassador—in chains. Pray that I may 20
speak of it boldly, as it is my duty to speak.

    You will want to know about my affairs, and how I am; Tychicus 21
will give you all the news. He is our dear brother and trustworthy
helper in the Lord's work. I am sending him to you on purpose to 22
let you know all about us, and to put fresh heart into you.

    Peace to the brotherhood and love, with faith, from God the 23
Father and the Lord Jesus Christ. God's grace be with all who love 24
our Lord Jesus Christ, grace and immortality.[a]

        [a] *Or* who love...Christ with love imperishable.

THE
LETTER OF PAUL TO THE
PHILIPPIANS

The Apostle and His Friends

1 FROM PAUL and Timothy, servants of Christ Jesus, to all those of God's people, incorporate in Christ Jesus, who live at Philippi, including their bishops and deacons.

2 Grace to you and peace from God our Father and the Lord Jesus Christ.

3, 4 I thank my God whenever I think of you; and when I pray for
5 you all, my prayers are always joyful, because of the part you have
6 taken in the work of the Gospel from the first day until now. Of one thing I am certain: the One who started the good work in you
7 will bring it to completion by the Day of Christ Jesus. It is indeed only right that I should feel like this about you all, because you hold me in such affection, and because, when I lie in prison or appear in the dock to vouch for the truth of the Gospel, you all share in the
8 privilege that is mine.*a* God knows how I long for you all, with
9 the deep yearning of Christ Jesus himself. And this is my prayer, that your love may grow ever richer and richer in knowledge and
10 insight of every kind, and may thus bring you the gift of true discrimination.*b* Then on the Day of Christ you will be flawless and
11 without blame, reaping the full harvest of righteousness that comes through Jesus Christ, to the glory and praise of God.

12 Friends, I want you to understand that the work of the Gospel has been helped on, rather than hindered, by this business of mine.
13 My imprisonment in Christ's cause has become common knowledge to all at headquarters*c* here, and indeed among the public at large;
14 and it has given confidence to most of our fellow-Christians to speak the word of God fearlessly and with extraordinary courage.

---

[a] *Or* I am justified in taking this view about you all, because I hold you in closest union, as those who, when I lie...of the Gospel, all share in the privilege that is mine.
[b] *Or* may teach you by experience what things are most worth while. [c] *Or* to all the imperial guard, *or* to all at the Residency (*Greek* Praetorium).

Some, indeed, proclaim Christ in a jealous and quarrelsome spirit; 15
others proclaim him in true goodwill, and these are moved by love 16
for me; they know that it is to defend the Gospel that I am where
I am. But the others, moved by personal rivalry, present Christ 17
from mixed motives, meaning to stir up fresh trouble for me as I
lie in prison.ᵃ What does it matter? One way or another, in pretence 18
or in sincerity, Christ is set forth, and for that I rejoice.

Yes, and rejoice I will, knowing well that the issue of it all will be 19
my deliverance, because you are praying for me and the Spirit of
Jesus Christ is given me for support.ᵇ For, as I passionately hope, 20
I shall have no cause to be ashamed, but shall speak so boldly that
now as always the greatness of Christ will shine out clearly in my
person, whether through my life or through my death. For to me 21
life is Christ, and death gain; but what if my living on in the body 22
may serve some good purpose? Which then am I to choose? I cannot
tell. I am torn two ways: what I should like is to depart and be with 23
Christ; that is better by far; but for your sake there is greater need 24
for me to stay on in the body. This indeed I know for certain: I shall 25
stay, and stand by you all to help you forward and to add joy to your
faith, so that when I am with you again, your pride in me may be 26
unbounded in Christ Jesus.

Only, let your conduct be worthy of the gospel of Christ, so that 27
whether I come and see you for myself or hear about you from a
distance, I may know that you are standing firm, one in spirit, one
in mind, contending as one man for the gospel faith, meeting your 28
opponents without so much as a tremor. This is a sure sign to them
that their doom is sealed, but a sign of your salvation, and one
afforded by God himself; for you have been granted the privilege 29
not only of believing in Christ but also of suffering for him. You and 30
I are engaged in the same contest; you saw me in it once, and, as
you hear, I am in it still.

IF THEN our common life in Christ yields anything to stir the heart, 2
any loving consolation, any sharing of the Spirit, any warmth of
affection or compassion, fill up my cup of happiness by thinking and 2
feeling alike, with the same love for one another, the same turn of
mind, and a common care for unity. Rivalry and personal vanity 3

[a] Or meaning to make use of my imprisonment to stir up fresh trouble. [b] Or
supplies me with all I need.

should have no place among you, but you should humbly reckon
4 others better than yourselves. You must look to each other's interest
and not merely to your own.

5   Let your bearing towards one another arise out of your life in Christ
6 Jesus.ᵃ For the divine nature was his from the first; yet he did not
7 think to snatch at equality with God,ᵇ but made himself nothing,
8 assuming the nature of a slave. Bearing the human likeness, revealed
in human shape, he humbled himself, and in obedience accepted
9 even death—death on a cross. Therefore God raised him to the
10 heights and bestowed on him the name above all names, that at the
name of Jesus every knee should bow—in heaven, on earth, and in
11 the depths—and every tongue confess, 'Jesus Christ is Lord', to
the glory of God the Father.

12   So you too, my friends, must be obedient, as always; even more,
now that I am away, than when I was with you. You must work out
13 your own salvation in fear and trembling; for it is God who works
in you, inspiring both the will and the deed, for his own chosen
purpose.

14, 15   Do all you have to do without complaint or wrangling. Show
yourselves guileless and above reproach, faultless children of God
in a warped and crooked generation, in which you shineᶜ like stars
16 in a dark worldᵈ and proffer the word of life.ᵉ Thus you will be my
pride on the Day of Christ, proof that I did not run my race in vain,
17 or work in vain. But if my life-blood is to crown that sacrifice which
is the offering up of your faith, I am glad of it, and I share my glad-
18 ness with you all. Rejoice, you no less than I, and let us share
our joy.

19 I HOPE (under the Lord Jesus) to send Timothy to you soon;
20 it will cheer me to hear news of you. There is no one else here who
sees things as I do, and takesᶠ a genuine interest in your concerns;
21 they are all bent on their own ends, not on the cause of Christ Jesus.
22 But Timothy's record is known to you: you know that he has been
at my side in the service of the Gospel like a son working under his
23 father. Timothy, then, I hope to send as soon as ever I can see how

[a] *Or* Have that bearing towards one another which was also found in Christ Jesus.
[b] *Or* yet he did not prize his equality with God. [c] *Or* ...generation. Shine out
among them... [d] *Or* in the firmament. [e] *Or* as the very principle of its life. [f] *Or*
no one else here like him, who takes...

things are going with me; and I am confident, under the Lord, that 24
I shall myself be coming before long.

I feel also I must send our brother Epaphroditus, my fellow- 25
worker and comrade, whom you commissioned to minister to my
needs. He has been missing all of you sadly, and has been distressed 26
that you heard he was ill. (He was indeed dangerously ill, but God 27
was merciful to him, and merciful no less to me, to spare me sorrow
upon sorrow.) For this reason I am all the more eager to send him, 28
to give you the happiness of seeing him again, and to relieve my
sorrow. Welcome him then in the fellowship of the Lord with whole- 29
hearted delight. You should honour men like him; in Christ's cause 30
he came near to death, risking his life to render me the service you
could not give.

And now, friends, farewell; I wish you joy in the Lord.   3

To REPEAT what I have written to you before is no trouble to me,
and it is a safeguard for you. Beware of those dogs and their mal- 2
practices. Beware of those who insist on mutilation—'circumcision'
I will not call it; we are the circumcised, we whose worship is 3
spiritual,*a* whose pride is in Christ Jesus, and who put no confidence
in anything external. Not that I am without grounds myself even 4
for confidence of that kind. If anyone thinks to base his claims on
externals, I could make a stronger case for myself: circumcised on 5
my eighth day, Israelite by race, of the tribe of Benjamin, a Hebrew
born and bred;*b* in my attitude to the law, a Pharisee; in pious zeal, 6
a persecutor of the church; in legal rectitude, faultless. But all such 7
assets I have written off because of Christ. I would say more: I 8
count everything sheer loss, because all is far outweighed by the
gain of knowing Christ Jesus my Lord, for whose sake I did in fact
lose everything. I count it so much garbage,*c* for the sake of gaining
Christ and finding myself incorporate in him, with no righteous- 9
ness of my own, no legal rectitude, but the righteousness which
comes*d* from faith in Christ, given by God in response to faith.
All I care for is to know Christ, to experience the power of his 10
resurrection, and to share his sufferings, in growing conformity

[a] *Some witnesses read* who worship God in the spirit; *others read* who worship by the
Spirit of God. [b] *Or* a Hebrew-speaking Jew of a Hebrew-speaking family. [c] *Or*
dung. [d] *Or* and in him finding that, though I have no righteousness of my own, no
legal rectitude, I have the righteousness which comes...

11 with his death, if only I may finally arrive at the resurrection from the dead.

12 It is not to be thought that I have already achieved all this. I have not yet reached perfection, but I press on, hoping to take hold of that

13 for which Christ once took hold of me. My friends, I do not reckon myself to have got hold of it yet. All I can say is this: forgetting what is behind me, and reaching out for that which lies ahead,

14 I press towards the goal to win the prize which is God's call to the life above, in Christ Jesus.

15 Let us then keep to this way of thinking, those of us who are mature. If there is any point on which you think differently, this

16 also God will make plain to you. Only let our conduct be consistent with the level we have already reached.

17 Agree together, my friends, to follow my example. You have us

18 for a model; watch those whose way of life conforms to it. For, as I have often told you, and now tell you with tears in my eyes, there are many whose way of life makes them enemies of the cross of

19 Christ. They are heading for destruction, appetite is their god, and

20 they glory in their shame. Their minds are set on earthly things. We, by contrast, are citizens of heaven, and from heaven we expect our

21 deliverer to come, the Lord Jesus Christ. He will transfigure the body belonging to our humble state, and give it a form like that of his own resplendent body, by the very power which enables him to

4 make all things subject to himself. Therefore, my friends, beloved friends whom I long for, my joy, my crown, stand thus firm in the Lord, my beloved!

2 I beg Euodia, and I beg Syntyche, to agree together in the Lord's

3 fellowship. Yes, and you too, my loyal comrade, I ask you to help these women, who shared my struggles in the cause of the Gospel, with Clement and my other fellow-workers, whose[a] names are in the book of life.

4 Farewell; I wish you all joy in the Lord. I will say it again: all joy be yours.

5 Let your magnanimity be manifest to all.

6 The Lord is near; have no anxiety, but in everything make your requests known to God in prayer and petition with thanksgiving.

7 Then the peace of God, which is beyond our utmost understanding,[b]

[a] *Some witnesses read* my fellow-workers, and the others whose... [b] *Or* of far more worth than human reasoning.

will keep guard over your hearts and your thoughts, in Christ Jesus.

And now, my friends, all that is true, all that is noble, all that is 8 just and pure, all that is lovable and gracious,*a* whatever is excellent and admirable—fill all your thoughts with these things.

The lessons I taught you, the tradition I have passed on, all that 9 you heard me say or saw me do, put into practice; and the God of peace will be with you.

IT IS A GREAT JOY to me, in the Lord, that after so long your care 10 for me has now blossomed afresh. You did care about me before for that matter; it was opportunity that you lacked. Not that I am 11 alluding to want, for I have learned to find resources in myself whatever my circumstances. I know what it is to be brought low, 12 and I know what it is to have plenty. I have been very thoroughly initiated into the human lot with all its ups and downs—fullness and hunger, plenty and want. I have strength for anything through him 13 who gives me power. But it was kind of you to share the burden of 14 my troubles.

As you know yourselves, Philippians, in the early days of my 15 mission, when I set out from Macedonia, you were the only congregation that were my partners in payments and receipts; for even at 16 Thessalonica you contributed to my needs, not once but twice over. Do not think I set my heart upon the gift; all I care for is the profit 17 accruing to you. However, here I give you my receipt for every- 18 thing—for more than everything; I am paid in full, now that I have received from Epaphroditus what you sent. It is a fragrant offering, an acceptable sacrifice, pleasing to God. And my God will supply 19 all your wants out of the magnificence of his riches in Christ Jesus. To our God and Father be glory for endless ages! Amen. 20

Give my greetings, in the fellowship of Christ, to each one of God's 21 people. The brothers who are now with me send their greetings to you, and so do all God's people here, particularly those who belong 22 to the imperial establishment.

The grace of our Lord Jesus Christ be with your spirit. 23

[a] *Or* of good repute.

341

THE
LETTER OF PAUL TO THE
COLOSSIANS

The Centre of Christian Belief

1 FROM PAUL, apostle of Christ Jesus commissioned by the
2 will of God, and our colleague Timothy, to God's people at
Colossae, brothers in the faith, incorporate in Christ.
Grace to you and peace from God our Father.

3 In all our prayers to God, the Father of our Lord Jesus Christ,
4 we thank him for you, because we have heard of the faith you hold
5 in Christ Jesus, and the love you bear towards all God's people. Both
spring from the hope stored up for you in heaven—that hope of which
6 you learned when the message of the true Gospel first came to you.
In the same way it is coming to men the whole world over; everywhere it is growing and bearing fruit as it does among you, and has
done since the day when you heard of the graciousness of God and
7 recognized it for what in truth it is. You were taught this by Epaphras,
our dear fellow-servant, a trusted worker for Christ on our*a* behalf,
8 and it is he who has brought us the news of your God-given love.*b*
9 For this reason, ever since the day we heard of it, we have not
ceased to pray for you. We ask God that you may receive from him
all wisdom and spiritual understanding for full insight into his will,
10 so that your manner of life may be worthy of the Lord and entirely
pleasing to him. We pray that you may bear fruit in active goodness
11 of every kind, and grow in the knowledge of God. May he strengthen
you, in his glorious might, with ample power to meet whatever comes
12 with fortitude, patience, and joy; and to give thanks*c* to the Father
who has made you fit to share the heritage of God's people in the
realm of light.

13 He rescued us from the domain of darkness and brought us away
14 into the kingdom of his dear Son, in whom our release is secured
15 and our sins forgiven. He is the image of the invisible God; his is

[a] *Some witnesses read* your. [b] *Or* your love within the fellowship of the Spirit.
[c] *Or* with fortitude and patience, and to give joyful thanks...

the primacy over[a] all created things. In him everything in heaven 16 and on earth was created, not only things visible but also the invisible orders of thrones, sovereignties, authorities, and powers: the whole universe has been created through him and for him. And he exists 17 before everything, and all things are held together in him. He is, 18 moreover, the head of the body, the church. He is its origin, the first to return from the dead, to be in all things alone supreme. For 19 in him the complete being of God, by God's own choice, came to dwell. Through him God chose to reconcile the whole universe to 20 himself, making peace through the shedding of his blood upon the cross—to reconcile all things, whether on earth or in heaven, through him alone.

Formerly you were yourselves estranged from God; you were his 21 enemies in heart and mind, and your deeds were evil. But now by 22 Christ's death in his body of flesh and blood God has reconciled you to himself, so that he may present you before himself as dedicated men, without blemish and innocent in his sight. Only you must 23 continue in your faith, firm on your foundations, never to be dislodged from the hope offered in the gospel which you heard. This is the gospel which has been proclaimed in the whole creation under heaven; and I, Paul, have become its minister.

It is now my happiness to suffer for you. This is my way of 24 helping to complete, in my poor human flesh, the full tale of Christ's afflictions still to be endured, for the sake of his body which is the church. I became its servant by virtue of the task assigned to me by 25 God for your benefit: to deliver his message in full; to announce 26 the secret hidden for long ages and through many generations, but now disclosed to God's people, to whom it was his will to make it 27 known—to make known how rich and glorious it is among all nations. The secret is this: Christ in[b] you, the hope of a glory to come.

He it is whom we proclaim. We admonish everyone without 28 distinction, we instruct everyone in all the ways of wisdom, so as to present each one of you as a mature member of Christ's body. To this end I am toiling strenuously with all the energy and power 29 of Christ at work in me. For I want you to know how strenuous 2 are my exertions for you and the Laodiceans and all who have never set eyes on me. I want them to continue in good heart and in the 2

[a] Or image of the invisible God, born before... [b] Or among.

unity of love, and to come to the full wealth of conviction which understanding brings, and grasp God's secret. That secret is Christ
3 himself; in him lie hidden all God's treasures of wisdom and know-
4 ledge. I tell you this to save you from being talked*ᵃ* into error by
5 specious arguments. For though absent in body, I am with you in spirit, and rejoice to see your orderly array and the firm front which your faith in Christ presents.

6 THEREFORE, SINCE Jesus was delivered to you as Christ and
7 Lord, live your lives in union with him. Be rooted in him; be built in him; be consolidated in the faith you were taught;*ᵇ* let your hearts
8 overflow with thankfulness. Be on your guard; do not let your minds be captured by hollow and delusive speculations, based on traditions of man-made teaching and centred on the elemental spirits*ᶜ* of the world and not on Christ.
9 For it is in Christ that the complete being of the Godhead dwells
10 embodied,*ᵈ* and in him you have been brought to completion. Every
11 power and authority in the universe is subject to him as Head. In him also you were circumcised, not in a physical sense, but by being divested of the lower nature; this is Christ's way of circumcision.
12 For in baptism*ᵉ* you were buried with him, in baptism also you were raised to life with him through your faith in the active power of God
13 who raised him from the dead. And although you were dead because of your sins and because you were morally uncircumcised, he has made you alive with Christ. For he has forgiven us all our sins;
14 he has cancelled the bond which pledged us to the decrees of the law. It stood against us, but he has set it aside, nailing it to the cross.
15 On that cross he discarded the cosmic powers and authorities like a garment; he made a public spectacle of them and led them*ᶠ* as captives in his triumphal procession.

16 ALLOW NO ONE therefore to take you to task about what you eat or drink, or over the observance of festival, new moon, or sabbath.
17 These are no more than a shadow of what was to come; the solid

[a] *Or* What I mean is this: no one must talk you... [b] *Or* by your faith, as you were taught. [c] *Or* rudimentary notions. [d] *Or* corporately. [e] *Or* ...nature, in the very circumcision of Christ himself; for in baptism... [f] *Or* he stripped himself of his physical body, and thereby boldly made a spectacle of the cosmic powers and authorities, and led them...; *or* he despoiled the cosmic powers and authorities, and boldly made a spectacle of them, leading them...

reality is Christ's. You are not to be disqualified by the decision of 18
people who go in for self-mortification and angel-worship, and try
to enter into some vision of their own. Such people, bursting with the
futile conceit of worldly minds, lose hold upon the Head; yet it is 19
from the Head that the whole body, with all its joints and ligaments,
receives its supplies, and thus knit together grows according to God's
design.

Did you not die with Christ and pass beyond reach of the elemen- 20
tal spirits*a* of the world? Then why behave as though you were still
living the life of the world? Why let people dictate to you: 'Do not 21
handle this, do not taste that, do not touch the other'—all of them 22
things that must perish as soon as they are used? That is to follow
merely human injunctions and teaching. True, it has an air of 23
wisdom, with its forced piety, its self-mortification, and its severity
to the body; but it is of no use at all in combating sensuality.

Were you not raised to life with Christ? Then aspire to the realm 3
above, where Christ is, seated at the right hand of God, and let 2
your thoughts dwell on that higher realm, not on this earthly life.
I repeat, you died; and now your life lies hidden with Christ in God. 3
When Christ, who is our life, is manifested, then you too will be 4
manifested with him in glory.

Then put to death those parts of you which belong to the earth— 5
fornication, indecency, lust, foul cravings, and the ruthless greed
which is nothing less than idolatry. Because of these, God's dreadful 6
judgement is impending; and in the life you once lived these are the 7
ways you yourselves followed. But now you yourselves must lay 8
aside all anger, passion, malice, cursing, filthy talk—have done with
them! Stop lying to one another, now that you have discarded the 9
old nature with its deeds and have put on the new nature, which is 10
being constantly renewed in the image of its Creator and brought
to know God. There is no question here of Greek and Jew, circum- 11
cised and uncircumcised, barbarian, Scythian, freeman, slave; but
Christ is all, and is in all.

Then put on the garments that suit God's chosen people, his own, 12
his beloved: compassion, kindness, humility, gentleness, patience.
Be forbearing with one another, and forgiving, where any of you 13
has cause for complaint: you must forgive as the Lord forgave you.
To crown all, there must be love, to bind all together and complete 14

[a] *Or* rudimentary notions.

15 the whole. Let Christ's peace be arbiter in your hearts: to this peace you were called as members of a single body. And be filled with
16 gratitude. Let the message of Christ dwell among you in all its richness. Instruct and admonish each other with the utmost wisdom. Sing thankfully in your hearts to God,[a] with psalms and hymns and
17 spiritual songs. Whatever you are doing, whether you speak or act, do everything in the name of the Lord Jesus, giving thanks to God the Father through him.

18 WIVES, BE SUBJECT to your husbands: that is your Christian duty.
19, 20 Husbands, love your wives and do not be harsh with them. Children, obey your parents in everything, for that is pleasing to God and is
21 the Christian way. Fathers, do not exasperate your children, for
22 fear they grow disheartened. Slaves, give entire obedience to your earthly masters, not merely with an outward show of service, to curry favour with men, but with single-mindedness, out of rever-
23 ence for the Lord. Whatever you are doing, put your whole heart
24 into it, as if you were doing it for the Lord and not for men, knowing that there is a Master who will give you your heritage as a reward for your service. Christ is the Master whose slaves you
25 must be. Dishonesty will be requited, and he has no favourites.
4 Masters, be just and fair to your slaves, knowing that you too have a Master in heaven.
2, 3 Persevere in prayer, with mind awake and thankful heart; and include a prayer for us, that God may give us an opening for preaching, to tell the secret of Christ; that indeed is why I am now in
4 prison. Pray that I may make the secret plain, as it is my duty to do.
5 Behave wisely towards those outside your own number; use the
6 present opportunity to the full. Let your conversation be always gracious, and never insipid; study how best to talk with each person you meet.

7 YOU WILL HEAR all about my affairs from Tychicus, our dear brother and trustworthy helper and fellow-servant in the Lord's
8 work. I am sending him to you on purpose to let you know all about
9 us and to put fresh heart into you. With him comes Onesimus, our trustworthy and dear brother, who is one of yourselves. They will tell you all the news here.

[a] *Some witnesses read* the Lord.

346

Aristarchus, Christ's captive like myself, sends his greetings; so 10 does Mark, the cousin of Barnabas (you have had instructions about him; if he comes, make him welcome), and Jesus Justus. Of the 11 Jewish Christians, these are the only ones who work with me for the kingdom of God, and they have been a great comfort to me. Greet- 12 ings from Epaphras, servant of Christ, who is one of yourselves. He prays hard for you all the time, that you may stand fast, ripe in conviction*a* and wholly devoted to doing God's will. For I can 13 vouch for him, that he works tirelessly for you and the people at Laodicea and Hierapolis. Greetings to you from our dear friend 14 Luke, the doctor, and from Demas. Give our greetings to the 15 brothers at Laodicea, and Nympha*b* and the congregation at her*c* house. And when this letter is read among you, see that it is also 16 read to the congregation at Laodicea, and that you in return read the one from Laodicea. This special word to Archippus: 'Attend 17 to the duty entrusted to you in the Lord's service, and discharge it to the full.'

This greeting is in my own hand—PAUL. Remember I am in 18 prison. God's grace be with you.

[a] *Or* stand fast, mature and complete... [b] *Or* Nymphas. [c] *Some witnesses read* his.

THE
FIRST LETTER OF PAUL TO THE
THESSALONIANS

Hope and Discipline

1 FROM PAUL, Silvanus, and Timothy to the congregation of Thessalonians who belong to God the Father and the Lord Jesus Christ.
Grace to you and peace.

2 We always thank God for you all, and mention you in our prayers
3 continually. We call to mind, before our God and Father, how your faith has shown itself in action, your love in labour, and your hope of
4 our Lord Jesus Christ in fortitude. We are certain, brothers beloved
5 by God, that he has chosen you and that^{*a*} when we brought you the Gospel, we brought it not in mere words but in the power of the Holy Spirit, and with strong conviction, as you know well. That is the kind of men we were at Thessalonica, and it was for your sake.

6 And you, in your turn, followed the example set by us and by the Lord; the welcome you gave the message meant grave suffering
7 for you, yet you rejoiced in the Holy Spirit; thus you have become
8 a model for all believers in Macedonia and in Achaia. From Thessalonica the word of the Lord rang out; and not in Macedonia and Achaia alone, but everywhere your faith in God has reached men's
9 ears. No words of ours are needed, for they themselves spread the news of our visit to you and its effect: how you turned from idols,
10 to be servants of the living and true God, and to wait expectantly for the appearance from heaven of his Son Jesus, whom he raised from the dead, Jesus our deliverer from the terrors of judgement to come.

2 You know for yourselves, brothers, that our visit to you was not
2 fruitless. Far from it; after all the injury and outrage which to your knowledge we had suffered at Philippi, we declared the gospel of God to you frankly and fearlessly, by the help of our God. A hard
3 struggle it was. Indeed, the appeal we make never springs from

[*a*] *Or* . . . chosen you, because. . .

348

error or base motive; there is no attempt to deceive; but God has 4
approved us as fit to be entrusted with the Gospel, and on those
terms we speak. We do not curry favour with men; we seek only the
favour of God, who is continually testing our hearts. Our words have 5
never been flattering words, as you have cause to know; nor, as God
is our witness, have they ever been a cloak for greed. We have never 6
sought honour from men, from you or from anyone else, although as
Christ's own envoys we might have made our weight felt; but we 7
were as gentle with you as a nurse caring fondly for her children.
With such yearning love we chose to impart to you not only the 8
gospel of God but our very selves, so dear had you become to us.
Remember, brothers, how we toiled and drudged. We worked for 9
a living night and day, rather than be a burden to anyone, while
we proclaimed before you the good news of God.

We call you to witness, yes and God himself, how devout and 10
just and blameless was our behaviour towards you who are believers.
As you well know, we dealt with you one by one, as a father deals 11
with his children, appealing to you by encouragement, as well as by
solemn injunctions, to live lives worthy of the God who calls you 12
into his kingdom and glory.

This is why we thank God continually, because when we handed 13
on God's message, you received it, not as the word of men, but as
what it truly is, the very word of God at*a* work in you who hold
the faith. You have fared like the congregations in Judaea, God's 14
people in Christ Jesus. You have been treated by your countrymen
as they are treated by the Jews, who killed the Lord Jesus and 15
the prophets*b* and drove us out, the Jews who are heedless of God's
will and enemies of their fellow-men, hindering us from speaking 16
to the Gentiles to lead them to salvation. All this time they have
been making up the full measure of their guilt, and now retribution
has overtaken them for good and all.*c*

MY FRIENDS, when for a short spell you were lost to us—lost to 17
sight, not to our hearts—we were exceedingly anxious to see you
again. So we did propose to come to Thessalonica—I, Paul, more 18
than once—but Satan thwarted us. For after all, what hope or joy 19
or crown of pride is there for us, what indeed but you, when we stand

[a] *Or* word of God who is at... [b] *Some witnesses read* their own prophets. [c] *Or*
now at last retribution has overtaken them.

20 before our Lord Jesus at his coming? It is you who are indeed our glory and our joy.

3 So when we could bear it no longer, we decided to remain alone
2 at Athens, and sent Timothy, our brother and God's fellow-worker*a* in the service of the gospel of Christ, to encourage you to stand
3 firm for the faith and, under all these hardships, not to be shaken;*b*
4 for you know that this is our appointed lot. When we were with you we warned you that we were bound to suffer hardship; and so it
5 has turned out, as you know. And thus it was that when I could bear it no longer, I sent to find out about your faith, fearing that the tempter might have tempted you and my labour might be lost.

6 But now Timothy has just arrived from Thessalonica, bringing good news of your faith and love. He tells us that you always think
7 kindly of us, and are as anxious to see us as we are to see you. And so in all our difficulties and hardships your faith reassures us about
8 you. It is the breath of life to us that you stand firm in the Lord.
9 What thanks can we return to God for you? What thanks for all the
10 joy you have brought us, making us rejoice before our God while we pray most earnestly night and day to be allowed to see you again and to mend your faith where it falls short?

11 May our God and Father himself, and our Lord Jesus, bring us
12 direct to you; and may the Lord make your love mount and overflow towards one another and towards all, as our love does towards you.
13 May he make your hearts firm, so that you may stand before our God and Father holy and faultless when our Lord Jesus comes with all those who are his own.

4 AND NOW, MY FRIENDS, we have one thing to beg and pray of you, by our fellowship with the Lord Jesus. We passed on to you the tradition of the way we must live to please God; you are indeed already following it, but we beg you to do so yet more thoroughly.
2 For you know what orders we gave you, in the name of the Lord
3 Jesus. This is the will of God, that you should be holy: you must
4 abstain from fornication; each one of you must learn to gain mastery
5 over his body, to hallow and honour it, not giving way to lust like
6 the pagans who are ignorant of God; and no man must do his

[a] *Or* and fellow-worker for God; *one witness has simply* and fellow-worker. [b] *Or* beguiled away.

brother wrong in this matter,^a or invade his rights, because, as we
told you before with all emphasis, the Lord punishes all such offences.
For God called us to holiness, not to impurity. Anyone therefore 7, 8
who flouts these rules is flouting, not man, but God who bestows
upon you his Holy Spirit.

About love for our brotherhood you need no words of mine, for 9
you are yourselves taught by God to love one another, and you are 10
in fact practising this rule of love towards all your fellow-Christians
throughout Macedonia. Yet we appeal to you, brothers, to do better
still. Let it be your ambition to keep calm and look after your own 11
business, and to work with your hands, as we ordered you, so that 12
you may command the respect of those outside your own number,
and at the same time may never be in want.

WE WANT YOU not to remain in ignorance, brothers, about those 13
who sleep in death; you should not grieve like the rest of men, who
have no hope. We believe that Jesus died and rose again; and so it 14
will be for those who died as Christians; God will bring them to life
with Jesus.^b

For this we tell you as the Lord's word: we who are left alive 15
until the Lord comes shall not forestall those who have died; because 16
at the word of command, at the sound of the archangel's voice and
God's trumpet-call, the Lord himself will descend from heaven;
first the Christian dead will rise, then we who are left alive shall join 17
them, caught up in clouds to meet the Lord in the air. Thus we
shall always be with the Lord. Console one another, then, with these 18
words.

About dates and times, my friends, we need not write to you, 5
for you know perfectly well that the Day of the Lord comes like 2
a thief in the night. While they are talking of peace and security, all 3
at once calamity is upon them, sudden as the pangs that come upon
a woman with child; and there will be no escape. But you, my 4
friends, are not in the dark, that the day should overtake you like
a thief.^c You are all children of light, children of day. We do not 5
belong to night or darkness, and we must not sleep like the rest, 6
but keep awake and sober. Sleepers sleep at night, and drunkards 7
are drunk at night, but we, who belong to daylight, must keep sober, 8

[a] *Or* must overreach his brother in his business (*or* in lawsuits). [b] *Or* will bring
them in company with Jesus. [c] *Some witnesses read* thieves.

armed with faith and love for breastplate, and the hope of salvation
9 for helmet. For God has not destined us to the terrors of judgement,
but to the full attainment of salvation through our Lord Jesus Christ.
10 He died for us so that we, awake or asleep, might live in company
11 with him. Therefore hearten one another, fortify one another—as
indeed you do.

12 WE BEG YOU, brothers, to acknowledge those who are working so
hard among you, and in the Lord's fellowship are your leaders and
13 counsellors. Hold them in the highest possible esteem and affection
for the work they do.

14   You must live at peace among yourselves. And we would urge
you, brothers, to admonish the careless, encourage the faint-hearted,
support the weak, and to be very patient with them all.

15   See to it that no one pays back wrong for wrong, but always aim
at doing the best you can for each other and for all men.

16, 17, 18   Be always joyful; pray continually; give thanks whatever happens;
for this is what God in Christ wills for you.

19, 20   Do not stifle inspiration, and do not despise prophetic utterances,
21 but bring them all to the test and then keep what is good in them
22 and avoid the bad of whatever kind.[a]

23   May God himself, the God of peace, make you holy in every part,
and keep you sound in spirit, soul, and body, without fault when our
24 Lord Jesus Christ comes. He who calls you is to be trusted; he will
do it.

25   Brothers, pray for us also.

26   Greet all our brothers with the kiss of peace.

27   I adjure you by the Lord to have this letter read to the whole
brotherhood.

28   The grace of our Lord Jesus Christ be with you!

[a] *Or* ...utterances. Put everything to the test; keep hold of what is good and avoid
every kind of evil.

THE
SECOND LETTER OF PAUL TO THE
THESSALONIANS

Hope and Discipline

FROM PAUL, Silvanus, and Timothy to the congregation 1
of Thessalonians who belong to God our Father and the Lord
Jesus Christ.

Grace to you and peace from God the Father and the Lord Jesus 2
Christ.

Our thanks are always due to God for you, brothers. It is right 3
that we should thank him, because your faith increases mightily,
and the love you have, each for all and all for each, grows ever
greater. Indeed we boast about you ourselves among the con- 4
gregations of God's people, because your faith remains so steadfast under all your persecutions, and all the troubles you endure.
See how this brings out the justice of God's judgement. It will 5
prove you worthy of the kingdom of God, for which indeed you are
suffering.

It is surely just that God should balance the account by sending 6
trouble to those who trouble you, and relief to you who are troubled, 7
and to us as well, when our Lord Jesus Christ is revealed from heaven
with his mighty angels in blazing fire. Then he will do justice upon 8
those who refuse to acknowledge God and upon those who will not
obey*a* the gospel of our Lord Jesus. They will suffer the punishment 9
of eternal ruin, cut off from the presence of the Lord and the splendour of his might, when on that great Day he comes to be glorified 10
among his own and adored among all believers; for you did indeed
believe the testimony we brought you.

With this in mind we pray for you always, that our God may 11
count you worthy of his calling, and mightily bring to fulfilment every
good purpose and every act inspired by faith, so that the name of our 12
Lord Jesus may be glorified in you, and you in him, according to
the grace of our God and the Lord Jesus Christ.

[a] *Or* justice upon those who refuse...and will not obey...

2 AND NOW, BROTHERS, about the coming of our Lord Jesus Christ
2 and his gathering of us to himself: I beg you, do not suddenly lose
your heads or alarm yourselves, whether at some oracular utterance,
or pronouncement, or some letter purporting to come from us,
3 alleging that the Day of the Lord is already here. Let no one deceive
you in any way whatever. That day cannot come before the final
rebellion against God, when wickedness will be revealed in human
4 form, the man doomed to perdition. He is the Enemy. He rises in his
pride against every god, so called, every object of men's worship, and
even takes his seat in the temple of God claiming to be a god himself.
5 You cannot but remember that I told you this while I was still
6 with you; you must now be aware of the restraining hand which
7 ensures that he shall be revealed only at the proper time. For already
the secret power of wickedness is at work, secret only for the present
8 until the Restrainer disappears from the scene. And then he will be
revealed, that wicked man whom the Lord Jesus will destroy with
the breath of his mouth, and annihilate by the radiance of his coming.
9 But the coming of that wicked man is the work of Satan. It will be
10 attended by all the powerful signs and miracles of the Lie, and all
the deception that sinfulness can impose on those doomed to destruction. Destroyed they shall be, because they did not open their minds
11 to love of the truth, so as to find salvation. Therefore God puts them
12 under a delusion, which works upon them to believe the lie, so that
they may all be brought to judgement, all who do not believe the
truth but make sinfulness their deliberate choice.

13 BUT WE ARE bound to thank God for you, brothers beloved by the
Lord, because from the beginning of time God chose you[a] to find
salvation in the Spirit that consecrates you, and in the truth that
14 you believe. It was for this that he called you through the gospel
we brought, so that you might possess for your own the splendour of
our Lord Jesus Christ.
15 Stand firm, then, brothers, and hold fast to the traditions which
16 you have learned from us by word or by letter. And may our Lord
Jesus Christ himself and God our Father, who has shown us such
love, and in his grace has given us such unfailing encouragement
17 and such bright hopes, still encourage and fortify you in every good
deed and word!

[a] *Some witnesses read* because God chose you as his firstfruits...

And now, brothers, pray for us, that the word of the Lord may have 3
everywhere the swift and glorious course that it has had among you,
and that we may be rescued from wrong-headed and wicked men; 2
for it is not all who have faith. But the Lord is to be trusted, and he 3
will fortify you and guard you from the evil one. We feel perfect 4
confidence about you, in the Lord, that you are doing and will
continue to do what we order. May the Lord direct your hearts 5
towards God's love and the steadfastness of Christ!

These are our orders to you, brothers, in the name of our Lord 6
Jesus Christ: hold aloof from every Christian brother who falls into
idle habits, and does not follow the tradition you received from us.
You know yourselves how you ought to copy our example: we were 7
no idlers among you; we did not accept board and lodging from 8
anyone without paying for it; we toiled and drudged, we worked
for a living night and day, rather than be a burden to any of you—
not because we have not the right to maintenance, but to set an 9
example for you to imitate. For even during our stay with you we 10
laid down the rule: the man who will not work shall not eat. We 11
mention this because we hear that some of your number are idling
their time away, minding everybody's business but their own. To 12
all such we give these orders, and we appeal to them in the name of
the Lord Jesus Christ to work quietly for their living.

My friends, never tire of doing right. If anyone disobeys our 13, 14
instructions given by letter, mark him well, and have no dealings
with him until he is ashamed of himself. I do not mean treat him as 15
an enemy, but give him friendly advice, as one of the family. May the 16
Lord of peace himself give you peace at all times and in all ways.[a]
The Lord be with you all.

The greeting is in my own hand, signed with my name, PAUL; 17
this authenticates all my letters; this is how I write. The grace[b] of 18
our Lord Jesus Christ be with you all.

[a] *Some witnesses read* at all times, wherever you may be. [b] *Or* ...letters. My message is this: the grace...

THE
FIRST LETTER OF PAUL TO
TIMOTHY

Church Order

1 FROM PAUL, apostle of Christ Jesus by command of God
2 our Saviour and Christ Jesus our hope, to Timothy his true-
born son in the faith.

Grace, mercy, and peace to you from God the Father and Christ
Jesus our Lord.

3 When I was starting for Macedonia, I urged you to stay on at
Ephesus. You were to command certain persons to give up teaching
4 erroneous doctrines and studying those interminable myths and
genealogies, which issue in mere speculation and cannot make known
God's plan for us, which works through faith.*a*

5 The aim and object of this command is the love which springs
from a clean heart, from a good conscience, and from faith that is
6 genuine. Through falling short of these, some people have gone
7 astray into a wilderness of words. They set out to be teachers of the
moral law, without understanding either the words they use or the
subjects about which they are so dogmatic.

8 We all know that the law is an excellent thing, provided we treat
9 it as law, recognizing that it is not aimed at good citizens, but at
the lawless and unruly, the impious and sinful, the irreligious and
10 worldly; at parricides and matricides, murderers and fornicators,
perverts, kidnappers, liars, perjurers—in fact all whose behaviour
11 flouts the wholesome teaching which conforms with the gospel
entrusted to me, the gospel which tells of the glory of God in his
eternal felicity.

12 I thank him who has made me equal to the task, Christ Jesus our
Lord; I thank him for judging me worthy of this trust and appoint-
13 ing me to his service—although in the past I had met him with
abuse and persecution and outrage. But because I acted ignorantly
14 in unbelief I was dealt with mercifully; the grace of our Lord

[a] Or cannot promote the faithful discharge of God's stewardship.

356

was lavished upon me, with the faith and love which are ours in
Christ Jesus.

Here are words you may trust, words that merit full acceptance: 15
'Christ Jesus came into the world to save sinners'; and among them
I stand first. But I was mercifully dealt with for this very purpose, 16
that Jesus Christ might find in me the first occasion for displaying
all his patience, and that I might be typical of all who were in future
to have faith in him and gain eternal life. Now to the King of all 17
worlds, immortal, invisible, the only God, be honour and glory for
ever and ever! Amen.

This charge, son Timothy, I lay upon you, following that prophetic 18
utterance which first pointed you out to me. So fight gallantly, armed 19
with faith and a good conscience. It was through spurning conscience that certain persons made shipwreck of their faith, among them 20
Hymenaeus and Alexander, whom I consigned to Satan, in the hope
that through this discipline they might learn not to be blasphemous.

FIRST OF ALL, then, I urge that petitions, prayers, intercessions, 2
and thanksgivings be offered for all men; for sovereigns and all in 2
high office, that we may lead a tranquil and quiet life in full observance of religion and high standards of morality. Such prayer is 3
right, and approved by God our Saviour, whose will it is that all 4
men should find salvation and come to know the truth. For there is 5
one God, and also one mediator between God and men, Christ Jesus,
himself man, who sacrificed himself to win freedom for all mankind, 6
so providing, at the fitting time, proof of the divine purpose; of this 7
I was appointed herald and apostle (this is no lie, but the truth), to
instruct the nations in the true faith.

It is my desire, therefore, that everywhere prayers be said by the 8
men of the congregation, who shall lift up their hands with a pure
intention, excluding angry or quarrelsome thoughts. Women again 9
must dress in becoming manner, modestly and soberly, not with
elaborate hair-styles, not decked out with gold or pearls, or expensive
clothes, but with good deeds, as befits women who claim to be 10
religious. A woman must be a learner, listening quietly and with 11
due submission. I do not permit a woman to be a teacher, nor must 12
woman domineer over man; she should be quiet. For Adam was 13
created first, and Eve afterwards; and it was not Adam who was 14
deceived; it was the woman who, yielding to deception, fell into sin.

15 Yet she will be saved through motherhood*a*—if only women continue in faith,*b* love, and holiness, with a sober mind.

3 There is a popular saying:*c* 'To aspire to leadership is an honourable
2 ambition.' Our leader, therefore, or bishop, must be above reproach, faithful to his one wife,*d* sober, temperate, courteous, hospitable, and
3 a good teacher; he must not be given to drink, or a brawler, but of a forbearing disposition, avoiding quarrels, and no lover of money.
4 He must be one who manages his own household well and wins obedience from his children, and a man of the highest principles.
5 If a man does not know how to control his own family, how can
6 he look after a congregation of God's people? He must not be a convert newly baptized, for fear the sin of conceit should bring upon him
7 a judgement contrived by the devil.*e* He must moreover have a good reputation with the non-Christian public, so that he may not be exposed to scandal and get caught in the devil's snare.

8 Deacons, likewise, must be men of high principle, not indulging in double talk, given neither to excessive drinking nor to money-
9 grubbing. They must be men who combine a clear conscience with
10 a firm hold on the deep truths of our faith. No less than bishops, they must first undergo a scrutiny, and if there is no mark against
11 them, they may serve. Their wives,*f* equally, must be women of high principle, who will not talk scandal, sober and trustworthy in
12 every way. A deacon must be faithful to his one wife,*d* and good
13 at managing his children and his own household. For deacons with a good record of service may claim a high standing and the right to speak openly on matters of the Christian faith.

14, 15 I am hoping to come to you before long, but I write this in case I am delayed, to let you know how men ought to conduct themselves in God's household, that is, the church of the living God, the pillar
16 and bulwark of the truth. And great beyond all question is the mystery of our religion:

> 'He who was manifested in the body,
> vindicated in the spirit,
> seen by angels;

[a] *Or* saved through the Birth of the Child, *or* brought safely through childbirth.
[b] *Or* if only husband and wife continue in mutual fidelity... [c] *Some witnesses read*
Here are words you may trust, *which some interpreters attach to the end of the preceding
paragraph.* [d] *Or* married to one wife, *or* married only once. [e] *Or* the judgement
once passed on the devil. [f] *Or* ...serve. Deaconesses...

who was proclaimed among the nations,
believed in throughout the world,
glorified in high heaven.'

THE SPIRIT SAYS expressly that in after times some will desert 4
from the faith and give their minds to subversive doctrines inspired
by devils, through the specious falsehoods of men whose own con- 2
science is branded with the devil's sign. They forbid marriage and 3
inculcate abstinence from certain foods, though God created them
to be enjoyed with thanksgiving by believers who have inward
knowledge of the truth. For everything that God created is good, 4
and nothing is to be rejected when it is taken with thanksgiving,
since it is hallowed by God's own word and by prayer. 5

By offering such advice as this to the brotherhood you will prove 6
a good servant of Christ Jesus, bred in the precepts of our faith and
of the sound instruction which you have followed. Have nothing to 7
do with those godless myths, fit only for old women. Keep yourself
in training for the practice of religion. The training of the body 8
does bring limited benefit, but the benefits of religion are without
limit, since it holds promise not only for this life but for the life to
come. Here are words you may trust, words that merit full accept- 9
ance: 'With this before us we labour and struggle,^{a} because^b we 10
have set our hope on the living God, who is the Saviour of all
men'—the Saviour, above all, of believers.

Pass on these orders and these teachings. Let no one slight you 11, 12
because you are young, but make yourself an example to believers in
speech and behaviour, in love, fidelity, and purity. Until I arrive 13
devote your attention to the public reading of the scriptures, to
exhortation, and to teaching. Do not neglect the spiritual endow- 14
ment you possess, which was given you, under the guidance of
prophecy, through the laying on of the hands of the elders as a
body.^{c}

Make these matters your business and your absorbing interest, 15
so that your progress may be plain to all. Persevere in them, keeping 16
close watch on yourself and your teaching; by doing so you will
further the salvation of yourself and your hearers.

[a] *Some witnesses read* suffer reproach. [b] *Or* since 'It holds promise...to come.'
These are words...acceptance. For this is the aim of all our labour and struggle,
since... [c] *Or* through your ordination as an elder.

5 Never be harsh with an elder; appeal to him as if he were your
2 father. Treat the younger men as brothers, the older women as
mothers, and the younger as your sisters, in all purity.
3 The status of widow is to be granted only to widows who are such
4 in the full sense. But if a widow has children or grandchildren,
then they should learn as their first duty to show loyalty to the
family and to repay what they owe to their parents and grandparents;
5 for this God approves. A widow, however, in the full sense, one
who is alone in the world, has all her hope set on God, and regularly
6 attends the meetings for prayer and worship night and day. But
7 a widow given over to self-indulgence is as good as dead. Add these
8 orders to the rest, so that the widows may be above reproach. But
if anyone does not make provision for his relations, and especially
for members of his own household, he has denied the faith and is
worse than an unbeliever.
9 A widow should not be put on the roll under sixty years of age.
10 She must have been faithful in marriage to one man, and must produce evidence of good deeds performed, showing whether she has
had the care of children, or given hospitality, or washed the feet of
God's people, or supported those in distress—in short, whether
she has taken every opportunity of doing good.
11 Younger widows may not be placed on the roll. For when their
passions draw them away from Christ, they hanker after marriage
12, 13 and stand condemned for breaking their troth with him. Moreover,
in going round from house to house they learn to be idle, and worse
than idle, gossips and busybodies, speaking of things better left
14 unspoken. It is my wish, therefore, that young widows shall marry
again, have children, and preside over a home; then they will
15 give no opponent occasion for slander. For there have in fact
been widows who have taken the wrong turning and gone to the
devil.
16 If a Christian man or woman has widows in the family, he must
support them himself;[a] the congregation must be relieved of the
burden, so that it may be free to support those who are widows in
the full sense of the term.
17 Elders who do well as leaders should be reckoned worthy of a
double stipend, in particular those who labour at preaching and

[a] *Some witnesses read* If a Christian woman has widows in her family, she must support
them herself.

teaching. For Scripture says, 'A threshing ox shall not be muzzled'; 18
and besides, 'the workman earns his pay'.

Do not entertain a charge against an elder unless it is supported 19
by two or three witnesses. Those who commit sins you must expose 20
publicly, to put fear into the others. Before God and Christ Jesus 21
and the angels who are his chosen, I solemnly charge you, maintain
these rules, and never pre-judge the issue, but act with strict impar-
tiality. Do not be over-hasty in laying on hands in ordination,ᵃ or 22
you may find yourself responsible for other people's misdeeds; keep
your own hands clean.

Stop drinking nothing but water; take a little wine for your 23
digestion, for your frequent ailments.

While there are people whose offences are so obvious that they 24
run before them into court, there are others whose offences have
not yet overtaken them. Similarly, good deeds are obvious, or even 25
if they are not, they cannot be concealed for ever.

All who wear the yoke of slavery must count their own masters 6
worthy of all respect, so that the name of God and the Christian
teaching are not brought into disrepute. If the masters are believers, 2
the slaves must not respect them any less for being their Christian
brothers. Quite the contrary; they must be all the better servants
because those who receive the benefit of their service are one with
them in faith and love.

THIS IS WHAT you are to teach and preach. If anyone is teaching 3
otherwise, and will not give his mind to wholesome precepts—I
mean those of our Lord Jesus Christ—and to good religious teaching,
I call him a pompous ignoramus. He is morbidly keen on mere 4
verbal questions and quibbles, which give rise to jealousy, quarrelling, slander, base suspicions, and endless wrangles: all typical of 5
men who have let their reasoning powers become atrophied and have
lost grip of the truth. They think religion should yield dividends;
and of course religion does yield high dividends, but only to the 6
man whose resources are within him. We brought nothing into the 7
world, because when we leave it we cannot take anything with us
either, but if we have food and covering we may rest content. 8
Those who want to be rich fall into temptations and snares and many 9
foolish harmful desires which plunge men into ruin and perdition.

[a] *Or* in restoring an offender by the laying on of hands.

10 The love of money is the root of all evil things, and there are some who in reaching for it have wandered from the faith and spiked themselves on many thorny griefs.

11 But you, man of God, must shun all this, and pursue justice,
12 piety, fidelity, love, fortitude, and gentleness. Run the great race of faith and take hold of eternal life. For to this you were called;
13 and you confessed your faith nobly before many witnesses. Now in the presence of God, who gives life to all things, and of Jesus Christ, who himself made the same noble confession and gave his testimony
14 to it before Pontius Pilate, I charge you to obey your orders irreproachably and without fault until our Lord Jesus Christ appears.
15 That appearance God will bring to pass in his own good time—God who in eternal felicity alone holds sway. He is King of kings and
16 Lord of lords; he alone possesses immortality, dwelling in unapproachable light. No man has ever seen or ever can see him. To him be honour and might for ever! Amen.

17 Instruct those who are rich in this world's goods not to be proud, and not to fix their hopes on so uncertain a thing as money, but upon
18 God, who endows us richly with all things to enjoy. Tell them to hoard a wealth of noble actions by doing good, to be ready to give
19 away and to share, and so acquire a treasure which will form a good foundation for the future. Thus they will grasp the life which is life indeed.

20 Timothy, keep safe that which has been entrusted to you. Turn a deaf ear to empty and worldly chatter, and the contradictions of
21 so-called 'knowledge', for many who lay claim to it have shot far wide of the faith.

Grace be with you all!

THE
SECOND LETTER OF PAUL TO
TIMOTHY

Character of a Christian Minister

FROM PAUL, apostle of Jesus Christ by the will of God, whose 1
promise of life is fulfilled in Christ Jesus, to Timothy his dear 2
son.

Grace, mercy, and peace to you from God the Father and our
Lord Jesus Christ.

I thank God—whom I, like my forefathers, worship with a pure 3
intention—when I mention you in my prayers; this I do constantly
night and day. And when I remember the tears you shed, I long 4
to see you again to make my happiness complete. I am reminded 5
of the sincerity of your faith, a faith which was alive in Lois your
grandmother and Eunice your mother before you, and which, I am
confident, lives in you also.

That is why I now remind you to stir into flame the gift of God 6
which is within you through the laying on of my hands. For the 7
spirit that God gave us is no craven spirit, but one to inspire strength,
love, and self-discipline. So never be ashamed of your testimony to 8
our Lord, nor of me his prisoner, but take your share of suffering for
the sake of the Gospel, in the strength that comes from God. It is 9
he who brought us salvation and called us to a dedicated life, not
for any merit of ours but of his own purpose and his own grace,
which was granted to us in Christ Jesus from all eternity, but has 10
now at length been brought fully into view by the appearance on
earth of our Saviour Jesus Christ. For he has broken the power of
death and brought life and immortality to light through the Gospel.

Of this Gospel I, by his appointment, am herald, apostle, and 11
teacher. That is the reason for my present plight; but I am not 12
ashamed of it, because I know who it is in whom[a] I have trusted,
and am confident of his power to keep safe what he has put into my
charge,[b] until the great Day. Keep before you an outline of the 13

[a] *Or* I know the one whom... [b] *Or* what I have put into his charge.

363

sound teaching which*a* you heard from me, living by the faith and
14 love which are ours in Christ Jesus. Guard the treasure put into our
charge, with the help of the Holy Spirit dwelling within us.
15   As you know, everyone in the province of Asia deserted me,
16 including Phygelus and Hermogenes. But may the Lord's mercy
rest on the house of Onesiphorus! He has often relieved me in my
17 troubles. He was not ashamed to visit a prisoner, but took pains to
18 search me out when he came to Rome, and found me. I pray that
the Lord may grant him to find mercy from the Lord on the great
Day. The many services he rendered at Ephesus you know better
than I could tell you.
2   Now therefore, my son, take strength from the grace of God which
2 is ours in Christ Jesus. You heard my teaching in the presence
of many witnesses; put that teaching into the charge of men you can
trust, such men as will be competent to teach others.
3   Take your share of hardship, like a good soldier of Christ Jesus.
4 A soldier on active service will not let himself be involved in civilian
affairs; he must be wholly at his commanding officer's disposal.
5,6 Again, no athlete can win a prize unless he has kept the rules. The
7 farmer who gives his labour has first claim on the crop. Reflect on
what I say, for the Lord will help you to full understanding.
8   Remember Jesus Christ, risen from the dead, born of David's line.
9 This is the theme of my gospel, in whose service I am exposed to
hardship, even to the point of being shut up like a common criminal;
10 but the word of God is not shut up. And I endure it all for the sake
of God's chosen ones, with this end in view, that they too may attain
the glorious and eternal salvation which is in Christ Jesus.
11   Here are words you may trust:

'If we died with him, we shall live with him;
12   If we endure, we shall reign with him.
        If we deny him, he will deny us.
13   If we are faithless, he keeps faith,
        For he cannot deny himself.'

14 GO ON REMINDING people of this, and adjure them before God
to stop disputing about mere words; it does no good, and is the ruin
15 of those who listen. Try hard to show yourself worthy of God's

[a] *Or* Keep before you as a model of sound teaching that which...

approval, as a labourer who need not be ashamed, driving a straight furrow, in your proclamation of the truth. Avoid empty and worldly 16 chatter; those who indulge in it will stray further and further into godless courses, and the infection of their teaching will spread like 17 a gangrene. Such are Hymenaeus and Philetus; they have shot wide 18 of the truth in saying that our resurrection has already taken place, and are upsetting people's faith. But God has laid a foundation, 19 and it stands firm, with this inscription: 'The Lord knows his own', and, 'Everyone who takes the Lord's name upon his lips must forsake wickedness.' Now in any great house there are not only utensils of 20 gold and silver, but also others of wood or earthenware; the former are valued, the latter held cheap. To be among those which are 21 valued and dedicated, a thing of use to the Master of the house, a man must cleanse himself from all those evil things;[a] then he will be fit for any honourable purpose.

Turn from the wayward impulses of youth, and pursue justice, 22 integrity, love, and peace with all who invoke the Lord in singleness of mind. Have nothing to do with foolish and ignorant speculations. 23 You know they breed quarrels, and the servant of the Lord must 24 not be quarrelsome, but kindly towards all. He should be a good teacher, tolerant, and gentle when discipline is needed for the 25 refractory. The Lord may grant them a change of heart and show them the truth, and thus they may come to their senses and escape from 26 the devil's snare, in which they have been caught and held at his will.[b]

You must face the fact: the final age of this world is to be a time 3 of troubles. Men will love nothing but money and self; they will 2 be arrogant, boastful, and abusive; with no respect for parents, no gratitude, no piety, no natural affection; they will be implacable 3 in their hatreds, scandal-mongers, intemperate and fierce, strangers to all goodness, traitors, adventurers, swollen with self-importance. 4 They will be men who put pleasure in the place of God, men who 5 preserve the outward form of religion, but are a standing denial of its reality. Keep clear of men like these. They are the sort that 6 insinuate themselves into private houses and there get miserable women into their clutches, women burdened with a sinful past, and led on by all kinds of desires, who are always wanting to be taught, 7 but are incapable of reaching a knowledge of the truth. As Jannes 8

[a] Or must separate himself from these persons. [b] Or escape from the devil's snare, caught now by God and made subject to his will.

and Jambres defied Moses, so these men defy the truth; they have lost the power to reason, and they cannot pass the tests of faith.

9 But their successes will be short-lived, for, like those opponents of Moses, they will come to be recognized by everyone for the fools they are.

10 But you, my son, have followed, step by step, my teaching and my manner of life, my resolution, my faith, patience, and spirit of

11 love, and my fortitude under persecutions and sufferings—all that I went through at Antioch, at Iconium, at Lystra, all the persecutions

12 I endured; and the Lord rescued me out of them all. Yes, persecution

13 will come to all who want to live a godly life as Christians, whereas wicked men and charlatans will make progress from bad to worse,

14 deceiving and deceived. But for your part, stand by the truths you have learned and are assured of. Remember from whom you learned

15 them; remember that from early childhood you have been familiar with the sacred writings which have power to make you wise and

16 lead you to salvation through faith in Christ Jesus. Every inspired scripture has its use for teaching the truth and refuting error, or for

17 reformation of manners and discipline in right living, so that the man who belongs to God may be efficient and equipped for good work of every kind.

4 Before God, and before Christ Jesus who is to judge men living and dead, I adjure you by his coming appearance and his reign,

2 proclaim the message, press it home on all occasions,*a* convenient or inconvenient, use argument, reproof, and appeal, with all the patience

3 that the work of teaching requires. For the time will come when they will not stand wholesome teaching, but will follow their own fancy

4 and gather a crowd of teachers to tickle their ears. They will stop

5 their ears to the truth and turn to mythology. But you yourself must keep calm and sane at all times; face hardship, work to spread the Gospel, and do all the duties of your calling.

6 As for me, already my life is being poured out on the altar, and the

7 hour for my departure is upon me. I have run the great race, I have

8 finished the course, I have kept faith. And now the prize awaits me, the garland of righteousness which the Lord, the all-just Judge, will award me on that great Day; and it is not for me alone, but for all who have set their hearts on his coming appearance.

[a] *Or* be on duty at all times.

Do your best to join me soon; for Demas has deserted me because 9, 10 his heart was set on this world; he has gone to Thessalonica, Crescens to Galatia,[a] Titus to Dalmatia; I have no one with me but Luke. 11 Pick up Mark and bring him with you, for I find him a useful assistant. Tychicus I have sent to Ephesus. When you come, bring 12, 13 the cloak I left with Carpus at Troas, and the books, above all my notebooks.

Alexander the copper-smith did me a great deal of harm. Retribu- 14 tion will fall upon him from the Lord. You had better be on your 15 guard against him too, for he violently opposed everything I said. At the first hearing of my case no one came into court to support me; 16 they all left me in the lurch; I pray that it may not be held against them. But the Lord stood by me and lent me strength, so that I might 17 be his instrument in making the full proclamation of the Gospel for the whole pagan world to hear; and thus I was rescued out of the lion's jaws. And the Lord will rescue me from every attempt to do 18 me harm, and keep me safe until his heavenly reign begins.[b] Glory to him for ever and ever! Amen.

Greetings to Prisca and Aquila, and the household of Onesiphorus. 19 Erastus stayed behind at Corinth, and I left Trophimus ill at 20 Miletus. Do try to get here before winter. 21 Greetings from Eubulus, Pudens, Linus, and Claudia, and from all the brotherhood here.

The Lord be with your spirit. Grace be with you all! 22

[a] *Or* Gaul; *some witnesses read* Gallia.   [b] *Or* from all that evil can do, and bring me safely into his heavenly kingdom.

THE
LETTER OF PAUL TO
TITUS

Training for the Christian Life

1 FROM PAUL, servant of God and apostle of Jesus Christ, marked as such by faith and knowledge and hope—the faith of God's chosen people, knowledge of the truth as our religion
2 has it, and the hope of eternal life.*a* Yes, it is eternal life that God,
3 who cannot lie, promised long ages ago, and now in his own good time he has openly declared himself in the proclamation which was entrusted to me by ordinance of God our Saviour.

4 To Titus, my true-born son in the faith which we share, grace and peace from God our Father and Christ Jesus our Saviour.

5 My intention in leaving you behind in Crete was that you should set in order what was left over, and in particular should institute elders in each town. In doing so, observe the tests I prescribed:
6 is he a man of unimpeachable character, faithful to his one wife,*b* the father of children who are believers, who are under no imputation
7 of loose living, and are not out of control? For as God's steward a bishop must be a man of unimpeachable character. He must not be overbearing or short-tempered; he must be no drinker, no brawler,
8 no money-grubber, but hospitable, right-minded, temperate, just,
9 devout, and self-controlled. He must adhere to the true doctrine, so that he may be well able both to move his hearers with wholesome teaching and to confute objectors.

10 There are all too many, especially among Jewish converts, who are out of all control; they talk wildly and lead men's minds astray.
11 Such men must be curbed, because they are ruining whole families
12 by teaching things they should not, and all for sordid gain. It was a Cretan prophet, one of their own countrymen, who said, 'Cretans
13 were always liars, vicious brutes, lazy gluttons'—and he told the

[a] *Or* apostle of Jesus Christ, to bring God's chosen people to faith and to a knowledge of the truth as our religion has it, with its hope for eternal life. [b] *See note on 1 Timothy 3. 2.*

truth! All the more reason why you should pull them up sharply, so that they may come to a sane belief, instead of lending their ears 14 to Jewish myths and commandments of merely human origin, the work of men who turn their backs upon the truth.

To the pure all things are pure; but nothing is pure to the tainted 15 minds of disbelievers, tainted alike in reason and conscience. They 16 profess to acknowledge God, but deny him by their actions. Their detestable obstinacy disqualifies them for any good work.

For your own part, what you say must be in keeping with whole- 2 some doctrine. Let the older men know that they should be sober, 2 high-principled, and temperate, sound in faith, in love, and in endurance. The older women, similarly, should be reverent in their 3 bearing, not scandal-mongers or slaves to strong drink; they must set a high standard, and school the younger women to be loving 4 wives and mothers, temperate, chaste, and kind, busy at home, 5 respecting the authority of their own husbands. Thus the Gospel will not be brought into disrepute.

Urge the younger men, similarly, to be temperate in all things, 6, 7 and set them a good example yourself. In your teaching, you must show integrity and high principle, and use wholesome speech to 8 which none can take exception. This will shame any opponent, when he finds not a word to say to our discredit.

Tell slaves to respect their masters' authority in everything, and 9 to comply with their demands without answering back; not to 10 pilfer, but to show themselves strictly honest and trustworthy; for in all such ways they will add lustre to the doctrine of God our Saviour.

For the grace of God has dawned upon the world with healing 11 for all mankind; and by it we are disciplined to renounce godless 12 ways and worldly desires, and to live a life of temperance, honesty, and godliness in the present age, looking forward to the happy fulfil- 13 ment of our hopes when the splendour of our great God and Saviour*a* Christ Jesus will appear. He it is who sacrificed himself for us, to set 14 us free from all wickedness and to make us a pure people marked out for his own, eager to do good.

These, then, are your themes; urge them and argue them. And 15 speak with authority: let no one slight you.

Remind them to be submissive to the government and the authori- 3 ties, to obey them, and to be ready for any honourable form of work;*b*

[a] *Or* of the great God and our Saviour... [b] *Or* ready always to do good.

2 to slander no one, not to pick quarrels, to show forbearance and a consistently gentle disposition towards all men.

3 For at one time we ourselves in our folly and obstinacy were all astray. We were slaves to passions and pleasures of every kind. Our days were passed in malice and envy; we were odious ourselves

4 and we hated one another. But when the kindness and generosity

5 of God our Saviour dawned upon the world, then, not for any good deeds of our own, but because he was merciful, he saved us through the water of rebirth and the renewing power of[a] the Holy Spirit.

6 For he sent down the Spirit upon us plentifully through Jesus Christ

7 our Saviour, so that, justified by his grace, we might in hope become

8 heirs to eternal life. These are words you may trust.

Such are the points I should wish you to insist on. Those who have come to believe in God should see that they engage in honourable occupations, which are not only honourable in themselves, but

9 also useful to their fellow-men.[b] But steer clear of foolish speculations, genealogies, quarrels, and controversies over the Law; they are unprofitable and pointless.

10 A heretic should be warned once, and once again; after that, have

11 done with him, recognizing that a man of that sort has a distorted mind and stands self-condemned in his sin.

12 When I send Artemas to you, or Tychicus, make haste to join me at Nicopolis, for that is where I have determined to spend the

13 winter. Do your utmost to help Zenas the lawyer and Apollos on

14 their travels, and see that they are not short of anything. And our own people must be taught to engage in honest employment to produce the necessities of life; they must not be unproductive.

15 All who are with me send you greetings. My greetings to those who are our friends in truth. Grace be with you all!

[a] *Or* the water of rebirth and of renewal by... [b] *Or* should make it their business to practise virtue. These precepts are good in themselves and useful to society. [c] *Or* our friends in the faith.

THE
LETTER OF PAUL TO
PHILEMON

A Runaway Slave

FROM PAUL, a prisoner of Christ Jesus, and our colleague 1 Timothy, to Philemon our dear friend and fellow-worker, and 2 Apphia our sister, and Archippus our comrade-in-arms, and the congregation at your house.

Grace to you and peace from God our Father and the Lord Jesus 3 Christ.

I thank my God always when I mention you in my prayers, 4 for I hear of your love and faith towards the Lord Jesus and towards 5 all God's people. My prayer is that your fellowship with us in our 6 common faith may deepen the understanding of all the blessings that our union with Christ brings us.[a] For I am delighted and 7 encouraged by your love: through you, my brother, God's people have been much refreshed.

Accordingly, although in Christ I might make bold to point out 8 your duty, yet, because of that same love, I would rather appeal to 9 you. Yes, I, Paul, ambassador as I am of Christ Jesus—and now his prisoner—appeal to you about my child, whose father I have become 10 in this prison.

I mean Onesimus, once so little use to you, but now useful indeed, 11 both to you and to me. I am sending him back to you, and in doing 12 so I am sending a part of myself. I should have liked to keep him 13 with me, to look after me as you would wish, here in prison for the Gospel. But I would rather do nothing without your consent, so that 14 your kindness may be a matter not of compulsion, but of your own free will. For perhaps this is why you lost him for a time, that you 15 might have him back for good, no longer as a slave, but as more than 16 a slave—as a dear brother, very dear indeed to me and how much dearer to you, both as man and as Christian.

If, then, you count me partner in the faith, welcome him as you 17

[a] *Or* that bring us to Christ.

371

18 would welcome me. And if he has done you any wrong or is in your
19 debt, put that down to my account. Here is my signature, PAUL;
    I undertake to repay—not to mention that you owe your very self to
20 me as well. Now brother, as a Christian, be generous with me, and
    relieve my anxiety; we are both in Christ!
21   I write to you confident that you will meet my wishes; I know that
22 you will in fact do better than I ask. And one thing more: have a
    room ready for me, for I hope that, in answer to your prayers, God
    will grant me to you.
23, 24   Epaphras, Christ's captive like myself, sends you greetings. So
    do Mark, Aristarchus, Demas, and Luke, my fellow-workers.
25   The grace of the Lord Jesus Christ be with your spirit!

A LETTER TO
HEBREWS

Christ Divine and Human

W HEN IN FORMER TIMES God spoke to our 1
forefathers, he spoke in fragmentary and varied fashion
through the prophets. But in this the final age he has 2
spoken to us in the Son whom he has made heir to the whole universe,
and through whom he created all orders of existence: the Son who is 3
the effulgence of God's splendour and the stamp of God's very being,
and sustains*a* the universe by his word of power. When he had
brought about the purgation of sins, he took his seat at the right hand
of Majesty on high, raised as far above the angels, as the title he has 4
inherited is superior to theirs.

For God never said to any angel, 'Thou art my Son; today I have 5
begotten thee', or again, 'I will be father to him, and he shall be my
son.' Again, when he presents the first-born to the world, he says, 6
'Let all the angels of God pay him homage.' Of the angels he says, 7

'He who makes his angels winds,
And his ministers a fiery flame';

but of the Son, 8

'Thy throne, O God, is for ever and ever,
And the sceptre*b* of justice is the sceptre of his kingdom.
Thou hast loved right and hated wrong; 9
Therefore, O God, thy God*c* has set thee above thy fellows,
By anointing with the oil of exultation.'

And again, 10

'By thee, Lord, were earth's foundations laid of old,
And the heavens are the work of thy hands.
They shall pass away, but thou endurest; 11
Like clothes they shall all grow old;
Thou shalt fold them up like a cloak; 12
Yes, they shall be changed like any garment.
But thou art the same, and thy years shall have no end.'

[a] Or bears along. [b] Or God is thy throne for ever and ever, And thy sceptre...
[c] Or Therefore God who is thy God...

373

13 To which of the angels has he ever said, 'Sit at my right hand
14 until I make thy enemies thy footstool'? What are they all but
ministrant spirits, sent out to serve, for the sake of those who are
to inherit salvation?

2 Thus we are bound to pay all the more heed to what we have
2 been told, for fear of drifting from our course. For if the word
spoken through angels had such force that any transgression or
3 disobedience met with due retribution, what escape can there be for
us if we ignore a deliverance so great? For this deliverance was first
announced through the lips of the Lord himself; those who heard
4 him confirmed it to us, and God added his testimony by signs, by
miracles, by manifold works of power, and by distributing the gifts of
the Holy Spirit at his own will.

5 For it is not to angels that he has subjected the world to come, which
6 is our theme. But there is somewhere a solemn assurance which runs:

'What is man, that thou rememberest him,
Or the son of man, that thou hast regard to him?
7 Thou didst make him for a short while lower than the angels;
Thou didst crown him with glory and honour;
8 Thou didst put all things in subjection beneath his feet.'

For in subjecting all things to him, he left nothing that is not subject.
9 But in fact we do not yet see all things in subjection to man. In
Jesus, however, we do see one who[a] for a short while was made lower
than the angels, crowned now with glory and honour because he
suffered death, so that, by God's gracious will, in tasting death he
should stand[b] for us all.
10 It was clearly fitting that God for whom and through whom all
things exist should, in bringing many sons to glory, make the leader
11 who delivers them perfect through sufferings. For a consecrating
priest and those whom he consecrates are all of one stock; and that
12 is why the Son does not shrink from calling men his brothers, when
he says, 'I will proclaim thy name to my brothers; in full assembly
13 I will sing thy praise'; and again, 'I will keep my trust fixed on him';
and again, 'Here am I, and the children whom God has given me.'
14 The children of a family share the same flesh and blood; and so he
too shared ours, so that through death he might break the power of

[a] *Or* in subjection to him. But we see Jesus, who... [b] *Some witnesses read* so that
apart from God he should taste death...

him who had death at his command, that is, the devil; and might 15
liberate those who, through fear of death, had all their lifetime been
in servitude. It is not angels, mark you, that he takes to himself, 16
but the sons of Abraham. And therefore he had to be made like 17
these brothers of his in every way, so that he might be merciful and
faithful as their high priest before God, to expiate the sins of the
people. For since he himself has passed through the test of suffering, 18
he is able to help those who are meeting their test now.

Therefore, brothers in the family of God, who share a heavenly 3
calling, think of the Apostle and High Priest of the religion we
profess,*a* who was faithful to God who appointed him. Moses also 2
was faithful in God's household; and Jesus, of whom I speak, has 3
been deemed worthy of greater honour than Moses, as the founder
of a house enjoys more honour than his household. For every house 4
has its founder; and the founder of all is God. Moses, then, was 5
faithful as a servitor in God's whole household; his task was to bear
witness to the words that God would speak; but Christ is faithful 6
as a son, set over his household. And we are that household of his,
if only we are fearless and keep our hope high.

'TODAY', therefore, as the Holy Spirit says— 7

'Today if you hear his voice,
Do not grow stubborn as in those days of rebellion, 8
At that time of testing in the desert,
Where your forefathers tried me and tested me, 9
And saw*b* the things I did for forty years.
And so, I was indignant with that generation 10
And I said, Their hearts are for ever astray;
They would not discern my ways;
As I vowed in my anger, they shall never enter my rest.' 11

See to it, brothers, that no one among you has the wicked, faithless 12
heart of a deserter from the living God; but day by day, while that 13
word 'Today' still sounds in your ears, encourage one another, so
that no one of you is made stubborn by the wiles of sin. For we 14
have become Christ's partners*c* if only we keep our original confidence firm to the end.

[a] Or of him whom we confess as God's Envoy and High Priest. [b] Or Though
they saw... [c] Or have been given a share in Christ.

375

15 　　When Scripture says, 'Today if you hear his voice, do not grow
16 stubborn as in those days of rebellion', who, I ask, were those who
　　heard and rebelled? All those, surely, whom Moses had led out of
17 Egypt. And with whom was God indignant for forty years? With
　　those, surely, who had sinned, whose bodies lay where they fell in
18 the desert. And to whom did he vow that they should not enter
19 his rest, if not to those who had refused to believe? We perceive that
　　it was unbelief which prevented their entering.

4 　　Therefore we must have before us the fear that while the promise
　　of entering his rest remains open, one or another among you should
2 be found to have missed his chance. For indeed we have heard the
　　good news, as they did. But in them the message they heard did no
　　good, because they brought no admixture of faith to the hearing of it.
3 It is we, we who have become believers, who enter the rest referred to
　　in the words, 'As I vowed in my anger, they shall never enter my rest.'
　　Yet God's work has been finished ever since the world was created;
4 for does not Scripture somewhere speak thus of the seventh day:
5 'God rested from his work on the seventh day'?—and once again in
6 the passage above we read, 'They shall never enter my rest.' The fact
　　remains that someone must enter it, and since those who first heard
7 the good news failed to enter through unbelief, God fixes another
　　day. Speaking through the lips of David after many long years, he
　　uses the words already quoted: 'Today if you hear his voice, do not
8 grow stubborn.' If Joshua had given them rest, God would not
9 thus have spoken of another day after that. Therefore, a sabbath rest
10 still awaits the people of God; for anyone who enters God's rest,
11 rests from his own work as God did from his. Let us then make
　　every effort to enter that rest, so that no one may fall by following this
　　evil example of unbelief.

12 　　For the word of God is alive and active. It cuts more keenly than
　　any two-edged sword, piercing as far as the place where life and
　　spirit, joints and marrow, divide. It sifts the purposes and thoughts
13 of the heart. There is nothing in creation that can hide from him;
　　everything lies naked and exposed to the eyes of the One with whom
　　we have to reckon.

14 　　Since therefore we have a great high priest who has passed through
　　the heavens, Jesus the Son of God, let us hold fast to the religion
15 we profess. For ours is not a high priest unable to sympathize with
　　our weaknesses, but one who, because of his likeness to us, has been

376

tested every way,[a] only without sin. Let us therefore boldly approach 16
the throne of our gracious God, where we may receive mercy and in
his grace find timely help.

The Shadow and the Real

FOR EVERY HIGH PRIEST is taken from among men and appointed 5
their representative before God, to offer gifts and sacrifices for
sins. He is able to bear patiently with the ignorant and erring, since 2
he too is beset by weakness; and because of this he is bound to make 3
sin-offerings for himself no less than for the people. And nobody 4
arrogates the honour to himself: he is called by God, as indeed Aaron
was. So it is with Christ; he did not confer upon himself the glory 5
of becoming high priest: it was granted by God, who said to him,
'Thou art my Son; today I have begotten thee'; as also in another 6
place he says, 'Thou art a priest for ever, in the succession of
Melchizedek.' In the days of his earthly life he offered up prayers 7
and petitions, with loud cries and tears, to God who was able to
deliver him from the grave. Because of his humble submission his
prayer was heard: son though he was, he learned obedience in the 8
school of suffering, and, once perfected, became the source of eternal 9
salvation for all who obey him, named by God high priest in the 10
succession of Melchizedek.

About Melchizedek we have much to say, much that is difficult 11
to explain, now that you have grown so dull of hearing. For indeed, 12
though by this time you ought to be teachers, you need someone
to teach you the ABC of God's oracles over again; it has come to
this, that you need milk instead of solid food. Anyone who lives 13
on milk, being an infant, does not know[b] what is right. But grown 14
men can take solid food; their perceptions are trained by long use to
discriminate between good and evil.

Let us then stop discussing the rudiments of Christianity. We 6
ought not to be laying over again the foundations of faith in God and
of repentance from the deadness of our former ways, by instruc- 2
tion[c] about cleansing rites and the laying-on-of-hands, about the

[a] *Or* who has been tested every way, as we are. [b] *Or* is incompetent to speak of...
[c] *Or* laying the foundations over again: repentance from the deadness of our former
ways and faith in God, instruction...

resurrection of the dead and eternal judgement. Instead, let us
3 advance towards maturity; and so we shall, if God permits.
4   For when men have once been enlightened, when they have had
5 a taste of the heavenly gift and a share in the Holy Spirit, when they
have experienced the goodness of God's word and the spiritual
6 energies of the age to come, and after all this have fallen away, it is
impossible to bring them again to repentance; for with their own
hands they are crucifying*a* the Son of God and making mock of
7 his death. When the earth drinks in the rain that falls upon it from
time to time, and yields a useful crop to those for whom it is culti-
8 vated, it is receiving its share of blessing from God; but if it bears
thorns and thistles, it is worthless and God's curse hangs over it;
9 the end of that is burning. But although we speak as we do, we are
convinced that you, my friends, are in the better case, and this makes
10 for your salvation. For God would not be so unjust as to forget all
that you did for love of his name, when you rendered service to his
11 people, as you still do. But we long for every one of you to show the
12 same eager concern, until your hope is finally realized. We want you
not to become lazy, but to imitate those who, through faith and
patience, are inheriting the promises.
13   When God made his promise to Abraham, he swore by himself,
14 because he had no one greater to swear by: 'I vow that I will bless
15 you abundantly and multiply your descendants.' Thus it was that
16 Abraham, after patient waiting, attained the promise. Men swear
by a greater than themselves, and the oath provides a confirmation
17 to end all dispute; and so God, desiring to show even more clearly
to the heirs of his promise how unchanging was his purpose, guaran-
18 teed it by oath. Here, then, are two irrevocable acts in which God
could not possibly play us false, to give powerful encouragement to
us, who have claimed his protection by grasping*b* the hope set before
19 us. That hope we hold. It is like an anchor for our lives, an anchor
20 safe and sure. It enters in through the veil, where Jesus has entered
on our behalf as forerunner, having become a high priest for ever in
the succession of Melchizedek.

7 THIS MELCHIZEDEK, king of Salem, priest of God Most High,
met Abraham returning from the rout of the kings and blessed him;

[*a*] *Or* crucifying again. [*b*] *Or* to give to us, who have claimed his protection, a
powerful incentive to grasp...

378

and Abraham gave him a tithe of everything as his portion. His 2
name, in the first place, means 'king of righteousness'; next he
is king of Salem, that is, 'king of peace'. He has no father, no 3
mother, no lineage; his years have no beginning, his life no end.
He is like the Son of God: he remains a priest for all time.

Consider now how great he must be for Abraham the patriarch 4
to give him a tithe of the finest of the spoil. The descendants of Levi 5
who take the priestly office are commanded by the Law to tithe
the people, that is, their kinsmen, although they too are descendants
of Abraham. But Melchizedek, though he does not trace his descent 6
from them, has tithed Abraham himself, and given his blessing to
the man who received the promises; and beyond all dispute the lesser 7
is always blessed by the greater. Again, in the one instance tithes 8
are received by men who must die; but in the other, by one whom
Scripture affirms to be alive. It might even be said that Levi, who 9
receives tithes, has himself been tithed through Abraham; for he 10
was still in his ancestor's loins when Melchizedek met him.

Now if perfection had been attainable through the Levitical 11
priesthood (for it is on this basis that the people were given the Law),
what further need would there have been to speak of another priest
arising, in the succession of Melchizedek, instead of the succession
of Aaron? For a change of priesthood must mean a change of law. 12
And the One here spoken of belongs to a different tribe, no member 13
of which has ever had anything to do with the altar. For it is very 14
evident that our Lord is sprung from Judah, a tribe to which Moses
made no reference in speaking of priests.

The argument becomes still clearer, if the new priest who arises 15
is one like Melchizedek, owing his priesthood not to a system of 16
earth-bound rules but to the power of a life that cannot be destroyed.
For here is the testimony: 'Thou art a priest for ever, in the succes- 17
sion of Melchizedek.' The earlier rules are cancelled as impotent 18
and useless, since the Law brought nothing to perfection; and a better 19
hope is introduced, through which we draw near to God.

How great a difference it makes that an oath was sworn! There was 20, 21
no oath sworn when those others were made priests; but for this
priest an oath was sworn, as Scripture says of him: 'The Lord has
sworn and will not go back on his word, "Thou art a priest for ever."'
How far superior must the covenant also be of which Jesus is 22
the guarantor! Those other priests are appointed in numerous 23

379

succession, because they are prevented by death from continuing in
24 office; but the priesthood which Jesus holds is perpetual, because he
25 remains for ever. That is why he is also able to save absolutely those
who approach God through him; he is always living to plead on their
behalf.
26   Such a high priest does indeed fit our condition—devout, guileless, undefiled, separated from sinners, raised high above the
27 heavens. He has no need to offer sacrifices daily, as the high priests
do, first for his own sins and then for those of the people; for this he
28 did once and for all when he offered up himself. The high priests
made by the Law are men in all their frailty; but the priest appointed
by the words of the oath which supersedes the Law is the Son, made
perfect now for ever.

8 NOW THIS IS my main point: just such a high priest we have, and
he has taken his seat at the right hand of the throne of Majesty in the
2 heavens, a ministrant in the real sanctuary, the tent pitched by the
3 Lord and not by man. Every high priest is appointed to offer gifts
and sacrifices: hence, this one too must have[a] something to offer.
4 Now if he had been on earth, he would not even have been a priest,
since there are already priests who offer the gifts which the Law
5 prescribes, though they minister in a sanctuary which is only a copy
and shadow of the heavenly. This is implied when Moses, about to
erect the tent, is instructed by God: 'See to it that you make every-
6 thing according to the pattern shown you on the mountain.' But
in fact the ministry which has fallen to Jesus is as far superior to
theirs as are the covenant he mediates and the promises upon which
it is legally secured.
7   Had that first covenant been faultless, there would have been no
8 need to look for a second in its place. But God, finding fault with
them, says, 'The days are coming, says the Lord, when I will conclude a new covenant with the house of Israel and the house of Judah.
9 It will not be like the covenant I made with their forefathers when
I took them by the hand to lead them out of Egypt; because they
did not abide by the terms of that covenant, and I abandoned them,
10 says the Lord. For the covenant I will make with the house of
Israel after those days, says the Lord, is this: I will set my laws in
their understanding and write them on their hearts; and I will be

[a] *Or* must have had.

their God, and they shall be my people. And they shall not teach 11
one another, saying to brother and fellow-citizen,*ª* "Know the Lord!"
For all of them shall know me, from small to great; I will be merciful 12
to their wicked deeds, and their sins I will remember no more at all.'
By speaking of a new covenant, he has pronounced the first one old; 13
and anything that is growing old and ageing will shortly disappear.

THE FIRST COVENANT indeed had its ordinances of divine service 9
and its sanctuary, but a material sanctuary. For a tent was prepared 2
—the first tent—in which was the lamp-stand, and the table with the
bread of the Presence; this is called the Holy Place. Beyond the 3
second curtain was the tent called the Most Holy Place. Here was 4
a golden altar of incense, and the ark of the covenant plated all over
with gold, in which were a golden jar containing the manna, and
Aaron's staff which once budded, and the tablets of the covenant;
and above it the cherubim of God's glory, overshadowing the place 5
of expiation. On these we cannot now enlarge.

Under this arrangement, the priests are always entering the first 6
tent in the discharge of their duties; but the second is entered only 7
once a year, and by the high priest alone, and even then he must take
with him the blood which he offers on his own behalf and for the
people's sins of ignorance. By this the Holy Spirit signifies that 8
so long as the earlier tent still stands, the way into the sanctuary
remains unrevealed. (All this is symbolic, pointing to the present 9
time.) The offerings and sacrifices there prescribed cannot give the
worshipper inward perfection. It is only a matter of food and drink 10
and various rites of cleansing—outward ordinances in force until the
time of reformation.

But now Christ has come, high priest of good things already in 11
being.*ᵇ* The tent of his priesthood is a greater and more perfect one,
not made by men's hands, that is, not belonging to this created
world; the blood of his sacrifice is his own blood, not the blood of 12
goats and calves; and thus he has entered the sanctuary once and
for all and secured an eternal deliverance. For if the blood of goats 13
and bulls and the sprinkled ashes of a heifer have power to hallow
those who have been defiled and restore their external purity, how 14
much greater is the power of the blood of Christ; he offered himself

[*a*] *Some witnesses read* brother and neighbour. [*b*] *Some witnesses read* good things
which were (*or* are) to be.

381

without blemish to God, a spiritual and eternal sacrifice; and his blood will cleanse our conscience from the deadness of our former ways and fit us for the service of the living God.

15 And therefore he is the mediator of a new covenant, or testament, under which, now that there has been a death to bring deliverance from sins committed under the former covenant, those whom God
16 has called may receive the promise of the eternal inheritance. For where there is a testament it is necessary for the death of the testator
17 to be established. A testament is operative only after a death: it cannot
18 possibly have force while the testator is alive. Thus we find that the
19 former covenant itself was not inaugurated without blood. For when, as the Law directed, Moses had recited all the commandments to the people, he took the blood of the calves, with water, scarlet wool, and marjoram, and sprinkled the law-book itself and all the people,
20 saying, 'This is the blood of the covenant which God has enjoined
21 upon you.' In the same way he also sprinkled the tent and all the
22 vessels of divine service with blood. Indeed, according to the Law, it might almost be said, everything is cleansed by blood and without the shedding of blood there is no forgiveness.
23 If, then, these sacrifices cleanse the copies of heavenly things, those heavenly things themselves require better sacrifices to cleanse
24 them. For Christ has entered, not that sanctuary made by men's hands which is only a symbol of the reality, but heaven itself, to
25 appear now before God on our behalf. Nor is he there to offer himself again and again, as the high priest enters the sanctuary
26 year by year with blood not his own. If that were so, he would have had to suffer many times since the world was made. But as it is, he has appeared once and for all at the climax of history to abolish
27 sin by the sacrifice of himself. And as it is the lot of men to die once,
28 and after death comes judgement, so Christ was offered once to bear the burden of men's sins,[a] and will appear a second time, sin done away, to bring salvation to those who are watching for him.

10 FOR THE LAW contains but a shadow, and no true image,[b] of the good things which were to come; it provides for the same sacrifices year after year, and with these it can never bring the worshippers
2 to perfection for all time.[c] If it could, these sacrifices would surely

[a] *Or* to remove men's sins. [b] *Some witnesses read* a shadow and likeness... [c] *Or* bring to perfection the worshippers who come continually.

have ceased to be offered, because the worshippers, cleansed once
for all, would no longer have any sense of sin. But instead, in these ₃
sacrifices year after year sins are brought to mind, because sins can ₄
never be removed by the blood of bulls and goats.

That is why, at his coming into the world, he says: ₅

> 'Sacrifice and offering thou didst not desire,
> But thou hast prepared a body for me.
> Whole-offerings and sin-offerings thou didst not delight in. ₆
> Then I said, "Here am I: as it is written of me in the scroll, ₇
> I have come, O God, to do thy will."'

First he says, 'Sacrifices and offerings, whole-offerings and sin- ₈
offerings, thou didst not desire nor delight in'—although the Law
prescribes them—and then he says, 'I have come to do thy will.' ₉
He thus annuls the former to establish the latter. And it is by the ₁₀
will of God that we have been consecrated, through the offering of
the body of Jesus Christ once and for all.

Every priest stands performing his service daily and offering ₁₁
time after time the same sacrifices, which can never remove sins.
But Christ offered for all time one sacrifice for sins, and took his ₁₂
seat at the right hand of God, where he waits henceforth until his ₁₃
enemies are made his footstool. For by one offering he has perfected ₁₄
for all time those who are thus consecrated. Here we have also the ₁₅
testimony of the Holy Spirit: he first says, 'This is the covenant ₁₆
which I will make with them after those days, says the Lord: I will
set my laws in their hearts and write them on their understanding';
then he adds, 'and their sins and wicked deeds I will remember ₁₇
no more at all.' And where these have been forgiven, there is no ₁₈
longer any offering for sin.

So NOW, MY FRIENDS, the blood of Jesus makes us free to enter ₁₉
boldly into the sanctuary by the new, living way which he has opened ₂₀
for us through the curtain, the way of his flesh.[a] We have, moreover, ₂₁
a great priest set over the household of God; so let us make our ₂₂
approach in sincerity of heart and full assurance of faith, our guilty
hearts sprinkled clean, our bodies washed with pure water. Let us ₂₃
be firm and unswerving in the confession of our hope, for the Giver
of the promise may be trusted. We ought to see how each of us may ₂₄

[a] *Or* through the curtain of his flesh.

25 best arouse others to love and active goodness, not staying away
from our meetings, as some do, but rather encouraging one another,
all the more because you see the Day drawing near.

26 For if we persist in sin after receiving the knowledge of the truth,
27 no sacrifice for sins remains: only a terrifying expectation of judge-
28 ment and a fierce fire which will consume God's enemies. If a man
disregards the Law of Moses, he is put to death without pity on
29 the evidence of two or three witnesses. Think how much more severe
a penalty that man will deserve who has trampled under foot the
Son of God, profaned the blood of the covenant by which he was
30 consecrated, and affronted God's gracious Spirit! For we know who
it is that has said, 'Justice is mine: I will repay'; and again, 'The
31 Lord will judge his people.' It is a terrible thing to fall into the
hands of the living God.

32 Remember the days gone by, when, newly enlightened, you met
33 the challenge of great sufferings and held firm. Some of you were
abused and tormented to make a public show, while others stood
34 loyally by those who were so treated. For indeed you shared the
sufferings of the prisoners, and you cheerfully accepted the seizure
of your possessions, knowing that you possessed something better
35 and more lasting. Do not then throw away your confidence, for it
36 carries a great reward. You need endurance, if you are to do God's
37 will and win what he has promised. For 'soon, very soon' (in the words
38 of Scripture), 'he who is to come will come; he will not delay; and
by faith my righteous servant shall find life; but if a man shrinks
39 back, I take no pleasure in him.' But we are not among those who
shrink back and are lost; we have the faith to make life our own.

A Call to Faith

11 AND WHAT IS FAITH? Faith gives substance[a] to our hopes, and
makes us certain of realities we do not see.
2 It is for their faith that the men of old stand on record.
3 By faith we perceive that the universe was fashioned by the word
of God, so that the visible came forth from the invisible.
4 By faith Abel offered a sacrifice greater than Cain's, and through

[a] *Or* assurance.

faith his goodness was attested, for his offerings had God's approval; and through faith he continued to speak after his death.

By faith Enoch was carried away to another life without passing 5 through death; he was not to be found, because God had taken him. For it is the testimony of Scripture that before he was taken he had pleased God, and without faith it is impossible to please him; for 6 anyone who comes to God must believe that he exists and that he rewards those who search for him.

By faith Noah, divinely warned about the unseen future, took good 7 heed and built an ark to save his household. Through his faith he put the whole world in the wrong, and made good his own claim to the righteousness which comes of faith.

By faith Abraham obeyed the call to go out to a land destined for 8 himself and his heirs, and left home without knowing where he was to go. By faith he settled as an alien in the land promised him, 9 living in tents, as did Isaac and Jacob, who were heirs to the same promise. For he was looking forward to the city with firm founda- 10 tions, whose architect and builder is God.

By faith even Sarah herself received strength to conceive, though 11 she was past the age, because she judged that he who had promised would keep faith; and therefore from one man, and one as good as 12 dead, there sprang descendants numerous as the stars or as the countless grains of sand on the sea-shore.

All these persons died in faith. They were not yet in possession 13 of the things promised, but had seen them far ahead and hailed them, and confessed themselves no more than strangers or passing travellers on earth. Those who use such language show plainly that 14 they are looking for a country of their own. If their hearts had been 15 in the country they had left, they could have found opportunity to return. Instead, we find them longing for a better country—I mean, 16 the heavenly one. That is why God is not ashamed to be called their God; for he has a city ready for them.

By faith Abraham, when the test came, offered up Isaac: he had 17 received the promises, and yet he was on the point of offering his only son, of whom he had been told, 'Through the line of Isaac your 18 posterity shall be traced.' For he reckoned that God had power even 19 to raise from the dead—and from the dead, he did, in a sense, receive him back.

By faith Isaac blessed Jacob and Esau and spoke of things to come. 20

21 By faith Jacob, as he was dying, blessed each of Joseph's sons, and
22 worshipped God, leaning on the top of his staff. By faith Joseph,
at the end of his life, spoke of the departure of Israel from Egypt,
and instructed them what to do with his bones.

23 By faith, when Moses was born, his parents hid him for three
months, because they saw what a fine child he was; they were not
24 afraid of the king's edict. By faith Moses, when he grew up, refused
25 to be called the son of Pharaoh's daughter, preferring to suffer
hardship with the people of God rather than enjoy the transient
26 pleasures of sin. He considered the stigma that rests on God's
Anointed greater wealth than the treasures of Egypt, for his eyes
27 were fixed upon the coming day of recompense. By faith he left
Egypt, and not because he feared the king's anger; for he was
resolute, as one who saw the invisible God.

28 By faith he celebrated the Passover and sprinkled the blood, so
29 that the destroying angel might not touch the first-born of Israel. By
faith they crossed the Red Sea as though it were dry land, whereas
the Egyptians, when they attempted the crossing, were drowned.

30 By faith the walls of Jericho fell down after they had been encircled
31 on seven successive days. By faith the prostitute Rahab escaped the
doom of the unbelievers, because she had given the spies a kindly
welcome.

32 Need I say more? Time is too short for me to tell the stories of
Gideon, Barak, Samson, and Jephthah, of David and Samuel and
33 the prophets. Through faith they overthrew kingdoms, established
justice, saw God's promises fulfilled. They muzzled ravening lions,
34 quenched the fury of fire, escaped death by the sword. Their weakness was turned to strength, they grew powerful in war, they put
35 foreign armies to rout. Women received back their dead raised to
life. Others were tortured to death, disdaining release, to win a
36 better resurrection. Others, again, had to face jeers and flogging,
37 even fetters and prison bars. They were stoned,ᵃ they were sawn in
two, they were put to the sword, they went about dressed in skins of
38 sheep or goats, in poverty, distress, and misery. They were too good
for this world. They were refugees in deserts and on the hills, hiding
39 in caves and holes in the ground. These also, one and all, are com-
memorated for their faith; and yet they did not enter upon the
40 promised inheritance, because, with us in mind, God had made a

[a] *Some witnesses insert* they were put to the question.

386

better plan, that only in company with us should they reach their
perfection.

AND WHAT OF OURSELVES? With all these witnesses to faith 12
around us like a cloud, we must throw off every encumbrance, every
sin to which we cling,*ᵃ* and run with resolution the race for which we
are entered, our eyes fixed on Jesus, on whom faith depends from 2
start to finish: Jesus who, for the sake of the joy that lay ahead of
him,*ᵇ* endured the cross, making light of its disgrace, and has taken
his seat at the right hand of the throne of God.

Think of him who submitted to such opposition from sinners: 3
that will help you not to lose heart and grow faint. In your struggle 4
against sin, you have not yet resisted to the point of shedding your
blood. You have forgotten the text of Scripture which addresses 5
you as sons and appeals to you in these words:

'My son, do not think lightly of the Lord's discipline,
Nor lose heart when he corrects you;
For the Lord disciplines those whom he loves;   6
He lays the rod on every son whom he acknowledges.'

You must endure it as discipline: God is treating you as sons. Can 7
anyone be a son, who is not disciplined by his father? If you escape 8
the discipline in which all sons share, you must be bastards and
no true sons. Again, we paid due respect to the earthly fathers who 9
disciplined us; should we not submit even more readily to our
spiritual Father, and so attain life? They disciplined us for this short 10
life according to their lights; but he does so for our true welfare,
so that we may share his holiness. Discipline, no doubt, is never 11
pleasant; at the time it seems painful, but in the end it yields for
those who have been trained by it the peaceful harvest of an honest
life. Come, then, stiffen your drooping arms and shaking knees, and 12, 13
keep your steps from wavering. Then the disabled limb will not be
put out of joint, but regain its former powers.

Aim at peace with all men, and a holy life, for without that no one 14
will see the Lord. See to it that there is no one among you who 15
forfeits the grace of God, no bitter, noxious weed growing up to
poison the whole, no immoral person, no one worldly-minded like 16

[*a*] *Or* every clinging sin; *one witness reads* the sin which all too readily distracts us.
[*b*] *Or* who, in place of the joy that was open to him, ...

387

17 Esau. He sold his birthright for a single meal, and you know that although he wanted afterwards to claim the blessing, he was rejected; for he found no way open for second thoughts, although he strove, to the point of tears, to find one.

18 REMEMBER WHERE you stand: not before the palpable, blazing
19 fire of Sinai, with the darkness, gloom, and whirlwind, the trumpet-blast and the oracular voice, which they heard, and begged to hear
20 no more; for they could not bear the command, 'If even an animal
21 touches the mountain, it must be stoned.' So appalling was the sight, that Moses said, 'I shudder with fear.'
22 No, you stand before Mount Zion and the city of the living God,
23 heavenly Jerusalem, before myriads of angels, the full concourse and assembly of the first-born citizens of heaven, and God the judge
24 of all, and the spirits of good men made perfect, and Jesus the mediator of a new covenant, whose sprinkled blood has better things
25 to tell than the blood of Abel. See that you do not refuse to hear the voice that speaks. Those who refused to hear the oracle speaking on earth found no escape; still less shall we escape if we refuse to
26 hear the One who speaks from heaven. Then indeed his voice shook the earth, but now he has promised, 'Yet once again I will shake
27 not earth alone, but the heavens also.' The words 'once again'—and only once—imply that the shaking of these created things
28 means their removal, and then what is not shaken will remain. The kingdom we are given is unshakable; let us therefore give thanks to God, and so worship him as he would be worshipped, with
29 reverence and awe; for our God is a devouring fire.

13 NEVER CEASE to love your fellow-Christians.
2 Remember to show hospitality. There are some who, by so doing, have entertained angels without knowing it.
3 Remember those in prison as if you were there with them; and those who are being maltreated, for you like them are still in the world.
4 Marriage is honourable; let us all keep it so, and the marriage-bond inviolate; for God's judgement will fall on fornicators and adulterers.
5 Do not live for money; be content with what you have; for God
6 himself has said, 'I will never leave you or desert you'; and so we can take courage and say, 'The Lord is my helper, I will not fear; what can man do to me?'

Remember your leaders, those who first spoke God's message to 7 you; and reflecting upon the outcome of their life and work, follow the example of their faith.

Jesus Christ is the same yesterday, today, and for ever. So do not 8,9 be swept off your course by all sorts of outlandish teachings; it is good that our souls should gain their strength from the grace of God, and not from scruples about what we eat, which have never done any good to those who were governed by them.

Our altar is one from which*a* the priests of the sacred tent have 10 no right to eat. As you know, those animals whose blood is brought 11 as a sin-offering by the high priest into the sanctuary, have their bodies burnt outside the camp, and therefore Jesus also suffered 12 outside the gate, to consecrate the people by his own blood. Let us 13 then go to him outside the camp, bearing the stigma that he bore. For here we have no permanent home, but we are seekers after the 14 city which is to come. Through Jesus, then, let us continually offer 15 up to God the sacrifice of praise, that is, the tribute of lips which acknowledge his name, and never forget to show kindness and to 16 share what you have with others; for such are the sacrifices which God approves.

Obey your leaders and defer to them; for they are tireless in 17 their concern for you, as men who must render an account. Let it be a happy task for them, and not pain and grief, for that would bring you no advantage.

Pray for us; for we are convinced that our conscience is clear; our 18 one desire is always to do what is right. All the more earnestly I ask 19 for your prayers, that I may be restored to you the sooner.

May the God of peace, who brought up from the dead our Lord 20 Jesus, the great Shepherd of the sheep, by the blood of the eternal covenant, make you perfect in all goodness so that you may do his 21 will, and may he make of us what he would have us be through Jesus Christ, to whom be glory for ever and ever! Amen.

I beg you, brothers, bear with this exhortation; for it is after all 22 a short letter. I have news for you: our friend Timothy has been 23 released; and if he comes in time he will be with me when I see you.

Greet all your leaders and all God's people. Greetings to you 24 from our Italian friends.

God's grace be with you all!   25

[a] *Or* one like that from which...

A LETTER OF

JAMES

Practical Religion

1 FROM JAMES, a servant of God and the Lord Jesus Christ. Greetings to the Twelve Tribes dispersed throughout the world.

2 My brothers, whenever you have to face trials of many kinds, 3 count yourselves supremely happy, in the knowledge that such 4 testing of your faith breeds fortitude, and if you give fortitude full play you will go on to complete a balanced character that will fall 5 short in nothing. If any of you falls short in wisdom, he should ask God for it and it will be given him, for God is a generous giver who 6 neither refuses nor reproaches anyone. But he must ask in faith, without a doubt in his mind; for the doubter is like a heaving sea 7 ruffled by the wind. A man of that kind must not expect the Lord 8 to give him anything; he is double-minded, and never can keep*a* a steady course.

9 The brother in humble circumstances may well be proud that 10 God lifts him up; and the wealthy brother must find his pride in being brought low. For the rich man will disappear like the flower 11 of the field; once the sun is up with its scorching heat the flower withers, its petals fall, and what was lovely to look at is lost for ever. So shall the rich man wither away as he goes about his business.

12 Happy the man who remains steadfast under trial, for having passed that test he will receive for his prize the gift of life promised 13 to those who love God. No one under trial or temptation should say, 'I am being tempted by God'; for God is untouched by evil,*b* and 14 does not himself tempt anyone. Temptation arises when a man is 15 enticed and lured away by his own lust; then lust conceives, and gives birth to sin; and sin full-grown breeds death.

16, 17 Do not deceive yourselves, my friends. All good giving and*c* every perfect gift comes from above, from the Father of the lights of heaven. With him there is no variation, no play of passing

[*a*] Or anything; a double-minded man never keeps... [*b*] Or God cannot be tempted by evil. [*c*] Or All giving is good, and...

shadows.*ᵃ* Of his set purpose, by declaring the truth, he gave us 18
birth to be a kind of firstfruits of his creatures.

Of that you may be certain, my friends. But each of you must 19
be quick to listen, slow to speak, and slow to be angry. For a man's 20
anger cannot promote the justice of God. Away then with all that is 21
sordid, and the malice that hurries to excess, and quietly accept the
message planted in your hearts, which can bring you salvation.

Only be sure that you act on the message and do not merely 22
listen; for that would be to mislead yourselves. A man who listens 23
to the message but never acts upon it is like one who looks in a
mirror at the face nature gave him. He glances at himself and goes 24
away, and at once forgets what he looked like. But the man who 25
looks closely into the perfect law, the law that makes us free, and
who lives in its company, does not forget what he hears, but acts
upon it; and that is the man who by acting will find happiness.

A man may think he is religious, but if he has no control over his 26
tongue, he is deceiving himself; that man's religion is futile. The 27
kind of religion which is without stain or fault in the sight of God our
Father is this: to go to the help of orphans and widows in their
distress and keep oneself untarnished by the world.

My BROTHERS, believing as you do in our Lord Jesus Christ, who 2
reigns in glory, you must never show snobbery. For instance, two 2
visitors may enter your place of worship, one a well-dressed man
with gold rings, and the other a poor man in shabby clothes. Suppose 3
you pay special attention to the well-dressed man and say to him,
'Please take this seat', while to the poor man you say, 'You can
stand; or you may sit here*ᵇ* on the floor by my footstool', do you 4
not see that you are inconsistent and judge by false standards?

Listen, my friends. Has not God chosen those who are poor in 5
the eyes of the world to be rich in faith and to inherit the kingdom he
has promised to those who love him? And yet you have insulted the 6
poor man. Moreover, are not the rich your oppressors? Is it not
they who drag you into court and pour contempt on the honoured 7
name by which God has claimed you?

If, however, you are observing the sovereign law laid down in 8
Scripture, 'Love your neighbour as yourself', that is excellent. But 9

[*a*] *Some witnesses read* no variation, or shadow caused by change.   [*b*] *Some witnesses*
read Stand where you are or sit here...; *others read* Stand where you are or sit...

if you show snobbery, you are committing a sin and you stand

10 convicted by that law as transgressors. For if a man keeps the whole law apart from one single point, he is guilty of breaking all of it.

11 For the One who said, 'Thou shalt not commit adultery', said also, 'Thou shalt not commit murder.' You may not be an adulterer, but

12 if you commit murder you are a law-breaker all the same. Always speak and act as men who are to be judged under a law of freedom.

13 In that judgement there will be no mercy for the man who has shown no mercy. Mercy triumphs over judgement.

14 MY BROTHERS, what use is it for a man to say he has faith when

15 he does nothing to show it? Can that faith save him? Suppose a

16 brother or a sister is in rags with not enough food for the day, and one of you says, 'Good luck to you, keep yourselves warm, and have plenty to eat', but does nothing to supply their bodily needs, what

17 is the good of that? So with faith; if it does not lead to action, it is in itself a lifeless thing.

18   But someone may object: 'Here is one who claims to have faith and another who points to his deeds.' To which I reply: 'Prove to me that this faith you speak of is real though not accompanied by

19 deeds, and by my deeds I will prove to you my faith.' You have faith enough to believe that there is one God. Excellent! The devils have

20 faith like that, and it makes them tremble. But can you not see,

21 you quibbler, that faith divorced from deeds is barren? Was it not by his action, in offering his son Isaac upon the altar, that our

22 father Abraham was justified? Surely you can see that faith was at work in his actions, and that by these actions the integrity of his

23 faith was fully proved. Here was fulfilment of the words of Scripture: 'Abraham put his faith in God, and that faith was counted to him as

24 righteousness'; and elsewhere he is called 'God's friend'. You see then that a man is justified by deeds and not by faith in itself.

25 The same is true of the prostitute Rahab also. Was not she justified by her action in welcoming the messengers into her house and

26 sending them away by a different route? As the body is dead when there is no breath left in it, so faith divorced from deeds is lifeless as a corpse.

3 MY BROTHERS, not many of you should become teachers, for you may be certain that we who teach shall ourselves be judged with

greater strictness. All of us often go wrong; the man who never 2
says a wrong thing is a perfect character, able to bridle his whole
being. If we put bits into horses' mouths to make them obey our 3
will, we can direct their whole body. Or think of ships: large they 4
may be, yet even when driven by strong gales they can be directed
by a tiny rudder on whatever course the helmsman chooses. So 5
with the tongue. It is a small member but it can make huge claims.*ᵃ*
What a huge stack of timber*ᵇ* can be set ablaze by the tiniest spark!
And the tongue is in effect a fire. It represents among our members 6
the world with all its wickedness; it pollutes our whole being; it
keeps the wheel of our existence red-hot, and its flames are fed by
hell. Beasts and birds of every kind, creatures that crawl on the 7
ground or swim in the sea, can be subdued and have been subdued
by mankind; but no man can subdue the tongue. It is an intractable 8
evil, charged with deadly venom. We use it to sing the praises of 9
our Lord and Father, and we use it to invoke curses upon our fellow-
men who are made in God's likeness. Out of the same mouth come 10
praises and curses. My brothers, this should not be so. Does a 11
fountain gush with both fresh and brackish water from the same
opening? Can a fig-tree, my brothers, yield olives,or a vine figs? 12
No more does salt water yield fresh.

WHO AMONG YOU is wise or clever? Let his right conduct give 13
practical proof of it, with the modesty that comes of wisdom. But 14
if you are harbouring bitter jealousy and selfish ambition in your
hearts, consider whether your claims are not false, and a defiance
of the truth. This is not the wisdom that comes from above; it is 15
earth-bound, sensual, demonic. For with jealousy and ambition 16
come disorder and evil of every kind. But the wisdom from above 17
is in the first place pure; and then peace-loving, considerate, and
open to reason; it is straightforward and sincere, rich in mercy and
in the kindly deeds that are its fruit. True justice is the harvest 18
reaped by peacemakers from seeds sown in a spirit of peace.

What causes conflicts and quarrels among you? Do they not 4
spring from the aggressiveness of your bodily desires? You want 2
something which you cannot have, and so you are bent on murder;
you are envious, and cannot attain your ambition, and so you
quarrel and fight. You do not get what you want, because you do not

[a] *Or* it is a great boaster. [b] *Or* What a huge forest...

3 pray for it. Or, if you do, your requests are not granted because you
pray from wrong motives, to spend what you get on your pleasures.
4 You false, unfaithful creatures! Have you never learned that love
of the world is enmity to God? Whoever chooses to be the world's
5 friend makes himself God's enemy. Or do you suppose that Scripture has no meaning when it says that the spirit which God implanted
6 in man turns towards envious desires? And yet the grace he gives is
stronger. Thus Scripture says, 'God opposes the arrogant and gives
7 grace to the humble.' Be submissive then to God. Stand up to the
8 devil and he will turn and run. Come close to God, and he will
come close to you. Sinners, make your hands clean; you who are
9 double-minded, see that your motives are pure. Be sorrowful,
mourn and weep. Turn your laughter into mourning and your
10 gaiety into gloom. Humble yourselves before God and he will lift
you high.
11 Brothers, you must never disparage one another. He who disparages a brother or passes judgement on his brother disparages the
law and judges the law. But if you judge the law, you are not keeping
12 it but sitting in judgement upon it. There is only one lawgiver and
judge, the One who is able to save life and destroy it. So who are
you to judge your neighbour?

13 A WORD with you, you who say, 'Today or tomorrow we will go
off to such and such a town and spend a year there trading and making
14 money.' Yet you have no idea what tomorrow will bring. Your life,
what is it? You are no more than a mist, seen for a little while and
15 then dispersing. What you ought to say is: 'If it be the Lord's will,
16 we shall live to do this or that.' But instead, you boast and brag,
17 and all such boasting is wrong. Well then, the man who knows the
good he ought to do and does not do it is a sinner.
5 Next a word to you who have great possessions. Weep and
2 wail over the miserable fate descending on you. Your riches have
3 rotted; your fine clothes are moth-eaten; your silver and gold have
rusted away, and their very rust will be evidence against you and
consume your flesh like fire. You have piled up wealth in an age
4 that is near its close. The wages you never paid to the men who
mowed your fields are loud against you, and the outcry of the
5 reapers has reached the ears of the Lord of Hosts. You have lived
on earth in wanton luxury, fattening yourselves like cattle—and the

day for slaughter has come. You have condemned the innocent and 6
murdered him; he offers no resistance.

Be patient, my brothers, until the Lord comes. The farmer looking 7
for the precious crop his land may yield can only wait in patience,
until the winter and spring rains have fallen. You too must be patient 8
and stout-hearted, for the coming of the Lord is near. My brothers, 9
do not blame your troubles on one another, or you will fall under
judgement; and there stands the Judge, at the door. If you want 10
a pattern of patience under ill-treatment, take the prophets who
spoke in the name of the Lord; remember: 'We count those happy 11
who stood firm.' You have all heard how Job stood firm, and you
have seen how the Lord treated him in the end. For the Lord is full
of pity and compassion.

ABOVE ALL THINGS, my brothers, do not use oaths, whether 'by 12
heaven' or 'by earth' or by anything else. When you say yes or no,
let it be plain 'Yes' or 'No', for fear that you expose yourselves to
judgement.

Is anyone among you in trouble? He should turn to prayer. Is 13
anyone in good heart? He should sing praises. Is one of you ill? He 14
should send for the elders of the congregation to pray over him and
anoint him with oil in the name of the Lord. The prayer offered in 15
faith will save the sick man, the Lord will raise him from his bed, and
any sins he may have committed will be forgiven. Therefore confess 16
your sins to one another, and pray for one another, and then you
will be healed. A good man's prayer is powerful and effective.
Elijah was a man with human frailties like our own; and when he 17
prayed earnestly that there should be no rain, not a drop fell on the
land for three years and a half; then he prayed again, and down came 18
the rain and the land bore crops once more.

My brothers, if one of your number should stray from the truth 19
and another succeed in bringing him back, be sure of this: any man 20
who brings a sinner back from his crooked ways will be rescuing
his soul from death and cancelling innumerable sins.

THE
FIRST LETTER OF
PETER

The Calling of a Christian

1 FROM PETER, apostle of Jesus Christ, to those of God's
   scattered people who lodge for a while in Pontus, Galatia,
2 Cappadocia, Asia, and Bithynia—chosen of old in the purpose
of God the Father, hallowed to his service by the Spirit, and
consecrated with the sprinkled blood of Jesus Christ.
   Grace and peace to you in fullest measure.
3 Praise be to the God and Father of our Lord Jesus Christ, who
in his mercy gave us new birth into a living hope by the resurrection
4 of Jesus Christ from the dead! The inheritance to which we are
born is one that nothing can destroy or spoil or wither. It is kept
5 for you in heaven, and you, because you put your faith in God, are
under the protection of his power until salvation comes—the salvation which is even now in readiness and will be revealed at the end of
time.
6 This is cause for great joy, even though now you smart for a little
7 while, if need be, under trials of many kinds. Even gold passes
through the assayer's fire, and more precious than perishable gold
is faith which has stood the test. These trials come so that your faith
may prove itself worthy of all praise, glory, and honour when Jesus
Christ is revealed.
8 You have not seen him, yet you love him; and trusting in him
now without seeing him, you are transported with a joy too great for
9 words, while you reap the harvest of your faith, that is, salvation
10 for your souls. This salvation was the theme which the prophets
pondered and explored, those who prophesied about the grace of
11 God awaiting you. They tried to find out what was the time,[a] and
what the circumstances, to which the spirit of Christ in them pointed,
foretelling the sufferings in store for Christ and the splendours to
12 follow; and it was disclosed to them that the matter they treated of

[a] *Or* who was the person...

was not for their time but for yours. And now it has been openly announced to you through preachers who brought you the Gospel in the power of the Holy Spirit sent from heaven. These are things that angels long to see into.

You must therefore be like men stripped for action, perfectly 13 self-controlled. Fix your hopes on the gift of grace which is to be yours when Jesus Christ is revealed. As obedient children, do not 14 let your characters be shaped any longer by the desires you cherished in your days of ignorance. The One who called you is holy; like him, 15 be holy in all your behaviour, because Scripture says, 'You shall be 16 holy, for I am holy.'

If you say 'our Father' to the One who judges every man impar- 17 tially on the record of his deeds, you must stand in awe of him while you live out your time on earth. Well you know that it was no perish- 18 able stuff, like gold or silver, that bought your freedom from the empty folly of your traditional ways. The price was paid in precious 19 blood, as it were of a lamb without mark or blemish—the blood of Christ. He was predestined before the foundation of the world, 20 and in this last period of time he was made manifest for your sake. Through him you have come to trust in God who raised him from the 21 dead and gave him glory, and so your faith and hope are fixed on God.

Now that by obedience to the truth you have purified your souls 22 until you feel sincere affection towards your brother Christians, love one another whole-heartedly with all your strength. You have been 23 born anew, not of mortal parentage but of immortal, through the living and enduring word of God.*a* For (as Scripture says) 24

'All mortals are like grass;
All their splendour like the flower of the field;
The grass withers, the flower falls;
But the word of the Lord endures for evermore.' 25

And this 'word' is the word of the Gospel preached to you.

Then away with all malice and deceit, away with all pretence and 2 jealousy and recrimination of every kind! Like the new-born infants 2 you are, you must crave for pure milk (spiritual milk, I mean), so that you may thrive upon it to your souls' health. Surely you have 3 tasted that the Lord is good.

So come to him, our living Stone—the stone rejected by men but 4

[a] *Or* through the word of the living and enduring God.

397

5 choice and precious in the sight of God. Come, and let yourselves
be built, as living stones, into a spiritual temple; become a holy
priesthood,*a* to offer spiritual sacrifices acceptable to God through
6 Jesus Christ. For it stands written:

> 'I lay in Zion a choice corner-stone of great worth.
> The man who has faith in it will not be put to shame.'

7 The great worth of which it speaks is for you who have faith. For
those who have no faith, the stone which the builders rejected has
8 become not only the corner-stone,*b* but also 'a stone to trip over, a
rock to stumble against'. They stumble when they disbelieve the
Word. Such was their appointed lot!

9   But you are a chosen race, a royal priesthood, a dedicated nation,
and a people claimed by God for his own, to proclaim the triumphs
of him who has called you out of darkness into his marvellous light.
10 You are now the people of God, who once were not his people;
outside his mercy once, you have now received his mercy.

11 DEAR FRIENDS, I beg you, as aliens in a foreign land, to abstain
12 from the lusts of the flesh which are at war with the soul. Let all
your behaviour be such as even pagans can recognize as good, and
then, whereas they malign you as criminals now, they will come to
see for themselves that you live good lives, and will give glory to
God on the day when he comes to hold assize.
13   Submit yourselves to every human institution for the sake of the
14 Lord, whether to the sovereign as supreme, or to the governor as
his deputy for the punishment of criminals and the commendation
15 of those who do right. For it is the will of God that by your good
conduct you should put ignorance and stupidity to silence.
16   Live as free men; not however as though your freedom were there
to provide a screen for wrongdoing, but as slaves in God's service.
17 Give due honour to everyone: love to the brotherhood, reverence to
God, honour to the sovereign.
18   Servants, accept the authority of your masters with all due submission, not only when they are kind and considerate, but even
19 when they are perverse. For it is a fine*c* thing if a man endure the
20 pain of undeserved suffering because God is in his thoughts. What

---

[*a*] *Or* a spiritual temple for the holy work of priesthood. [*b*] *Or* the apex of the
building. [*c*] *Or* creditable.

credit is there in fortitude when you have done wrong and are beaten for it? But when you have behaved well and suffer for it, your fortitude is a fine thing*ᵃ* in the sight of God. To that you were 21 called, because Christ suffered*ᵇ* on your behalf, and thereby left you an example; it is for you to follow in his steps. He committed no sin, 22 he was convicted of no falsehood; when he was abused he did not 23 retort with abuse, when he suffered he uttered no threats, but committed his cause to the One who judges justly. In his own person 24 he carried our sins to*ᶜ* the gallows, so that we might cease to live for sin and begin to live for righteousness. By his wounds you have been healed. You were straying like sheep, but now you have turned 25 towards the Shepherd and Guardian of your souls.

In the same way you women must accept the authority of your 3 husbands, so that if there are any of them who disbelieve the Gospel they may be won over, without a word being said, by observing 2 the chaste and reverent behaviour of their wives. Your beauty should 3 reside, not in outward adornment—the braiding of the hair, or jewellery, or dress—but in the inmost centre of your being, with 4 its imperishable ornament, a gentle, quiet spirit, which is of high value in the sight of God. Thus it was among God's people in days 5 of old: the women who fixed their hopes on him adorned themselves by submission to their husbands. Such was Sarah, who obeyed 6 Abraham and called him 'my master'. Her children you have now become, if you do good and show no fear.

In the same way, you husbands must conduct your married life 7 with understanding: pay honour to the woman's body, not only because it is weaker, but also because you share together in the grace of God which gives you life. Then your prayers will not be hindered.

To sum up: be one in thought and feeling, all of you; be full of 8 brotherly affection, kindly and humble-minded. Do not repay 9 wrong with wrong, or abuse with abuse; on the contrary, retaliate with blessing, for a blessing is the inheritance to which you yourselves have been called.

> 'Whoever loves life and would see good days   10
> Must restrain his tongue from evil
> And his lips from deceit;
> Must turn from wrong and do good,   11
> Seek peace and pursue it.

[*a*] *Or* is creditable. [*b*] *Some witnesses read* died. [*c*] *Or* on.

12   For the Lord's eyes are turned towards the righteous,
          His ears are open to their prayers;
          But the Lord's face is set against wrong-doers.'

13 WHO IS GOING to do you wrong if you are devoted to what is good?
14 And yet if you should suffer for your virtues, you may count your-
15 selves happy. Have no fear of them:*a* do not be perturbed, but hold
the Lord Christ in reverence in your hearts.*b* Be always ready with
your defence whenever you are called to account for the hope that
16 is in you, but make that defence with modesty and respect. Keep
your conscience clear, so that when you are abused, those who malign
17 your Christian conduct may be put to shame. It is better to suffer
for well-doing, if such should be the will of God, than for doing
18 wrong. For Christ also died*c* for our sins*d* once and for all. He, the
just, suffered for the unjust, to bring us to God.

In the body he was put to death; in the spirit he was brought to
19 life. And in the spirit he went and made his proclamation to the
20 imprisoned spirits. They had refused obedience long ago, while God
waited patiently in the days of Noah and the building of the ark,
and in the ark a few persons, eight in all, were brought to safety
21 through the water. This water prefigured the water of baptism through
which you are now brought to safety. Baptism is not the washing
away of bodily pollution, but the appeal made to God by a good
conscience; and it brings salvation through the resurrection of
22 Jesus Christ, who entered heaven after receiving the submission of
angelic authorities and powers, and is now at the right hand of God.
4   Remembering that Christ endured bodily suffering, you must arm
yourselves with a temper of mind like his. When a man has thus
2 endured bodily suffering he has finished with sin, and for the rest
of his days on earth he may live, not for the things that men desire,
3 but for what God wills. You had time enough in the past to do all
the things that men want to do in the pagan world. Then you lived
in licence and debauchery, drunkenness, riot, and tippling, and the
4 forbidden worship of idols. Now, when you no longer plunge with
them into all this reckless dissipation, they cannot understand it, and
5 they vilify you accordingly; but they shall answer for it to him who

[a] *Or* Do not fear what they fear. [b] *Or* hold Christ in reverence in your hearts, as
Lord. [c] *Some witnesses read* suffered. [d] *Some witnesses read* for sins; *others read*
for us.

stands ready to pass judgement on the living and the dead. Why was 6
the Gospel preached to those who are dead? In order that, although
in the body they received the sentence common to men, they might
in the spirit be alive with the life of God.

The end of all things is upon us, so you must lead an ordered and 7
sober life, given to prayer. Above all, keep your love for one another 8
at full strength, because love cancels innumerable sins. Be hos- 9
pitable to one another without complaining. Whatever gift each of 10
you may have received, use it in service to one another, like good
stewards dispensing the grace of God in its varied forms. Are you 11
a speaker? Speak as if you uttered oracles of God. Do you give
service? Give it as in the strength which God supplies. In all things
so act that the glory may be God's through Jesus Christ; to him
belong glory and power for ever and ever. Amen.

MY DEAR FRIENDS, do not be bewildered by the fiery ordeal that 12
is upon you, as though it were something extraordinary. It gives you 13
a share in Christ's sufferings, and that is cause for joy; and when his
glory is revealed, your joy will be triumphant. If Christ's name is 14
flung in your teeth as an insult, count yourselves happy, because then
that glorious Spirit which is the Spirit of God is resting upon you.
If you suffer, it must not be for murder, theft, or sorcery,[a] nor for 15
infringing the rights of others. But if anyone suffers as a Christian, 16
he should feel it no disgrace, but confess that name to the honour
of God.

The time has come for the judgement to begin; it is beginning 17
with God's own household. And if it is starting with you, how will
it end for those who refuse to obey the gospel of God? And if it is 18
hard enough for the righteous to be saved, what will become of the
impious and sinful? So even those who suffer, if it be according 19
to God's will, should commit their souls to him—by doing good;
their Maker will not fail them.

And now I appeal to the elders of your community, as a fellow- 5
elder and a witness of Christ's sufferings, and also a partaker in
the splendour that is to be revealed. Tend that flock of God whose 2
shepherds you are, and do it, not under compulsion, but of your
own free will, as God would have it; not for gain but out of sheer
devotion; not tyrannizing over those who are allotted to your care, 3

[a] *Or* other crime.

4 but setting an example to the flock. And then, when the Head Shepherd appears, you will receive for your own the unfading garland of glory.

5 In the same way you younger men must be subordinate to your elders. Indeed, all of you should wrap yourselves in the garment of humility towards each other, because God sets his face against the
6 arrogant but favours the humble. Humble yourselves then under
7 God's mighty hand, and he will lift you up in due time. Cast all your cares on him, for you are his charge.

8 Awake! be on the alert! Your enemy the devil, like a roaring lion,
9 prowls round looking for someone to devour. Stand up to him, firm in faith, and remember that your brother Christians are going
10 through the same kinds of suffering while they are in the world. And the God of all grace, who called you into his eternal glory in Christ, will himself, after your brief suffering, restore, establish, and streng-
11 then you on a firm foundation. He holds dominion for ever and ever. Amen.

12 I write you this brief appeal through Silvanus, our trusty brother as I hold him, adding my testimony that this is the true grace of God. In this stand fast.

13 Greetings from her who dwells in Babylon, chosen by God like
14 you, and from my son Mark. Greet one another with the kiss of love.

Peace to you all who belong to Christ!

THE
SECOND LETTER OF
PETER

The Remedy for Doubt

FROM SIMEON PETER, servant and apostle of Jesus 1
Christ, to those who through the justice of our God and
Saviour Jesus Christ share our faith and enjoy equal privilege
with ourselves.

Grace and peace be yours in fullest measure, through the know- 2
ledge of God and Jesus our Lord.

His divine power has bestowed on us everything that makes for 3
life and true religion, enabling us to know the One who called us
by his own splendour and might. Through this might and splendour 4
he has given us his promises, great beyond all price, and through
them you may escape the corruption with which lust has infected
the world, and come to share in the very being of God.

With all this in view, you should try your hardest to supplement 5
your faith with virtue, virtue with knowledge, knowledge with self- 6
control, self-control with fortitude, fortitude with piety, piety with 7
brotherly kindness, and brotherly kindness with love.

These are gifts which, if you possess and foster them, will keep 8
you from being either useless or barren in the knowledge of our
Lord Jesus Christ. The man who lacks them is short-sighted and 9
blind; he has forgotten how he was cleansed from his former sins.
All the more then, my friends, exert yourselves to clinch God's 10
choice and calling of you. If you behave so, you will never come
to grief. Thus you will be afforded full and free admission into the 11
eternal kingdom of our Lord and Saviour Jesus Christ.

And so I will not hesitate to remind you of this again and again, 12
although you know it and are well grounded in the truth that has
already reached you. Yet I think it right to keep refreshing your 13
memory so long as I still lodge in this body. I know that very soon 14
I must leave it; indeed our Lord Jesus Christ has told me so.*a* But 15

[a] Or I must leave it, as our Lord Jesus Christ told me.

I will see to it that after I am gone you will have means of remembering these things at all times.

16 It was not on tales artfully spun that we relied when we told you of the power of our Lord Jesus Christ and his coming; we saw him
17 with our own eyes in majesty, when at the hands of God the Father he was invested with honour and glory, and there came to him from the sublime Presence a voice which said: 'This is my Son, my Beloved,*a*
18 on whom my favour rests.' This voice from heaven we ourselves heard; when it came, we were with him on the sacred mountain.
19 All this only confirms for us the message of the prophets,*b* to which you will do well to attend, because it is like a lamp shining in a murky place, until the day breaks and the morning star rises to illuminate your minds.

20 BUT FIRST note this: no one can interpret any prophecy of Scrip-
21 ture by himself. For it was not through any human whim that men prophesied of old; men they were, but, impelled by the Holy Spirit, they spoke the words of God.
2 But Israel had false prophets as well as true; and you likewise will have false teachers among you. They will import disastrous heresies, disowning the very Master who bought them, and bringing
2 swift disaster on their own heads. They will gain many adherents to their dissolute practices, through whom the true way will be brought
3 into disrepute. In their greed for money they will trade on your credulity with sheer fabrications.

But the judgement long decreed for them has not been idle;
4 perdition waits for them with unsleeping eyes. God did not spare the angels who sinned, but consigned them to the dark pits of hell,*c*
5 where they are reserved for judgement. He did not spare the world of old (except for Noah, preacher of righteousness, whom he preserved with seven others), but brought the deluge upon that world
6 of godless men. The cities of Sodom and Gomorrah God burned to ashes, and condemned them to total destruction, making them
7 an object-lesson for godless men in future days. But he rescued Lot, who was a good man, shocked by the dissolute habits of the
8 lawless society in which he lived; day after day every sight, every

[a] *Or* This is my only Son. [b] *Or* And in the message of the prophets we have something still more certain. [c] *Some witnesses read* consigned them to darkness and chains in hell.

sound, of their evil courses tortured that good man's heart. Thus 9
the Lord is well able to rescue the godly out of trials, and to reserve
the wicked under punishment until the day of judgement.

Above all he will punish those who follow their abominable lusts. 10
They flout authority; reckless and headstrong, they are not afraid
to insult celestial beings, whereas angels, for all their superior 11
strength and might, employ no insults in seeking judgement against
them before the Lord.

These men are like brute beasts, born in the course of nature to 12
be caught and killed. They pour abuse upon things they do not
understand; like the beasts they will perish, suffering hurt for the 13
hurt they have inflicted. To carouse in broad daylight is their idea
of pleasure; while they sit with you at table they are an ugly blot on
your company, because they revel in their own deceptions.[a]

They have eyes for nothing but women, eyes never at rest from 14
sin. They lure the unstable to their ruin; past masters in mercenary
greed, God's curse is on them! They have abandoned the straight 15
road and lost their way. They have followed in the steps of Balaam
son of Beor, who consented to take pay for doing wrong, but was 16
sharply rebuked for his offence when the dumb beast spoke with a
human voice and put a stop to the prophet's madness.

These men are springs that give no water, mists driven by a storm; 17
the place reserved for them is blackest darkness. They utter big, 18
empty words, and make of sensual lusts and debauchery a bait to
catch those who have barely begun to escape from their heathen
environment. They promise them freedom, but are themselves slaves 19
of corruption; for a man is the slave of whatever has mastered him.
They had once escaped the world's defilements through the know- 20
ledge of our Lord and Saviour Jesus Christ; yet if they have entangled
themselves in these all over again, and are mastered by them, their
plight in the end is worse than before. How much better never to 21
have known the right way, than, having known it, to turn back and
abandon the sacred commandments delivered to them! For them 22
the proverb has proved true: 'The dog returns to its own vomit',
and, 'The sow after a wash rolls in the mud again.'

THIS IS NOW my second letter to you, my friends. In both of 3
them I have been recalling to you what you already know, to rouse

[a] *Or* in their mock love-feasts; *some witnesses read* in their love-feasts.

2 you to honest thought. Remember the predictions made by God's own prophets, and the commands given by the Lord and Saviour through your apostles.

3 Note this first: in the last days there will come men who scoff 4 at religion and live self-indulgent lives, and they will say: 'Where now is the promise of his coming? Our fathers have been laid to their rest, but still everything continues exactly as it has always been since the world began.'

5 In taking this view they lose sight of the fact[a] that there were heavens and earth long ago, created by God's word out of water 6 and with water; and by water that first world was destroyed, the 7 water of the deluge. And the present heavens and earth, again by God's word, have been kept in store for burning; they are being reserved until the day of judgement when the godless will be destroyed.

8 And here is one point, my friends, which you must not lose sight of: with the Lord one day is like a thousand years and a thousand 9 years like one day. It is not that the Lord is slow in fulfilling his promise, as some suppose, but that he is very patient with you, because it is not his will for any to be lost, but for all to come to repentance.

10 But the Day of the Lord will come; it will come, unexpected as a thief. On that day the heavens will disappear with a great rushing sound, the elements will disintegrate in flames, and the earth with all that is in it will be laid bare.[b]

11 Since the whole universe is to break up in this way, think what sort of people you ought to be, what devout and dedicated lives 12 you should live! Look eagerly for the coming of the Day of God and work to hasten it on; that day will set the heavens ablaze until they 13 fall apart, and will melt the elements in flames. But we have his promise, and look forward to new heavens and a new earth, the home of justice.

14 With this to look forward to, do your utmost to be found at peace 15 with him, unblemished and above reproach in his sight. Bear in mind that our Lord's patience with us is our salvation, as Paul, our friend and brother, said when he wrote to you with his inspired 16 wisdom. And so he does in all his other letters, wherever he speaks of this subject, though they contain some obscure passages, which the

[a] *Or* They choose to overlook the fact... [b] *Some witnesses read* will be burnt up.

ignorant and unstable misinterpret to their own ruin, as they do the other scriptures.*ᵃ*

But you, my friends, are forewarned. Take care, then, not to let 17 these unprincipled men seduce you with their errors; do not lose your own safe foothold. But grow in the grace and in the knowledge 18 of our Lord and Saviour Jesus Christ.*ᵇ* To him be glory now and for all eternity!

[a] *Or* his other writings. [b] *Or* But grow up, by the grace of our Lord and Saviour Jesus Christ, and by knowing him.

THE
FIRST LETTER OF
JOHN

Recall to Fundamentals

1 IT WAS THERE from the beginning; we have heard it; we have seen it with our own eyes; we looked upon it, and felt it with our own hands; and it is of this we tell. Our theme is the

2 word of life. This life was made visible; we have seen it and bear our testimony; we here declare to you the eternal life which dwelt

3 with the Father and was made visible to us. What we have seen and heard we declare to you, so that you and we together may share in a common life, that life which we share with the Father and his Son

4 Jesus Christ. And we write this in order that the joy of us all may be complete.

5 Here is the message we heard from him and pass on to you:

6 that God is light, and in him there is no darkness at all. If we claim to be sharing in his life while we walk in the dark, our words and

7 our lives are a lie; but if we walk in the light as he himself is in the light, then we share together a common life, and we are being cleansed from every sin by the blood of Jesus his Son.

8 If we claim to be sinless, we are self-deceived and strangers to the

9 truth. If we confess our sins, he is just, and may be trusted to for-

10 give our sins and cleanse us from every kind of wrong; but if we say we have committed no sin, we make him out to be a liar, and then his word has no place in us.

2 My children, in writing thus to you my purpose is that you should not commit sin. But should anyone commit a sin, we have one to plead our cause*a* with the Father, Jesus Christ, and he is just.

2 He is himself the remedy for the defilement of our sins, not our sins only but the sins of all the world.

3 Here is the test by which we can make sure that we know him:

4 do we keep his commands? The man who says, 'I know him', while he disobeys his commands, is a liar and a stranger to the truth;

[a] *Literally* we have an advocate...

but in the man who is obedient to his word, the divine love has indeed 5
come to its perfection.

Here is the test by which we can make sure that we are in him: who- 6
ever claims to be dwelling in him, binds himself to live as Christ
himself lived. Dear friends, I give you no new command. It is the 7
old command which you always had before you; the old command is
the message which you heard at the beginning. And yet again it is 8
a new command that I am giving you—new in the sense that the
darkness is passing and the real light already shines. Christ has
made this true, and it is true in your own experience.

A man may say, 'I am in the light'; but if he hates his brother, 9
he is still in the dark. Only the man who loves his brother dwells in 10
light: there is nothing to make him stumble. But one who hates his 11
brother is in darkness; he walks in the dark and has no idea where
he is going, because the darkness has made him blind.

I write to you, my children, because your sins have been forgiven 12
for his sake.*

I write to you, fathers, because you know him who is and has 13
been from the beginning.*

I write to you, young men, because you have mastered the evil
one.

To you, children, I have written because you know the Father.

To you, fathers, I have written because you know him who is and 14
has been from the beginning.*

To you, young men, I have written because you are strong;
God's word is in you, and you have mastered the evil one.

Do not set your hearts on the godless world or anything in it. 15
Anyone who loves the world is a stranger to the Father's love.
Everything the world affords, all that panders to the appetites, or 16
entices the eyes, all the glamour of its life, springs not from the
Father but from the godless world. And that world is passing away 17
with all its allurements, but he who does God's will stands for
evermore.

MY CHILDREN, this is the last hour! You were told that Antichrist 18
was to come, and now many antichrists have appeared; which proves

[a] *Or* forgiven, since you bear his name. [b] *Or* him whom we have known from the
beginning.

19 to us that this is indeed the last hour. They went out from our company, but never really belonged to us; if they had, they would have stayed with us. They went out, so that it might be clear that not all in our company truly belong to it.[a]

20 You, no less than they, are among the initiated;[b] this is the gift of
21 the Holy One, and by it you all have knowledge.[c] It is not because you are ignorant of the truth that I have written to you, but because you know it, and because lies, one and all, are alien to the truth.

22 Who is the liar? Who but he that denies that Jesus is the Christ?
23 He is Antichrist, for he denies both the Father and the Son: to deny the Son is to be without the Father; to acknowledge the Son is to have
24 the Father too. You therefore must keep in your hearts that which you heard at the beginning; if what you heard then still dwells in
25 you, you will yourselves dwell in the Son and also in the Father. And this is the promise that he himself gave us, the promise of eternal life.

26, 27 So much for those who would mislead you. But as for you, the initiation[d] which you received from him stays with you; you need no other teacher, but learn all you need to know from his initiation, which is real and no illusion. As he taught you, then, dwell in him.

28 Even now, my children, dwell in him, so that when he appears
29 we may be confident and unashamed before him at his coming. If you know that he is righteous, you must recognize that every man
3 who does right is his child. How great is the love that the Father has shown to us! We were called God's children, and such we are;[e] and the reason why the godless world does not recognize us is that
2 it has not known him. Here and now, dear friends, we are God's children; what we shall be has not yet been disclosed, but we know that when it is disclosed[f] we shall be like him,[g] because we shall
3 see him as he is. Everyone who has this hope before him purifies himself, as Christ is pure.

4 To commit sin is to break God's law: sin, in fact, is lawlessness.
5 Christ appeared, as you know, to do away with sins, and there is no
6 sin in him. No man therefore who dwells in him is a sinner; the sinner has not seen him and does not know him.

7 My children, do not be misled: it is the man who does right who is

[a] *Or* that none of them truly belong to us. [b] *Literally* have an anointing (*Greek* chrism). [c] *Some witnesses read* you have all knowledge. [d] *Literally* the anointing. [e] *Or* We are called children of God! Not only called, we really are his children. [f] *Or* when he appears. [g] *Or* we are God's children, though he has not yet appeared; what we shall be we know, for when he does appear we shall be like him.

righteous, as God is righteous; the man who sins is a child of the 8
devil, for the devil has been a sinner from the first; and the Son of
God appeared for the very purpose of undoing the devil's work.

A child of God does not commit sin, because the divine seed 9
remains in him; he cannot be a sinner, because he is God's child.
That is the distinction between the children of God and the children 10
of the devil: no one who does not do right is God's child, nor is
anyone who does not love his brother. For the message you have 11
heard from the beginning is this: that we should love one another;
unlike Cain, who was a child of the evil one and murdered his 12
brother. And why did he murder him? Because his own actions
were wrong, and his brother's were right.

My brothers, do not be surprised if the world hates you. We for 13, 14
our part have crossed over from death to life; this we know, because
we love our brothers. The man who does not love is still in the realm
of death, for everyone who hates his brother is a murderer, and no 15
murderer, as you know, has eternal life within him. It is by this 16
that we know what love is: that Christ laid down his life for us.
And we in our turn are bound to lay down our lives for our brothers.
But if a man has enough to live on, and yet when he sees his brother 17
in need shuts up his heart against him, how can it be said that the
divine love*a* dwells in him?

My children, love must not be a matter of words or talk; it must 18
be genuine, and show itself in action. This is how we may know 19
that we belong to the realm of truth, and convince ourselves in his
sight that even if our conscience condemns us, God is greater than 20
our conscience*b* and knows all.

Dear friends, if our conscience does not condemn us, then we can 21
approach God with confidence, and obtain from him whatever we 22
ask, because we are keeping his commands and doing what he
approves. This is his command: to give our allegiance to his Son 23
Jesus Christ and love one another as he commanded. When we keep 24
his commands we dwell in him and he dwells in us. And this is
how we can make sure that he dwells within us: we know it from the
Spirit he has given us.

[*a*] *Or* that love for God... [*b*] *Or* and reassure ourselves in his sight in matters where
our conscience condemns us, because God is greater than our conscience...; *or* and yet
we shall do well to convince ourselves that if even our own conscience condemns us, still
more will God who is greater than conscience...

4 BUT DO NOT trust any and every spirit, my friends; test the spirits,
to see whether they are from God, for among those who have gone
2 out into the world there are many prophets falsely inspired. This
is how we may recognize the Spirit of God: every spirit which
acknowledges that Jesus Christ has come in the flesh is from God,
3 and every spirit which does not thus acknowledge Jesus is not from
God. This is what is meant by 'Antichrist';[a] you have been told that
he was to come, and here he is, in the world already!

4   But you, my children, are of God's family, and you have the
mastery over these false prophets, because he who inspires you is
5 greater than he who inspires the godless world. They are of that
world, and so therefore is their teaching; that is why the world
6 listens to them. But we belong to God, and a man who knows God
listens to us, while he who does not belong to God refuses us a
hearing. That is how we distinguish the spirit of truth from the
spirit of error.

7   Dear friends, let us love one another, because love is from God.
8 Everyone who loves is a child of God and knows God, but the un-
9 loving know nothing of God. For God is love; and his love was
disclosed to us in this, that he sent his only Son into the world to
10 bring us life. The love I speak of is not our love for God, but the
love he showed to us in sending his Son as the remedy for the defile-
11 ment of our sins. If God thus loved us, dear friends, we in turn are
12 bound to love one another. Though God has never been seen by
any man, God himself dwells in us if we love one another; his love
is brought to perfection within us.

13   Here is the proof that we dwell in him and he dwells in us: he
14 has imparted his Spirit to us. Moreover, we have seen for ourselves,
and we attest, that the Father sent the Son to be the saviour of the
15 world, and if a man acknowledges that Jesus is the Son of God,
16 God dwells in him and he dwells in God. Thus we have come to know
and believe the love which God has for us.

God is love; he who dwells in love is dwelling in God, and God
17 in him. This is for us the perfection of love, to have confidence on the
day of judgement, and this we can have, because even in this world
18 we are as he is. There is no room for fear in love; perfect love
banishes fear. For fear brings with it the pains of judgement, and
19 anyone who is afraid has not attained to love in its perfection. We

[a] *Or* This is the spirit of Antichrist.

412

love because he loved us first. But if a man says, 'I love God', 20
while hating his brother, he is a liar. If he does not love the brother
whom he has seen, it cannot be that he loves God whom he has not
seen. And indeed this command comes to us from Christ himself: 21
that he who loves God must also love his brother.

Everyone who believes that Jesus is the Christ is a child of God, 5
and to love the parent means to love his child; it follows that when 2
we love God and obey his commands we love his children too. For 3
to love God is to keep his commands; and they are not burdensome,
because every child of God is victor over the godless world. The 4
victory that defeats the world is our faith, for who is victor over the 5
world but he who believes that Jesus is the Son of God?

This is he who came with water and blood: Jesus Christ. He 6
came, not by water alone, but by water and blood; and there is the
Spirit to bear witness, because the Spirit is truth. For there are 7, 8
three witnesses, the Spirit, the water, and the blood, and these three
are in agreement. We accept human testimony, but surely divine 9
testimony is stronger, and this threefold testimony is indeed that
of God himself, the witness he has borne to his Son. He who believes 10
in the Son of God has this testimony in his own heart, but he who
disbelieves God, makes him out to be a liar, by refusing to accept
God's own witness to his Son. The witness is this: that God has 11
given us eternal life, and that this life is found in his Son. He who 12
possesses the Son has life indeed; he who does not possess the Son
of God has not that life.

THIS LETTER is to assure you that you have eternal life. It is 13
addressed to those who give their allegiance to the Son of God.

We can approach God with confidence for this reason: if we make 14
requests which accord with his will he listens to us; and if we know 15
that our requests are heard, we know also that the things we ask for
are ours.

If a man sees his brother committing a sin which is not a deadly 16
sin, he should pray to God for him, and he will grant him life—
that is, when men are not guilty of deadly sin. There is such a thing
as deadly sin, and I do not suggest that he should pray about that;
but although all wrongdoing is sin, not all sin is deadly sin. 17

We know that no child of God is a sinner; it is the Son of God 18
who keeps him safe, and the evil one cannot touch him.

19 We know that we are of God's family, while the whole godless world lies in the power of the evil one.

20 We know that the Son of God has come and given us understanding to know him who is real; indeed we are in him who is real, since we are in his Son Jesus Christ. This is the true God, this is eternal

21 life. My children, be on the watch against false gods.

THE
SECOND LETTER OF
JOHN

Truth and Love

1 THE ELDER to the Lady chosen by God, and her children, whom I love in truth—and not I alone but all who know the

2 truth—for the sake of the truth that dwells among us and will be with us for ever.

3 Grace, mercy, and peace shall be with us from God the Father and from Jesus Christ the Son of the Father, in truth and love.

4 I was delighted to find that some of your children are living by the

5 truth, as we were commanded by the Father. And now I have a request to make of you. Do not think I am giving a new command; I am recalling the one we have had before us from the beginning:

6 let us love one another. And love means following the commands of God. This is the command which was given you from the beginning, to be your rule of life.

7 Many deceivers have gone out into the world, who do not acknowledge Jesus Christ as coming in the flesh. These are the persons

8 described as the Antichrist, the arch-deceiver. Beware of them, so that you may not lose all that we worked for, but receive your reward in full.

9 Anyone who runs ahead too far, and does not stand by the

doctrine of the Christ, is without God; he who stands by that doctrine possesses both the Father and the Son. If anyone comes to you 10 who does not bring this doctrine, do not welcome him into your house or give him a greeting; for anyone who gives him a greeting 11 is an accomplice in his wicked deeds.

I have much to write to you, but I do not care to put it down in 12 black and white. But I hope to visit you and talk with you face to face, so that our joy may be complete. The children of your Sister, 13 chosen by God, send their greetings.

THE
THIRD LETTER OF
JOHN

Trouble in the Church

THE ELDER to dear Gaius, whom I love in truth.   1
My dear Gaius, I pray that you may enjoy good health, 2
and that all may go well with you, as I know it goes well with your soul. I was delighted when friends came and told me how true 3 you have been; indeed you are true in your whole life. Nothing 4 gives me greater joy than to hear that my children are living by the truth.

My dear friend, you show a fine loyalty in everything that you 5 do for these our fellow-Christians, strangers though they are to you. They have spoken of your kindness before the congregation here. 6 Please help them on their journey in a manner worthy of the God we serve. It was on Christ's work that they went out; and they would 7 accept nothing from pagans. We are bound to support such men, and 8 so play our part in spreading the truth.

I sent a letter to the congregation, but Diotrephes, their would-be 9 leader, will have nothing to do with us. If I come, I will bring up 10 the things he is doing. He lays baseless and spiteful charges against us; not satisfied with that, he refuses to receive our friends, and he interferes with those who would do so, and tries to expel them from the congregation.

11   My dear friend, do not imitate bad examples, but good ones. The well-doer is a child of God; the evil-doer has never seen God.

12   Demetrius gets a good testimonial from everybody—yes, and from the truth itself. I add my testimony, and you know that my testimony is true.

13   I have much to write to you, but I do not care to set it down with
14   pen and ink. I hope to see you very soon, and we will talk face to face. Peace be with you. Our friends send their greetings. Greet our friends individually.

A LETTER OF

JUDE

The Danger of False Belief

FROM JUDE, servant of Jesus Christ and brother of James, 1
to those whom God has called, who live in the love of God the
Father and in the safe keeping of Jesus Christ.
Mercy, peace, and love be yours in fullest measure. 2

My friends, I was fully engaged in writing to you about our salva- 3
tion—which is yours no less than ours—when it became urgently
necessary to write at once and appeal to you to join the struggle in
defence of the faith, the faith which God entrusted to his people once
and for all. It is in danger from certain persons who have wormed 4
their way in, the very men whom Scripture long ago marked down
for the doom they have incurred. They are the enemies of religion;
they pervert the free favour of our God into licentiousness, disowning Jesus Christ, our only Master and Lord.*ª*

You already know it all, but let me remind you how the Lord,*ᵇ* 5
having once delivered the people of Israel out of Egypt, next time
destroyed those who were guilty of unbelief. Remember too the 6
angels, how some of them were not content to keep the dominion
given to them but abandoned their proper home; and God has
reserved them for judgement on the great Day, bound beneath the
darkness in everlasting chains. Remember Sodom and Gomorrah 7
and the neighbouring towns; like the angels, they committed fornication and followed unnatural lusts; and they paid the penalty in
eternal fire, an example for all to see.

So too with these men today. Their dreams lead them to defile 8
the body, to flout authority, and to insult celestial beings. In con- 9
trast, when the archangel Michael was in debate with the devil,
disputing the possession of Moses's body, he did not presume to condemn him in insulting words,*ᶜ* but said, 'May the Lord rebuke you!'

But these men pour abuse upon things they do not understand; 10
the things they do understand, by instinct like brute beasts, prove

[a] Or disowning our one and only Master, and Jesus Christ our Lord. [b] Some witnesses
read Jesus (which might be understood as Joshua). [c] Or to charge him with blasphemy.

11 their undoing. Alas for them! They have gone the way of Cain; they have plunged into Balaam's error for pay; they have rebelled like Korah, and they share his doom.

12 These men are a blot on your love-feasts, where they eat and drink without reverence. They are shepherds who take care only of themselves. They are clouds carried away by the wind without giving rain, trees that in season bear no fruit, dead twice over and pulled

13 up by the roots. They are fierce waves of the sea, foaming shameful deeds; they are stars that have wandered from their course, and the place for ever reserved for them is blackest darkness.

14 It was to them that Enoch, the seventh in descent from Adam, directed his prophecy when he said: 'I saw the Lord come with his

15 myriads of angels, to bring all men to judgement and to convict all the godless of all the godless deeds they had committed, and of all the defiant words which godless sinners had spoken against him.'

16 They are a set of grumblers and malcontents. They follow their lusts. Big words come rolling from their lips, and they court favour

17 to gain their ends. But you, my friends, should remember the pre-

18 dictions made by the apostles of our Lord Jesus Christ. This was the warning they gave you: 'In the final age there will be men who pour scorn on religion, and follow their own godless lusts.'

19 These men draw a line between spiritual and unspiritual persons,

20 although they are themselves*a* wholly unspiritual. But you, my friends, must fortify yourselves in your most sacred faith. Continue

21 to pray in the power of the Holy Spirit. Keep yourselves in the love of God, and look forward to the day when our Lord Jesus Christ in his mercy will give eternal life.

22, 23 There are some doubting souls who need your pity;*b* snatch them from the flames and save them.*c* There are others for whom your pity must be mixed with fear; hate the very clothing that is contaminated with sensuality.

24 Now to the One who can keep you from falling and set you in the

25 presence of his glory, jubilant and above reproach, to the only God our Saviour, be glory and majesty, might and authority, through Jesus Christ our Lord, before all time, now, and for evermore. Amen.

[*a*] Or These men create divisions; they are... [*b*] *Some witnesses read* There are some who raise disputes; these you should refute. [*c*] *So one witness; the rest read* some you should snatch from the flames and save.

THE
REVELATION
OF JOHN

THE REVELATION
OF JOHN

THIS IS THE REVELATION given by God to Jesus 1
Christ. It was given to him so that he might show his
servants what must shortly happen. He made it known by
sending his angel to his servant John, who, in telling all that he saw, 2
has borne witness to the word of God and to the testimony of
Jesus Christ.[a]

Happy is the man who reads, and happy those who listen to the 3
words of this prophecy and heed what is written in it. For the hour
of fulfilment is near.

A Message from Christ to the Churches

JOHN to the seven churches in the province of Asia. 4
Grace be to you and peace, from him who is and who was and
who is to come, from the seven spirits before his throne, and from 5
Jesus Christ, the faithful witness, the first-born from the dead and
ruler of the kings of the earth.

To him who loves us and freed us from our sins with his life's
blood, who made of us a royal house, to serve as the priests of his God 6
and Father—to him be glory and dominion for ever and ever! Amen.

Behold, he is coming with the clouds! Every eye shall see him, 7
and among them those who pierced him; and all the peoples of the
world shall lament in remorse. So it shall be. Amen.

'I am the Alpha and the Omega', says the Lord God, who is and 8
who was and who is to come, the sovereign Lord of all.

I, John, your brother, who share with you in the suffering and the 9
sovereignty and the endurance which is ours in Jesus—I was on the
island called Patmos because I had preached God's word and borne
my testimony to Jesus. It was on the Lord's day, and I was caught 10
up by the Spirit; and behind me I heard a loud voice, like the sound

[a] Or has borne his testimony to the word of God and to Jesus Christ.

11 of a trumpet, which said to me, 'Write down what you see on a scroll and send it to the seven churches: to Ephesus, Smyrna, Pergamum,
12 Thyatira, Sardis, Philadelphia, and Laodicea.' I turned to see whose voice it was that spoke to me; and when I turned I saw seven stand-
13 ing lamps of gold, and among the lamps one like a son of man, robed
14 down to his feet, with a golden girdle round his breast. The hair of his head was white as snow-white wool, and his eyes flamed like
15 fire; his feet gleamed like burnished brass refined in a furnace, and
16 his voice was like the sound of rushing waters. In his right hand he held seven stars, and out of his mouth came a sharp two-edged sword; and his face shone like the sun in full strength.
17 When I saw him, I fell at his feet as though dead. But he laid his right hand upon me and said, 'Do not be afraid. I am the first and
18 the last, and I am the living one; for I was dead and now I am alive
19 for evermore, and I hold the keys of death and Hades. Write down therefore what you have seen, what is now, and what will be hereafter.
20 'Here is the secret meaning of the seven stars which you saw in my right hand, and of the seven lamps of gold: the seven stars are the angels of the seven churches, and the seven lamps are the seven churches.

2 'To the angel of the church at Ephesus write:
'"These are the words of the One who holds the seven stars in his
2 right hand and walks among the seven lamps of gold: I know all your ways, your toil and your fortitude. I know you cannot endure evil men; you have put to the proof those who claim to be apostles but
3 are not, and have found them false. Fortitude you have; you have
4 borne up in my cause and never flagged. But I have this against you:
5 you have lost your early love. Think from what a height you have fallen; repent, and do as you once did. Otherwise, if you do not
6 repent, I shall come to you and remove your lamp from its place. Yet you have this in your favour: you hate the practices of the Nico-
7 laitans, as I do. Hear, you who have ears to hear, what the Spirit says to the churches! To him who is victorious I will give the right to eat from the tree of life that stands in the Garden of God."
8 'To the angel of the church at Smyrna write:
'"These are the words of the First and the Last, who was dead
9 and came to life again: I know how hard pressed you are, and poor—

422

and yet you are rich; I know how you are slandered by those who claim to be Jews but are not—they are Satan's synagogue. Do 10 not be afraid of the suffering to come. The Devil will throw some of you into prison, to put you to the test; and for ten days you will suffer cruelly. Only be faithful till death, and I will give you the crown of life. Hear, you who have ears to hear, what the Spirit says 11 to the churches! He who is victorious cannot be harmed by the second death.'

'To the angel of the church at Pergamum write: 12

'"These are the words of the One who has the sharp two-edged sword: I know where you live; it is the place where Satan has his 13 throne. And yet you are holding fast to my cause. You did not deny your faith in me even at the time when Antipas, my faithful witness, was killed in your city, the home of Satan. But I have 14 a few matters to bring against you: you have in Pergamum some that hold to the teaching of Balaam, who taught Balak to put temptation in the way of the Israelites. He encouraged them to eat food sacrificed to idols and to commit fornication, and in the same way you 15 also have some who hold the doctrine of the Nicolaitans. So repent! 16 If you do not, I shall come to you soon and make war upon them with the sword that comes out of my mouth. Hear, you who have ears to 17 hear, what the Spirit says to the churches! To him who is victorious I will give some of the hidden manna; I will give him also a white stone, and on the stone will be written a new name, known to none but him that receives it.'

'To the angel of the church at Thyatira write: 18

'"These are the words of the Son of God, whose eyes flame like fire and whose feet gleam like burnished brass: I know all your 19 ways, your love and faithfulness, your good service and your fortitude; and of late you have done even better than at first. Yet I have 20 this against you: you tolerate that Jezebel, the woman who claims to be a prophetess, who by her teaching lures my servants into fornication and into eating food sacrificed to idols. I have given her time 21 to repent, but she refuses to repent of her fornication. So I will 22 throw her on to a bed of pain,*a* and plunge her lovers into terrible suffering, unless they forswear what she is doing; and her children 23 I will strike dead. This will teach all the churches that I am the searcher of men's hearts and thoughts, and that I will reward each

[a] *One witness reads* into a furnace.

423

24 one of you according to his deeds. And now I speak to you others in Thyatira, who do not accept this teaching and have had no experience of what they like to call the deep secrets of Satan; on you I will

25 impose no further burden. Only hold fast to what you have, until

26 I come. To him who is victorious, to him who perseveres in doing my will to the end, I will give authority over the nations—that same

27 authority which I received from my Father—and he shall rule them

28 with an iron rod, smashing them to bits like earthenware; and I will

29 give him also the morning star. Hear, you who have ears to hear, what the Spirit says to the churches!"

3 'To the angel of the church at Sardis write:

'"These are the words of the One who holds the seven spirits of God, the seven stars: I know all your ways; that though you have a

2 name for being alive, you are dead. Wake up, and put some strength into what is left, which must otherwise die! For I have not found any

3 work of yours completed in the eyes of my God. So remember the teaching you received; observe it, and repent. If you do not wake up, I shall come upon you like a thief, and you will not know the moment

4 of my coming. Yet you have a few persons in Sardis who have not polluted their clothing. They shall walk with me in white, for so

5 they deserve. He who is victorious shall thus be robed all in white; his name I will never strike off the roll of the living, for in the presence of my Father and his angels I will acknowledge him as mine.

6 Hear, you who have ears to hear, what the Spirit says to the churches!"

7 'To the angel of the church at Philadelphia write:

'"These are the words of the holy one, the true one, who holds the key of David; when he opens none may shut, when he shuts none

8 may open: I know all your ways; and look, I have set before you an open door, which no one can shut. Your strength, I know, is small, yet you have observed my commands and have not disowned my

9 name. So this is what I will do: I will make those of Satan's synagogue, who claim to be Jews but are lying frauds, come and fall down at your feet; and they shall know that you are my beloved people.

10 Because you have kept my command and stood fast, I will also keep you from the ordeal that is to fall upon the whole world and test its

11 inhabitants. I am coming soon; hold fast what you have, and let no

12 one rob you of your crown. He who is victorious—I will make him a pillar in the temple of my God; he shall never leave it. And I will write the name of my God upon him, and the name of the city of my

God, that new Jerusalem which is coming down out of heaven from
my God, and my own new name. Hear, you who have ears to hear, 13
what the Spirit says to the churches!"
 'To the angel of the church at Laodicea write: 14
'"These are the words of the Amen, the faithful and true witness,
the prime source of all God's creation: I know all your ways; you 15
are neither hot nor cold. How I wish you were either hot or cold!
But because you are lukewarm, neither hot nor cold, I will spit you 16
out of my mouth. You say, 'How rich I am! And how well I have 17
done! I have everything I want in the world.' In fact, though you
do not know it, you are the most pitiful wretch, poor, blind, and
naked. So I advise you to buy from me gold refined in the fire, to 18
make you truly rich, and white clothes to put on to hide the shame
of your nakedness, and ointment for your eyes so that you may see.
All whom I love I reprove and discipline. Be on your mettle there- 19
fore and repent. Here I stand knocking at the door; if anyone hears 20
my voice and opens the door, I will come in and sit down to supper
with him and he with me. To him who is victorious I will grant a place 21
on my throne, as I myself was victorious and sat down with my
Father on his throne. Hear, you who have ears to hear, what the 22
Spirit says to the churches!"'

The Opening of the Sealed Book

AFTER THIS I looked, and there before my eyes was a door 4
opened in heaven; and the voice that I had first heard speaking
to me like a trumpet said, 'Come up here, and I will show you
what must happen hereafter.' At once I was caught up by the Spirit. 2
There in heaven stood a throne, and on the throne sat one whose 3
appearance was like the gleam of jasper and cornelian; and round the
throne was a rainbow, bright as an emerald. In a circle about this 4
throne were twenty-four other thrones, and on them sat twenty-four
elders, robed in white and wearing crowns of gold. From the throne 5
went out flashes of lightning and peals of thunder. Burning before
the throne were seven flaming torches, the seven spirits of God,
and in front of it stretched what seemed a sea of glass, like a sheet 6
of ice.

In the centre, round the throne itself, were four living creatures,
7 covered with eyes, in front and behind. The first creature was like
a lion, the second like an ox, the third had a human face, the fourth
8 was like an eagle in flight. The four living creatures, each of them
with six wings, had eyes all over, inside and out; and by day and by
night without a pause they sang:

> 'Holy, holy, holy is God the sovereign Lord of all, who was,
> and is, and is to come!'

9 As often as the living creatures give glory and honour and thanks
to the One who sits on the throne, who lives for ever and ever,
10 the twenty-four elders fall down before the One who sits on the
throne and worship him who lives for ever and ever; and as they lay
their crowns before the throne they cry:

> 11   'Thou art worthy, O Lord our God, to receive glory and honour
> and power, because thou didst create all things; by thy will they
> were created, and have their being!'

5 Then I saw in the right hand of the One who sat on the throne a
scroll, with writing inside and out, and it was sealed up with seven
2 seals. And I saw a mighty angel proclaiming in a loud voice, 'Who
3 is worthy to open the scroll and to break its seals?' There was no
one in heaven or on earth or under the earth able to open the scroll
4 or to look inside it. I was in tears because no one was found who was
5 worthy to open the scroll or to look inside it. But one of the elders
said to me: 'Do not weep; for the Lion from the tribe of Judah, the
Root of David, has won the right to open the scroll and break its
seven seals.'
6 Then I saw standing in the very middle of the throne, inside the
circle of living creatures and the circle of elders,*a* a Lamb with the
marks of slaughter upon him. He had seven horns and seven eyes,
the eyes which are the seven spirits of God sent out over all the
7 world. And the Lamb went up and took the scroll from the right
8 hand of the One who sat on the throne. When he took it, the four
living creatures and the twenty-four elders fell down before the
Lamb. Each of the elders had a harp, and they held golden bowls
9 full of incense, the prayers of God's people, and they were singing
a new song:

[a] *Or* standing between the throne, with the four living creatures, and the elders...

'Thou art worthy to take the scroll and to break its seals, for thou wast slain and by thy blood didst purchase for God men of every tribe and language, people and nation; thou hast made of them a 10 royal house, to serve our God as priests; and they shall reign upon earth.'

Then as I looked I heard the voices of countless angels. These 11 were all round the throne and the living creatures and the elders. Myriads upon myriads there were, thousands upon thousands, and 12 they cried aloud:

'Worthy is the Lamb, the Lamb that was slain, to receive all power and wealth, wisdom and might, honour and glory and praise!'

Then I heard every created thing in heaven and on earth and under 13 the earth and in the sea, all that is in them, crying:

'Praise and honour, glory and might, to him who sits on the throne and to the Lamb for ever and ever!'

And the four living creatures said, 'Amen', and the elders fell 14 down and worshipped.

THEN I watched as the Lamb broke the first of the seven seals; 6 and I heard one of the four living creatures say in a voice like thunder, 'Come!' And there before my eyes was a white horse, and 2 its rider held a bow. He was given a crown, and he rode forth, conquering and to conquer.

When the Lamb broke the second seal, I heard the second creature 3 say, 'Come!' And out came another horse, all red. To its rider was 4 given power to take peace from the earth and make men slaughter one another; and he was given a great sword.

When he broke the third seal, I heard the third creature say, 5 'Come!' And there, as I looked, was a black horse; and its rider held in his hand a pair of scales. And I heard what sounded like 6 a voice from the midst of the living creatures, which said, 'A whole day's wage for a quart of flour, a whole day's wage for three quarts of barley-meal! But spare the olive and the vine.'

When he broke the fourth seal, I heard the voice of the fourth crea- 7 ture say, 'Come!' And there, as I looked, was another horse, sickly 8 pale; and its rider's name was Death, and Hades came close behind.

To him was given power over a quarter of the earth, with the right to kill by sword and by famine, by pestilence and wild beasts.

9 When he broke the fifth seal, I saw underneath[a] the altar the souls of those who had been slaughtered for God's word and for the testi-
10 mony they bore. They gave a great cry: 'How long, sovereign Lord, holy and true, must it be before thou wilt vindicate us and avenge
11 our blood on the inhabitants of the earth?' Each of them was given a white robe; and they were told to rest a little while longer, until the tally should be complete of all their brothers in Christ's service who were to be killed as they had been.

12 Then I watched as he broke the sixth seal. And there was a violent
13 earthquake; the sun turned black as a funeral pall and the moon all red as blood; the stars in the sky fell to the earth, like figs shaken
14 down by a gale; the sky vanished, as a scroll is rolled up, and every
15 mountain and island was moved from its place. Then the kings of the earth, magnates and marshals, the rich and the powerful, and all men, slave or free, hid themselves in caves and mountain
16 crags; and they called out to the mountains and the crags, 'Fall on us and hide us from the face of the One who sits on the throne
17 and from the vengeance of the Lamb.' For the great day of their vengeance has come, and who will be able to stand?

7 After this I saw four angels stationed at the four corners of the earth, holding back the four winds so that no wind should blow on
2 sea or land or on any tree. Then I saw another angel rising out of the east, carrying the seal of the living God; and he called aloud to the four angels who had been given the power to ravage land and sea:
3 'Do no damage to sea or land or trees until we have set the seal
4 of our God upon the foreheads of his servants.' And I heard the number of those who had received the seal. From all the tribes of
5 Israel there were a hundred and forty-four thousand: twelve thou-sand from the tribe of Judah, twelve thousand from the tribe of
6 Reuben, twelve thousand from the tribe of Gad, twelve thousand from the tribe of Asher, twelve thousand from the tribe of Naphtali,
7 twelve thousand from the tribe of Manasseh, twelve thousand from the tribe of Simeon, twelve thousand from the tribe of Levi, twelve
8 thousand from the tribe of Issachar, twelve thousand from the tribe of Zebulun, twelve thousand from the tribe of Joseph, and twelve thousand from the tribe of Benjamin.

[a] *Or* at the foot of...

After this I looked and saw a vast throng, which no one could 9
count, from every nation, of all tribes, peoples, and languages,
standing in front of the throne and before the Lamb. They were
robed in white and had palms in their hands, and they shouted 10
together:

'Victory to our God who sits on the throne, and to the Lamb!'

And all the angels stood round the throne and the elders and the 11
four living creatures, and they fell on their faces before the throne
and worshipped God, crying: 12

'Amen! Praise and glory and wisdom, thanksgiving and honour,
power and might, be to our God for ever and ever! Amen.'

Then one of the elders turned to me and said, 'These men that 13
are robed in white—who are they and from where do they come?'
But I answered, 'My lord, you know, not I.' Then he said to me, 14
'These are the men who have passed through the great ordeal; they
have washed their robes and made them white in the blood of the
Lamb. That is why they stand before the throne of God and minister 15
to him day and night in his temple; and he who sits on the throne
will dwell with them. They shall never again feel hunger or thirst, 16
the sun shall not beat on them nor any scorching heat, because the 17
Lamb who is at the heart of the throne will be their shepherd and
will guide them to the springs of the water of life; and God will wipe
all tears from their eyes.'

Now when the Lamb broke the seventh seal, there was silence 8
in heaven for what seemed half an hour. Then I looked, and the 2
seven angels that stand in the presence of God were given seven
trumpets.

Then another angel came and stood at the altar, holding a golden 3
censer; and he was given a great quantity of incense to offer with the
prayers of all God's people upon the golden altar in front of the
throne. And from the angel's hand the smoke of the incense went 4
up before God with the prayers of his people. Then the angel took 5
the censer, filled it from the altar fire, and threw it down upon the
earth; and there were peals of thunder, lightning, and an earthquake.

The Powers of Darkness Conquered

6 THEN THE seven angels that held the seven trumpets prepared to blow them.

7 The first blew his trumpet; and there came hail and fire mingled with blood, and this was hurled upon the earth. A third of the earth was burnt, a third of the trees were burnt, all the green grass was burnt.

8 The second angel blew his trumpet; and what looked like a great blazing mountain was hurled into the sea. A third of the sea was 9 turned to blood, a third of the living creatures in it died, and a third of the ships on it foundered.

10 The third angel blew his trumpet; and a great star shot from the sky, flaming like a torch; and it fell on a third of the rivers and 11 springs. The name of the star was Wormwood; and a third of the water turned to wormwood, and men in great numbers died of the water because it had been poisoned.

12 The fourth angel blew his trumpet; and a third part of the sun was struck, a third of the moon, and a third of the stars, so that the third part went dark and a third of the light of the day failed, and of the night.

13 Then I looked, and I heard an eagle calling with a loud cry as it flew in mid-heaven: 'Woe, woe, woe to the inhabitants of the earth when the trumpets sound which the three last angels must now blow!'

9 Then the fifth angel blew his trumpet; and I saw a star that had fallen to the earth, and the star was given the key of the shaft of the 2 abyss. With this he opened the shaft of the abyss; and from the shaft smoke rose like smoke from a great furnace, and the sun and the air 3 were darkened by the smoke from the shaft. Then over the earth, out of the smoke, came locusts, and they were given the powers 4 that earthly scorpions have. They were told to do no injury to the grass or to any plant or tree, but only to those men who had not 5 received the seal of God on their foreheads. These they were allowed to torment for five months, with torment like a scorpion's sting; 6 but they were not to kill them. During that time these men will seek death, but they will not find it; they will long to die, but death will elude them.

In appearance the locusts were like horses equipped for battle. 7
On their heads were what looked like golden crowns; their faces
were like human faces and their hair like women's hair; they had 8
teeth like lions' teeth, and wore breastplates like iron; the sound 9
of their wings was like the noise of horses and chariots rushing to
battle; they had tails like scorpions, with stings in them, and in their 10
tails lay their power to plague mankind for five months. They had 11
for their king the angel of the abyss, whose name, in Hebrew, is
Abaddon, and in Greek, Apollyon, or the Destroyer.

The first woe has now passed. But there are still two more to 12
come.

The sixth angel then blew his trumpet; and I heard a voice 13
coming from between the horns of the golden altar that stood in the
presence of God. It said to the sixth angel, who held the trumpet: 14
'Release the four angels held bound at the great river Euphrates!'
So the four angels were let loose, to kill a third of mankind. They 15
had been held ready for this moment, for this very year and month,
day and hour. And their squadrons of cavalry, whose count I heard, 16
numbered two hundred million.

This was how I saw the horses and their riders in my vision: 17
They wore breastplates, fiery red, blue, and sulphur-yellow; the
horses had heads like lions' heads, and out of their mouths came
fire, smoke, and sulphur. By these three plagues, that is, by the 18
fire, the smoke, and the sulphur that came from their mouths, a
third of mankind was killed. The power of the horses lay in their 19
mouths, and in their tails also; for their tails were like snakes, with
heads, and with them too they dealt injuries.

The rest of mankind who survived these plagues still did not 20
abjure the gods their hands had fashioned, nor cease their worship
of devils and of idols made from gold, silver, bronze, stone, and wood,
which cannot see or hear or walk. Nor did they repent of their 21
murders, their sorcery, their fornication, or their robberies.

THEN I SAW another mighty angel coming down from heaven. 10
He was wrapped in cloud, with the rainbow round his head; his
face shone like the sun and his legs were like pillars of fire. In his 2
hand he held a little scroll unrolled. His right foot he planted on
the sea, and his left on the land. Then he gave a great shout, like the 3
roar of a lion; and when he shouted, the seven thunders spoke. I was 4

about to write down what the seven thunders had said; but I heard
a voice from heaven saying, 'Seal up what the seven thunders have
5 said; do not write it down.' Then the angel that I saw standing on
6 the sea and the land raised his right hand to heaven and swore by him
who lives for ever and ever, who created heaven and earth and the
7 sea and everything in them: 'There shall be no more delay; but
when the time comes for the seventh angel to sound his trumpet,
the hidden purpose of God will have been fulfilled, as he promised
to his servants the prophets.'

8   Then the voice which I heard from heaven was speaking to me
again, and it said, 'Go and take the open scroll in the hand of the
9 angel that stands on the sea and the land.' So I went to the angel
and asked him to give me the little scroll. He said to me, 'Take it,
and eat it. It will turn your stomach sour, although in your mouth
10 it will taste sweet as honey.' So I took the little scroll from the angel's
hand and ate it, and in my mouth it did taste sweet as honey; but
when I swallowed it my stomach turned sour.

11   Then they said to me, 'Once again you must utter prophecies over
peoples and nations and languages and many kings.'

11   I was given a long cane, a kind of measuring-rod, and told: 'Now
go and measure the temple of God, the altar, and the number of the
2 worshippers. But have nothing to do with the outer court of the
temple; do not measure that; for it has been given over to the Gentiles, and they will trample the Holy City underfoot for forty-two
3 months. And I have two witnesses, whom I will appoint to prophesy,
dressed in sackcloth, all through those twelve hundred and sixty days.'
4 These are the two olive-trees and the two lamps that stand in the
5 presence of the Lord of the earth. If anyone seeks to do them harm,
fire pours from their mouths and consumes their enemies; and thus
6 shall the man die who seeks to do them harm. These two have the
power to shut up the sky, so that no rain may fall during the time
of their prophesying; and they have the power to turn water to blood
7 and to strike the earth at will with every kind of plague. But when
they have completed their testimony, the beast that comes up from
the abyss will wage war upon them and will defeat and kill them.
8 Their corpses will lie in the street of the great city, whose name in
allegory is Sodom, or Egypt, where also their Lord was crucified.
9 For three days and a half men from every people and tribe, of every
language and nation, gaze upon their corpses and refuse them burial.

All men on earth gloat over them, make merry, and exchange pre- 10
sents; for these two prophets were a torment to the whole earth. But 11
at the end of the three days and a half the breath of life from God
came into them; and they stood up on their feet to the terror of all
who saw it. Then a loud voice was heard speaking to them from 12
heaven, which said, 'Come up here!' And they went up to heaven
in a cloud, in full view of their enemies. At that same moment there 13
was a violent earthquake, and a tenth of the city fell. Seven thousand
people were killed in the earthquake; the rest in terror did homage
to the God of heaven.

The second woe has now passed. But the third is soon to come. 14
Then the seventh angel blew his trumpet; and voices were heard 15
in heaven shouting:

'The sovereignty of the world has passed to our Lord and his
Christ, and he shall reign for ever and ever!'

And the twenty-four elders, seated on their thrones before God, 16
fell on their faces and worshipped God, saying: 17

'We give thee thanks, O Lord God, sovereign over all, who art
and who wast, because thou hast taken thy great power into thy
hands and entered upon thy reign. The nations raged, but thy 18
day of retribution has come. Now is the time for the dead to be
judged; now is the time for recompense to thy servants the prophets, to thy dedicated people, and all who honour thy name,
both great and small, the time to destroy those who destroy the
earth.'

Then God's temple in heaven was laid open, and within the temple 19
was seen the ark of his covenant. There came flashes of lightning and
peals of thunder, an earthquake, and a storm of hail.

NEXT APPEARED a great portent in heaven, a woman robed with 12
the sun, beneath her feet the moon, and on her head a crown of
twelve stars. She was pregnant, and in the anguish of her labour she 2
cried out to be delivered. Then a second portent appeared in heaven: 3
a great red dragon with seven heads and ten horns; on his heads were
seven diadems, and with his tail he swept down a third of the stars 4
in the sky and flung them to the earth. The dragon stood in front
of the woman who was about to give birth, so that when her child

433

5 was born he might devour it. She gave birth to a male child, who is destined to rule all nations with an iron rod. But her child was
6 snatched up to God and his throne; and the woman herself fled into the wilds, where she had a place prepared for her by God, there to be sustained for twelve hundred and sixty days.
7 Then war broke out in heaven. Michael and his angels waged war
8 upon the dragon. The dragon and his angels fought, but they had
9 not the strength to win, and no foothold was left them in heaven. So the great dragon was thrown down, that serpent of old that led the whole world astray, whose name is Satan, or the Devil—thrown down to the earth, and his angels with him.
10 Then I heard a voice in heaven proclaiming aloud: 'This is the hour of victory for our God, the hour of his sovereignty and power, when his Christ comes to his rightful rule! For the accuser of our brothers is overthrown, who day and night accused them before our
11 God. By the sacrifice of the Lamb they have conquered him, and by the testimony which they uttered;[a] for they did not hold their
12 lives too dear to lay them down. Rejoice then, you heavens and you that dwell in them! But woe to you, earth and sea, for the Devil has come down to you in great fury, knowing that his time is short!'
13 When the dragon found that he had been thrown down to the earth, he went in pursuit of the woman who had given birth to the
14 male child. But the woman was given two great eagle's wings, to fly to the place in the wilds where for three years and a half she
15 was to be sustained, out of reach of the serpent. From his mouth the serpent spewed a flood of water after the woman to sweep her away
16 with its spate. But the earth came to her rescue and opened its mouth and swallowed the river which the dragon spewed from his
17 mouth. At this the dragon grew furious with the woman, and went off to wage war on the rest of her offspring, that is, on those who keep God's commandments and maintain their testimony to Jesus.
13 He took his stand on the sea-shore.

Then[b] out of the sea I saw a beast rising. It had ten horns and seven heads. On its horns were ten diadems, and on each head
2 a blasphemous name. The beast I saw was like a leopard, but its feet were like a bear's and its mouth like a lion's mouth. The dragon
3 conferred upon it his power and rule, and great authority. One of its

[a] *Or* the word of God to which they bore witness. [b] *Some witnesses read* . . . testimony to Jesus. Then I stood by the sea-shore and . . .

434

heads appeared to have received a death-blow; but the mortal wound
was healed. The whole world went after the beast in wondering
admiration. Men worshipped the dragon because he had conferred 4
his authority upon the beast; they worshipped the beast also, and
chanted, 'Who is like the Beast? Who can fight against it?'

The beast was allowed to mouth bombast and blasphemy, and was 5
given the right to reign for forty-two months. It opened its mouth 6
in blasphemy against God, reviling his name and his heavenly dwelling.*a* It was also allowed to wage war on God's people and to defeat 7
them, and was granted*b* authority over every tribe and people,
language and nation. All on earth will worship it, except those whose 8
names the Lamb that was slain keeps in his roll of the living, written
there since the world was made.

Hear, you who have ears to hear! Whoever is meant for prison, 9, 10
to prison he goes. Whoever takes the sword to kill, by the sword he
is bound to be killed. Here the fortitude and faithfulness of God's
people have their place.

Then I saw another beast, which came up out of the earth; it 11
had two horns like a lamb's, but spoke like a dragon. It wielded all 12
the authority of the first beast in its presence, and made the earth
and its inhabitants worship this first beast, whose mortal wound
had been healed. It worked great miracles, even making fire come 13
down from heaven to earth before men's eyes. By the miracles it was 14
allowed to perform in the presence of the beast it deluded the inhabitants of the earth, and made them erect an image in honour
of the beast that had been wounded by the sword and yet lived. It 15
was allowed to give breath to the image of the beast, so that it could
speak, and could cause all who would not worship the image to be
put to death. Moreover, it caused everyone, great and small, rich 16
and poor, slave and free, to be branded with a mark on his right hand
or forehead, and no one was allowed to buy or sell unless he bore this 17
beast's mark, either name or number. (Here is the key; and anyone 18
who has intelligence may work out the number of the beast. The
number represents a man's name, and the numerical value of its
letters is six hundred and sixty-six.)

[a] *Some witnesses read* reviling his name and his dwelling-place, that is, those that
live in heaven. [b] *Some witnesses read* It was granted... (*omitting the words* was
also...them, and).

435

Visions of the End

14 THEN I LOOKED, and on Mount Zion stood the Lamb, and with him were a hundred and forty-four thousand who had his name
2 and the name of his Father written on their foreheads. I heard a sound from heaven like the noise of rushing water and the deep roar
3 of thunder; it was the sound of harpers playing on their harps. There before the throne, and the four living creatures and the elders, they were singing a new song. That song no one could learn except the hundred and forty-four thousand, who alone from the whole
4 world had been ransomed. These are men who did not defile themselves with women, for they have kept themselves chaste, and they follow the Lamb wherever he goes. They have been ransomed as the
5 firstfruits of humanity for God and the Lamb. No lie was found in their lips; they are faultless.
6 Then I saw an angel flying in mid-heaven, with an eternal gospel to proclaim to those on earth, to every nation and tribe,
7 language and people. He cried in a loud voice, 'Fear God and pay him homage; for the hour of his judgement has come! Worship him who made heaven and earth, the sea and the water-springs!'
8 Then another angel, a second, followed, and he cried, 'Fallen, fallen is Babylon the great, she who has made all nations drink the fierce wine of[a] her fornication!'
9 Yet a third angel followed, crying out loud, 'Whoever worships the beast and its image and receives its mark on his forehead or hand,
10 he shall drink the wine of God's wrath, poured undiluted into the cup of his vengeance. He shall be tormented in sulphurous flames
11 before the holy angels and before the Lamb. The smoke of their torment will rise for ever and ever, and there will be no respite day or night for those who worship the beast and its image or receive
12 the mark of its name.' Here the fortitude of God's people has its place—in keeping God's commands and remaining loyal to Jesus.
13 Moreover, I heard a voice from heaven, saying, 'Write this: "Happy are the dead who die in the faith of Christ! Henceforth",[b]

[a] Or drink the wine of God's wrath upon... [b] Or Assuredly.

436

says the Spirit,[a] "they may rest from their labours; for they take with them the record of their deeds."'

Then as I looked there appeared a white cloud, and on the cloud 14 sat one like a son of man. He had on his head a crown of gold and in his hand a sharp sickle. Another angel came out of the temple 15 and called in a loud voice to him who sat on the cloud: 'Stretch out your sickle and reap; for harvest-time has come, and earth's crop is over-ripe.' So he who sat on the cloud put his sickle to the earth and 16 its harvest was reaped.

Then another angel came out of the heavenly temple, and he also 17 had a sharp sickle. Then from the altar came yet another, the angel 18 who has authority over fire, and he shouted to the one with the sharp sickle: 'Stretch out your sickle, and gather in earth's grape-harvest, for its clusters are ripe.' So the angel put his sickle to the 19 earth and gathered in its grapes, and threw them into the great winepress of God's wrath. The winepress was trodden outside the 20 city, and for two hundred miles around blood flowed from the press to the height of the horses' bridles.

Then I saw another great and astonishing portent in heaven: seven **15** angels with seven plagues, the last plagues of all, for with them the wrath of God is consummated.

I saw what seemed a sea of glass shot with fire, and beside the sea 2 of glass, holding the harps which God had given them, were those who had won the victory over the beast and its image and the number of its name.

They were singing the song of Moses, the servant of God, and the 3 song of the Lamb, as they chanted:

'Great and marvellous are thy deeds, O Lord God, sovereign over all; just and true are thy ways, thou king of the ages.[b] Who 4 shall not revere thee, Lord, and do homage to thy name? For thou alone art holy. All nations shall come and worship in thy presence, for thy just dealings stand revealed.'

After this, as I looked, the sanctuary of the heavenly Tent of 5 Testimony was thrown open, and out of it came the seven angels with 6 the seven plagues. They were robed in fine linen, clean and shining, and had golden girdles round their breasts. Then one of the four 7

[a] *Some witnesses read* "...the dead who henceforth die in the faith of Christ!" "Yes," says the Spirit...   [b] *Some witnesses read* king of the nations.

living creatures gave the seven angels seven golden bowls full of
8 the wrath of God who lives for ever and ever; and the sanctuary
was filled with smoke from the glory of God and his power, so that
no one could enter it until the seven plagues of the seven angels
were completed.

16   Then from the sanctuary I heard a loud voice, and it said to the
seven angels, 'Go and pour out the seven bowls of God's wrath on
the earth.'

2   So the first angel went and poured his bowl on the earth; and foul
malignant sores appeared on those men that wore the mark of the
beast and worshipped its image.

3   The second angel poured his bowl on the sea, and it turned to
blood like the blood from a corpse; and every living thing in the sea
died.

4   The third angel poured his bowl on the rivers and springs, and
they turned to blood.

5   Then I heard the angel of the waters say, 'Just art thou in these
6 thy judgements, thou Holy One who art and wast; for they shed the
blood of thy people and of thy prophets, and thou hast given them
7 blood to drink. They have their deserts!' And I heard the altar cry,
'Yes, Lord God, sovereign over all, true and just are thy judgements!'

8   The fourth angel poured his bowl on the sun; and it was allowed
9 to burn men with its flames. They were fearfully burned; but they
only cursed the name of God who had the power to inflict such
plagues, and they refused to repent or do him homage.

10   The fifth angel poured his bowl on the throne of the beast; and
its kingdom was plunged in darkness. Men gnawed their tongues
11 in agony, but they only cursed the God of heaven for their pains and
sores, and would not repent of what they had done.

12   The sixth angel poured his bowl on the great river Euphrates;
and its water was dried up, to prepare the way for the kings from
the east.

13   Then I saw coming from the mouth of the dragon, the mouth of
the beast, and the mouth of the false prophet, three foul spirits like
14 frogs. These spirits were devils, with power to work miracles. They
were sent out to muster all the kings of the world for the great day
15 of battle of God the sovereign Lord. ('That is the day when I come
like a thief! Happy the man who stays awake and keeps on his
clothes, so that he will not have to go naked and ashamed for all to

see!') So they assembled the kings at the place called in Hebrew 16
Armageddon.

Then the seventh angel poured his bowl on the air; and out of the 17
sanctuary came a loud voice from the throne, which said, 'It is over!'
And there followed flashes of lightning and peals of thunder, and a 18
violent earthquake, like none before it in human history, so violent
it was. The great city was split in three; the cities of the world fell 19
in ruin; and God did not forget Babylon the great, but made her
drink the cup which was filled with the fierce wine of his vengeance.
Every island vanished; there was not a mountain to be seen. Huge 20, 21
hailstones, weighing perhaps a hundredweight, fell on men from the
sky; and they cursed God for the plague of hail, because that plague
was so severe.

THEN ONE of the seven angels that held the seven bowls came 17
and spoke to me and said, 'Come, and I will show you the judgement
on the great whore, enthroned above the ocean. The kings of the 2
earth have committed fornication with her, and on the wine of her
fornication men all over the world have made themselves drunk.'
In the Spirit he carried me away into the wilds, and there I saw 3
a woman mounted on a scarlet beast which was covered with blasphemous names and had seven heads and ten horns. The woman 4
was clothed in purple and scarlet and bedizened with gold and
jewels and pearls. In her hand she held a gold cup, full of obscenities
and the foulness of her fornication; and written on her forehead was 5
a name with a secret meaning: 'Babylon the great, the mother of
whores and of every obscenity on earth.' The woman, I saw, was 6
drunk with the blood of God's people and with the blood of those
who had borne their testimony to Jesus.

As I looked at her I was greatly astonished. But the angel said 7
to me, 'Why are you so astonished? I will tell you the secret of the
woman and of the beast she rides, with the seven heads and the ten
horns. The beast you have seen is he who once was alive, and is 8
alive no longer, but has yet to ascend out of the abyss before going
to perdition. Those on earth whose names have not been inscribed
in the roll of the living ever since the world was made will all be
astonished to see the beast; for he once was alive, and is alive no
longer, and has still to appear.

'But here is the clue for those who can interpret it. The seven 9

439

10 heads are seven hills on which the woman sits. They represent also seven kings,^a of whom five have already fallen, one is now reigning, and the other has yet to come; and when he does come he is only

11 to last for a little while. As for the beast that once was alive and is alive no longer, he is an eighth—and yet he is one of the seven, and

12 he is going to perdition. The ten horns you saw are ten kings who have not yet begun to reign, but who for one hour are to share with

13 the beast the exercise of royal authority; for they have but a single purpose among them and will confer their power and authority upon

14 the beast. They will wage war upon the Lamb, but the Lamb will defeat them, for he is Lord of lords and King of kings, and his victory will be shared by his followers, called and chosen and faithful.'^b

15 Then he said to me, 'The ocean you saw, where the great whore sat, is an ocean of peoples and populations, nations and languages.

16 As for the ten horns you saw, they together with the beast will come to hate the whore; they will strip her naked and leave her desolate,

17 they will batten on her flesh and burn her to ashes. For God has put it into their heads to carry out his purpose, by making common cause and conferring their sovereignty upon the beast until all that

18 God has spoken is fulfilled. The woman you saw is the great city that holds sway over the kings of the earth.'

18 After this I saw another angel coming down from heaven; he came with great authority and the earth was lit up with his splendour.

2 Then in a mighty voice he proclaimed, 'Fallen, fallen is Babylon the great! She has become a dwelling for demons, a haunt for every

3 unclean spirit, for every foul and loathsome bird. For all nations have drunk deep of^c the fierce wine of her fornication; the kings of the earth have committed fornication with her, and merchants the world over have grown rich on her bloated wealth.'

4 Then I heard another voice from heaven that said: 'Come out of her, my people, lest you take part in her sins and share in her plagues.

5 For her sins are piled high as heaven, and God has not forgotten her

6 crimes. Pay her back in her own coin, repay her twice over for her

7 deeds! Double for her the strength of the potion she mixed! Mete out grief and torment to match her voluptuous pomp! She says in her heart, "I am a queen on my throne! No mourning for me, no

8 widow's weeds!" Because of this her plagues shall strike her in a

[a] *Or* emperors. [b] *Or* ...kings, and his followers are faithful men, called and selected for service. [c] *Other witnesses read* have been ruined by...

single day—pestilence, bereavement, famine, and burning—for mighty is the Lord God who has pronounced her doom!'

The kings of the earth who committed fornication with her and 9 wallowed in her luxury will weep and wail over her, as they see the smoke of her conflagration. They will stand at a distance, for horror 10 at her torment, and will say, 'Alas, alas for the great city, the mighty city of Babylon! In a single hour your doom has struck!'

The merchants of the earth also will weep and mourn for her, 11 because no one any longer buys their cargoes, cargoes of gold and 12 silver, jewels and pearls, cloths of purple and scarlet, silks and fine linens; all kinds of scented woods, ivories, and every sort of thing made of costly woods, bronze, iron, or marble; cinnamon and spice, 13 incense, perfumes and frankincense; wine, oil, flour and wheat, sheep and cattle, horses, chariots, slaves, and the lives of men. 'The fruit 14 you longed for', they will say, 'is gone from you; all the glitter and the glamour are lost, never to be yours again!' The traders in 15 all these wares, who gained their wealth from her, will stand at a distance for horror at her torment, weeping and mourning and 16 saying, 'Alas, alas for the great city, that was clothed in fine linen and purple and scarlet, bedizened with gold and jewels and pearls! Alas that in one hour so much wealth should be laid waste!' 17

Then all the sea-captains and voyagers, the sailors and those who traded by sea, stood at a distance and cried out as they saw the smoke 18 of her conflagration: 'Was there ever a city like the great city?' They 19 threw dust on their heads, weeping and mourning and saying, 'Alas, alas for the great city, where all who had ships at sea grew rich on her wealth! Alas that in a single hour she should be laid waste!'

But let heaven exult over her; exult, apostles and prophets and 20 people of God; for in the judgement against her he has vindicated your cause!

Then a mighty angel took up a stone like a great millstone and 21 hurled it into the sea and said, 'Thus shall Babylon, the great city, be sent hurtling down, never to be seen again! No more shall the 22 sound of harpers and minstrels, of flute-players and trumpeters, be heard in you; no more shall craftsmen of any trade be found in you; no more shall the sound of the mill be heard in you; no more shall 23 the light of the lamp be seen in you; no more shall the voice of the bride and bridegroom be heard in you! Your traders were once the merchant princes of the world, and with your sorcery you deceived all the nations.'

24   For the blood of the prophets and of God's people was found in her, the blood of all who had been done to death on earth.

19   After this I heard what sounded like the roar of a vast throng in heaven; and they were shouting:

2   'Alleluia! Victory and glory and power belong to our God, for true and just are his judgements! He has condemned the great whore who corrupted the earth with her fornication, and has avenged upon her the blood of his servants.'

3   Then once more they shouted:

'Alleluia! The smoke goes up from her for ever and ever!'

4   And the twenty-four elders and the four living creatures fell down and worshipped God as he sat on the throne, and they too cried:

'Amen! Alleluia!'

5   Then a voice came from the throne which said:

'Praise our God, all you his servants, you that fear him, both great and small!'

6   Again I heard what sounded like a vast crowd, like the noise of rushing water and deep roars of thunder, and they cried:

'Alleluia! The Lord our God, sovereign over all, has entered on
7   his reign! Exult and shout for joy and do him homage, for the wedding-day of the Lamb has come! His bride has made herself
8   ready, and for her dress she has been given fine linen, clean and shining.'

(Now the fine linen signifies the righteous deeds of God's people.)

9   Then the angel said to me, 'Write this: "Happy are those who are invited to the wedding-supper of the Lamb!"' And he added, 'These
10   are the very words of God.' At this I fell at his feet to worship him. But he said to me, 'No, not that! I am but a fellow-servant with you and your brothers who bear their testimony to Jesus. It is God you must worship. Those who bear testimony to Jesus are inspired like the prophets.'[a]

[a] *Or* . . . worship. For testimony to Jesus is the spirit that inspires prophets.

442

THEN I SAW heaven wide open, and there before me was a white 11
horse; and its rider's name was Faithful and True, for he is just in
judgement and just in war. His eyes flamed like fire, and on his 12
head were many diadems. Written upon him was a name known to
none but himself, and he was robed in a garment drenched in blood.[a] 13
He was called the Word of God, and the armies of heaven followed 14
him on white horses, clothed in fine linen, clean and shining. From 15
his mouth there went a sharp sword with which to smite the nations;
for he it is who shall rule them with an iron rod, and tread the winepress of the wrath and retribution of God the sovereign Lord. And 16
on his robe and on his leg there was written the name: 'King of
kings and Lord of lords.'

Then I saw an angel standing in the sun, and he cried aloud to all 17
the birds flying in mid-heaven: 'Come and gather for God's great
supper, to eat the flesh of kings and commanders and fighting men, 18
the flesh of horses and their riders, the flesh of all men, slave and free,
great and small!' Then I saw the beast and the kings of the earth 19
and their armies mustered to do battle with the Rider and his army.
The beast was taken prisoner, and so was the false prophet who had 20
worked miracles in its presence and deluded those that had received
the mark of the beast and worshipped its image. The two of them
were thrown alive into the lake of fire with its sulphurous flames.
The rest were killed by the sword which went out of the Rider's 21
mouth; and all the birds gorged themselves on their flesh.

Then I saw an angel coming down from heaven with the key of 20
the abyss and a great chain in his hands. He seized the dragon, that 2
serpent of old, the Devil or Satan, and chained him up for a thousand
years; he threw him into the abyss, shutting and sealing it over him, 3
so that he might seduce the nations no more till the thousand years
were over. After that he must be let loose for a short while.

Then I saw thrones, and upon them sat those to whom judgement 4
was committed. I could see the souls of those who had been beheaded
for the sake of God's word and their testimony to Jesus, those who
had not worshipped the beast and its image or received its mark on
forehead or hand. These came to life again and reigned with Christ
for a thousand years, though the rest of the dead did not come to 5
life until the thousand years were over. This is the first resurrection.
Happy indeed, and one of God's own people, is the man who shares 6

[a] *Some witnesses read* spattered with blood.

443

in this first resurrection! Upon such the second death has no claim; but they shall be priests of God and of Christ, and shall reign with him for the thousand years.

7 When the thousand years are over, Satan will be let loose from
8 his dungeon; and he will come out to seduce the nations in the four quarters of the earth and to muster them for battle, yes, the hosts of
9 Gog and Magog, countless as the sands of the sea. So they marched over the breadth of the land and laid siege to the camp of God's people and the city that he loves. But fire came down on them from
10 heaven and consumed them; and the Devil, their seducer, was flung into the lake of fire and sulphur, where the beast and the false prophet had been flung, there to be tormented day and night for ever.

11 Then I saw a great white throne, and the One who sat upon it; from his presence earth and heaven vanished away, and no place was
12 left for them. I could see the dead, great and small, standing before the throne; and books were opened. Then another book was opened, the roll of the living. From what was written in these books the
13 dead were judged upon the record of their deeds. The sea gave up its dead, and Death and Hades gave up the dead in their keeping;
14 they were judged, each man on the record of his deeds. Then Death
15 and Hades were flung into the lake of fire. This lake of fire is the second death; and into it were flung any whose names were not to be found in the roll of the living.

21 THEN I SAW a new heaven and a new earth, for the first heaven and the first earth had vanished, and there was no longer any sea.
2 I saw the holy city, new Jerusalem, coming down out of heaven from
3 God, made ready like a bride adorned for her husband. I heard a loud voice proclaiming from the throne: 'Now at last God has his dwelling among men! He will dwell among them and they shall be his people,
4 and God himself will be with them.*ᵃ* He will wipe every tear from their eyes; there shall be an end to death, and to mourning and crying and pain; for the old order has passed away!'
5 Then he who sat on the throne said, 'Behold! I am making all things new!' And he said to me, 'Write this down; for these words
6 are trustworthy and true. Indeed', he said, 'they are already fulfilled. For I am the Alpha and the Omega, the beginning and the end. A draught from the water-springs of life will be my free gift to the

[a] *Some witnesses read* God-with-them shall himself be their God (*see Isaiah 7. 14; 8. 8*).

thirsty. All this is the victor's heritage; and I will be his God and 7
he shall be my son. But as for the cowardly, the faithless, and the 8
vile, murderers, fornicators, sorcerers, idolaters, and liars of every
kind, their lot will be the second death, in the lake that burns with
sulphurous flames.'

Then one of the seven angels that held the seven bowls full of the 9
seven last plagues came and spoke to me and said, 'Come, and I will
show you the bride, the wife of the Lamb.' So in the Spirit he 10
carried me away to a great high mountain, and showed me the holy
city of Jerusalem coming down out of heaven from God. It shone 11
with the glory of God; it had the radiance of some priceless jewel,
like a jasper, clear as crystal. It had a great high wall, with twelve 12
gates, at which were twelve angels; and on the gates were inscribed
the names of the twelve tribes of Israel. There were three gates to 13
the east, three to the north, three to the south, and three to the west.
The city wall had twelve foundation-stones, and on them were the 14
names of the twelve apostles of the Lamb.

The angel who spoke with me carried a gold measuring-rod, to 15
measure the city, its wall, and its gates. The city was built as a square, 16
and was as wide as it was long. It measured by his rod twelve
thousand furlongs, its length and breadth and height being equal.
Its wall was one hundred and forty-four cubits high, that is, by 17
human measurements, which the angel was using. The wall was 18
built of jasper, while the city itself was of pure gold, bright as clear
glass. The foundations of the city wall were adorned with jewels of 19
every kind, the first of the foundation-stones being jasper, the second
lapis lazuli, the third chalcedony, the fourth emerald, the fifth sar- 20
donyx, the sixth cornelian, the seventh chrysolite, the eighth beryl,
the ninth topaz, the tenth chrysoprase, the eleventh turquoise, and
the twelfth amethyst. The twelve gates were twelve pearls, each gate 21
being made from a single pearl. The streets of the city were of pure
gold, like translucent glass.

I saw no temple in the city; for its temple was the sovereign Lord 22
God and the Lamb. And the city had no need of sun or moon to 23
shine upon it; for the glory of God gave it light, and its lamp was
the Lamb. By its light shall the nations walk, and the kings of the 24
earth shall bring into it all their splendour. The gates of the city 25
shall never be shut by day—and there will be no night. The wealth 26
and splendour of the nations shall be brought into it; but nothing 27

unclean shall enter, nor anyone whose ways are false or foul, but only those who are inscribed in the Lamb's roll of the living.

22 Then he showed me the river of the water of life, sparkling like
2 crystal, flowing from the throne of God and of the Lamb down the middle of the city's street. On either side of the river stood a tree of life, which yields twelve crops of fruit, one for each month of the year. The leaves of the trees serve for the healing of the nations,
3 and every accursed thing shall disappear. The throne of God and of
4 the Lamb will be there, and his servants shall worship him; they
5 shall see him face to face, and bear his name on their foreheads. There shall be no more night, nor will they need the light of lamp or sun, for the Lord God will give them light; and they shall reign for evermore.

6 THEN HE SAID to me, 'These words are trustworthy and true. The Lord God who inspires the prophets has sent his angel to
7 show his servants what must shortly happen. And, remember, I am coming soon!'

Happy is the man who heeds the words of prophecy contained in
8 this book! It is I, John, who heard and saw these things. And when I had heard and seen them, I fell in worship at the feet of the angel
9 who had shown them to me. But he said to me, 'No, not that! I am but a fellow-servant with you and your brothers the prophets and those who heed the words of this book. It is God you must
10 worship.' Then he told me, 'Do not seal up the words of prophecy
11 in this book, for the hour of fulfilment is near. Meanwhile, let the evil-doer go on doing evil and the filthy-minded wallow in his filth, but let the good man persevere in his goodness and the dedicated man be true to his dedication.'

12 'Yes, I am coming soon, and bringing my recompense with me,
13 to requite everyone according to his deeds! I am the Alpha and the Omega, the first and the last, the beginning and the end.'
14 Happy are those who wash their robes clean! They will have the right to the tree of life and will enter by the gates of the city.
15 Outside are dogs, sorcerers and fornicators, murderers and idolaters, and all who love and practise deceit.
16 'I, Jesus, have sent my angel to you with this testimony for the churches. I am the root and scion of David, the bright morning star.'

'Come!' say the Spirit and the bride.   17
'Come!' let each hearer reply.

Come forward, you who are thirsty; accept the water of life, a free gift to all who desire it.

For my part, I give this warning to everyone who is listening to 18 the words of prophecy in this book: should anyone add to them, God will add to him the plagues described in this book; should any- 19 one take away from the words in this book of prophecy, God will take away from him his share in the tree of life and the Holy City, described in this book.

He who gives this testimony speaks: 'Yes, I am coming soon!'   20
Amen. Come, Lord Jesus!

The grace of the Lord Jesus be with you all.[a]   21

[a] *Some witnesses read* with all; *others read* with all God's people; *others read* with God's people; *some add* Amen.